AT&T Global Messaging

Of Related Interest

Baker · Networking the Enterprise
Baker · Network Security: How to Plan for It and Achieve It
Bates · Wireless Networked Communications
Black · Network Management Standards
Enck/Beckman · LAN to WAN Interconnection
Fatah · Electronic Mail Systems: A Network Manager's Guide
Goralski · An Introduction to ATM Networking
Grinberg · Computer/Telecom Integration
Kessler · ISDN 2d Edition
Minoli · Analyzing Outsourcing
Minoli · 1st, 2nd, & Next Generation LANs
Ouellette · The PEN Connection: A Guide to PEN Computing
Pecar · The McGraw-Hill Telecommunications Factbook
Sokol · From EDI to Electronic Commerce
Szuprowicz · Multimedia Networking

To order or to receive additional information on these or any other McGraw-Hill titles, please call 1-800-822-8158 in the United States. In other countries, contact your local McGraw-Hill representative. **BC15XXA**

AT&T Global Messaging

The AT&T EasyLink
Services Sourcebook

Ira Hertzoff

McGraw-Hill, Inc.
New York   San Francisco   Washington, D.C.   Auckland   Bogotá
Caracas   Lisbon   London   Madrid   Mexico City   Milan
Montreal   New Delhi   San Juan   Singapore
Sydney   Tokyo   Toronto

Library of Congress Cataloging-in-Publication Data

Hertzoff, Ira (date)
    AT&T global messaging : the AT&T EasyLink Services Sourcebook /
      p.   cm.
    Includes bibliographical references and index.
    ISBN 0-07-028459-8
    1. Electronic mail systems. 2. Telematics. 3. Business
communication. I. Title: AT and T global messaging.
  HE6239.E54H47   1995
  384.3'4—dc20
                                                                        95-899
                                                                                 CIP

Copyright © 1995 by Ira Hertzoff. All rights reserved. Printed in the United States of America. Except as permitted under the United States Copyright Act of 1976, no part of this publication may be reproduced or distributed in any form or by any means, or stored in a database or retrieval system, without the prior written permission of the publisher.

1 2 3 4 5 6 7 8 9 0   DOC/DOC   9 0 9 8 7 6 5 4

ISBN 0-07-028459-8

The sponsoring editor for this book was Marjorie Spencer, the editing supervisor was Caroline R. Levine, and the production supervisor was Pamela A. Pelton.

Printed and bound by R. R. Donnelley & Sons Company.

McGraw-Hill books are available at special quantity discounts to use as premiums and sales promotions, or for use in corporate training programs. For more information, please write to the Director of Special Sales, McGraw-Hill, Inc., 11 West 19th Street, New York, NY 10011; or contact your local bookstore.

        This book is printed on recycled, acid-free paper containing a minimum of 50% recycled de-inked fiber.

Information contained in this work has been obtained by McGraw-Hill, Inc., from sources believed to be reliable. However, neither McGraw-Hill nor its authors guarantees the accuracy or completeness of any information published herein, and neither McGraw-Hill nor its authors shall be responsible for any errors, omissions, or damages arising out of use of this information. This work is published with the understanding that McGraw-Hill and its authors are supplying information, but are not attempting to render engineering or other professional services. If such services are required, the assistance of an appropriate professional should be sought.

Trademarks

A-GATE is a trademark of ON-Technology Corporation Software.
ABA/net is a registered service mark of the American Bar Association.
Advantis, AS/400, Office Vision for IBM AS/400, OfficeAccess for IBM AS/400, OSME, PROFS, DISOSS, SNADS, System 36/38, MVS, and JES are trademarks of IBM, Inc.
All-in-1, VMS, and MRXII are trademarks of DEC, Inc.
AT&T, AT&T EasyLink Services, AT&T Mail, EasyLink, InfoMaster, NCR, RediList, Safari, ACCUNET, ACCUMASTER, and StarGROUP are registered trademarks of AT&T. AT&T FYI service is a service mark of AT&T.
EMBARC is a registered trademark of Motorola, Inc.
FormFlow is a trademark of Delrina Technologies.
InstantCom and InstantCom//MS are trademarks of Instant Information Inc.
Intel is a registered trademark of Intel Corporation.
Investment ANALY$T is a registered trademark of Telebase Systems, Inc.
Investment ANALY$T is a servicemark of Telebase Systems.
LEXIS/NEXIS, PUBCITE, ECLIPSE EXPRESS, and NEXIS EXPRESS are trademarks of Reed-Elsevier, Inc.
Macintosh is a registered trademark of Apple Computer, Inc.
Microsoft, MS, MS-DOS, MS WORD, Microsoft Word, Microsoft Excel, MS Windows, and Microsoft Windows are registered trademarks, and Windows is a trademark of Microsoft Corporation.
Mobidem is a trademark of Ericsson GE.
NetWare Directory Services, WordPerfect Office, and Novell NetWare are registered trademarks of Novell Inc
Official Airline Guide Electronic Edition is a trademark of Official Airline Guides, Inc.
OpenView, HP DESK 3000, and OpenMail 9000 are trademarks of Hewlett-Packard, Inc.
PostScript is a registered trademark of Adobe Systems Inc.
RAM Mobile Data is a business venture between RAM Broadcasting and BellSouth.
Telescript is a registered trademark of General Magic, Inc.
UNIX is a registered trademark of X/Open Company, Ltd.
WESTLAW is a registered trademark of West Publishing Company.

Trademarks, service marks, and registered trademarks are used for product identification only and may be registered in some jurisdictions by their owners.

To Joyce, Hilary, and Andrew

Contents

Foreword xiii

Introduction xvii

How to Use This Book xxiii

1. AT&T EasyLink Services 1

    AT&T Firsts 5

2. AT&T Global Messaging Applications 11

    Benefits and Applications 15

    AT&T Mail Business Advantages 17

    Business Applications 19

    Work Process Improvements 22

    Financial Messaging Applications 24

    AT&T Enhanced FAX Applications 27

    AT&T EDI Applications 31

    AT&T Enhanced Telex Applications 40

    Closed User Groups 41

3. Virtual Workplaces 47

    Telecommuting 49

    AT&T School of Business 52

    AT&T EasyLink Services Telecommuting Offerings ... 53

    Mobile Messaging Benefits 56

    Mobile Messaging Developments 63

    AT&T PersonaLink Services 64

Contents

4. Public Messaging Networks 67
   VAN and Internet Accountability 68
   Commercial Messaging Networks 69
   Messaging Network Management 70
   Integrated AT&T EasyLink Services Network Management 83
   Commercial Network Security 84
   Business Continuity and Disaster Recovery 87
   VAN Reliability 88

5. AT&T Business Multimedia Services 91
   AT&T NetWare Connect Services 92
   The AT&T–Novell Alliance 93
   AT&T Network Notes 94
   Collaborative Platform 95
   AT&T Network Notes 100

6. Global Messaging Architecture 107
   Strategy 108
   AT&T EasyLink Services Vision 109
   Unified Messaging Architecture 114
   AT&T Network Notes 117
   AT&T Global Messaging Services 118
   Network Design, Access, and Operations 122
   AT&T EasyLink Standards Support 131
   Sales and Support Structure 146

7. AT&T Mail 149
   Overview 149
   AT&T Mail Advanced Features 163

Contents

Message and Format Options 170

8. Personal Computer Software 177

Stand-alone PC Connectivity 178

Microsoft Mail Remote for Windows 200

Microsoft/AT&T Mail Benefits 201

9. AT&T FORMsolutions 203

FORMsolutions Options 210

10. AT&T Mail Connectivity 219

LAN Email Package Support 220

Microsoft-AT&T Strategic Relationship 225

Microsoft Mail for PC Networks 227

StarGROUP Services for MS MAIL 233

InstantCom//MS for LAN 238

Midrange Systems 240

Mainframes 244

UNIX 247

AT&T Mail Gateway400 Service 248

11. AT&T EDI 251

International EDI Services 253

Transaction Types 254

Purchase Order Example 255

EDI Standards 258

AT&T EDI Architecture 259

Investment Protection 259

International Access 261

Connectivity 261

VAN Interconnections 263
ASC X12 Mailbag 264
EDI Message Enveloping 264
Network Interface and Translation Software 265
EDI Software Certification Program 265
Value-Added Software Supplier Program (VASS) 266
UMA Envelopes and EDI Interchange 266
FreeForm Conversion Service 269
Hardware and Software Platforms 269
Online Administration 274
Audit Trails 276
X12 Mailbag/TA3 Acknowledgment 278
Security 278
Pricing 278
Billing 279
Support 280
Professional Services Support Programs 282
Global Subscriber Support Services 282

12. AT&T FAXsolutions 285

AT&T Enhanced FAX 289
AT&T SDN Enhanced FAX 306
AT&T FAX Catalog 307
Fax Services 316
FreeForm Conversion 319

13. AT&T Information Services 321

Information Distribution 325

Contents

PUBCITE	327
NEXIS EXPRESS	331
ECLIPSE EXPRESS	333
Interactive Information Services	336
14. AT&T Global Telex Services	367
Global Access	368
15. AT&T Professional Services	373
Program Design	375
Consulting and Design	375
Installation and Implementation	376
Ramping	377
AT&T Organizational Units	379
AT&T Business Units	379
AT&T's Joint Ventures and Alliances	381
Glossary	387
Bibliography	396
Index	397

Foreword

It was just over 150 years ago that Samuel Morse sent his first telegraph from the United States Capitol, and it's just shy of 100 years since Guglielmo Marconi sent his first wireless telegraph message from England. And once again, it looks like messaging technology is poised to change radically the way people operate their businesses.

Now that AT&T's messaging services have expanded from their North American base into Europe, Australia, China, Japan, and elsewhere, business relationships can cross oceans, borders, and even the International Date Line.

How fortunate we are to have a roadmap to consult for the AT&T Mail service! When I read an early version of *AT&T Global Messaging*, I learned something new every few pages, even though I've been using the AT&T Mail network on a daily basis since 1986. For example, I learned that I could receive faxes with the Access Plus front-end software package, and that messages could be read to me over the telephone by the AT&T MailTalk voice synthesizer.

Over the years, AT&T Mail has become an indispensable part of my business. AT&T Mail is the reason that as a reporter I can work from home and while traveling. Though there are plenty of messaging services to choose from, this is the one that's kept me in touch through every hotel room from Belgium to Bartlesville. More than once, an article has made it to press on time because of the availability and the reliability of the AT&T Mail network.

Thanks to the combination of low-cost computers and reliable data communications, people in different places routinely use messaging technology to work together, even in cases where they've never met, and in situations where, owing to the difference between their time zones, it is unlikely that they are ever in the office at the same moment.

Thus, AT&T's electronic messaging services have made it possible to operate a business independently of both time and location; messages can be written in one place at one time, and then received and read at another location in another time zone.

As the first examples of wireless messaging appear, it seems that it will not be long before people will be able to send and receive messages even from a moving vehicle. Some of the off-the-shelf technology described within this book allows people to literally take the office with them, packed into a carry-on bag or a briefcase.

Brand new services such as AT&T PersonaLink Services make it possible to send multimedia messages that contain not only words, but handwriting, drawings, musical recordings, and even dancing animations, as well. The inexpensive multimedia PCs now available to household buyers are eminently capable of processing such messages.

Whatever the shape of future innovations in messaging, AT&T is likely to be at the forefront. As a company, it is perhaps the biggest consumer of the messaging services that it develops. Many of its employees depend on email to keep in touch while working from home or while traveling. Some of them have likely coined the term "road warrior" to refer to colleagues who carry pagers, phones, and laptops with them wherever they go. (Employees have been known to take laptops to the beach, so that faxes can be sent from the shore!)

Hopefully, this book will provide its readers with enough inspiration to help them think of new uses for the network, plus enough clues to help them get their new applications up and running. The possibilities are limitless. Even though this is an industry whose roots are more than a century old, it seems never to cease reinventing itself.

Eric Arnum
Editor, *EMMS*, The Electronic Messaging Industry Newsletter
AT&T MAIL ID !earnum

Acknowledgments

This book describes the electronic messaging services provided by AT&T. Over the past six years, the management, developers, product managers, technical support, and media relations staffs of AT&T EasyLink Services have encouraged its writing and provided the insights and technical materials which made this book possible. In many cases, their suggestions made this work better. Without exception, AT&T insisted that all conclusions and content be my own.

I would like to acknowledge Ed Lopez of AT&T EasyLink Services media relations who arranged for the initial access to AT&T EasyLink Services staff for the purpose of starting this book. Tanya Kobishcha, who arranged for the assistance of her marketing managers, fully supported this work with the unrestricted access to information that AT&T has provided on other projects. The AT&T EasyLink Services subject matter experts provided both their technical insights and comments on style which added much to the content and clarity of the text. Irene Cortes, Laura Carpenter and Margaret Varian coordinated the technical reviews and were especially helpful in arranging for access to materials. The staff of Product Marketing, Product Management, Strategic Planning, Professional Relations, and Public Relations were instrumental in reviewing the content. Gordon Bridge, formerly AT&T EasyLink Services' president, created the atmosphere which made the AT&T EasyLink Services offering a pleasure to write about. I look forward to someday writing about his new leadership role in AT&T messaging which involves the development of consumer messaging services, using intelligent agent technologies.

My editor, Marjorie Spencer of McGraw-Hill, provided the direction and the resources that made this work possible. Joyce Hertzoff, my wife, dusted off her proofreading skills and performed heroically in repeatedly going through every word in this book. Her suggestions added much to the work.

Introduction

Electronic Commerce, Electronic Messaging

Electronic commerce is the natural extension of available computer and communication technology from intra-business applications to inter-business applications. Inter-business applications smooth communications between business partners. Electronic messaging is the term used to describe the transmission of multimedia messages.

The rise of distributed computing and local area networks in the late 1980s allowed businesses to employ a broad range of hardware and software. The flexibility resulted in the building of internal communications systems which were often incompatible with other systems, both inside and outside the enterprise. Therefore, enterprises found that automation improved overall efficiency, but also made communications more difficult. Electronic mail, then found in some office automation packages designed for internal one-to-one communications, has today developed into a powerful external communications tool as well. This global electronic messaging allows the enterprise and its customers, suppliers, and business partners to share and manage information regardless of form.

The various components of electronic messaging, which include email, fax, electronic data exchange (EDI), telex, and information services, provide the flexibility needed for conducting truly global business.

AT&T Mail transports messages electronically around the globe, instantaneously. An application example would be an important sales update simultaneously broadcast to multiple, dispersed locations which use differing technologies for receipt of messages.

AT&T FAXsolutions provides a range of application solutions which add capability to existing applications and fax equipment. These solutions provide advanced capabilities to high-volume fax users without the need for additional equipment or phone lines and add functionality to other AT&T messaging systems.

AT&T EDI allows inter-enterprise exchange of paperless business documents such as invoices, purchase orders, and price lists. The AT&T EasyLink Services network provides the standards-based applications and support for electronic commerce worldwide, eliminating technology, time, and distance barriers among business partners who may be using different computer systems and protocols.

AT&T Global Telex is enhanced and combined with newer forms of business communication, allowing a truly integrated electronic commerce and messaging system which protects older technology investments while enhancing their capabilities.

AT&T Information Services provides both mail-based and interactive access to public and private information sources which support business growth.

In November 1989, after first seeing AT&T Mail, I started my Network Management column in *LAN Technology* magazine with:

> AT&T has redefined electronic mail for LAN'S. I predict this set of E-mail products will rank right up there with AT&T's development of the transistor, UNIX, C, and the universal telephone network.

AT&T EasyLink Services' expanding set of messaging services and products is well on its way to being counted among those other AT&T innovations. AT&T Network Notes and AT&T NetWare Connect extend the use of mail-enabled databases to the public client/server environment to end the distinction between on- and off-network operations. The universal inbox, which supports email, fax, voice, and other multimedia messages, provides a strong foundation.

In 1994, AT&T EasyLink Services became part of the AT&T Business Multimedia Services business unit. This unit is charged with developing the business services and products rapidly developing from the convergence

Introduction   xix

of data and communications technologies. The first products of this unit, AT&T NetWare Connect and AT&T Network Notes, are currently in pilot test and represent the next stage of messaging. AT&T NetWare Connect provides the basis for groupware applications such as the replicated databases of AT&T Network Notes. AT&T Network Notes is a public network–based implementation of Lotus Notes. The products allow business users to collaborate in ways never before possible.

The range of applications goes from desktop purchasing to virtual workgroups formed and reformed to meet business objectives without regard to location resources, technical skills, organizational boundaries, distance, or time.

AT&T's public data services (PDS) are strong individually. They are much stronger collectively, as each service builds on the others and extends their reach and scope. AT&T Mail and AT&T Global Telex use AT&T Enhanced FAX to deliver messages to fax destinations. AT&T EDI's reach and scope are also extended by its integration with AT&T Mail, AT&T Global Telex, and AT&T Enhanced FAX. AT&T Information Services uses the facilities of AT&T Mail and AT&T Enhanced FAX both as delivery mechanisms and as the basis for unique services such as PUBCITE, a subscription-based current awareness service. AT&T EasyLink Services will provide messaging services to AT&T NetWare Connect and AT&T Network Notes. Conversely, these new services will enhance AT&T EasyLink Services.

This book was written using AT&T EasyLink Services as the message transport and for research services. AT&T Mail served as an integrating mechanism between reviewers and participants with differing technical capabilities. In some cases, messages were sent by paper delivery; in others, AT&T Enhanced FAX was used to receive comments and integrate them with email responses.These products build upon AT&T's role in business messaging, which can be traced back to the days of the first public electrically transmitted message. The products and services of AT&T Business Multimedia Services are built on the common foundation which supports AT&T's goal of universal connectivity and anywhere, anytime communications. The tables below, provided by EMMS newsletter and used by permission, show AT&T EasyLink Services' position in the electronic commerce market.

1994 E-Mail & File-to-Fax Services Revenue

Carrier	Revenue	Share
AT&T EasyLink/BCS	150	25.0%
GE Information Services	115	19.2%
Sprint Multimedia	55	9.2%
CompuServe	52	8.7%
MCI Business Networks	50	8.3%
Prodigy	35	5.8%
America Online	30	5.0%
Infonet	26	4.3%
Stentor/WordLinx	26	4.3%
Graphnet	24	4.0%
Advantis	14	2.3%
Other	23	3.8%
Total	$600	100%
Email Only	$515	86%
File-to-fax only	$85	14%

Estimates in US $ Millions; revised Jan 30, 1995

Source: EMMS

1994 EDI Services Revenue

Carrier		Share
GE Information Services	120	34.3%
Sterling	60	17.1%
Advantis	55	15.7%
AT&T EasyLink/BCS	22	6.3%
MCI Business Networks	10	2.9%
Stentor/WorldLinx	8	2.3%
Other	75	21.4%
Total	$350	100%

Estimates in US $ Millions; revised Jan 30, 1995

Source: EMMS

1994 Enhanced Fax Services Market
(Fax Broadcast and File-to-Fax)

Carrier	Revenue	Share
Xpedite	40	14.0%
Graphnet	29	10.2%
Sprint Multimedia	27	9.5%
MCI Business Networks	26	9.1%
BOCs	13	4.6%

1994 Enhanced Fax Services Market
(Fax Broadcast and File-to-Fax)

Carrier	Revenue	Share
Cable & Wireless	12	4.2%
GE Information Services	10	3.5%
Other	80	28.1%
Total	$285	100%
Fax Broadcast Only	$200	70%
File-to-Fax Only	$85	30%

Estimates in US $ Millions; revised Jan 30, 1995

Source: EMMS

How to Use This Book

Who This Book Is For

This book is an overview of AT&T Global Messaging directed at managerial users in high-volume operations with global messaging responsibilities. The book does not cover consumer messaging applications. It is an overview of a very large system and, while some operating features are covered, is not intended as a substitute for the individual service and software manuals.

How This Book Is Organized

This book covers a variety of services and, therefore, covers these services from multiple perspectives, as it would be an unlikely reader who worked in each of the areas covered.

The book provides a brief history of AT&T's 150 years in business messaging, an overview of some common business messaging applications, an overview of virtual offices, and a discussion of the benefits of commercial public networks as compared to the Internet. These sections are written from a management perspective.

The book continues with chapters dealing with specific services. These include a chapter on the exceptionally significant public data services called AT&T NetWare Connect and AT&T Network Notes, a discussion of the AT&T messaging architecture which forms the base for AT&T EasyLink Services' messaging offerings, and discussions of AT&T Mail. The AT&T Mail discussions are divided into an overview which covers the AT&T Mail functions used interactively, a chapter on AT&T Mail stand-alone software, one on AT&T Mail enhanced applications, and one on platform- and application-connectivity considerations.

AT&T's X.400-based EDI is covered separately, as EDI is primarily an application-to-application messaging function. The chapter on AT&T Enhanced FAX covers this enabling service, which adds functions to other services, existing fax equipment, and customer resources. The chapter on AT&T Information Services, a vast collection of information tools and resources, attempts to provide enough information to show both the power and ease of use of this unique service for users who have limited experience with such services. Chapters on AT&T Telex and the AT&T Professional Services operation, which supports customers in using the other services, complete the text.

How to Use This Book

Readers who want an overview of AT&T Global Messaging should read Chapters 1 to 5. Readers who are considering the Internet or the building of their own messaging networks should read Chapters 6 and 7.

Readers who want an overview of AT&T Mail should read Chapter 6, "Global Messaging Architecture," Chapter 7, "AT&T Mail," Chapter 8, "AT&T FORMsolutions," and Chapter 9, "Connectivity."

Readers who want information on AT&T EDI, AT&T Information Services, "AT&T Telex," or "AT&T Professional Services" can read those chapters and Chapter 2.

The appendixes include a glossary and other background materials.

Chapter 1

AT&T EasyLink Services

AT&T EasyLink Services provides electronic mail, EDI, enhanced telex, and information services; it is the industry leader in mailboxes supported, messages switched, and messaging revenue. AT&T is noted for its innovations in organizational structure, technology, and capital formation which support continuing development of its globally connective services. The company, founded by Alexander Graham Bell, whose ambition was to end the hearing impaired's disconnection from society, continues to break down communication barriers domestically and globally; its services, products, tools, and innovations continue to improve many aspects of life and make us all well connected.[1]

The company's strategic vision of universal communications service is expressed in an 1878 letter from Alexander Graham Bell to venture capitalists. The vision's implementation and the resulting changes in society are well documented and will not be covered here other than to note that the company developed franchising to support its rapid growth; was instrumental in the development of radio, television, radar, and computers; became one of the first major employers of women; built communications which supported suburban growth, skyscraper, and business decentralization; and designed, financed, and built the first communication satellite for its own use.[3,4]

The company made major contributions to military technology during both world wars, including World War II's radar, fire control computers, and integrated voice/teletypewriter networks. After the war, AT&T was one of the prime contractors on air defense weapons systems, including Nike and the DEW line; underwater systems, such as the anti-submarine acoustic arrays; airborne and submarine radars; and tactical and strategic defense systems such as the inertial ballistic missile guidance system, which later opened the doors to the space age. AT&T developed key aspects of command, control, and communications systems such as the Strategic Air Command's NORAD; managed nuclear weapons production through its Scandia Laboratories operation; and developed NASA's management systems for the 1960s Apollo manned space flight program. AT&T Bellcomm created the management system that controlled the space program's contractors; put man on the moon and mission-critical into business terminology. Those systems engineering documents are enshrined in the National Air and Space Museum, Smithsonian Institution, Washington, D.C.[2]

Globally available communications are widely considered to have been instrumental in ending the cold war by ending the isolation of the Communist countries.

The telephone, invented by Bell in 1876, grew out of his work as a teacher of the hearing impaired. Bell first met Gardiner Greene Hubbard, who later became his partner and father-in-law, on April 8, 1872. Bell, Hubbard, and Thomas Sanders signed an agreement to develop telecommunications, later known as the "Bell Patent Association," on February 27, 1875. Bell did the inventing, the others financed the effort, and all shared in the patents which resulted.[5]

Elisha Gray filed his telephone caveat on February 14, 1876, but Bell had filed for the basic telephone patent earlier that day. A caveat, a confidential report of an unperfected invention, can serve as proof of the first date of invention. AT&T had established its earlier date of invention by getting its patent application to the patent office first. The patent was granted on March 7, 1876, and the first telephone message, — "Mr. Watson, come here, I want you!" — was received on March 10, 1876. It is the first call for emergency assistance, a use whose mission-critical messaging requirements spurred the service reliability that became an AT&T hallmark.

By autumn 1876, it was obvious to the members of the Bell Patent Association that satisfying the demand for telephone service was going to require extraordinary amounts of capital. Consequently, Hubbard tried to sell the telephone patent for $100,000. The offer was made to Western Union, a well-capitalized company, built on Samuel Morse's invention of telegraphy. Western Union rejected the offer. It wanted to concentrate its resources on its profitable telegraphy operations. The common wisdom was that telegraphy was more suitable for general (business) communication, and the voice telephone was only an electrical toy. This rejection of new messaging technology stands witness to a monumental business blunder, as Western Union lost its chance at the future of communications.

As the telephone business grew, it finally attracted the attention of Western Union. The technology of the day had created extensive district (local) telegraph systems and long distance telegraph networks. The Bell company wanted the telephone to replace the telegraph as the messaging system for business-to-business communication. Western Union was highly profitable and well established. It now owned the Gray caveat as well as other telephone patents and had a legal army. By the spring of 1878, Western Union's entry into the telephone business had dried up Bell's growth, business, and capital; Western Union had its second chance at the future.

Shortly thereafter, in the strangest twist of messaging history, Western Union and Bell reached an agreement to end their competition. Some authorities speculate that this may have been a result of Western Union's coming to believe that its telephone patent claims were invalid. Others attribute the action to its need to defend against a corporate takeover by the famous raider Jay Gould. Western Union divested its telephone patents under the agreement reached on November 10, 1879, in what was then viewed as a brilliant business decision.

Western Union got a monopoly of the telegraph market secured by concessions contained in the agreement. Telephone use was limited to "personal conversation" and was not to be used for the transmission of general business messages, market quotations, or news for sale or publication which competed with Western Union. The company also got a 20 percent royalty on telephone rental income for 17 years. The level of telephone technology, in 1878, limited telephone exchanges to a 15-mile radius and prevented the use of the telephone for long distance communications.

Bell got a 15 percent commission for message transfer to Western Union over much of the country. It also got the freedom to grow without significant competition as it consolidated its market position, technology development, and operating practices to the point where, in 1909, AT&T acquired control of Western Union by purchasing 30 percent of its stock and AT&T's president, Theodore N. Vail, became president of Western Union as well.

The companies shared a common headquarters at 15 Dey Street. Vail and E. J. Hall viewed telegraph and telephone service as complementary services, whose value was proportional to the combined number of people connected, rather than as technological rivals. Combining the messaging and telephone service under common leadership spurred the growth of each until the government, to ensure competition between telegraphy and telephony, forced their separation in 1913. AT&T prospered and Western Union weakened over the next 70 years.

As a consequence of the Modification of Final Judgment, the Bell System was dissolved at midnight, December 31, 1983, when AT&T separated from the regional Bell operating companies, which now provide local telephone service. AT&T's Bell Laboratories still carries the name and logo of the former Bell System as it engages in the research and product and service development which AT&T uses to manage its own operations and which it makes available to others.

AT&T is now unregulated except in the area of long distance services and competes subject to market forces in all other areas of operations. It ended 1993 with 2.4 million stockholders, — it is the most widely held U.S. stock; in 1992 it had revenues of $67,156,000,000; earnings per share of $2.94 (before accounting charges); a return on average common equity of 29%; and 308,700 employees, with close to 52,000 working outside the United States.

Today, AT&T provides communication services globally, having transformed itself from a company concentrating on its U.S. operations and international long distance services to one operating in about 100 countries with local operations, support, and service. Its worldwide networks carry about 175 million voice, data, video, and facsimile messages each business day. The company's mission statement is:

> *We are dedicated to being the world's best at bringing people together — giving them easy access to each other and to the information and services they want and need — anytime, anywhere.*

AT&T EasyLink Services' current scope and functionality is best viewed in tandem with the company that developed it. AT&T EasyLink Services grew out of the coordinating messaging network that AT&T uses to link its far-flung colossal operations into a unified entity. The EDI functions that are needed to support long distance billing, the email that links hundreds of thousands of employees, the management functions and the fax messages needed for a high-technology operation of great scale and scope are the basis for services offered over AT&T EasyLink Services' public network. They run on the same software and hardware platforms which support AT&T's own global operations and which have allowed the company to restructure itself to one-third its former size, enter new markets such as credit cards on a vast scale, execute takeovers such as NCR and McCaw, and integrate the acquisitions with athletic grace and speed.

AT&T Firsts

- Commercial trans-Atlantic telephone service (1927)
- Electrical digital computer (1937)
- Transistor (1947)
- Laser (1958)

- Communications satellite, Telstar (1962)
- Commercial lightwave system (1977)
- Universal Messaging Architecture (1983)
- Karmarkar linear programming algorithm (1987)
- Commercial ISDN long distance network service (1988)
- Optical digital processor (1990)
- Full-color, motion videophone that operates on regular phone lines (1992)
- First corporate double winner of the Malcolm Baldrige National Quality Award (1992)
- Commercial multimedia messaging service, PersonaLink (1994)

AT&T is organized, in the main, into four groups: Communications Services, Multimedia Products and Services, Network Systems, and Global Information Solutions. Within these groups, business units concentrate on defined markets. On August 30, 1994, AT&T EasyLink Services, which had been a separate business unit, became part of the AT&T Business Multimedia Services unit, which has responsibility for a variety of advanced messaging services. The combined unit is able to better meet customer needs in such areas as electronic commerce, workgroup collaboration, and information access and distribution.

AT&T acquired Western Union Corporation's Business Services group, containing its EasyLink electronic mail, telex, and packet-switched services, for $180 million on December 31, 1990. Bell had set out to advance telegraph messaging technology by developing a harmonic telegraph to send multiple messages over a single wire. Early experiments showed that the telephone was also practical, and the Bell Patent Associates' intention was to work in both messaging and telephony. The acquisition reactivated the vision of universal service articulated by Edward J. Hall and Theodore N. Vail by making global connectivity the AT&T EasyLink Services hallmark.

Western Union's EasyLink PTS prompt, telegraphy's "Proceed To Send," remains in use and is a reminder of Western Union's role in messaging

AT&T EasyLink Services

development. AT&T incorporated Western Union's last contribution to messaging, its switching centers in Missouri and Virginia, and adopted the Western Union trademark, EasyLink, for its global messaging services.

> *Cycles transfer power through chains made up from links; most links are made of plates and pins pressed together with great force; one type, the easylink, completes a chain without stress or undue effort.*

AT&T EasyLink Services' position, high on AT&T's organizational chain, testifies to messaging's importance to the company, a company that owes its very existence to being first with a business message at the patent office. Today AT&T EasyLink Services' range of products, support, and functions shows what can be done with the mix of capital, organization, and research foreseen by its founders.

The year 1994 was the 150th anniversary of the first electronic messaging demonstration by Western Union's founder, who played a critical role in AT&T EasyLink Services history. On May 24, 1844, Samuel Morse sent the first public message from Baltimore, Maryland to Washington, D.C. The message content was *"What Hath God Wrought."*

Bell Letter, March 25, 1878

Kensington, March 25, 1878.

To the capitalists of the Electric Telephone Company:

Gentlemen — It has been suggested that at this, our first meeting, I should lay before you a few ideas, concerning the future of the electric telephone, together with any suggestions that occur to me in regard to the best mode of introducing the instrument to the public.

The telephone may be briefly described as an electrical contrivance for reproducing in distant places, the tones and articulations of a speaker's voice, so that conversation can be carried on by word of mouth between persons in different rooms, in different streets, or in different towns.

The great advantage it possesses over every other form of electrical apparatus consists in the fact that it requires no skill to operate the instrument. All other telegraphic machines produce signals which require to be translated by experts, and such instruments are therefore extremely limited in their application, but the telephone actually speaks, and for this reason it can be utilized for nearly every purpose for which speech is employed.

At the present time we have a perfect network of gas pipes and water pipes throughout our large cities. We have main pipes laid under the streets communicating by side pipes with the various dwellings, enabling the members — to draw their supplies of gas and water from a common source.

In a similar manner it is conceivable that cables of telephone wires could be laid under ground, or suspended overhead, communicating by branch wires with private dwellings, counting houses, shops, manufactories, etc. uniting them through the main cable with a central office where the wire could be connected as desired, establishing direct communication between any two places in the city. Such a plan as this, though impracticable at the present moment, will, I firmly believe, be the outcome of the introduction of the telephone to the public. Not only so, but I believe in the future wires will unite the head offices of telephone companies in different cities, and a man in one part of the country may communicate by word of mouth with another in a distant place.

In regard to other present uses for the telephone, the instrument can be supplied so cheaply as to compete on favorable terms with speaking tubes, bells and annunciators, as a means of communication between different parts of the house. This seems to be a very favorable application of the telephone, not only on account of the large number of telephones that would be wanted, but because it would lead eventually to the plan of intercommunication referred to above. I would therefore recommend that special arrangements be made for the introduction of the telephone into hotels and private buildings in place of the speaking tubes and annunciators, at present employed. Telephones sold for this purpose could be stamped or numbered in such a way as to distinguish them from those employed for business purposes, and an agreement could be signed by the purchaser that the telephones should become forfeited to the company if used for other purposes than those specified in the agreement.

It is probable that such a use of the telephone would speedily become popular, and that as the public became accustomed to the telephone in their houses they would recognize the advantage of a system of intercommunication.

In conclusion, I would say that it seems to me that the telephone should immediately be brought prominently before the public, as a means of communication between bankers, merchants, manufacturers, wholesale and retail dealers, dock companies, water companies, police offices, fire stations, newspaper offices, hospitals and public buildings and for use in railway offices, in mines and other operations.

Although there is a great field for the telephone in the immediate present, I believe there is still greater in the future. By bearing in mind the great object to be ultimately achieved, I believe that the telephone company cannot only secure for itself a business of the most remunerative kind, but also benefit the public in a way that has never been previously attempted.

I am, gentlemen, your obedient servant,

                    Alexander Graham Bell

Chapter 2

AT&T Global Messaging Applications

AT&T Global Messaging's qualities grow from its design as a method of universal connectivity within enterprises, between enterprises, and in mission-critical applications. It extends the power of local messaging systems by attaching them to a worldwide public network of exceptional reach and reliability. The combination of public and private communications provides the business manager with a set of tools to add faster "time-to-market" benefits to new and existing information processes. Business has changed, and today business advances at the speed of communications. This speed means more than just the speed of the link. It now includes the narrowing of the time from idea to implementation, the ability to communicate from anywhere to everywhere, and the building of messaging applications which go far beyond the basics of electronic mail.

AT&T EasyLink Services supports both open and closed user groups. User groups are software-defined private messaging networks, resident on the AT&T Mail network, which provide their members with special services. ABA/net, the network of the American Bar Association, is an

AT&T Mail closed user group that is discussed later in this chapter as an example of the customization and services provided to enterprise-level users.

AT&T EasyLink Services positions itself as the communications enabler of choice for global formal applications that are mission-critical. Applications are mission-critical if their performance is essential to an enterprise's operational requirements. These applications are an integral part of a specific and functional business process and, as such, generate a stream of transactions that are predictable, either in form or in content. Examples are purchase orders, price notifications, claims processing, inventory reporting, and other process-linked functions.

The service is unique in that its primary focus is high-volume, mission-critical applications rather than interpersonal messaging or informal messaging. Informal non-structured messages are those which are not integrally tied to a specific application or repetitive function. AT&T offers advanced consumer-oriented messaging services through AT&T PersonaLink Services.

AT&T EasyLink Services concentrates on supplying the messaging resources necessary for mission-critical applications. These applications may be characterized as distribution (one-to-many) and information gathering (many-to-one). Mission- or function-critical applications characteristically require security, reliability, accountability, and, often, global support, which can be provided only on a network designed and managed to support such applications. These classes of applications are essential to an enterprise's economic success and, often, to its competitive position.

Formal applications can be viewed in terms of their positioning in the organization. The responsible managers may be operations and functional heads — the head of sales for sales automation; the head of purchasing for purchase orders; the head of Information Systems for automating and selecting systems to replace manual or older automated systems — and/or cross-functional committees charged with finding solutions to key problems.

AT&T Global Messaging Applications

These types of applications require

- System reliability
- Ease of use
- Preservation and enhancement of in-place investments
- Mail-enabling application tool availability
- Professional services
- Demonstrable cost-benefits over existing and current alternatives

Most enterprises today have some form of in-house messaging systems. In legacy environments, these are generally mainframe and midrange systems running office automation and mail software. In newer environments, often these messaging systems are LANs running email software. When such messaging systems exist, then the manager's requirement is often for a mission-critical-level backbone. This is a globally connective messaging system which provides a backbone messaging capability to be used for the interconnection of stand-alone systems and remote locations. This is an application-independent application. Often, the initial messaging approach is to consider the existing corporate wide area network (WAN) that is or may be installed.

AT&T EasyLink Services provides a strong connectivity backbone in those cases where there is no installed WAN or other in-house messaging connectivity solution such as the Soft*Switch Central product and the enterprise prefers not to design, implement, and manage a WAN for messaging purposes. AT&T EasyLink Services provides a strong interconnection backbone option for the manager of communications or information services who prefers to off-load this responsibility. The features essential in a public messaging solution for this environment are

- Reliability
- System and LAN connectivity
- Global connectivity
- X.400 support and ADMD interconnection
- System transparency
- Corporate directory capability

- Support of multiple delivery methods (fax, telex, paper, etc.)
- Internet mail access
- Flexible billing
- Professional services

Network traffic is often driven by the need to have applications communicate across systems, locations, or functional groups and the need to extend reach and functionality to business partners who may be globally dispersed. Direct network links to external networks, such as X.400 public services and a variety of private systems, are often viewed as undesirable, since managing a large number of outside connections is costly and difficult. Enterprises seek other alternatives that can absorb substantial growth in application complexity and volume but that are application-independent.

Many companies that have installed and managed their own messaging and backbone network find that they no longer wish to maintain and manage those network functions which are not central to their own business operations. In those cases, a professional external group can manage these networks or the functions can be outsourced to a value-added network (VAN), such as AT&T EasyLink Services. The chief financial officers of companies, who are increasingly trying to reduce costs and focus their companies on their core strengths, often initiate such decisions. AT&T offers private messaging network management services through its Professional Services organization.

AT&T Mail, because of its public network basis, is appropriate for any enterprise with high-reliability, high-volume message requirements. Message volume, range, and mission-critical nature are more appropriate decision points than size, industry, or degree of automation. The decision to use AT&T EasyLink Services' messaging services is often based on the need to support the most mission-critical communications with exceptional availability and reliability. These needs include the ability to communicate

- With multiple locations
- With business partners

AT&T Global Messaging Applications 15

- With other companies
- Internationally
- With multiple electronic mail systems
- With multiple applications
- With one or more mainframe or midrange computers
- With LANs
- Using wired and wireless devices
- Using multiple message types
- Using multiple delivery options

AT&T's integrated line of public and private messaging, wired and wireless connectivity, computers, and communications services is capable of meeting almost any combination of such requirements with the flexibility provided by a full-service messaging provider. No other vendor offers a comparably robust suite of email, fax, telex, information services, mobile messaging services, and related products with single-source availability and support.

Benefits and Applications

AT&T Mail brings people and information closer together regardless of location or time differences. This total messaging solution gives businesses of all types and sizes a new way to improve their market position by providing the capability to transmit and exchange information faster and more efficiently. The total messaging solution improves communications in the following areas:

- Within a single department of a company
- Between departments in a single company
- Between locations of a single company
- Between companies
- Between companies and their customers

- Between companies and their business partners

AT&T Mail enhances the potential of existing computer systems, networks, or applications without requiring additional major investments and without causing serious disruption to productivity. The demand for electronic mail comes from companies of all sizes, representing all industrial and vertical markets, that seek a single, comprehensive, flexible, cost-effective, end-to-end solution. Enterprises view the following as key global messaging requirements:

Fast, effective delivery of messages	Reliable person-to-person communication that eliminates repetitive telephone tag; ensures delivery of memos, letters, and other business documents; and enables customers to overcome time zone differences.
Wide distribution of a single message	The ability to easily send a single message to a wide audience regardless of the recipients' location, organization, or system. The information can be destined for a department, company, or community of interest, including individuals without access to any form of automated service.
Reliable, simple exchange of business transactions	The ability to transmit memos, letters, spreadsheets, EDI, or forms swiftly and accurately.
International messaging	The ability to communicate effectively anytime, anyplace to anywhere in the world without limitations resulting from time zones, equipment used, systems used, or the type of information exchanged.

AT&T Mail works as an adhesive to combine networks of user groups with a common need to communicate as a cohesive unit. These groups may work at different functions or in multiple locations but can be linked together through the public messaging network for either permanent or temporary workgroup integration and information sharing. An example is a multinational manufacturer with headquarters in New York which needs a business communications system to integrate the activities of individual workgroups. These workgroups need to communicate among them-

AT&T Global Messaging Applications 17

selves, share information with other divisions, and report back to the corporate office. AT&T Mail provides the company with the broad connectivity it requires while protecting the company's existing computer system investment, enhancing individual and overall productivity, and providing an environment for controlled growth without unnecessary investment.

AT&T Mail redefines the messaging process into an ongoing series of controlled business transactions which are ideal for linking office automation and business applications. When positioned as an application-oriented service, it is especially effective in improving, simplifying, and speeding document processing.

AT&T Mail Business Advantages

AT&T Mail messaging services provide the following features, products, or services which directly address the need for business to work cheaper, faster, easier, and better with the same or diminished resources.

Ease of Use	No special training is required to create, read, or send messages.
Accountability	All messages are assigned a log number and can be identified by address, subject, date, length, and status.
Immediate Start-Up	Use can begin immediately.
Worldwide Access	Customers can use AT&T Mail globally. Messages can be sent anywhere in the world with delivery options such as AT&T EasyLink Services' MailFAX, Enhanced Telex, Internet gateway, and AT&T Mail 400 Service. Alternative delivery methods provide wider distribution capabilities to non-subscribers.
Versatility	AT&T Mail offers multiple gateway interfaces, numerous delivery options, and service features to meet virtually all communications needs. It is a powerful, easy-to-use system that goes far

beyond conventional electronic messaging and lets a business customize its network and products to meet its specific needs, whether public, private, or a combination of both.

Growth	AT&T Mail enables companies to automate a single person, group, or company. The enterprise can start with a small system or a single service and expand communication capabilities at any time while maintaining established systems and standards.
Investment Protection	AT&T Mail provides a flexible operating environment, giving subscribers the benefits of long-term investment protection, integration ease, and enhanced application portability. Support for existing systems and software allows for simple integration with in-place systems. AT&T Mail lets subscribers connect to the service over their existing computer equipment, which can be any combination of desktop, LAN, mobile, mainframe, midrange, UNIX, or X.400 installed systems.
Connectivity	AT&T Mail offers a connectivity solution for every user. The solution supports terminals, PCs, LANs, and most common office automation applications running on minis or mainframes. Connectivity is transparent to the user and can accommodate both the mobile and the stationary user.
One-Stop Shopping	AT&T Mail is a single integrated message solution for management and workgroup networking which provides messaging tools and every other element needed to make them work effectively. It also addresses the needs of the enterprise by supporting both intra- and inter-enterprise messaging needs.
Increased Productivity	Customers require an increasing amount of information that must be delivered in short time frames and in a form that can be used to control operations and speed decision making. AT&T

AT&T Global Messaging Applications

Mail meets these needs by giving instant access, both domestically and internationally, to important documents and confirming delivery of these documents, speeding decision making and eliminating time zone differences.

Multi-location Delivery — Messages and documents can be sent to any number of users, located worldwide, simultaneously, by either email, fax, or telex.

Business Applications

Messaging applications found in most enterprises present the following needs and opportunities:

Multi-location Communication — In-house systems rarely support messaging outside of the operation; they often address only the mail needs of campus users. AT&T Mail supports one of the most valuable applications in any enterprise. That is, it provides reliable, quick communications between locations, including the home office, branch offices, remote sales locations, mobile workers, telecommuters, and business partners. These locations may be geographically dispersed in domestic or international locations. Telephone tag is lessened because of the use of store and forward messaging. Communications are delivered to one location or broadcast to many in a single unbroken operation. Files, forms, and information can be shared, and spreadsheets or word processing documents can be developed and revised efficiently over email. Meeting dates and calendars can easily be synchronized, both inside and outside of the enterprise.

Customer Service — Memos and newsletters can be developed and sent using AT&T Mail. These items can be prepared using a computer and sent to the AT&T

Mail Service for delivery to a variety of devices, including email boxes, fax machines, telex machines, and postal mail. AT&T Mail Shared Folders and AT&T Mail Catalog are exceptional distribution methods for price update bulletins, safety alerts, and software fixes with anywhere, anytime access or delivery.

Finance Operations

Exceptional time savings can be achieved by automating the purchasing, invoicing, and credit collections processes. AT&T EasyLink Services provides the links that allow internal systems to connect to the outside world and accelerate cash flow. Orders and invoices can be sent worldwide electronically to speed order processing and speed deliveries. AT&T MailFAX is often well suited to environments where trading partners have not yet agreed upon EDI trading. Such systems, which decrease the time between the ordering of a product and the receipt of goods, have demonstrated impressive returns on the system investment by reaching and maintaining ideal inventory levels. An additional benefit is that out-of-stock conditions can be reduced, improving customer satisfaction.

Financial Management

Spreadsheets can be developed and revised by globally distributed individuals using AT&T Mail to route the documents to reviewers inside and outside the enterprise. This procedure can lead to quicker, more timely, and more profitable decisions. AT&T Mail Project Codes, shown on monthly bills, can be used to categorize costs associated with specific cost centers and allow chargeback to the appropriate entity. This can be a valuable billing tool for professional services providers.

Telemarketing/ Marketing

Client lead information can be transferred between Telemarketing/Marketing and branch locations quickly and easily; follow-up phone calls, appointment confirmations, letters, and notices can all be integrated easily over AT&T Mail's varied and robust delivery options: email, fax, telex, U.S. mail or courier. AT&T Mail broadcast capabilities using these delivery options make it easy to target specific prospective clients for email, fax, or direct mail campaigns.

Sales Automation	AT&T Mail can greatly increase the productivity of the sales force while improving the communication between headquarters and field sales. Email can be used to transmit sales and route reports, distribute sales leads, store and disseminate proposal boilerplate, distribute electronic newsletters, communicate pricing promotions, and keep staff aware of price changes. AT&T Mail integration with sales force automation software can multiply sales effectiveness.
Electronic Bulletin Boards	Most businesses or organizations have the need to distribute information to multiple outlets and delivery points quickly and easily. This can be done efficiently and effectively using AT&T Shared Folders, AT&T Mail Catalog, and AT&T Information Services InfoBoards for pricing information, product information, personnel information or job postings, and a variety of other information. These applications include external or internal newsletters, product information bulletins, pricing bulletins, wordprocessing or spreadsheet files, software fixes or updates, and form depositories.
Human Resources	Electronic messaging provides human resources with an opportunity to redefine its role in a corporate environment. Human resources is automating recruitment and hiring, benefits and insurance reporting, satisfaction surveys, and vouchering through the use of mail-enabled

	intelligent electronic forms, shared folders, and email.
Research Organizations	Access to AT&T Information Services allows research organizations of legal firms, multi-national firms, and educational centers to conveniently locate, access, and distribute research information. AT&T adds reach and delivery options and allows researchers to either do their own searching or receive results from internal or external library specialists over AT&T Mail. These services offer powerful ways to increase office productivity. The information obtained from the vast amounts of data, records, files, and abstracts is much more convenient to use and results are obtained faster over AT&T Mail. AT&T Information Services provide speed and convenience in research. It is possible to access over 900 databases over AT&T Mail, have the free services of a reference librarian, and receive only one bill at the end of the month for those services interactively used or requested through email.

Work Process Improvements

Messaging is not only a new technology but a new work process as well. Public messaging networks facilitate the unification of an enterprise's functional islands, eliminating the redundant handling of data. This reduces the potential for error and integrates a variety of reliable electronic media into critical business processes. Users increase the efficiency of their operations and the level of their customers' satisfaction, resulting in significant competitive advantages.

Petrochemical Companies	Petrochemical companies rely on electronic messaging because of the inherent interdependency of their operations. One company alone has 28,000 corporate users that communicate with thousands of electronic

mailboxes worldwide. For this company, the problem was how to extend its reach to worldwide customers and suppliers. Proprietary solutions were quickly discarded as it became apparent that only an international, public messaging network could keep pace with technology advances, work with the company's existing hardware, and allow users of equipment from various vendors to communicate.

The solution was to connect the internal system to a public messaging network which consolidated and managed faxes and existing email. This use of AT&T Mail makes internal and external communications simpler and more effective, and provides protection against changing technology. Another major petroleum company uses electronic messaging to help it adjust to worldwide events. An unexpected result is the improvement of relationships with global suppliers as the cost of doing business with them actually decreases. For example, freeing the branch in Tokyo from having its staff available during New York working hours, a fourteen-hour time difference, produced significant savings in overtime.

Air Express Companies	Air express companies find that electronic messaging permits customers and suppliers to interact in a way that is simple and effective. Customers need information about package delivery status, and the carrier's ability to provide timely package status information is often as important to customers as timely package delivery. The ability to respond to customers who inquire about shipment status and to notify them about package delivery are critical air express carrier service components. AT&T EasyLink Services' email and Enhanced FAX allow both people and computers to respond to business needs on a customized, time-of-day, or seasonal

basis. The carrier pays only for messages that are sent, so networking dollars are spent more wisely.

Travel Information Network

A well-known travel information network is a successful example of electronic commerce. This operating division of a major airline serves travel agencies at 14,000 locations in the United States, and another 1,700 in Canada. These travel agents send faxes using AT&T EasyLink Services. Travel agent clients stay right at their workstations while sending a travel itinerary rather than printing it and using a fax machine.

Financial Messaging Applications

One key advantage of sending spreadsheet and other computer files by electronic mail, instead of by fax or by regular mail, is that the recipient can develop the information further before sending it on to another person. The recipient can extract key data from the file, incorporate it into a written financial report, and attach that file to an email message. Thus, financial analysts can move the same data around the world, constantly refining and revising it and using it in a variety of reports. A second key advantage is the simultaneous reception of broadcast email such as interest rates or earnings reports at globally distributed locations.

Public networks offering an extensive number of messaging products now play a primary role in sending or receiving vital business information. Millions of worldwide subscribers to these powerful networks share information with trading partners, bringing them all closer together and, in the process, redefining modern transactions. They collaborate around the world using a large variety of electronic messaging tools — decreasing decision times from days to minutes, from hours to seconds.

Messaging cuts across all organizational levels, shortening the line of command and the psychological distance between top management and staff. The increased responsiveness contributes directly to the sharpen-

AT&T Global Messaging Applications 25

ing of a business's global competitive edge. Electronic messaging offers powerful information management tools to its users.

AT&T EasyLink Services FORMsolutions

AT&T EasyLink Services' FORMsolutions, a set of mail-enhanced forms products, uses the AT&T Mail network to provide value-added communication services and intelligent electronic forms. The global connectivity of AT&T Mail allows electronic forms to be used off-campus with business partners, mobile workers, and remote locations. The integration of intelligent electronic forms and the AT&T Mail global public messaging capabilities supports automation of all stages of the forms process. The stages include design, fill-in, distribution, and processing. The benefits of mail-enabled intelligent forms begin with immediate delivery of form data and continue with automatic processing without human intervention or wasted paper. The elimination of paper from storage, waste, and obsolescence can result in large cost reductions in addition to the increased productivity obtained.

Forms process automation savings are achieved by reducing the time spent completing and processing business paper forms. The automation of these processes is made possible by switching from paper to electronic methods. The faster processing of electronic forms substantially reduces the time needed to complete a business process and provides the enterprise with a competitive advantage.

Electronic forms can be used in any area where paper forms are cumbersome and expensive to use and there is a need for a quickly and accurately structured data collection. Application examples are:

- Mobile employee automation
- Inventory control
- Expense reporting
- Corporate training registration
- Purchasing automation
- Insurance agent data collection

- Human resource applications
- In-house travel services

AT&T EasyLink Services' FORMsolutions provides cost savings for the implementing enterprise. The savings directly attributable to improved form development and processing are found in the following areas:

- Paper forms production
- Form completion errors
- Postage or express mail
- Warehousing cost of forms
- Form distribution freight
- Obsolete form waste
- Employee time spent completing forms

AT&T EasyLink Services' FORMsolutions provides strategic advantages to the implementing enterprise. The strategic advantages are achieved by providing the following:

- Competitive edge in process and procedure
- Information availability and timeliness
- Reduced transaction time
- Improved customer support
- Reduced operating costs
- Improved control of forms and information content
- Improved personnel productivity
- Accuracy of corporate information

AT&T EasyLink Services' FORMsolutions allows intelligent electronic forms to be anywhere, at any time and extends the reach of intelligent electronic forms beyond the campus to business partners, mobile workers, and remote locations. This is achieved through the tight integration of the electronic form software and AT&T Mail.

AT&T Enhanced FAX Applications

AT&T Enhanced FAX offers a wide range of value-added features for companies with high-volume fax operations. AT&T MailFAX and AT&T EasyLink integrate fax into the desktop computer environment for companies that have migrated to electronic mail. AT&T Enhanced FAX services provide an effective set of network-based improvements for fax transmission and delivery. These services support the transmission of text and pictures to any number of locations. Time-saving features include multiple redialing and simultaneous broadcast of information to locations predefined in a stored address list. Some application examples are:

Fax from Host Applications or Personal Computers	When a stand-alone fax machine is used to transmit documents created on a computer, time is wasted printing the document, walking to the fax machine, waiting for the fax to be free, dialing until the other machine answers, sending the document, and waiting until the original can be removed. With AT&T EasyLink Fax, the document is sent straight from the host or personal computer to virtually any fax machine in the world.
Fax Business Forms from a Computer	AT&T EasyLink Services FAXAFORM allows storage of form images, including logos, graphics, text, signatures, and fonts, on the network. Variable data is created on a computer, merged with the appropriate form on the network, and sent to the recipient list. An AT&T EasyLink Services customer uses this system in plant maintenance and repair. Buyers use a mainframe purchase order application. The system then retrieves the appropriate fax number from a database and faxes the order to the supplier.
Private Fax Mailboxes	Incoming faxes are electronically stored in the subscriber's private mailbox until the subscriber, using the mailbox ID and password, specifies the fax delivery point. The subscriber may use any Group III fax machine or compatible device,

located anywhere, to retrieve the faxes received at the mailbox.

Computer users with AT&T Enhanced FAX accounts may dial into the AT&T Enhanced FAX mailbox and download faxes using a fax modem and software. Computer users with AT&T Mail accounts, AT&T Enhanced FAX accounts, and Combined Mailboxes may retrieve faxes and email in a single session. Retrieved faxes are managed locally, in the same manner and with the same tools as email.

AT&T FAX Catalog

AT&T FAX Catalog offers a fast and inexpensive way to provide up-to-date information to large groups of customers, sales organizations, and employees. Following voice prompts, the caller indicates the desired document and the phone number of a fax machine anywhere in the world. The document is faxed to that machine. Callers can be asked questions using voice prompts, and the information can be transcribed to tape, disk, or paper to create a marketing database. Credit cards can be verified within the service prior to information release if documents are being sold.

Integrated Fax, Email, and Telex

Companies that do business often need the ability to deliver messages originating on email or telex to fax machines. Companies with electronic mail systems often need to communicate with customers or clients that rely on fax machines. AT&T Enhanced FAX extends the reach of these systems to include delivery to a fax machine.

Broadcast Fax

Faxes, from fax machine or computer, can be broadcast to hundreds or even thousands of recipients through AT&T Enhanced FAX using distribution lists which can be uploaded or stored on the network. Stored lists can be selected with a one-key command. Large broadcasts can be scheduled to take advantage of lower overnight rates.

AT&T Global Messaging Applications

Some typical AT&T Enhanced FAX applications, by industry, are discussed below.

Insurance

AT&T Enhanced FAX provides the means for agencies to keep their representatives aware of new policies, rates, and other important information. Using AT&T Enhanced FAX, insurance agencies can

- Transmit new policy changes and rate information to all field representatives with a single call.
- Protect confidential financial information in a personal fax mailbox.
- Allow agents who are out of the office immediate access to their important fax messages.
- Increase efficiency by letting office staff send fax messages without worrying about busy signals.

Sales

AT&T Enhanced FAX provides the means for sales operations to give the entire sales force quick access to pricing updates, new product information, and promotional materials. Traveling sales executives can respond quickly to customer requests, for inventory status, production schedules, and delivery dates. All representatives can have immediate access to product changes and new product availability.

Sales operations using AT&T Enhanced FAX can:

- Fax the latest price changes to the entire sales force with just a single call.
- Allow executives to access fax messages — including new leads, delivery schedules, and promotional updates — while traveling virtually anywhere in the world.
- Improve customer service by immediately forwarding new and revised orders to all appropriate parties.
- Protect confidential product information by assigning personal fax mailboxes to key sales executives.

Engineering

AT&T Enhanced FAX provides the means for engineers to establish fast, efficient ways to communicate with clients, suppliers, and the firm's field engineers. Specifications, technical evaluations, new procedures, designs, and drawings can be sent to decision makers quickly and confidentially. Engineers using AT&T Enhanced FAX can:

- Quickly transmit designs at high resolution to a list of suppliers and corporate executives.
- Send analysis reports to a list of executives worldwide with just a single call.
- Allow engineers to retrieve reports, designs, specifications, and other documents quickly from virtually anywhere in the world through use of the AT&T Enhanced FAX mailbox.
- Protect confidential reports and specs by assigning user ID codes and passwords to key corporate personnel.

Hospitality

AT&T Enhanced FAX provides the means for hospitality management to improve communications with travel agencies, tour operators, and corporate meeting planners. Hospitality management can efficiently communicate with individual properties concerning the latest information on convention planning, banquet scheduling, and room availability. Hospitality management, with AT&T Enhanced FAX, can:

- Fax new promotional information to travel agents, tour operators, and planners with just a single call.
- Give traveling executives immediate access to fax documents from virtually any touch-tone phone in the world.
- Fax banquet and meeting room designs at high resolution to corporate meeting planners immediately.
- Safeguard confidential fax messages by assigning a personal fax mailbox to selected management executives.

AT&T Enhanced FAX provides similar benefits in other business applications using standard fax machines as the delivery point. Executives in

AT&T Global Messaging Applications 31

large and small companies can use AT&T Enhanced FAX to send and receive information anytime, almost anywhere. The service expands fax operations to allow the user to:

- Send the same document to multiple locations.
- Receive faxes on the road.
- Send confidential material.
- Make sure the fax has actually been received.
- Avoid redialing a busy number.
- Send faxes straight from a computer.
- Provide documents on demand.

AT&T Enhanced FAX features are designed to support high-volume fax users. The ability to consolidate delivery reporting, detailed billing, and related network services makes the management of large fax operations easier and more effective. AT&T Enhanced FAX network resources allow high-volume use with the assurance that the needed fax equipment, telephone lines, and staffing are available at all times. These services allow the fax to be used as a key tool in electronic commerce by removing the limitations found in typical fax operations.

AT&T EDI Applications

Electronic Data Interchange (EDI) is the phrase used to describe the inter-enterprise exchange of business transactions, such as purchase orders, invoices, or CAD/CAM information, in standard formats over communication links computer-to-computer. EDI allows enterprises to move from costly paper-based inter-enterprise business processes to paperless exchange of business transactions with trading partners. EDI promotes greater efficiency, time saving, and cost savings in business operations.

Until EDI, business was conducted primarily on paper. The use of business forms to exchange information between trading partners is too slow, costly, and inaccurate to support just-in-time global commerce. The growth of the service economy and the amount of data associated with the manufacture and sale of new communications and information products and services also require more timely and economical methods of business data exchange. The widespread use of computers and communications in business provides the base for EDI, the cost-effective way to communicate and process business data.

The information for a paper purchase order is written, typed, or computer-printed on a multipart form; this is a slow process with many opportunities for error. Once the document is produced, it is sent to the supplier through mail, express, or fax. If the purchase order is mailed, then it will spend several days in transit. If the purchase order is faxed, then it will still have to be entered into the supplier's order entry system, with additional delay and possible errors. Acknowledgments, confirmations, tracking, and corrections introduce additional delays, possible errors, and added costs. The problem becomes critical when just-in-time manufacturing depends on timely, low-cost inventory control at the buyer, supplier, subsupplier, and transit levels. EDI provides a strategic business advantage to those companies which take advantage of the opportunities to improve operations.

When paper-based processes are replaced with electronic equivalents, the enterprise benefits from lower inventory and float, increased productivity of its clerical staff, and faster response to market changes. AT&T's role is to provide the public network resources necessary for inter-enterprise operations, allowing its customers to concentrate their resources on developing those processes which are unique to the company and which affect its bottom line.

AT&T views EDI as more than a way to transmit business documents between companies. A thoroughly implemented EDI solution encompasses the "seamless" integration and automation of a company's external business transactions with its internal accounting systems, inventory control, procurement, operations, and back-office systems and functions.

For most companies, EDI implementation is still at the concept stage. Companies which have seen EDI benefits understood the need for high-level management endorsement of an inter-departmental implementation plan. EDI is not a technical issue; it is a business issue. The process of establishing the infrastructure of EDI, which includes the network services, software, applications interfaces, and hardware, is just the beginning. Companies that have automated current paper documents and processes have discovered that they have merely automated archaic business practices. The first step in re-engineering a business to achieve EDI benefits is cross-functional analysis of company business practices. EDI can be the catalyst for innovation by developing practices that convey strategic benefits to a corporation. These benefits include items such as improved customer satisfaction, better time to market, greater process flexibility, enhanced on-time delivery performance, and superior quality of products and services. A good example of "changing the way we do business" is demonstrated in a quick response or just-in-time environment.

An example is the shift seen in the retail industry. Until EDI, inventory management was the retailer's responsibility in a traditional retailer-manufacturer environment. With EDI, the retailer and manufacturer allocate inventory replenishment. The retailer can provide point-of-sale and inventory data from automated systems to the manufacturer. Information sharing outside the bounds of each enterprise reaps the benefits of competitive advantage, cost reduction, more efficient inventory management, and customer satisfaction that are not possible using traditional function separation.

A recent EDI Group Ltd. survey of EDI customers showed that error rate reduction ranged from 25 to 50 percent while processing costs were reduced from $3.00 to $7.00 per document. These savings, while very substantial, are small compared to the savings from lower inventories, higher order fill levels, and the other benefits of just-in-time manufacturing. Other benefits include less paper handling and tracking effort, allowing the redeployment of staff to building relationships with customers and more effective sales efforts by reducing the efforts involved in order processing and order entry error correction. The resulting improved customer service and satisfaction also affects the bottom line. EDI promotes the integration of business operations and systems between business partners, tying customers to suppliers, as the enhanced working relationship provides competitive advantages.

Transportation	The transportation industry uses EDI to communicate with carriers of various sorts, such as truck, rail, and ships. EDI shipping documents include order entry, bills of lading, customs documentation, and shipment status. For the shipper, the most critical message is the shipment status. Shippers must manage their company's inventory even when it is in the possession of the carrier. Shippers must know where the freight is at any time. Before EDI, tracking shipments was a tedious, time-consuming process. Customers would receive their orders late, sometimes damaged, or not at all.

With the EDI Shipment Status transaction, a shipper can track carrier performance and respond with fast, accurate answers when customers inquire about order delivery. In this application, the shipper can electronically monitor the exact location and status of each shipment of inventory. Carriers feed the shipper's computerized freight management system with the EDI Shipment Status. This application promotes efficient inventory management, reduces costs, and improves customer service. |
| Retail | Quick response has been used in the retail industry for many years. Stock keeping unit (SKU) level sales data is captured at the point-of-sale at the retailer's store location. The information is transmitted to the retailer's headquarters application system. Using this data, standard electronic documents such as purchase orders, advance ship notices, invoices, and adjustments flow between the retailer's and manufacturer's computers over EDI without manual intervention. EDI is a key enabling technology for a quick response implementation.

In a quick response implementation, costs are |

	reduced as a result of reduced manual intervention. Revenues are increased because of improved "in stock" position. Speedy stock replenishment keeps the retailer's shelves constantly replenished, resulting in a higher level of customer satisfaction. EDI also enhances information flow between retailers and manufacturers and their suppliers, banks, and transportation companies
Grocery	Efficient consumer response (ECR) is a grocery-industry strategy in which distributors and suppliers work together to bring better value to grocery consumers. Distributors and suppliers jointly focus on the efficiency of the total grocery supply system, rather than the efficiency of individual components, to reduce total system costs, inventories, and physical assets while improving the consumer's choice of high-quality, fresh grocery products. The ultimate goal of ECR is to enable distributors and suppliers to work together as business allies to maximize consumer satisfaction and minimize cost. Companies can use the VAN of their choice, and the VANs provide the connectivity between the various networks and operating environments. AT&T has interconnects with all the major VANS.
Utility	A very large utility authority is a power supplier to utility boards, utility companies, and distributors, and directly to major companies within seven southeastern states. It has over 10,000 active vendors and suppliers to whom it issues 200,000 releases on blanket contracts and 50,000 requests for quotation (RFQ) annually. The authority, using AT&T EasyLink Services as its EDI VAN, launched a pilot program in early 1993, and in late spring, began operations with its trading partners. It now has over 150 trading partners exchanging standard computer-to-computer EDI and about 235 smaller

trading partners receiving RFQs and purchase orders over FreeForm Conversion Service. AT&T EDI's FreeForm Conversion Service is used to allow suppliers with limited technical capabilities to participate in the EDI program. This service allows the authority to send human-readable EDI documents to fax machines.

Human Resources

AT&T was a pioneer in the application of EDI to human resources. In 1992, AT&T participated in the Workgroup for EDI pilot project with its insurance carriers. The Workgroup for EDI is a coalition of health-care providers urging the industry-wide adoption of EDI prior to 1996. X12 EDI standards for the insurance and health-care industry have been developed and approved for the employee enrollment, eligibility data, claim submission, and claim payment/remittance advice processes. The Healthcare Financing Administration (HCFA), which administers Medicare, has mandated that all providers must submit claims using EDI by the end of 1994.

Petroleum

A very large oil company uses AT&T EDI to send invoices to its distributors around the world. In this application, the company sends the standard EDI invoice to its distributor in the UK. The distributor then sends a standard EDI remittance advice document to the oil company's bank and a copy to the oil company.

These transactions take place in a matter of minutes rather than the days — or weeks typical in a paper-based invoice transaction. The oil company gets paid faster, but all trading partners benefit, as EDI speeds up all the processes. Issues of "float" in this application are greatly diminished or eliminated altogether because the trading partners work together to make the processes work. In many cases, a company overcomes the "float game" by offering its customers a discount for paying electronically (or, alternatively, the payer asks the receiver of the payment to give a discount). Benefits in this application are much the same as for other EDI applications — documents are processed faster and more accurately, and cash flow is greatly improved.

AT&T External EDI Applications

As a corporation, AT&T is committed to using EDI in all facets of its business. This effort began in 1983 when the AT&T purchasing organization implemented EDI with four suppliers. Today that organization is exchanging EDI documents with over 300 suppliers world-wide. AT&T Network Systems business unit conducts all of its business with the regional Bell operating companies (RBOCs) over EDI in all of the applications described below. In 1992 over 1.5 million transactions were exchanged using EDI. AT&T intends to remain at the forefront of EDI implementation. Its vision is to continue deploying EDI programs, recognizing the value of EDI in cost reduction efforts, quality initiatives, and its business process re-engineering. The corporate treasury organization ties all the EDI programs together in a financial EDI program.

Purchasing	AT&T is exchanging nearly 2 million transactions, such as purchase orders, shipping notices, and forecast data, annually. The purchasing organization extends its EDI capabilities globally with implementations in the Netherlands, Ireland, and Hong Kong.
Order Processing	AT&T has responded to customer requests and accepts customer orders for AT&T products using EDI.
Invoicing	AT&T is also actively implementing EDI in its Financial Operations Centers. In 1993 over 1 million invoices were processed using AT&T EDI, bringing substantial cost savings over paper processing.

Network Services Billing	AT&T bills its large telecommunications customers using the consolidated services transaction set. AT&T participated with the Telecom Forum in the development of this standard, which is designed to provide telecommunications invoice data in detail.
Human Resources	AT&T was the first corporation to implement EDI in Human Resources. Its HR organization, using AT&T EDI, deployed EDI for the first time in 1993, implementing the benefits enrollment transaction set. This followed participation on the Workgroup for EDI (WEDI) pilot project with the insurance carriers Travelers, Prudential, and Empire Blue Cross & Blue Shield. By using EDI in benefits enrollment, AT&T estimates that if it can reduce costs by only 1 percent, a savings of about $15 million per year will be realized.
Shipment Tracking	In 1993 the Network Systems business unit introduced the use of the standard EDI shipment tracking transaction to track the shipment and delivery of AT&T products to its customers. A continuous stream of tracking information is provided to AT&T by its carriers. When a customer calls AT&T to determine the status of a delivery, AT&T is able to give the exact status information. This is a major step forward in satisfying its customers.
Inter-company Transactions	AT&T has taken EDI beyond commercial applications and is now providing services to support the exchange of inter-company transactions over EDI. A first step in this direction is to provide all the business units with the capability of electronically processing invoices currently processed by paper. This is expected to provide the business units with major cost savings.

Future Applications	AT&T, as a corporation, is committed to implementing EDI for additional business processes in the future.
AT&T Treasury	AT&T is working with its financial institutions to integrate the use of EDI and electronic funds transfer (EFT) using AT&T EDI for financial data transmittal. The remittance/payment advice transaction set is sent over AT&T EDI to approximately 250 suppliers, freight carriers, and customers. In addition, AT&T Treasury has been working with its banks to implement the X12 standard Account Analysis transaction set and to move lockbox transactions using a standard EDI transaction set. The benefits of implementing financial EDI include quality improvements, cost containment, and improved cash flow, which improve a corporate treasury. Companies that have implemented just-in-time and quick response programs often implement financial EDI as part of those programs. Companies involved in re-engineering processes also find that financial EDI is more effective than the traditional approach of speeding up non-automated financial processes, as it extends time saving and automation to suppliers. Many companies have recognized the strategic value of closing the loop in their EDI programs by implementing financial EDI.

AT&T Internal EDI Applications

EDI has, up to now, been used primarily for conducting business with external customers and suppliers. The EDI support group in Greensboro, North Carolina, has taken EDI one step beyond that. It is now providing services to support the exchange of inter-company transactions over EDI. Its initial project is to provide every business unit and division with the capability to electronically process invoices that it currently receives from the vendor and sends through U.S. mail to the Atlanta and Orlando Financial Operations Centers (FOCs) for processing.

This group is currently working with 275 vendors, suppliers, and transportation companies. Several business units are using a Supply Tech package to electronically enter accounting information and send it over EDI to the FOCs. The impact of using EDI is a 35 to 40 percent invoice processing cost savings to the business units. The Network Systems installation division has implemented the "Internal EDI" process in seven regions. When this is fully implemented, the division anticipates savings in excess of $1 million. The EDI Support Group in Greensboro has tracked the EDI processes and found that processing costs were actually reduced by 50 percent. Furthermore, 95 percent of EDI messages go through error-free, improving the rate of errors on invoicing by 25 percent.

AT&T Enhanced Telex Applications

Banking · A New Jersey bank uses AT&T Enhanced Telex's connectivity and security for its international transactions of letters of credit, money transfers, foreign exchange, and collection. The public messaging network helps automate what were once unconnected work processes. When transaction instructions arrive from a customer, the transaction is immediately initiated, a telex message is sent to a correspondent bank, and a copy is faxed to the customer over the messaging network. The customer is informed that the transaction is completed, and the bank is secure in knowing that a telex message is accepted around the world. AT&T EasyLink Telex has made value-added changes to integrate telex into electronic commerce. AT&T EasyLink Services allows the sending of a telex from a desktop computer, receipt of a telex in an electronic mailbox, and converting a telex message to a fax or electronic mail message for resending. Telexes can be sent from an IBM AS/400 mid-range computer or from a LAN with automatic test-key authentication connected to AT&T EasyLink Services.

Closed User Groups

ABA/net is a service of the American Bar Association which functions as a closed user group on AT&T EasyLink Services. This service is an example of the customization and special features available using AT&T EasyLink Services. With this service, lawyers can use email to communicate with colleagues and collaborate on projects without regard to distance or time of day. This service allows law firms to share resources and perform research at a distance. They may also exchange files and messages with related services such as court reporters.

As AT&T Mail is a public messaging service, lawyers are equally able to communicate with clients and use all of the AT&T Mail services. A corporation using AT&T EasyLink Services therefore could establish communications between its legal department and its outside lawyers to form virtual workgroups. These workgroups could coordinate litigation support materials and avoid duplication of effort, resulting in lower legal costs.

The following description of ABA/net shows how a closed user group can use customized services to benefit its members. Other groups could select different research services more suitable for their purposes.

ABA/net provides a wide range of services to enhance and expand legal practice. The service, hosted on AT&T EasyLink Services, provides affordable access 24 hours a day, 7 days a week with most types of computer and word processing equipment common in law offices to a wide variety of legal and general business services, including

- LEXIS/NEXIS service
- WESTLAW

- Feature-rich AT&T EasyLink Electronic Communication Services
- Over 900 research databases
- News-clipping services
- On-line legal conferences
- ABA Master calendar

Services similar to those provided by ABA/net can be developed for other groups with services adjusted for that group's specific requirements. These features are not available to the general AT&T EasyLink Services subscriber. ABA/net's services are as follows:

ABA/net Colleague Directory	This is a directory containing email, telephone, background, and specialty information. It allows lawyers to enter a detailed profile of their background and specialty areas. This profile, which can be updated using ABA/net at any time, is the directory listing. The directory allows lawyers to locate colleagues in a specific geographic area or with a certain area of specialty. The ABA/net Colleague Directory is searchable, using menu screens, for other ABA/net subscribers who could be of assistance with a question or problem. The ABA/net Colleague Directory is an example of a special-purpose directory listing. This type of listing could be used for an association or as an enterprise-wide directory accessible by mobile and fixed location employees but not by outsiders.
ABA/net Master Calendar	This is a calendar of meetings conducted or sponsored by the ABA which can be searched using dates, locations, and sponsors of ABA meetings across the country. Private or public calendars can be built for any purpose, with access restricted to group members or available to all AT&T EasyLink Services subscribers. These calendars could be provided to fax users through the AT&T FAX Catalog, the AT&T Mail Auto-response, or FYI's bulletin-board-like feature.

AT&T Global Messaging Applications

Legal Conferencing	This ABA/net feature is a threaded message system which builds on the structure of email to provide an ordered record of message flow. Electronic conferencing is a means for a group of people in different locations, at different times, to efficiently discuss issues and develop solutions. It provides a vehicle for group discussions with the ability to identify the participants and their contributions to the ongoing discussion. A member of a conference submits an item or topic, which is automatically tagged with the originator's name and date of entry. Other members read the item and are prompted for a response. Their responses are automatically associated with the original item. Conferences may be open, or they may be restricted to a limited user community designated by the organizer.
AT&T Mail Legal Applications	Most law firms conduct business with clients located throughout the country, and efficient communication with them is essential. Communicating with support services, such as real estate brokers, title companies or other services, is improved. Communications with clients can be by email or fax, and the same message can be sent to multiple recipients using different delivery methods. Law firms can prepare documents in one office and send them in machine-readable form to another before forwarding them to the client.

Legal Research Services

ABA/net includes gateways to specialized legal services as part of its closed user group hosted on AT&T EasyLink Services. Other services can be provided to support other closed user group requirements.

ABA/net LEXIS/NEXIS	ABA/net provides a gateway to the LEXIS/NEXIS legal research services for its members.

ABA/net WESTLAW	ABA/net subscribers can access WESTLAW by selecting it from the ABA/net menu on their computer screen. WESTLAW provides access to one of the largest law libraries in the world, available 24 hours each weekday, 22 hours on Saturday, and 18 hours on Sunday.
ABA/net FAXsolutions	The private fax mailbox is part of a complete family of fax services designed to help the lawyer communicate more effectively through the fax machine. The private fax mailbox provides confidential access to faxes from anywhere at any time. Computer-generated faxes and broadcast are suitable for large-scale information distribution. AT&T FAX Catalog allows information to be requested as needed and either distributed free or charged for as desired. The subscriber can combine AT&T MailFAX with other delivery options, such as electronic mail and postal services.
ABA/net Information Services	These information services expand research capabilities to include the world's largest collection of databases and investment without the expense and inconvenience of individual subscriptions. Overall research costs can be decreased because of reduced connect time and fewer search requests. Inexperienced users are able to conduct searches quickly and efficiently.
ABA/net Customized Communications Software	Access PLUS has been customized specifically for ABA/net users with enhanced access to LEXIS/NEXIS and WESTLAW. Special configuration settings for each service simplify connection, and macros permit easy use of the service features. Both the LEXIS/NEXIS services and WESTLAW recognize certain character combinations as commands. For example, typing .np followed by the Enter key in the LEXIS/NEXIS services results in the next page being displayed. To make things easier, Access PLUS maps the

AT&T Global Messaging Applications

character combinations recognized by these legal services into function keys, so that F1 selects the next page. Access PLUS also lists the commands in a menu. Configuration files also have been created to simplify printing to disk or printer using the unique interactive commands for these legal services.

Chapter 3

Virtual Workplaces

The term *virtual workplace* describes a business strategy promoting independent and flexible work environments based on the use of portable office technology. These environments may include virtual offices such as satellite locations, hotel rooms, or an automobile. Enterprises can reduce office rent expenses by having employees in non-traditional locations, such as home or field locations. The establishment of more stringent environmental regulations has made telecommuting increasingly attractive.

Productivity also improves. AT&T's southwestern division of business network sales, which piloted AT&T's internal use of the virtual workplace concept, found that its real estate costs were cut in half, while productivity increased by 45 percent during a two-year trial.

AT&T EasyLink Services supports the AT&T virtual workplace concept by providing public messaging services which allow workers to be nomadic without the need to acquire, deploy, manage, and support mountains of equipment. The virtual office today can fit into a small briefcase. AT&T EasyLink Services adds the network services which allow today's mobile workers and professionals to operate no matter where they are.

AT&T EasyLink Services provides an exceptionally complete set of products and services to support the mobile, remote, or telecommuting worker who frequently uses a combination of wired and wireless connections. Mobile workers often need wireless connectivity from a variety of devices, including palm-sized pagers and electronic organizers, as well as laptop and notebook computers. Remote workers may be in distant locations or difficult-to-integrate smaller offices. Telecommuters are workers who generally interact with others and use applications more than messaging. Telecommuting is a useful solution to Clean Air Act compliance, required by U.S. law in eleven states and discussed later in this chapter.

AT&T Mail's strong platform supports both wired and wireless communications through its mailbox, which simplifies location-independent messaging. The AT&T EasyLink Services mailbox allows the easy integration of electronic messaging with the reach and effectiveness of mobile-enabling technologies when combined with additional equipment and a wireless service provider. AT&T Mail provides the messaging infrastructure so that the sender can create a message which is transported to the end user over any or all of the enabling or receiving technologies.

AT&T Mobile Messaging is the term used to describe the AT&T product range supporting these location-independent workers; it covers pagers, organizers, portable computers, software, gateways, and the related AT&T EasyLink Services' public network services. The product integration and support allow the network manager to support such workers without the need for extensive central hardware, modem pools, or administrative costs. Almost any mobile or remote device can be supported by use of AT&T Mail. The administrative and hardware burdens are shifted from the enterprise network to the public network, reducing cost and effort. An example is the reduced number of modems required to support mobile users. In a sales support example, enough modems and telephone lines must be available to support the expected users during a peak time period to prevent call blocking.

The public network provides almost unlimited ports, allowing mobile workers to call in, using a single toll-free number, and be assured of an available port. The central location calls in periodically, using a single link,

Virtual Workplaces   49

and picks up messages. The network administrator does not have to install multiple modems, phone lines, or toll-free access to its location, as these services are provided by AT&T Mail. The costs using AT&T Mail are variable and depend on usage. Equipment installed by an enterprise would have higher fixed costs which do not vary with usage, and the public mail system therefore provides economic benefits.

The combination of AT&T EasyLink Services, wireless connection technology, and laptop computers provides the mobile worker with a powerful tool set. A secretary can send a message to a mobile manager using the combination of AT&T EasyLink Services and wireless connectivity. This type of messaging allows the recipient to receive a message at any time and at any location within wireless service areas. With the combination of AT&T EasyLink Services and wireless connectivity, the mobile manager and field worker can keep in constant communication with the home office, client, or suppliers.

Telecommuting

Telecommuter is the term used to describe a person who works from a remote location to avoid the costs and time involved in commuting. The telecommuter is not a traveler for business purposes but is someone who uses telecommunications to partially or totally replace his or her presence at the office. In the United States, federal, state, and local governments are beginning enforcement under the 1990 Clean Air Act. In 11 states, the act requires that the number of cars on the road for commuting be reduced to improve air quality. The act mandates business compliance and provides severe penalties for companies which fail to implement the commuting reductions. Telecommuting is a useful method for business compliance. On September 20, 1994, AT&T's employees were encouraged to work from home during a "Telecommuting Day" demonstration of the potential.

Eleven states have been assigned federal pollution designations of *severe* or *extreme* and are required to impose mandatory Employer Trip Reduction Provisions (ETRP) on employers within the designated states. These designated states are California, Connecticut, Delaware, Illinois,

Indiana, Maryland, New Jersey, New York, Pennsylvania, Texas, and Wisconsin, with Massachusetts in an optional classification. Employer Trip Reduction Provisions require each employer with 100 or more employees in designated areas to increase the average vehicle occupancy for all trips by not less than 25 percent. Corporations must begin complying with the Clean Air Act, with detailed plans submitted in 1994, implementation in 1995, and compliance documentation submitted in 1996. Corporate van- and car-pool programs have reduced traffic congestion to a degree, but not to a point where the reductions satisfy the Clean Air Act requirements. Telecommuting is an option for meeting the requirements, as telecommuting can reduce the number of cars on the road.

AT&T EasyLink Services provides services whose management costs are spread over all users to reduce requirements for in-house management of the messaging network and related services. AT&T Mail is a stable messaging network with the features needed to support broadcast, message security, and global send and receipt of messages anywhere and at any time. AT&T EasyLink Services provides the shared resources which allow large numbers of employees to begin telecommuting without the need for large modem pools, administrative resources, or phone lines.

The AT&T EasyLink Services Telecommuting set of products and services consists of a series of modular consulting service bundles designed to assist corporations in complying with state laws associated with the requirements of Section 182 (d) (1) (B) of the 1990 Federal Clean Air Act Amendments. The modules of the Telecommuting product are designed to fit corporate management processes for problem solving and project implementation. These processes generally consist of the following phases.

Information Gathering and Problem Definitions

Information is gathered from a variety of sources, including databases, business library searches, and the use of surveys, interviews, and other data gathering tools.

Virtual Workplaces

Identifying and Quantifying Alternatives	Identifiy and evaluate a series of alternatives. Evaluations generally include financial, operational, personnel, and strategic considerations as appropriate.
Selecting Alternatives	Select an alternative or series of alternatives that is most congruent with corporate objectives and available resources.
Implement Alternatives	Obtain the necessary executive approvals, design and implement appropriate communication programs, develop and execute implementation plans, provide project management as necessary, and monitor to completion.
Assess Performance and Modify Activities as Appropriate	Assess performance against benchmarks and implement corrective actions as necessary.

Professional Services

Consulting, Team Support, and Baseline Establishment	This module makes available knowledgeable consultants to provide support for the client's Clean Air Act Compliance Team and to provide coordination and project management for the other AT&T product and service providers. Additionally, this module will establish a baseline for the client by conducting an employee survey and entering the results in a tracking database.
Implementation Support	This module of the Telecommuting product provides continuing project management support, training for the client's Clean Air Act Compliance Team and the client's employees as appropriate, provided by the AT&T School of Business, access to telecommuting product equipment packages

	from AT&T Global Information Solutions and AT&T Paradyne, and messaging service packages from AT&T EasyLink Services.
Compliance Monitoring and Documentation	This module provides for the continued tracking of the client's sites, continued access to the products and services provided in the Implementation Support module, and documentation to support demonstration of compliance with the law.

AT&T School of Business

AT&T, through its School of Business, offers its customers formal training in various aspects of electronic commerce. Courses in the AT&T Virtual Workplace Education Series assist enterprises in dealing with the issues of electronic commerce. Some examples are:

The Virtual Workplace	Defines key virtual workplace concepts and explores the virtual workplace as a major competitive advantage for businesses.
Defining the Virtual Workplace	Explores general virtual workplace concepts relevant to any business. Answers questions about it, and permits interactive discovery and analysis of virtual workplace issues of particular impact to the client's organization.
Designing Your Virtual Workplace	Determines how to identify the best candidates for the virtual workplace environment and approach to the client's business. Creates a blueprint specific to the business's needs and goals.
Building a Business Case for Your Virtual Workplace	Following a review of AT&T Business Case procedures, applies project analysis and business modeling techniques to the blueprint created in preceding courses.

Virtual Workplaces

Implementing Your Virtual Workplace	Considers the factors for purchasing and/or installing the technological and communications tools that the virtual workplace plan requires. Reviews practical aspects such as safety and liability. Finally, defines the process required for effective communications, organization and productivity.
Working in the Virtual Workplace	Provides a look at how to work outside the traditional office and excel in the new environment — how to maintain communications, manage and organize time, control distractions, manage information, and much more.
Managing in the Virtual Workplace	Provides a variety of interactive and diagnostic exercises with practical guidelines on how to manage by results and outputs. Topics, from performance management to objective setting, are geared to unique challenges posed by the virtual workplace environment.
Virtual Workplace Technology Making it Work for You	Provides an in-depth look at numerous hardware and software offerings as well as communication services available. Topics include: AT&T EasyLink Services, Business Impact of Mobile Networked Commuting, and the Portable Marketplace Sales Support and Marketing programs.

AT&T EasyLink Services Telecommuting Offerings

AT&T EasyLink Services offers multiple products and services which support development of a virtual office environment. Messaging, EDI, and mobile technologies support both mobile and telecommuting workers and can be used in compliance programs to reduce travel.

- AT&T Mail
- FAXsolutions

Chapter Three

- FORMsolutions
- AT&T Mail
- Connectivity for laptops, notebooks and personal computers
- Pen-based offerings, pagers, organizers, and personal digital assistants (PDAs).
- Mail-enabled forms
- Wireless connectivity
- MailTALK
- Unified Message Mailbox
- Information Services

Mobile messaging provides location-independent communications by combining the flexibility of AT&T Mail with the mobility of portable devices such as personal organizers or laptops with cellular or wireless modems. Information can be sent and received from anywhere to anywhere without the restriction of a wired network mail system or the need for a phone line. The mobile worker can choose the type of device to be used for messaging and the method of connection and can switch between wired and wireless connectivity without special configuration or account requirements. The traveler does not have to consider the local resources as a limitation. Location-independent messaging increases productivity, as the mobile worker can receive messages using any device, including touch-tone phones and MailTALK, pagers, personal organizers, computers, or PDAs and switch as desired among them. AT&T EasyLink Services' store-and-forward architecture acts as a buffer, allowing all parties to work at whatever time is desired while making information immediately available. All devices other than pagers and MailTALK can create messages for global distribution using any of the AT&T Mail delivery techniques to communicate with the office, or to work from any location, reducing the need for offices.

Mobile connectivity is provided by a range of technologies and software. Transmission technologies include cellular telephony, satellite transmission to pagers, and two-way packet radio. End-user devices include portable computers, pagers, personal organizers, and pen-based devices. Portable computers, including laptop, notebook, and palmtop computers,

Virtual Workplaces 55

are used by the mobile worker who needs a strong computing platform for applications such as word processing and spreadsheets. Personal organizers are used by the mobile worker who uses calendaring, address book, and other limited applications but who does not need general-purpose application capability. Paging devices are used by the mobile worker who needs near real-time message delivery. Pen-point devices are used where keyboards are difficult to use or not desired by the end user. There is significant overlap between these devices. AT&T Mail's mobile messaging support isolates the sender from the mechanics of the recipient's device. The email message can be received on any supported device, and the end user may change the device as desired as long as appropriate software is used. Any subscriber can send fax messages to almost anywhere in the world using either a wired or a wireless modem. Wireless modem users have the ability to use all AT&T Mail options.

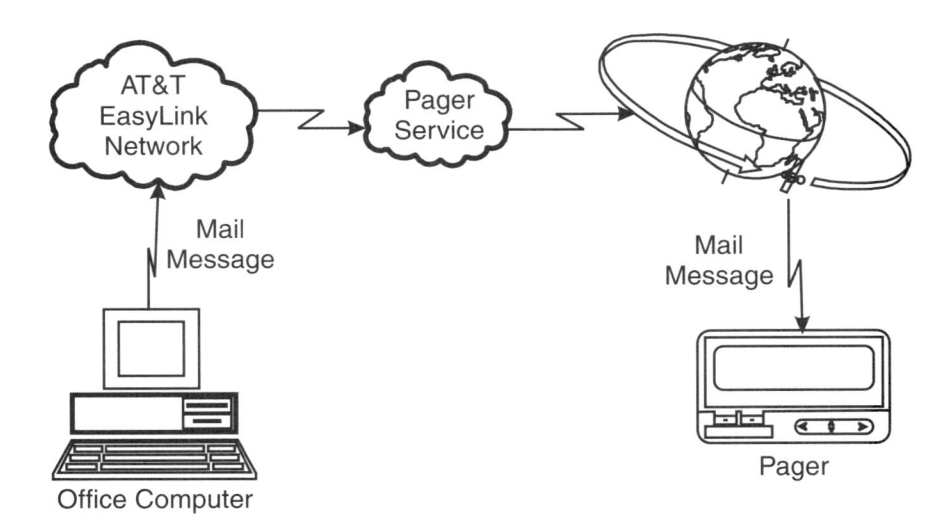

Figure 3-1 **Email to pager** AT&T EasyLink Services uses pager services such as EMBARC and SkyTel to transmit email to pagers.

Wide-area radio frequency (RF) transmission can be used for both one- and two-way data flow. One-way data flow is used in pagers. A pager service transmits a pager ID and message using radio. The pager recognizes its ID and displays the incoming digital message. In two-way service, the receiving unit also sends data back to the carrier, which forwards the data to AT&T Mail.

RF modems come in two types. One does packet assembly and disassembly in software and is carrier-specific. The other uses a modified RF modem which supports standard AT modem commands and can be used with standard software. RF modems connect only to compatible service providers and are referred to as fixed-endpoint services.

Mobile Messaging Benefits

Communications is a key tool of almost any enterprise. The ability to keep mobile and remote workers and business partners involved and aware of events in the workplace and to provide access to enterprise information, resources, and tools provides a business with competitive advantage.

Some examples are:

- Critical information is received and disseminated in a timely matter.
- Information can be sent, and received, from anywhere to anywhere.
- Physical availability of these facilities is no longer an issue.
- Communications are efficient and effective.
- Productivity is increased, and "phone tag" is greatly reduced.
- Customer satisfaction is increased as timely information arrives.

Pagers supporting AT&T EasyLink access include:

SkyTel   AT&T EasyLink Services and SkyTel, a leader in satellite paging, have created a service that turns a palm-sized pager into an enhanced electronic messaging system. The SkyMail service uses a

Virtual Workplaces 57

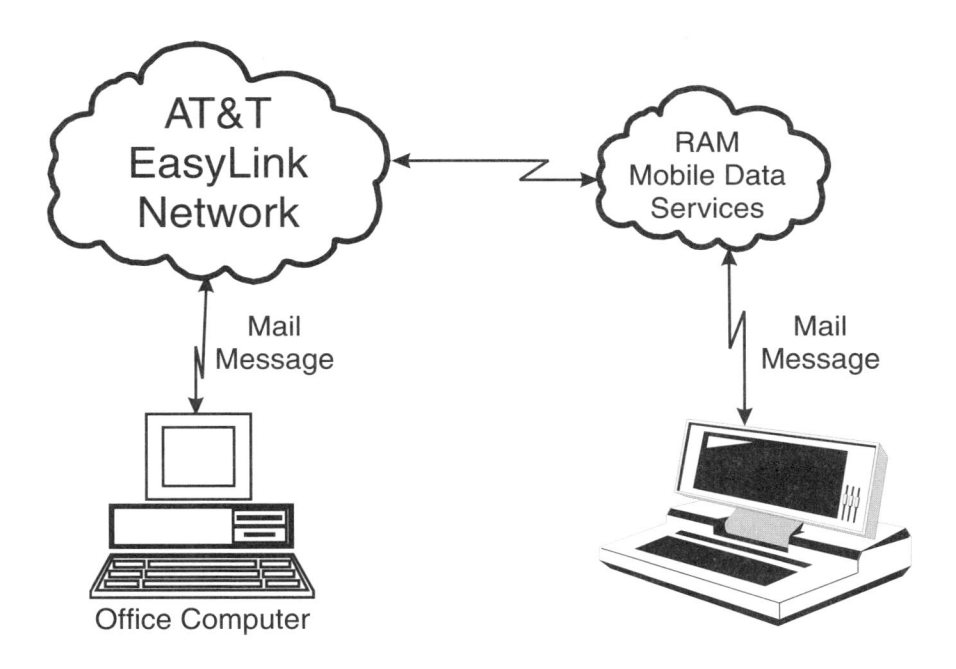

Figure 3-2 **Bi-directional wireless** Bi-directional wireless data access uses radio-frequency modems.

SkyWord pager to receive and display electronic mail messages transmitted using AT&T EasyLink Services to virtually anywhere throughout the country and, eventually, throughout the world. The message can be read, stored on the pager, deleted, or downloaded to a laptop or notebook computer. As many as 20 messages of up to 240 characters each can be stored on the pager. An unlimited number of messages can be stored on a computer using AT&T Mail Access PLUS messaging software. Messages are sent to a SkyTel address using any AT&T Mail software. The message is sent by AT&T EasyLink Services to the SkyTel network, where it is uploaded to a satellite which downloads it to hundreds of SkyTel ground stations and then to SkyTel transmitters, which send it to the pager.

EMBARC — EMBARC (Electronic Mail Broadcasts to A Roaming Computer) is Motorola's wireless delivery service, which connects to AT&T Mail as a delivery option. EMBARC integrates the immediacy and reliability of paging with the data-storage capabilities of portable computers and allows users to send messages containing up to 32,000 characters. These messages can be linked together, by using special software, to form a single file. EMBARC also allows senders to broadcast their messages simultaneously to a number of receivers, a feature that is useful for updating the same file on several remote machines. Its functional advantages are that it can be used effectively for broadcasting file updates or broadcast messages in addition to individual messages. These broadcast or single-recipient messages may be substantial in size. EMBARC uses radio broadcast methods to send information from a central provider to one or many receivers. It uses a one-way data channel at 930 to 931 MHz, licensed to Motorola. Messages can be sent through the AT&T Mail system and received by laptops or palmtops equipped with special receivers such as NewStream, SkyStream, or the PCMCIA-based NewsCard.

Wireless data network services providing bi-directional access to AT&T EasyLink services are currently provided by RAM Mobile Data Services.

RAM Mobile Data Services — AT&T EasyLink Service and RAM Mobile Data Services, a leading wireless data network provider, provide a bi-directional wireless messaging service using AT&T Mail Access PLUS for Windows software and connecting to the RAM Mobile Data Networks with an Intel

Virtual Workplaces

Mobidem AT modem.

The Intel Mobidem AT modem is a small device which supports the AT command data communications set. The Intel Mobidem AT modem makes two-way communications easy by simply connecting to the serial port of the notebook or laptop computer. The previewing capability of AT&T's Mail Access PLUS for Windows allows users to select which messages to download wirelessly using the RAM Mobile Data Networks and the Intel wireless modem.

Mobile workers can use the AT&T Mail network over RAM Mobile Data Services to send and receive electronic messages without a wired telephone connection. RAM Mobile Data Services provides packet radio data communications in over 6,300 U.S. cities and towns covering over 90 percent of the U.S. urban business population. RAM Mobile Data architecture incorporates MOBITEX packet switching technology that offers users fast-response and cost-effective access to the RAM network. The transparent roaming feature of the network allows users to travel anywhere in the United States without needing extra access codes or incurring additional charges. Access to the network is via the Intel Mobidem AT modem.

The combination of RAM Mobile Data Services, Intel Mobidem AT modems, and AT&T Mail Access PLUS for Windows software provides location-independent messaging in the United States. Messages may be sent and received through AT&T EasyLink Services without a phone line.

AT&T EasyLink Services provides AT&T Mail Wireless through an agreement with RAM Mobile

Data Services. The AT&T EasyLink Services' subscriber obtains a RAM Mobile Data Services wireless account, wireless and wired AT&T Mail support, and an integrated bill from AT&T EasyLink Services.

Mobile Messaging Supporting Software

Microsoft Mail Remote for Windows is electronic mail software which allows mobile workers with computers and modems to use AT&T EasyLink Services. Microsoft Mail Remote for Windows users can dial into their LAN as well as communicate using the full range of AT&T Mail features for worldwide connectivity.

The AT&T Mail Driver is bundled with Microsoft Mail Remote for Windows. After users subscribe to AT&T Mail, they are ready to send and receive electronic mail, fax, or telex messages on the road or at home. Microsoft Mail Remote for Windows users can communicate with over 40 million private and public electronic mail subscribers worldwide, as well as millions of fax machines, telex terminals, and postal addresses. Corporations can use the Microsoft Mail Remote for Windows package to assure that being out of the office doesn't mean being out of touch.

Microsoft Mail Remote for Windows offers advanced features for email users on the road. See Chapter 8, page 199.

Access PLUS for Windows

Access PLUS for Windows, version 2.5.1 or higher, provides extensive support for wireless communications using either a packet radio network or a cellular telephone and modem. The subscriber can connect in a wireless mode to AT&T Mail using a computer and wireless modems. These connects fall into two primary classes:

Packet radio network

Cellular network

Packet radio access requires a radio modem and packet radio account. The AT&T Mail network is reached by use of a radio modem connection

Virtual Workplaces

to a local base station with radio transmitter and receiver. The radio modem is used in place of the modem-to-telephone-line connection. The packet radio vendor provides a gateway to the AT&T Mail service, permitting wireless connectivity to AT&T Mail. Wireless connectivity using packet radio is provided by RAM Mobile Data Services.

Cellular phone access to AT&T Mail requires a cellular telephone, compatible modem, and cellular phone service. The AT&T Mail network is reached by use of a modem connected to a cellular phone which connects to a local base station with a radio transmitter and receiver. The cellular phone is used in place of the standard telephone line connection. Therefore, all AT&T Mail services are available over a wireless connection from any location with cellular phone access.

Access PLUS for Windows includes several advanced features which allow subscribers to use wireless mail more effectively. One such feature is the ability to maintain multiple configurations and to select the appropriate one as needed. This allows a subscriber to switch between a communications setup for a wired modem and others for wireless use from a menu. Another advanced feature is the ability to access the AT&T Mail account in a preview mode, review messages, and then download only selected ones while maintaining the connection.

In standard operation, messages are downloaded as a group and then reviewed offline. This is practical for wired operation but can cause both time and cost problems with wireless operations should, for example, a 2-Mb graphics or fax message be downloaded over a wireless connection. The subscriber should consider effective transmission cost and speed in relation to the value of the message prior to downloading. When the message is of a time-critical nature, then wireless downloading may be desired. In other cases, the message may remain on the AT&T Mail network until a more cost-effective connection can be made. The Access PLUS for Windows preview mode provides the ability to select messages for downloading and will be covered in detail here. See Chapter 8, page 179 for other features of Access PLUS which support messaging functions common to both wired and wireless operations.

Preview Mail

The Preview Mail feature displays a listing of messages located in remote folders on the AT&T Mail service. In normal mode, messages are first downloaded to the PC and then reviewed. In Preview Mail mode, the message headers are reviewed and only selected messages are downloaded in a single session and connection. This feature allows the subscriber to preview messages, select messages to be downloaded to local folders on the PC, and then download selected messages in a single connection to AT&T Mail. The subscriber may decide to receive only messages that require immediate attention or to download small messages to conserve local disk space. In Preview Mail, the subscriber manages costs by controlling connect time and the individual messages to be downloaded over either wireless or wired modems. Both new mail and information in other AT&T Mail folders may be previewed. The Access

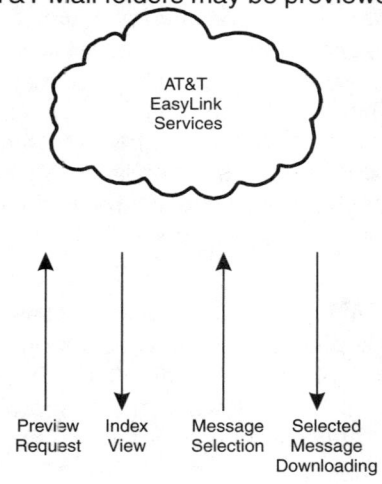

Figure 3-3 **Preview mode** In preview mode, the subscriber selects messages for downloading while online.

PLUS Preview Mail feature can be used over either a wireless or a wired AT&T Mail connection.

The Preview Mail window provides an index-level view of messages in remote folders on the AT&T Mail service. Index-level view is the listing of message headers showing information such as addressee, subject, date, size, type, and comments for each message. A running total of the number of selected messages and the approximate total size of the selected messages is displayed to indicate the amount of data that will be downloaded if the user decides to receive the selected messages. Messages cannot be read in Preview mode but must be downloaded from AT&T Mail to the local PC for reading. The downloaded messages can then be selected for reading using standard Access PLUS for Windows commands.

Preview mode must be terminated by exiting the Preview Mail window using the Exit command. As a precaution, users connected to AT&T Mail who are not performing any activity are presented with a dialog box to confirm whether they want to stay connected. Disconnection is automatic if there is no response to this dialog box within 30 seconds.

Mobile Messaging Developments

Microsoft Mobile Companions

Microsoft has announced that it will include connectivity to AT&T Mail with Microsoft At Work's operating platform for hand-held devices. AT&T EasyLink Services has announced that it will support Microsoft At Work, a new architecture for the workplace that will simplify communication for office workers and mobile professionals. Microsoft's vision is to equip most office devices with Microsoft At Work software that will let information flow seamlessly among them. Those devices include machines that until now had no communication capabilities, such as printers and copiers, as well as machines that had some communication capabilities, such as facsimile machines, telephones, laptop and notebook computers, hand-held devices, and desktop computers.

The Microsoft Mobile Companion operating system is being supported under the strategic agreement between AT&T and Microsoft to closely link their mail initiatives. The agreement also supports Microsoft's strategy of extending the Windows desktop to portable devices. The mobile products are to contain robust communications and come with APIs and toolkits. Significant hardware partners include Sharp Electronics, Toshiba, Zenith Data Systems, and others. Microsoft Mobile Companions combine a Windows-like user interface, personal convenience, and communications and have links to the AT&T Mail network with full support of AT&T Mail messaging and a toolkit for the development of mail-enabled applications.

AT&T PersonaLink Services

This service provides mobile intelligent messaging using personal digital assistant (PDA) devices and AT&T PersonaLink Services. AT&T PersonaLink is a consumer-oriented service and is of interest to managers of mobile workers because it is being developed with intelligent agents and wireless messaging as key components. These facilities and the personal communicators in development by many manufacturers may well represent the future of mobile messaging.

Electronic "intelligent assistants" are pieces of software that can be customized easily to reflect a person's unique messaging and information retrieval requirements. The intelligent assistants are available at retail, in products by Sony and others, using Telescript technology, which is a new communications language developed by General Magic, Inc. Telescript technology is designed to bring the advantages of electronic communication to millions of people who are not comfortable using technology. These intelligent assistants use the AT&T PersonaLink Services network to carry out the user's instructions to find, buy, and sell products and services; filter available information to locate what the customer requested; and save the customer time by performing mail filtering and other complex transactions.

Intelligent assistants are messages which the network interprets as commands. The subscriber fills out a form which creates the assistant, and

Virtual Workplaces

the assistant executes on the network, traveling from location to location to execute its functions. This is similar to a PostScript document which is interpreted as a program by a PostScript printer. Intelligent agents can expire at a predetermined time or after their task is complete. They perform tasks on the network which otherwise would require extensive knowledge and effort on the part of the subscriber. Multiple intelligent assistants can work on behalf of a user at multiple locations at one time.

Customers will be able to subscribe to AT&T PersonaLink Services when they buy a personal communicator or other device with Telescript language capabilities. Every subscriber to AT&T PersonaLink Services will be assigned a mailbox, or address. Subscribers also will be able to communicate with other people who have devices with Telescript technology. Sony, one of the partners in the General Magic alliance, has introduced personal communications devices using the Telescript technology.

Chapter 4

Public Messaging Networks

Corporate success increasingly depends on the enterprise's ability to effectively exploit distributed information resources and computing power for competitive advantage. The availability, reliability, maintainability, and security of the public messaging networks will become the corporate link to the outside world and a key component of the enterprise's ability to compete in fast-moving global markets. The vendor's ability to manage and control these public messaging networks in close coordination with major customers is a dominant concern and a critical differentiator between messaging services.

High-quality of network management makes a messaging network suitable for mission-critical applications. Network management provides the security, reliability, and availability which ensures that the message gets to its destination on a timely basis, in the intended form, and without being disclosed to unauthorized snoopers. AT&T is noted for its network management expertise, and AT&T EasyLink Services provides advanced network management as one of its most significant value-adds.

VAN and Internet Accountability

Accountability is a service provided to a corporate network buyer when it contracts with a commercial value-added network vendor. Accountability differentiates a commercial service from a non-commercial service. When a commercial network does not perform, the accountability is clear. This accountability is especially important when the public network is used to support financial systems. Systems which lack this feature are not suitable for some operations where proof of transport is a necessary condition of establishing liability. A commercial enterprise that procures network services has a fiduciary responsibility to its shareholders. It must ensure that critical features are present before it uses any network for commercial purposes that may materially affect its operations.

The Internet, however, lacks critical components of security, such as accountability and support service, which maintain the effectiveness of its underlying highly reliable protocols, such as TCP/IP. Investments in encryption software and firewalls by commercial users can protect against some of these shortcomings. However, reliability, accountability and support are inherent Internet shortcomings. Without central management and an assured revenue base, these problems cannot be solved. Commercial services, such as AT&T EasyLink Services, have the central management and revenue base to provide the essential management systems and control needed to support mission-critical applications today. The Internet is a high-risk environment, and it is not prudent for commercial enterprises to consider the Internet for applications that directly and materially support the enterprise's key operations. Examples of such applications which belong only on commercial networks include EDI, enterprise backbone network services, mission-critical applications, banking services, and other applications directly affecting the bottom line of the business or life safety. For such applications, enterprises should either contract with reputable, responsible public network providers or construct their own private messaging networks. Security is both a management and a technical problem which requires an enterprise building its own messaging network to consider how and under what conditions it can connect to the outside world.

Commercial Messaging Networks

Commercial messaging networks differ in concept from the use-at-your-own-risk structure of the Internet. AT&T EasyLink Services is a messaging network which provides services to subscribers on a commercial basis. Embedded in the word *commercial* are critical management and security services which are best evaluated by comparison with the well-known Internet. The Internet is a shared resource network where access to the network is paid for, either by the user or by others, but access to resources is, at present, free and unlimited. AT&T's messaging network includes components which make it an industrial-strength network carrier suitable for the most mission-critical operations. These components are security, reliability, accountability, and support. These ancillary services are provided on a formal basis with adequate dedicated resources paid for by the income from fee-based services. Industrial-strength commercial messaging networks are managed by profit-making organizations, such as AT&T EasyLink Services, to provide the predictable level of public network services that a prudent manager demands for any mission-critical operation.

The Internet, in contrast, is a group of inexpensive global networks available for commercial use and suitable for sub-critical operations such as personal mail, information retrieval, personal messaging, industry and professional forums, non-proprietary information sharing, and other non-critical communication applications. The Internet provides exceptional functionality in these areas. Commercial networks have to provide access to these services while maintaining the management and security which provide the stability needed for mission-critical operations. The Internet started as an academic and government research network over military physical resources. It now grows by donated publicly available resources. It is essentially unmanaged and operates by consensus of its service providers. Consensus is reached using an informal structure, without chain of command or responsibility. The consensus building and large universe of developers make the Internet an essential messaging tool, but also make it unsuitable as the transport for mission-critical applications.

Messaging Network Management

Managing the ensemble of message processing elements which make up a globally distributed messaging network is a significant undertaking and must include all relevant elements. A global messaging management system unifies and coordinates the management system domains found in local and wide area networking. Network management standards also define models for fault management (problem management), performance management, security management, accounting management, and configuration management. Network management architecture is directed toward the integration of multiple stand-alone network management systems. This approach provides new options in implementing and managing multi-vendor networks and eliminates the restraints of proprietary single-vendor systems.

Three classes of management are addressed by sophisticated commercial network management architectures such as AT&T EasyLink Services Enterprise Network Management. The first is management of the physical network domain, which includes systems in the corporate facilities, the local telephone company, the messaging carrier, and the long distance or interchange carrier. These domains may vary in size from small (a 1000-node LAN) to medium (the Chicago local telephone system) to immense (AT&T Long Distance). Each of these network domains generates information that must be accessible and manageable. The degree of management required will vary, but at the very least the management system must allow the operator to reroute traffic and reconfigure the network to bypass the failed element in the case of a failure somewhere in the messaging network. The second level consists of the management systems that handle operations, administration, and maintenance of network components. This level contains the tools that most LAN administrators use.

The third level is integrated network management. This level provides end-to-end network management for both voice and data networks that form the network management customer's information network. The quality of network management is greatly influenced by how well network operating system specific management tools are integrated into a system for quality network management. The Internet's lack of management structure and predictable income limits its ability to develop and maintain integrated network management.

AT&T's Network Management Expertise

AT&T's network management architecture implementation operates by accessing element management systems used to manage each element, and integrating multiple element management tools into a common management system. The integrated management tools are updated in real time as the management systems receive and coordinate information from element management systems, report end-to-end network status, and isolate network faults.

AT&T has a long history of developing leading-edge approaches to managing multi-vendor networks. AT&T introduced its implementation of the OSI standard for multi-vendor network management, called Unified Network Management Architecture (UNMA), in 1987. UNMA is a comprehensive, international-standards-based, three-layered architecture which links management system domains to manage local and wide area networks: premises equipment, local exchange networks, and interchange services. Layer 1 contains the network elements, such as networking equipment and services in customer locations, local exchange carrier networks, and interchange or long distance networks. Layer 2 contains the management systems that control the operation, administration, and maintenance of the network elements found in layer 1. Layer 3 is the family of integrated network management systems. A Network Management Protocol (NMP) was specified as the interface between element management systems and the integrated network management system. Using this "network to manage networks," managers can integrate management functions across network elements on a single system.

Network management can therefore respond quickly and accurately to keep the network at peak efficiency. The intent is to concentrate scarce technical resources rather than scatter them among multiple network management centers, and to collect them while integrating network management functions into a single system. This is a logical concentration of network management resources, not a physical one. The network management configuration database includes the names and locations of network elements, and information regarding how the elements connect to one another. With this information, and maps of the network, the network management application provides the administrator with a real-time graphic display of network status. The information contained in the configuration database is also displayed graphically.

When a network fault goes above the predetermined threshold level and sets off an alarm, the network management application traces the fault and displays it on the network map. The operator can zoom in on that map portion, verify and isolate the problem, and immediately take steps to correct it. Faults can be defined as degraded, failed, or critical, and are depicted in yellow, orange, or red to convey severity and importance.

An extremely important feature of the architecture enables a network operator to indicate alarm ownership, to help prevent other system operators from taking conflicting corrective action. Alarm correlation is performed using internal logic and information from the configuration database. Alarms are compared as they are received, and secondary alarms linked to the original problem are suppressed. With alarm correlation, network managers can work quickly to solve the problem. The network management station uses high-resolution graphics, icons, simple menus and commands, help screens, and a mouse. Operators can access more than one function and management system simultaneously, and several operators can work concurrently at separate workstations in a fully coordinated environment.

AT&T also provides network management to enterprises that want to draw on its expertise to consolidate the management of complex, far-flung information systems and telecommunications networks which are commonly managed as separate functions today. A family of software services, called AT&T OneVision Network Management Solutions, provides customers with integrated monitoring and management of non-homogeneous networking components in use throughout an enterprise. The coordinated management of computers, local area networks, telecom management systems, transmission lines, private branch exchanges, modems, and multiplexers provided by different vendors improves reliability and reduces costs. The overall reliability of corporate messaging networks depends both on the management of the private portions and on the reliability of the public service.

Public Messaging Networks

AT&T's OneVision Network Management Solutions will use platform software based on AT&T's BaseWorX and Hewlett-Packard's OpenView with software from NetLabs Inc. and third-party providers. AT&T plans to make its computing, communications, and services offerings manageable with OneVision applications. AT&T Business Communications Services will use the OneVision product family to enhance ACCUMASTER Management Services. The company delivered network management applications during 1994 for products and services in several communications and computing areas.

AT&T EasyLink Services Enterprise Network Management

The AT&T EasyLink Services Enterprise Network Management system provides end-to-end network management for the AT&T messaging network. Networks without this level of end-to-end network management, such as the Internet and many VANs, are unsuitable for mission-critical operations. AT&T has developed an automated management platform that incorporates the UNMA principles for messaging networks. The management platform integrates element management systems provided with element products. This is accomplished by custom software. The management platform monitors and manages the elements which make up AT&T EasyLink Services. These include message transfer agents (MTA), mail gateways, and switches. The UNMA-model-based implementation uses management software, configuration databases, and problem databases to identify and control most problems with little or no operator intervention.

This messaging management platform uses the Simple Network Management Protocol (SNMP) and internally developed software to produce the integrated environment used to manage off-the-shelf products in a modular and scalable manner. The AT&T EasyLink Services' network management design also can be used in private messaging networks and is adaptable to large distributed corporate environments with equipment, applications, and messaging systems from multiple vendors. The platform may be made available to large AT&T EasyLink Services' customers who desire to perform administrative functions from a customer premises-based graphical interface.

The AT&T EasyLink Services' management platform is built on Hewlett-Packard's OpenView, a leading SNMP platform. An operator at an EasyLink operations center OpenView console can delegate management tasks to multiple element management systems distributed throughout the world, respond to alarms according to predetermined routines, act on such alarms in accordance with predetermined standards, and act on requests from the element managers. These functions can be distributed and redistributed to control points as operating conditions warrant.

The managed elements include UNIX hosts and UNIX operating systems which support the AT&T EasyLink Services' Message Transfer Agents (MTAs), UNIX workstations, and personal computers which function as gateways, front-end processors, routers, AT&T Datakit switches, fiberhubs, modems, and related components. This managed equipment is found at each of the AT&T EasyLink Services nodes around the world which perform the messaging network switching and service provisioning. The network management view is centralized, but management is distributed using the element managers. AT&T has patented local intelligent monitors to perform network management functions including performance monitoring, alarm filtering, configuration management, and event thresholding.

The intelligent monitors track activity in message queues in the MTAs using databases which contain all management attributes and variables present on the AT&T EasyLink Services network. One example would be a filled delivery queue. The queue, on reaching a predetermined threshold, triggers an alert from the monitor software to the local element manager. The element manager, using its knowledge base, can then determine if the problem report is valid. If the problem report is not valid, then the element manager does not take action. If the problem report is valid, then the element manager can remove the corrupted message, place it in temporary memory, correct it, and add it back into the queue. The central OpenView console is notified when the problem requires determination or action at a higher level than the element manager. The system provides early warning of potential problems, allowing most problems to be corrected before the messaging user is affected. Element managers are able to use alarm messages and deduce probable cause using expert system–based fault, configuration, and performance management applications. The management applications share a common

Public Messaging Networks

data repository, allowing access to common connectivity, physical topology, routing, asset, configuration, and other information.

Unified Network Management Architecture defines network elements, element management systems, and an integrator and is the foundation for the AT&T EasyLink Services Enterprise Network Management system, which provides a unified framework for managing the AT&T EasyLink Services' messaging network. Element management systems focus on a distinct class of network element and provide a single point of monitoring and management control for the entire class. Each element management system also contributes its own automation capabilities, which can repair problems which are element-specific. The AT&T EasyLink Services network has three classes of element management systems:

- Access network management systems
- Backbone transport network management systems
- Processing node management systems

The functions provide a unified portal into the entire messaging network for the network operators by intelligently combining the data from multiple element management systems. Real-time expert systems within the integrator provide self-healing features for network-wide problems. User interface displays and commands are consistent for all management systems; management functions use common meanings and procedures for the jobs performed; objects managed by the system conform to a consistent, common set of definitions, structures, and naming conventions; and methods for communication between the management systems and the managed objects and/or managed elements, as well as between management systems, are prespecified and maintain consistency. The use of an open system platform permits development of network management applications, such as fault, performance, configuration, and others, using industry standard application programming interfaces (API). This attention to detail contributes greatly to the reliability and performance of AT&T EasyLink Services Network Management and, therefore, to the reliability and availability of the managed messaging network.

AT&T EasyLink Services has designed its network management systems to hierarchically escalate the events and alarms originating from each of the processing nodes to its immediate element management system. This provides the basis for quick problem isolation and resolution.

AT&T EasyLink Services Integrated Network Management System detects different problem conditions and identifies hierarchical resolution methods. This involves the development of intermediate filters which handle some frequent events and perform some focused time-limited reasoning. These filters pass unresolved problem conditions and/or faults to a higher management system with more reasoning and inferencing capabilities.

Proactive and Reactive Response

Proactive problem detection uses a monitoring system, such as a messaging application manager (MAM), which periodically examines the messaging applications, operating system, and other processor-related conditions. This monitoring system looks for conditions indicating that a problem is developing. An example would be a queue length exceeding a threshold or growing traffic congestion. The MAM identifies potential or developing faults and has the ability to automatically take corrective action in response to certain potential problem conditions.

Reactive problem detection occurs in response to a problem after an error condition is detected by the component. Some problems or faults are reported by various subsystems of the messaging application, the operating system, or other components of the network. A messaging fault manager is responsible for handling these reactive faults.

Backbone Transport Network (WAN) Management

The backbone transport network is a WAN, and its management is referred to as WAN management. The WAN management system monitors the backbone network from a central location. The backbone network is monitored for alarms. Traffic and other reports are automatically generated. The WAN management system also provides capabilities for remotely accessing, administering, and configuring WAN components. The WAN management system therefore provides all the tools the administrator needs to centrally manage the backbone network. Most WAN ele-

Public Messaging Networks

ment vendors have their own set of management tools complying with the SNMP protocol and provide an enterprise-specific management information base (MIB). The WAN management system provides features and functions that include

- Centralized configuration management to ease network setup and expansion
- Real-time performance and error analysis to enhance network performance tuning
- Real-time event and fault monitoring to simplify problem identification and isolation

The WAN network element managers provide dynamic fault visibility known as SNMP Traps and node event logs. Node event messages configured as faults in SNMP Traps are forwarded to the appropriate WAN manager and may directly alert an operator or be further filtered, consolidated, and escalated to the integrated network management system. The WAN element manager displays the faults along with all the necessary management information, such as severity codes, message texts, and other information. The WAN management system also performs other related tasks, such as custom filtering, traffic routing and management, and blocking.

Access and Egress Network Facilities Management

A key element in managing a messaging network for mission-critical use is the suitability of the facilities and ports that terminate on the provider's premises. AT&T EasyLink Services directly monitors these facilities and ports as a prerequisite for properly engineering the access and egress messaging network facilities to ensure that they are suitable for the messaging services customer's intended use.

The access and egress facilities monitoring system is a device used to test, report, and log exceptional events. The system bridges onto the tip and ring pair of the circuits to measure traffic characteristics and monitor transmission quality. This monitoring system is used to effectively manage and troubleshoot most problems associated with the AT&T EasyLink Services messaging network's access and egress facilities. This includes items such as:

- Total number of calls that each circuit accepted in the last measuring period, usually called peg count.

- Percentage of calls on each circuit that violated the predefined signal level threshold.

- Total number of calls and the number of calls that were blocked for a group of circuits during its busiest hour of the day, called busy hour traffic. For a given type of messaging service a group of circuits are usually bundled and monitored based on their individual service-level guarantees.

- Total number of calls for a group of circuits that were grouped together based on their characteristics, called group traffic report.

- Consolidated report of various problems occurring for the entire set of circuits, including, but not limited to, circuits that have Ring No Answer, Connection Information, or other problems. This is an exception report and may be integrated within an overall fault management system for further correlation and consolidation.

Configuration and Physical Management

The configuration and physical management of the AT&T EasyLink Services' messaging network are closely related functions that are essential to managing the messaging services, Most management systems' primary focus is on fault management built on manual physical topology and configuration information. These manual techniques frequently fail to accurately reflect the objects within the messaging network and, even more frequently, do not accurately reflect the relationships between the numerous managed objects. This condition is often found in large global networks built using multi-vendor components and devices. AT&T EasyLink Services Integrated Network Management Platform provides several tools and systems which support overall configuration management.

The configuration or physical management of AT&T EasyLink Services Messaging Network resources tracks the network infrastructure and its connectivity. Inventory or asset management documents network resources, but configuration management is a much more dynamic process and describes the state and parameters of these messaging network resources. Configuration management includes setting parameters and changing the states of managed objects. A messaging network's configuration typically is described in terms of physical connections such as its circuits and routers and logical connections such as its core messaging services and applications. Configuration management also keeps track of network connectivity based on geography of the nodes and messaging functions.

A major challenge in effectively managing a messaging network is the development of a efficient methodology that supports the network operators in the solution of both physical and logical networking issues in a way which integrates well with existing management tools. AT&T EasyLink Services has developed a robust and comprehensive management platform which provides a set of tools that addresses the key functional needs of managing the logical components of the network, managing the messaging network's physical infrastructure, and managing the requests to induce changes to the network's logical and physical components.

The AT&T EasyLink Services network management system can, when necessary after a problem is identified, create and automatically dispatch a trouble ticket to resolve the problem. This occurs after extensive interaction with the expert system to ascertain the nature of the actual problem, and after correlation with other problems, if any, and previous trouble tickets related to the particular problem. The ticket automatically includes physical location information, work history, asset information, and an end-to-end circuit trace. The trace shows all possible physical components that could be involved in the particular failure. For software components, the system points to the exact messaging service or its component that is experiencing an outage or problem. The integrated network management system provides connectivity management information in addition to configuration information. This system gives the operator a graphical display of the physical locations of all WAN networking equipment, including hubs, routers, patch panels, switches, and other managed units. This system also provides connectivity information, such as port configurations, circuits lists, routing tables, and other relevant settings. The connectivity of all of these items is tracked, maintained, and available online for immediate and real-time access using a standard presentation interface.

The AT&T EasyLink Services' network operators are provided with a dynamic, real-time correlation between seemingly different problem conditions and problem resolution techniques by linking the logical management capabilities with physical topology or configuration information along with an expert system. This correlation information provides the means to solve messaging network problems more quickly. This, in turn, minimizes downtime and improves network reliability and diagnostic and repair activities.

AT&T EasyLink Services' integrated management infrastructure provides a centralized information source for network problem resolution as well as the work flow process for dispatching and effecting change. A predefined work flow process automatically validates the trouble report with the expert system to verify its authenticity, correlates with other similar problem conditions, and then routes the ticket appropriately. The system provides for controlled network operator overrides.

AT&T EasyLink Services Performance Management

AT&T EasyLink Services performance management capabilities include mechanisms which monitor and analyze the performance of the managed network and its associated messaging services. The results of performance analysis trigger diagnostic testing procedures and can initiate configuration changes required to maintain the prescribed level of service or performance. Performance management procedures collect and distribute data on the current state of the messaging network, maintain and analyze performance logs, and track compliance with service-level objectives and other predefined performance measures.

The integrated management infrastructure supports varied management applications which perform differing aspects of performance management. The fault management application, for example, provides the capability to set thresholds and conditions which indicate unacceptable performance levels. This setting is in the form of rules, and the fault management application provides automatic reporting when established thresholds are violated. Historical data is used to track the performance of the messaging network over time and for trend analysis. Other management applications within the integrated management platform utilize

Public Messaging Networks

the performance data to do network tuning and optimization. This includes correlation of network events by the expert system.

Key functions of the performance management application include performance event monitoring, identifying performance thresholds, performance analysis, control, and administration. Performance event monitoring facilities provide real-time monitoring of management data and filtering of non-performance-related information. The performance analysis facilities collect measurements from the managed objects that make up the messaging services network. They provide a means for creation and maintenance of an historical database of performance statistics for the managed objects while analyzing the current performance statistics to detect faults. The performance analysis facilities provide the essential correlation of the current statistics with historical data to predict long-term trends for capacity planning.

The performance management application statistics formulas use raw data over a time period together with selected specific characteristics of the messaging services and associated networking devices to compute performance statistics for different messaging services within the AT&T EasyLink Services network. Some key measures are: alarm count, traffic volume, availability and reliability of the network, speed of service, accessibility of the network, call completion ratio, message volume based on type of message, and WAN statistics.

AT&T EasyLink Services Network performance measures are grouped into three main categories: availability, reliability, and serviceability.

An end user's evaluation of messaging service availability is influenced by a combination of several factors. A measurement set is defined and measured for the end user by identifying the following:

- Components involved in end user access into the messaging services network
- Scheduled and unscheduled outages for the various messaging network software and hardware components

- Failures, causes, and their end user outage time consequence for all the elements in the network by effect (this is done by mapping into network elements, deriving end user outage time, and quantifying by the number of user sessions interrupted or the time a messaging service is unavailable).
- Appropriate weights

This approach identifies the degree to which each component contributes to the unavailability of the messaging network from an end user's perspective. This form of availability measurement takes an inside-out approach, rather than treating the messaging network as a black box and measuring customer availability from the outside. The approach provides customer availability data and also identifies component-level failures and their causes.

An end user's evaluation of messaging service reliability is based on the perception that the messaging network is doing what the customer expects it to do. A measurement set is defined and measured for the end user by identifying the following:

- Mailbox-to-mailbox delivery time
- Message delivery to the endpoint within the preset service-level objective
- Speed of service
- Appropriate weights

These reliability measurements can differ by messaging services type. Video, voice, interactive multimedia, fax, X400, EDI, and others may have differing reliability standards.

An end user's evaluation of messaging service serviceability is based on the perception that availability and reliability do not vary. Serviceability is also known as operability of the network and refers to the measurement of the speed with which network operations can perform network service and bring the affected service back online before end users notice any major degradation of service. A measurement set is defined and measured for the end user by identifying items such as the following:

- Number of alarms that the network operators have to respond to or take action on

- Number of corrupted messages (dead letters) requiring human intervention

Integrated AT&T EasyLink Services Network Management

A primary reason for AT&T EasyLink Services Enterprise Network Management integration of different element management systems is to provide tools to coordinate the end-to-end management of the AT&T EasyLink Services distributed messaging services network, which consists of multi-vendor products and services. This requires sophisticated but user-friendly interfaces which ideally present multiple management and support systems in a uniform and consistent manner. The integration motivation is to collect all status reports and alarm signals, no matter what brand of equipment they come from, and present network operators with only the most useful and urgent information. The system provides color-coded overview maps of the network, but also allows operators to zoom in on details as needed. Expert system software or other rule-based software systems filter incoming events and alarms, give detailed advice, and can even act automatically to reroute traffic around a failed component or subsystem.

The standards selected for management of the AT&T EasyLink Services messaging services network include X11/Motif as the graphical user interface (GUI) and Simple Network Management Protocol (SNMP) as the communication protocol between elements, element management systems, and other management systems, including integrated management systems and Structured Query Language (SQL) for database management system interfacing. The use of SNMP as the management information communication protocol requires definition of managed objects and development of a management information base (MIB) for all the managed components and messaging services. This methodology requires that objects conform to a consistent, common set of definitions, structures, and naming conventions.

AT&T EasyLink Services Messaging Network Integrated Management also provides for the future management of additional and evolving messaging services and networking architectures. The management system architecture and design is a platform for the rapid deployment of new network management applications and services. It is therefore rapidly extensible in areas including platform and infrastructure, standards conformance, expert system enhancement, and integrated relational database. Some standards include

- Graphical User Interface: X11/Motif, OSF/DME, etc.
- Management Communication: OSF/DME, XOM/XMP API access to SNMP, SNMPII, CMIP, CMOT, and CMOL protocols
- Database Management System: SQL (ANSI standard, etc.) or OSQL (object-oriented structured query language) for object-oriented database management system

Commercial Network Security

Commercial network security is a facet of network management and the network provider's responsibility. The prerequisite for security is a stable, well-managed distributed network. Reliable networks can be made more secure, but poorly managed or unstable networks cannot be unless they are stabilized first. Multiple security layers, tightly integrated into the network management process, protect against failures of any individual security measure. Security layers protect specific functions against threats such as disaster, interception, and fraud. The selection of effective and appropriate security techniques requires both management skills and technical knowledge. Policy must be established and approved and procedures derived and implemented to create a security strategy and tactical approach. Improper selection and application of network security measures degrades performance, increases costs, and provides only minimally effective protection.

Reliability is both more complex and more important to mission-critical work. The commercial network provides intensively managed capacity planning, consistent response time, carefully planned and tested disaster recovery, and continuous staff training. These services are covered by

Public Messaging Networks

the service fees paid to the commercial network. On non-commercial networks, the question is how the services are provided if they exist at all and whose management standards are being used.

In terms of reliability, comparing AT&T EasyLink Services to the Internet is similar to comparing air express to the post office. The post office, like the Internet, is certainly capable of delivering most messages eventually. However, when an enterprise wants its message to be delivered within a scheduled interval, it chooses air express.

Messages carry tracking and audit data. The organization that is responsible is clearly identifiable. The support organization is also clearly identifiable. These features are supported by the messaging charges. Economies of scale lower these costs for all users. Such systems are difficult and costly to develop. They are not found on non-commercial messaging networks such as the Internet. The lack of management structure, tools, and resources found in non-commercial applications makes the use of such networks for mission-critical applications a high-risk venture.

The Internet was developed to enhance communications between researchers who functioned in an open environment. The protocols used, such as TCP/IP, SMTP, and UUCP, and the software used, such as Finger, World Read, Archie, and Mosaic, allow users to interrogate distant machines and link to them in real time. It is easily possible to monitor other communication sessions on target machines. There are two major security breaches possible. One is eavesdropping, where information is obtained by unauthorized people without altering or destroying the original information, and the other is impersonation, where a user assumes a false identity to use another's authority, privilege, or resource.

Messages sent over the Internet are fully exposed because data packets are relayed through several unknown computers between sender and receiver and the packets are in plain text. These routers may or may not be secure, but there is no way to know. Messages may be captured and viewed at any point, on or off the Internet. Encryption provides protection at substantial cost. Encryption works by increasing the work factor needed to read a message. While no encryption measure is infallible, the theory is that the effort or work needed to decrypt the message will discourage the unauthorized reader. However, management and distribution of encryption keys is a major and difficult task. This cost alone is often enough to make the cost of the Internet's free messaging equal or greater than that of the value-added commercial network. VANs offer security. Security is one of the value-added services provided, together with the other mission-critical services essential to commercial customers such as accountability, reliability, and support services.

AT&T EasyLink Services acts as a firewall or barrier between a company's internal network and the outside world. An enterprise considering the use of the Internet with a direct connection would have to build the equivalent of AT&T's internal corporate network security system and should factor the costs of firewall design, operation, and maintenance into its economic evaluation. A firewall is an interface computer which runs with a limited, carefully structured and managed set of software and hardware. AT&T's internal corporate firewalls consist of two dedicated computers, one connected to the Internet and the other connected to the corporation's own network. The external machine examines all incoming traffic and forwards only the "safe" packets to its internal counterpart, and it will accept outgoing traffic only from the internal gateway machine, so that an attacker attempting to transfer information illicitly out of AT&T's domain would be unable to do so without subverting the internal gateway. The internal gateway, meanwhile, accepts incoming traffic only from the external one, so that if unauthorized packets do somehow find their way to it, they cannot pass. A firewall is usually a computer that is connected to a company's internal systems and to the external network, so that any traffic that goes between the two must go through it. Programming on the firewall computer limits the kinds of connections that can be made between the inside and outside and who can make them. It determines the integrity of messages passed to it and blocks access to dangerous software and files.

Managing encryption and building firewalls is expensive. Some companies have the skill; others consider this to be a key VAN advantage. AT&T EasyLink Services permits only email to pass through its messaging network and, therefore, provides this essential protection for the corporate network as an inherent part of its VAN service.

AT&T EasyLink Services ensures the security of its services and its associated networks by several proactive methods. An annual AT&T EasyLink Services network security audit is performed by AT&T Corporate Security & Auditing. The audit findings are provided to responsible AT&T EasyLink Services personnel, including key vice presidents and the business unit president. AT&T EasyLink Services is required to formally respond to the corporate audit and to provide a corrective action plan for any adverse findings.

Multi-level access control is designed into the AT&T EasyLink Services network. The customer access level provides access only to a specific account. Access to that account must be in the form of a user ID and an associated password. Secondary user passwords are available. The user ID and password combination will allow access only to that account. Other accounts, operator functions,and maintenance functions cannot be accessed. This is an AT&T EasyLink Services design feature.

Data encryption may be used to transmit proprietary, restricted, or otherwise sensitive information and data at the user's option.

Business Continuity and Disaster Recovery

AT&T EasyLink Services provides multiple measures to ensure its operation under abnormal conditions. These include pre-planning of prevention and mitigation measures. Specific tasks includes risk assessment, preventive actions, and disaster/recovery development and testing. AT&T Corporate Security and Auditing requires AT&T EasyLink Services to perform an annual risk assessment, Problem items which are identified in the risk assessment are items or tasks that do not provide adequate controls. A formal plan of action must be drawn up to correct or resolve identified deficiencies, if any.

This category also includes items such as physical security, fire and other hazard prevention, off-site storage of backups, and related items. Disaster recovery planning includes the development of a global strategy for implementing the strategy and annual disaster plan testing with at least annual reviews by AT&T Corporate Security & Auditing.

Disaster recovery procedures, the operations during a crisis, include the testing of the roles and responsibilities of the various teams which are assigned disaster recovery tasks as described in the AT&T EasyLink Services disaster recovery procedures. Procedures are updated on a monthly basis, are provided to persons on a need to know basis, and are stored both on paper and electronically offsite. Testing, on at least an annual basis, is an AT&T EasyLink Services requirement.

Business recovery procedures, the operations after a crisis, include the testing of the roles and responsibilities for resuming normal operations and the implementation of procedures to go from disaster mode back to normal mode.

VAN Reliability

Reliability refers to network performance, which is affected by availability, fault tolerance or redundancy, error or disaster recovery, and responsiveness. The question is, how can a relatively informal structure, such as the Internet, provide the underpinnings needed to ensure commercial-level reliability? The Internet's open access, available to anyone, anywhere, creates the conditions which make extended loss of Internet messaging a real and continuing possibility. The management control which protects against events which cause denial of messaging use is a key VAN reliability feature.

An example of what can happen on the Internet occurred in 1988, when a rogue program released by Robert T. Morris Jr., a Cornell graduate student, shut down most Internet traffic for several days. The program tried to get into AT&T EasyLink Services' network but could not gain entry and did not affect service. This was a result of well-defined and well-implemented management controls. A VAN provides these services as part of its commercial service.

Public Messaging Networks

AT&T EasyLink Services is structured, designed, provisioned, maintained, and secured to support mission-critical operations.

Chapter 5

AT&T Business Multimedia Services

AT&T Business Multimedia Services (BMS), a member of the AT&T Communications Services Group, concentrates on developing collaborative uses of network technology. AT&T EasyLink Services is a part of that organization. This positioning reflects the growing importance of multimedia in business functions. Two announced services point the way to the integration of public multimedia data services with strong messaging support. AT&T has joined forces with Lotus Development Corporation and Novell Inc. to provide AT&T Network Notes and AT&T NetWare Connect.

The extensive connectivity and functionality of AT&T NetWare Connect Services and AT&T Network Notes will provide enterprises with tools that enable fast start-up time, cost-effectiveness, and a secure environment. Some benefits for both enterprises and individual users are:

- Enable electronic commerce with fast start-up time
- Connect to remote sites, customers, and suppliers
- Enable desktop purchasing — create a new market for goods and services

- Link information and transactions to speed the purchasing process
- Build teams across geographic boundaries and time zones
- Integrate corporate knowledge with public information for competitive advantage
- Provide easy information navigation and searching
- Communicate with customers for closer relationships
- Collaborate with suppliers for reduced development cycles
- Extend electronic boundaries beyond the enterprise for intercorporate communications
- Access information services: news, weather, shopping, banking, etc.
- Provide an electronic market for business services and products
- Enable end-to-end technical support, problem isolation, and trouble management
- Distribute software electronically within and between corporate boundaries
- Provide online customer support and training

AT&T NetWare Connect Services

The development objectives for AT&T NetWare Connect Services were to combine the quality, performance, and reliability of the AT&T network with the directory services, network management, security, connectivity, and ease of use of Novell's networking technology. AT&T NetWare Connect Services was designed to:

- Provide easy access to public, commercial, and private network services over a single, highly secure connection.
- Offer a high-performance, secure, manageable, and reliable infrastructure, based on Novell NetWare 4.x Directory Services, that supports business application services.
- Create an open platform for easy development of applications.

The AT&T–Novell Alliance

The increased demand for fast communications has created a complex web of routers, bridges, gateways, and protocols to carry information at high speed between users. Businesses require LAN-type performance over WAN connections to remain competitive. Businesses also require easy operation and maintenance of their networks. AT&T and Novell developed AT&T NetWare Connect Services to build a platform for business and WAN applications where open participation can take place. The alliance objective is to provide efficient and cost-effective WAN connectivity with ubiquitous access, and rich functionality and features.

Novell provides networking products and services which have enabled people to seamlessly access information and network resources from anywhere in the network. Novell and AT&T, with AT&T NetWare Connect Services, will expand connectivity from within an enterprise to suppliers, customers, and partners while maintaining the security and integrity of corporate resources.

Novell Technology and AT&T NetWare Connect Services

The Novell technologies used in AT&T NetWare Connect Services are:

NetWare Directory Services (NDS)	NetWare Directory Services is a distributed database which provides seamless, global access to network resources regardless of their physical location. NDS, the AT&T NetWare Connect Services foundation, allows users to browse through directories of information similar to a local telephone directory. NDS is based on object-oriented technology, and, therefore, subdirectories of publicly accessible resources can be created within an organization and then, if desired, connected to AT&T NetWare Connect Services.
NetWare Security	When a network is extended beyond corporate boundaries, the network requires sophisticated security features to protect network integrity and

corporate data. AT&T NetWare Connect Services uses Novell's established multi-layered security technology to help ensure that security requirements are met. NetWare security features such as user authentication and digital signature per packet technology are incorporated in AT&T NetWare Connect Services.

Novell Dial-in Services — AT&T NetWare Connect Services uses Novell technology to provide dial-in services to global networks. Novell consolidates core communications resources on a single integrated and scalable platform, eliminating the need to have separate modems and phone lines for each mobile user.

AT&T Network Notes

The development objective for AT&T Network Notes was to combine the quality, performance, and reliability of the AT&T network using AT&T NetWare Connect to create an advanced environment for electronic work collaboration anywhere, at any time. AT&T Network Notes provides advanced collaborative network services to enterprise users and

- Enables businesses to create applications that meet specific needs, such as sales automation and virtual office (these are described later in this book).
- Promotes information flow and electronic commerce among business partners, customers, and suppliers.
- Provides access to many advanced directory and messaging services.
- Permits electronic catalog distribution.
- Supports electronic ordering.

Collaborative Platform

The objective of providing enterprise users with a collaborative platform was achieved by combining the AT&T communications experience, powerful Lotus business applications, and Novell network expertise. AT&T will deliver wide-area services for communications and collaborative applications that will be accessible from virtually anywhere and at any time. AT&T NetWare Connect Services is a WAN infrastructure that allows users to connect easily to a variety of services, information sources, and applications. Users may select either NetWare Internet Packet Exchange (IPX) or Transmission Control Protocol/Internet Protocol (TCP/IP) routing with high levels of security and performance.

AT&T NetWare Connect Services provides an environment where open participation can take place over both private and public data networks. Businesses will be able to make information available across AT&T NetWare Connect Services, people will be able to access the information easily, and developers will be able to build horizontal and vertical applications using application programming interfaces (APIs). AT&T NetWare Connect Services enables businesses to integrate customers and suppliers into their network to improve product development and distribution, decrease the time to market for products and services, and reduce operating costs.

Businesses will have an enhanced, reliable, and secure environment for information flow and collaborative work without incurring the costs of supporting and staffing private networks because AT&T will provide, manage, administer, and maintain the hardware and software components of the network. The same quality standards that AT&T follows today for its worldwide communications network will also be applied to AT&T NetWare Connect Services.

Functions and Features

AT&T NetWare Connect Services, like AT&T EasyLink Services, expands connectivity options while maintaining the investment in existing networks. AT&T NetWare Connect Services will be based on familiar network technology and provide the following features:

- NetWare IPX and TCP/IP routing in the AT&T network
- Easy connection through a choice of access methods
- Security
- Electronic mail and gateways
- Directory services
- Registration services
- Open protocols
- Network management
- Software development kits (SDK)

Access Options

Users can access AT&T NetWare Connect Services from their existing networks using Novell or other network operating systems and the following access options:

Dedicated Access	AT&T InterSpan Frame Relay Service at port speeds of 64, 128, 256, 384, 512, and 768 kbps and 1.024 and 1.544 Mbps.
Dial-up Access	Access over AT&T InterSpan Information Access Service dial-up data service, enabling remote access to data services at speeds ranging from 300 bps to 14.4 kbps using 950-XXXX local service.
Planned Enhancements	AT&T NetWare Connect Services will support direct access using leased lines, X.25, ISDN, ATM, and wireless access.

AT&T InterSpan Frame Relay and Information Access Service

AT&T InterSpan Frame Relay Service is a public data protocol conversion service for applications that generate bursty traffic and require high connectivity, high bandwidth, and low latency. AT&T InterSpan Frame Relay Service provides fast, reliable LAN interconnections over a wide area and supports complex distributed computing applications without dedicated, point-to-point leased lines. Frame relay is a network interface standard based on statistical multiplexing. AT&T InterSpan Frame Relay Service conforms to both national (ANSI) and international (ITU-T) frame relay interface standards. Some of the highlights of the AT&T InterSpan Frame Relay Service include

- Protocol conversion.
- Nationwide service ubiquity with access coordination.
- Integrated access.
- Multiple interface speed options.
- Public virtual circuit (PVC) service with up to 252 PVCs per interface.
- Global addressing. A single address can be used from anywhere in the network to address a given location.

AT&T InterSpan Information Access Service is a data communications service that connects remote or mobile callers to AT&T NetWare Connect Services. Connection is made only after the caller enters a login ID, a password, and an optional randomly generated number from a security token. Information Access Service is planning local dial-up access from all major U.S. cities at speeds up to 28.8 kbps for remote callers. Some of the highlights of Information Access Service include

- A single sign-on sequence for all locations
- Flexible data speeds from 300 bps to 14.4 kbps
- Access speeds automatically detected by Information Access Service
- 950-XXXX local access
- A variable session inactivity timer that can be set for each login ID

Security

The connection of private and public networks for collaborative processing makes security provisions for information protection and privacy major business concerns. AT&T NetWare Connect Services includes Novell's multi-level security options designed to protect intellectual data from unauthorized users. Access control, with integral login and password checks, and standard NetWare encryption are part of the design specifications. AT&T and Novell work together to help ensure that security requirements are met. Some key security features are

User Authentication	Provided by the public key technology of Novell NetWare Directory Services.
Digital Signatures	Novell NetWare software will provide per packet verification to prevent unauthorized users from transmitting packets by impersonating authorized users.
Login and Password Verification	AT&T NetWare Connect and AT&T InterSpan Information Access Service provide complementary security features. Information Access Service supports the use of security tokens, using randomly generated numbers, as added protection for dial-up accounts.

Electronic Mail and Gateways

Public messaging service access for AT&T Network Notes and AT&T NetWare Connect Services users will initially be provided by AT&T EasyLink Services. These services will be accessible using popular application software packages and common messaging interfaces. AT&T NetWare Connect Services will support messaging hub capabilities for Novell Global Message Handling System (MHS), Simple Message Transfer Protocol (SMTP), X.400, and other selected messaging systems, allowing native mode transport of messages between private mailboxes.

A centralized root directory, based on NetWare 4.x Directory Services, will provide global directory capabilities. The directory will simplify the administrative tasks of large, complex networks and provide features such

AT&T Business Multimedia Services 99

as network "white pages" and "yellow pages," cross-network directory synchronization, listed and unlisted directory entries, and reverse address translation (physical to logical address translation). Directory interoperability is a strategic direction for AT&T NetWare Connect Services.

Businesses will be able to make part or all of their directories available to customers and suppliers. Users will be able to navigate easily to other users' addresses and to resources on the network using the Novell Global Network Directory System.

Network Management

AT&T will manage and monitor facilities through its global Network Operations Center (NOC). The NOC will be the focal point for trouble reporting, isolation of network faults, and problem resolution. Network management provides round-the-clock monitoring of performance and traffic. Advanced reports provide sophisticated measurements and analyses for precise adjustment of capacity and congestion-free operation. Traffic engineering and performance systems keep network efficiency at high levels. Frequently scheduled backups and disaster recovery provisions will provide the traditional AT&T data protection and consistent availability.

Software Development Kits

Software development kits (SDK) will be available for developers who wish to create vertical or horizontal applications for public use or for users who wish to develop custom applications. SDKs will provide the same capabilities for the AT&T NetWare Connect Services environment that they provide for applications in a LAN environment. This compatibility includes Lotus Notes applications designed for LANs. AT&T, Novell, and Lotus have committed to extend the current SDKs to support network capabilities that will evolve over time.

AT&T Network Notes

AT&T Network Notes will allow people over a wide geographic area to share ideas and knowledge, work on documents or view images together, access information from databases, and connect to services and information. AT&T Network Notes combines AT&T's expertise in wide-area communications networks and Lotus Notes' open platform to create a globally available platform for sharing knowledge and building business applications.

AT&T Network Notes enables business to access integrated applications, share ideas and knowledge, and streamline many internal and external processes for increased productivity and cost savings. The service will provide access to a cost-effective, secure, and reliable client/server computing environment accessed through AT&T NetWare Connect Services. The service is based on Lotus Notes and supports most Lotus Notes 3.0 capabilities. AT&T Network Notes allows

- People to do collaborative work across distances, organizations, and enterprises
- Businesses to streamline processes; cut operating, distribution, and postal costs; and increase profits
- Service and information providers to make their offers widely available
- Developers to build customized applications to perform collaborative functions that were previously impractical or impossible

AT&T Network Notes supports the development and deployment of document-oriented applications. Examples of such applications include customer tracking, status reporting, project management, information distribution, discussions, and electronic mail. AT&T Network Notes provides inter-LAN database replication and mail routing, and supports all popular network operating systems. Some examples of AT&T Network Notes functions and features are

- Distributed and automatically replicated document databases
- Support for automatic tracking of document versions
- Access to private and public directories and to a directory of databases

AT&T Business Multimedia Services

- Access to external public and private information sources
- Optical character recognition (OCR) capability
- Document processing with full support for compound documents consisting of text, numeric fields, keywords, graphics, images, and rich text supporting multiple fonts, color, and mixed data types
- Integrated support for computer conferencing, broadcast dissemination, executive information systems, and mail-enabled applications
- Fully searchable document database with extensive customization options
- Import and export filters for spreadsheets, major word processing programs, and standard graphic file formats
- Comprehensive security measures to control access to databases and to help ensure secure delivery of messages
- Electronic mail with private mailboxes and access to AT&T Mail and to other messaging systems through AT&T Mail's large number of gateways, including SMTP and MHS
- Background replication of databases
- Context-sensitive online help with hypertext links

AT&T Network Notes will support adhoc flexibility in the creation of workgroups. An AT&T Network Notes user will often be a member of several logical workgroups at the same time. These can be for each project and each special interest area. There are no geographical, organizational, or enterprise barriers to membership. This unique capability allows any AT&T Network Notes user to be part of a discussion when given access by the discussion's manager. AT&T Network Notes users can be either active participants or observers. The role can vary by discussion, permitting flexible, dynamic information exchange to enhance cooperation, collaboration, and the free exchange of ideas and knowledge.

Business Application Areas

AT&T Network Notes and AT&T NetWare Connect Services provide a platform for applications designed to help enterprises reduce cost, streamline processes, and operate more efficiently in global markets.

The major application areas for AT&T NetWare Connect Services fall into the following categories:

Electronic Information Exchange	Electronic Information Exchange applications will allow users to access and search a variety of information sources. Users will be able to navigate easily through a variety of popular publications and public data sources, access business news, and customize individual searches using intelligent agents and filters made available by AT&T NetWare Connect Services.
Electronic Collaboration	Support for collaborative applications will enable people from different areas of a company or from different companies, anywhere, at any time, to work together without regard to time, distance, or organization.
Electronic Commerce	Universal access from the desktop over LANs will allow companies to transact commercial activities, reduce the time interval between production and sales, and reach a large customer base. Service or product suppliers will be able to create electronic catalogs and make them widely accessible via AT&T NetWare Connect Services.

Some examples of applications that can be developed using AT&T NetWare Connect Services as a communications backbone are

- Extended enterprise
- Sales automation
- Virtual office
- Process re-engineering
- Software distribution
- Customer support and training

AT&T NetWare Connect Services' open platform and published APIs allow third-party developers to build applications such as

- Messaging and email gateway

AT&T Business Multimedia Services 103

- Disaster recovery
- Medical imaging
- Online libraries and news and information services
- Language translation services
- Desktop purchasing
- Legal service interfaces
- Bulletin board applications
- Public help desk applications
- Video catalogs
- Classified ads
- Remote printing
- Product literature distribution
- Enhanced Internet gateways
- Interoperability with other directory and security systems

Application Examples

The following are examples of how businesses may use AT&T NetWare Connect Services to reduce cost, streamline processes, and operate more efficiently. These examples show the possibilities when the LAN is extended globally.

Businesses will be able to extend their private networks to include business partners such as consultants, suppliers, and lawyers while preserving the internal network's privacy and security. Some possible applications will allow extended enterprises to

- Collaborate with suppliers for reduced development cycles.
- Communicate with customers for closer relationships.
- Build teams across geographic boundaries and time zones.

- Integrate corporate knowledge with public information for competitive advantage.

A possible scenario would be an auto parts distributor with warehouses throughout the East Coast. The distributor has a private network that connects the main office with all of the warehouses but wants to make two enhancements to the network.

The distributor wishes to include major auto repair shops in the network so that they can order parts, make changes (add or delete items), and track order status electronically. The benefits would be reducing the paperwork, speeding up the ordering process, and reducing the time required to make changes and process returned merchandise. These benefits, when achieved, would translate into cost savings and competitive advantage. The desired security would be to limit access to the network to selected repair shops and to limit access to specific areas of the network so that unauthorized users would not be able to access information such as vendor accounts. The distributor would also want to expand the capabilities of the network to include connectivity to auto parts manufacturers and to AT&T Mail.

AT&T NetWare Connect Services can be used to extend the distributor's network to reach beyond its present boundaries and provide the ability to access other networks, information sources, and mail services in a cost-effective manner.

A sales automation scenario would be a sales office in a large manufacturing facility. AT&T Network Notes and AT&T NetWare Connect Services can be used to automate the sales process by defining a workgroup of people who have responsibilities for processing the forms, and automating the steps of the approval process. Sales contracts can then be completed electronically in significantly less time and at a lower cost.

A government sales scenario might be a corporation that deals with the federal government and maintains a large staff whose main function is to prepare, process, and submit all RFPs. The work consists of filling out forms and preparing documents according to strict U.S. government specifications, obtaining the appropriate approvals from corporate man-

AT&T Business Multimedia Services 105

agers, and submitting the paperwork to government officials. The process is not automated and is quite costly.

AT&T NetWare Connect Services and AT&T Network Notes can be used to streamline the process by

- Defining the major work categories, identifying the steps in each category and the individual(s) responsible for each step, building a work flow process, and creating workgroups with restricted access on AT&T Network Notes
- Replacing all paper forms with electronic ones (by scanning them) and creating a database of forms
- Establishing electronic connections with all corporate managers whose input and/or approvals are needed
- Creating electronic routing slips that keep track of information such as time and date of review, name and title of reviewer, document version, and status (i.e., approved/rejected)
- Automatically routing approved forms to the next person, as identified in the work flow
- Automatically returning rejected forms, with comments, for correction
- Establishing a central point for printing and distribution of completed forms

Software distribution applications, using AT&T NetWare Connect Services as a backbone, can be used to distribute software and manage licenses more efficiently within private networks. Software distribution applications will also be available on public networks, providing many businesses with new methods of obtaining software and content from vendors.

Training and technical support at the desktop, over AT&T NetWare Connect Services, can be provided by training organizations. This will enable electronic access for resolving problems quickly, adding users and privileges, and even training users. In addition, users of customer support applications will be able to access vendors' technical support centers using interactive, online services. Training for new programs and procedures will be supplied electronically, enabling companies to keep their employees informed of new trends and technologies.

Chapter 6

Global Messaging Architecture

Enterprises can now link local- and wide-area-network–based message systems to public electronic messaging services integrating remote sites and users easily and economically. The integration architecture provides local workers, mobile workers, telecommuters, and business partners with the resources and support of the enterprise regardless of where they are, their access method, or their computing platform. Every user may use authorized resources of the enterprise network and of the AT&T EasyLink Services public network to draw on the resources and support of the enterprise as a whole.

Unified Messaging Architecture (UMA), U.S. Patent 4837798, is AT&T's strategic blueprint for global public client/server and virtual private multimedia networks. UMA is the architectural definition for a global multimedia messaging network with interfaces and extensions that maintain compatibility with current market-accepted standards. The architecture provides for enterprise and workgroup LAN/WAN integration, standards-based interfaces with public and private messaging systems, a consistent development environment, exceptional system management tools, an intuitive consistent administrative interface, and a logical multimedia unified mailbox.

AT&T Unified Messaging Architecture is an integrating environment which supports global enterprises by providing the public network infrastructure for the development, provisioning, and operation of new strategic applications as well as for the integration of existing data, applications, and communications systems. The architecture supports business partner, enterprise, and workgroup computing with network software tools that help store, access, and manage multiple types of data and which coordinate cross-environment and geographic resources. The architecture's workflow automation provisions leverage existing computing resources for controlling the execution of recurring tasks or processes across enterprise and geographic boundaries. The software supports automatic initiation, routing, and execution of process steps and incorporates process management tools.

Strategy

AT&T EasyLink Services is one of AT&T's messaging arms and is responsible for developing and implementing new messaging functionality. This includes items such as

- LAN gateways
- Mobile messaging support
- Mail-enabled intelligent forms
- UNIX connectivity
- EDI support
- Enhanced Macintosh support
- External connectivity for PersonaLink
- Internal email within AT&T
- Messaging to and from the Internet
- Messaging support for AT&T SDN customers
- Evolving standard support

Global Messaging Architecture

- Globalization
- Directory enhancements
- Unified Messaging mailbox
- Multimedia support enhancements

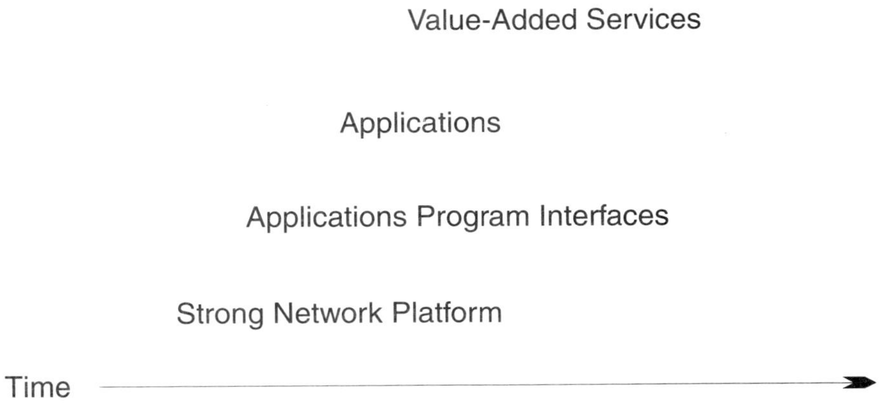

Value-Added Services

Applications

Applications Program Interfaces

Strong Network Platform

Time ─────────────────────────────────➤

Figure 6-1 **AT&T EasyLink Direction** The strategic direction shows the migration to value-added services.

AT&T EasyLink Services Vision

AT&T EasyLink Services supports messaging for the business market and is one of the primary organizational units implementing anytime, anywhere messaging to "change the way business does business." Other organizations within AT&T are responsible for consumer messaging.

AT&T EasyLink Services provides a reliable network platform with robust network management tools, superior directory capability, standards compliancy, and the ability to connect to virtually anything the market requires.

AT&T EasyLink Services supports industry standard applications programming interfaces (APIs) and provides application enabling tools for software development. The APIs and software toolkits, together with strategic partners, provide the ability to deliver complex mission-critical applications for vertical and horizontal markets. AT&T EasyLink Services is evolving from its role as a strong network platform provider to its future as the leading provider of value-added messaging services.

Users can use many devices. These can be stand-alone wired or wireless PCs, LAN shared resources, phones and fax machines, host terminals, and a new class of handheld personal digital assistants (PDAs). AT&T EasyLink Services is committed to supporting the technology and device interfaces the market requires in a user-transparent manner which defines and implements truly global anytime, anywhere communications. This allows the customer to use the service with the most cost-effective hardware, software, and staff investment, maximum customization options, and adherence to standards.

AT&T's strategic direction for support of its worldwide customer base's increasingly complex mission-critical business and computing environments is defined in its Unified Messaging Architecture (UMA). This architecture guides the development of globally distributed messaging systems for those who must extend messaging from desktops, workgroups, and enterprise systems to business partners, mobile workers, and remote sites worldwide.

AT&T's Unified Messaging Architecture is a patented, integrated messaging network architecture which has three major objectives:

- One network interface for all services
- One network account for all services
- One network session for all services

The UMA strategy is to support and achieve customer business goals. UMA's building blocks are a set of public network architectural services, interfaces, and facilities which incorporate the following:

Global Messaging Architecture

Interconnect-ability	The facilities and protocols for worldwide messaging, permitting UMA-compatible systems to connect to one another and to non-UMA systems
Interoperability	The protocols between services and applications allowing functions such as electronic mail and file exchanges
Cooperative processing	The facilities allowing users to transparently access resources irrespective of network location
Heterogeneity	The support of network operation and growth by providing coexistence and migration paths
Application portability	An industry standard interface set allowing AT&T EasyLink Services customers maximum access to software solutions
Consistent human interface	A harmonious group of human interface services and guidelines
Scalability	A platform family encompassing a wide range of computing power

AT&T's definition of an architecture is "a set of standard relationships that enable different computers, subsystems, applications, and system software to operate together." UMA is based on existing and emerging open standards that are widely accepted, in the public domain, or reasonably licensable and well defined.

Client/Server Operations

AT&T defines cooperative computing as the process by which two or more software programs, communicating through message passing, jointly participate in performing a business task. UMA, through standard application programming interfaces (APIs), allows system services, data, and applications to be distributed across network processing nodes. Within UMA, AT&T has defined the model for cooperative processing as client/server and uses the following definitions of client/server.

Client and server processes communicate by exchanging industry-standard, open-protocol formatted messages. Processes often execute under different operating environments and reside on separate physical processors. An example is a DOS email client process working collaboratively with an email server process running under UNIX.

UMA is based on the client/server view of an open, standards-based, cooperative computing system. The architecture provides reusable application code and data while allowing the customer to select solutions based on individual needs. UMA also permits development of information solutions in small, modular steps optimized for each user class while maintaining overall efficiency.

Clients	A client is defined as an application process that meets a unique need of a specific user or user class. Client applications request services from other processes and are called client processes.
Servers	A server is an application process that meets general needs or functions shared by classes of users. Server applications fill service requests from other processes and are called server processes.
Client Processes	Client processes satisfy user or user class requirements, provide human interfaces, invoke computing services, and perform calculations on user request. Examples would be to answer a mail message or to store a mail message in a local file. Client processes may be written by users or professional developers and can be executed on any appropriate processor. The processor may reside on a desktop or in a computer center. A client process can interact with other client processes, such as electronic mail or videoconferencing. Often, a person may concurrently execute multiple client processes under a common human interface on a desktop processor.

Global Messaging Architecture

Server Processes	Server processes are mechanisms that enterprises use to consistently define and enforce common practices throughout their operations. Server processes are commonly written and maintained by professional developers and may reside on any appropriate processor in a user department or in a computer center. They normally support multiple concurrent client processes and utilize the services of other servers.

A client/server operation would be a software process which manages client information storage and retrieval. A specific example is an invoicing software process or server invoked by any client process wishing to invoice a customer. The server logic is responsible for invoice creation, EDI transmission, posting to the accounts receivable server, inventory adjustment, revenue posting, and sales commission posting.

Equivalent object classes would be customer, order, invoice, and ledger for object-oriented implementations. Client processes then trigger methods against these objects to complete a task such as invoicing. The server is defined as the control for formatting and distributing information about its process. Server processes are general-purpose and reusable, invoked by client requests using appropriate open system interfaces.

Public Server Processes	Server processes implemented on a common carrier or fee-for-service basis provide cross-enterprise functions such as email transport, EDI, information retrieval, telex, and network-based fax. These servers reside on AT&T EasyLink Services hardware and communications platforms. They are globally accessible by registered enterprises and individuals. Government or other communications link limitations may restrict access method or service use from any specific location.

Servers, by definition, enforce enterprise standards. Public servers carry this to the inter-enterprise level by defining and enforcing the standards necessary for communications between and within public and enterprise messaging systems. UMA servers are open standards–based, providing ISO standard services such as X.400 mail and EDI. As public servers, they provide the full benefits of the open systems approach without the development and deployment costs. Public server standards-based computing extends the reach of existing systems and networks globally. Translation services, running as client applications on non-standard but common computing platforms, allow existing LANs or mainframe systems to globally interconnect within and without the enterprise.

This public server approach also permits use of lower-cost microcomputer technology while retaining the flexibility to use mainframe solutions as needed to achieve the most cost-effective mix. Consistency is maintained by housing common or standard services in server processes invoked by client processes. Application development time and costs are reduced by combining the client/server model with an integrated tool set, standard interfaces, and advanced storage techniques. User productivity is enhanced by delivering all information, regardless of how or where stored, through a consistent, integrated user interface running on desktop processors with object-oriented and graphical presentation. Organizational operation is enhanced by improved access to information through cooperative processing. Cost-effectiveness is enhanced by the geographical, computing resource, storage, and network flexibility inherent in UMA.

Unified Messaging Architecture

AT&T Unified Messaging Architecture is a "new way of messaging." Its objective is to help each customer make effective use of information technology for managing rapidly changing business environments. Each customer's unique needs are supported in a manner that adds value to activities which vary both between and within individual organizations,

Global Messaging Architecture

and even within workgroups. AT&T EasyLink Services' mission statement is:

> To apply information technology to meet the needs of our global customers for global messaging applications.
>
> To provide the highest quality, integrated, multimedia messaging services, products, and related value-added network offerings.
>
> To be the worldwide leader in messaging services.

The client/server model allows those persons responsible for a process or resource to directly control the development priorities of application automation. This approach results in a stronger link between business priorities and the automation efforts. UMA's objective is to isolate the user from technical and network issues and to allow him or her to concentrate on business concerns. This is accomplished by use of the client and server process concepts.

Client processes are of two types. One interacts with and supports a business client in completing a set of business tasks in a single session. The other, a batch client, is typically timer-initiated and does not interact with human users.

Server processes also are of two types. One manages storing and retrieving information and is an information storage server. The other is an activity server, which automates standard business activity. Both can be invoked by either client or server request. The server function parallels organizational responsibility for the data or activity.

Groupware

Groupware such as Lotus Notes allows users to work cooperatively using LAN-based client/server applications. The public server concept allows these functions to be made available globally and to remote offices while off-loading the network operation, management, administration, and provisioning (OAMP) through use of the AT&T public network. The standards-based public network also simplifies cross-platform interoperability. The ITU X.400 messaging and addressing standards enhance groupware interoperability because they are platform-independent. Scheduling, a popular groupware function, often uses email as its transport.

Windows NT and Windows '95 tightly integrate AT&T Mail email services into the desktop operating system. Messaging transport is the basis for a new category of productivity applications including intelligent email, structured messaging, and workflow automation. Productivity applications focus on work that occurs on a single desktop. Workgroup applications promote work that takes place between desktops, within workgroups, inside enterprises, and among business partners.

Lotus Notes Release 3 is a multiple-platform client/server application which provides multiple information type creation and distribution, supporting messages, documents, and graphics in its own text database. Notes contains Imagery Software image-enabled technology and workflow primitives. Lotus Notes groupware is a tool for relatively unstructured or ad hoc teams such as research and development teams, with a database that has associated documents and support files.

Notes is organized in groups of six macro folders, each with up to thirty databases, accessed from a single graphical interface. Notes Rich Text Format support allows bit-mapped images to be entered beside text. Planned enhancements include voice response, video, and real-time screen-sharing features. Notes will also operate over high-speed links, allowing replication of Notes documents containing video clips. Lotus Notes will perform flow control over WAN links, based on bandwidth availability, with the Notes software managing traffic. Lotus may add shared white-board capability, allowing globally distributed users to make changes in real time to their shared screen.

AT&T Network Notes

AT&T Network Notes, based on Lotus Notes, is a service which allows enterprises to create a new class of applications, which can be public, cross-enterprise, workgroup, or desktop level. These applications can enhance information flow and electronic commerce between business partners, customers, and suppliers.

Third-party developers using AT&T Network Notes development tools will be able to create a wide range of industry-specific or cross-business applications, such as sales automation, virtual offices, extended enterprises, and process re-engineering. These can be limited to a closed user group or made globally accessible to the public.

AT&T will deploy AT&T Network Notes servers using AT&T InterSpan Frame Relay Service to support dial-up and dedicated access from LANs and personal computers. This eliminates the distinction between LAN and WAN. The network-based service extends LAN functions worldwide, while the store-and-forward messaging transports of AT&T's Unified Messaging Architecture eliminate time differences, distance, and computing platforms as barriers to electronic commerce.

UMA's flexibility and its client/server modular approach allow the customer to establish application phasing as its services are provisioned and currently available globally. UMA supports client process access as if such processes were locally resident and eliminates conceptual differences between local, regional, national, or global servers. UMA enhances the corporate organizational and cultural environment by providing an open, cooperative infrastructure for worldwide information access. Application development is enhanced by a modular client/server model and, especially, by the shared resource of public servers. The provisioning of new technology such as AT&T Network Notes is enhanced by the AT&T public network's flexible run-time environment.

AT&T Global Messaging Services

AT&T EasyLink Services is a worldwide public messaging service with secure message transport and value-added capabilities for email, EDI, information services, telex, and enhanced fax services. The comprehensive offering adds value to transport, user, and network administration functions and provides usage-based billing. The service supports input from a variety of devices, including fax machines, asynchronous terminals, personal computers (PCs), UNIX system processors, a wide variety of mainframe computers, local area networks, groupware, and many handheld and mobile devices. It includes worldwide email connectivity to many cooperating systems that conform to MHS X.400 (the ITU recommendation for electronic mail interchange).

The messaging platform supports a number of interrelated services in a common architecture. It supports the services offered today, and will serve as the foundation for future services.

The Unified Messaging Architecture is covered by U.S. Patent 4837798, titled COMMUNICATION SYSTEM HAVING UNIFIED MESSAGING.

The patent abstract gives a brief summary of the architecture.

> Unified messaging is a concept that provides for a single electronic mailbox for different types of messages. The mailbox can be on a user's host computer, PBX, PC, etc. and the user has consistent facilities available to originate, receive and manipulate messages. Messages can be translated from one media to another for reception, and a single message may be composed of parts that use different native media. The message recipient has a single controllable point of contact where all messages can be scanned and/or viewed.

The Global Messaging platform is AT&T's strategic computing platform

Global Messaging Architecture 119

for business messaging. A computing platform is a set of **networking components**, computing hardware, and operating system software implemented as the technological base upon which a set of **server processes** are developed. The GMS platform is based upon AT&T's **Unified Messaging Architecture**, which contains two sub-architectures.

AT&T MAIL	AT&T FAXsolutions	AT&T EDI	AT&T Information Services	Future Services
Universal Messaging Architecture				
Message Transfer Architecture		Content Description Architecture		
Network Platform				

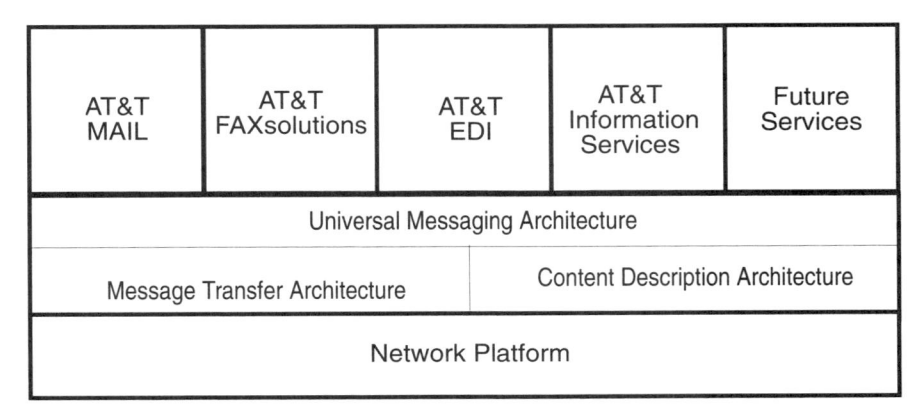

Figure 6-2 **Unified Messaging Architecture** The messaging applications are built on the Message Transfer Architecture and Content Description Architecture.

Message Transfer Architecture (MTA) — MTA defines the format of the message/envelope.

Content Description Architecture — CDA defines the format of the common envelope's contents, such as email, EDI, or fax. The common envelope currently supports multimedia data, such as text, image, voice, video, and graphics.

Messaging services are added as server processes to the core store-and-forward network. These servers provide the specific functions and capabilities available to the customer in specific services. Gateways and interfaces to customer systems and public networks are also server processes.

Server Process Groupings

AT&T EasyLink Services classes its individual services implemented as one or more server processes into broad classes as follows:

AT&T Mail
: AT&T EasyLink Services provides global public messaging services which permit customers to communicate with almost anyone anywhere on the planet using a variety of strong delivery methods. These include wire and wireless electronic mailbox delivery, X.400, text and graphic to fax, telex, paging, voice, and paper delivery by post and express (overnight and 4-hour). Delivery modes may be separately selected for each recipient of a single message. Users can send standard text messages, graphics, spreadsheets, and other binary files, allowing software delivery through email. The store-and-forward mail capability also provides a platform for a variety of mail-enabled applications using AT&T Mail features such as Shared Folders, AT&T Mail Catalog, Forms, Auto-Forwarding, and Auto-Reply. The Interactive Forms feature allows creation and administration of purchase orders, registration requests, and other documents for use within an enterprise in a parallel manner to AT&T EDI, which is structured for use between enterprises.

AT&T FAXsolutions
: AT&T EasyLink Services provides the most extensive range of fax services, some of which are enhanced fax-to-fax using store-and-forward servers and services and PC text-to-fax and graphic-to-fax store-and-forward technology. The

Global Messaging Architecture

full fax service range is described in Chapter 12, "AT&T FAXsolutions."

AT&T Electronic Data Interchange (EDI)	EDI supports electronic commerce in a cost-effective and globally connective manner. EDI supports inter-enterprise electronic exchange of business transactions (such as purchase orders and invoices, among others) in standard formats between business partners. AT&T EDI offers businesses the essential elements needed for worldwide EDI implementations, including network design, systems, software, and implementation support. AT&T's EDI network is based on ITU MHS X.400, the internationally accepted messaging standard, permitting easy connection to business partners on all continents while providing interconnections and conversion services for the less reliable and less secure older EDI systems. These EDI services are available on a variety of subscription bases and are described in Chapter 11, "AT&T EDI."
AT&T Information Services	AT&T Mail users have simple, fast, and cost-effective access to the world's largest collection of online interactive databases, informational services, online news wires, and flexible research services under a user-friendly menuing system. Users of these services are charged only for usage and do not have to maintain separate subscriptions or administer different accounts for each service. Access is included in the AT&T Mail subscription cost. These services may be used anytime from anywhere over land or wireless connections. These are described in Chapter 13, "AT&T Information Services."

Network Design, Access, and Operations

AT&T's Global Messaging and Information Services network has physical node sites distributed around the world, with several more being deployed each year. AT&T EasyLink Services network node designations refer to actual processing capabilities at the location, not to a remote access point for an out-of-country processing site. AT&T's Global Messaging Service network is truly distributed, with tightly coupled globally distributed computers. Its multi-node configuration permits rapid relocation of server processes and user files in the event of a disaster. The loss of one physical site does not affect connections or functionality of the unaffected node sites. This interconnection provides redundant backup between node sites. Within a site, processors are logically redundant and storage mirrored with a direction toward a fully fault-tolerant platform.

The globally distributed AT&T multi-processor nodes are currently connected through AT&T Datakit Virtual Circuit Switches for wide-area networking. The Datakit switch uses ACCUNET T1.5 and multiple 56-kilobyte circuits to interconnect geographically dispersed nodes and fiber optics to interconnect co-located nodes at a processing center. Frame relay connections are being added to support AT&T NetWare Connectivity and AT&T Network Notes. End-user access and interprocessor communications are through the Datakit network, and increases in processor power and supported user connections are by adding nodes.

Virtual circuit connections, between and within nodes, are established using AT&T Datakit Virtual Circuit Switch processors. The Datakit service concept, a communication service or host-based service coupled with a UNIX system file structure, establishes "virtual" machines which can reside on any node processor. Therefore, when a physical processor is unavailable, all services can be restored on other node processors without the need to reconfigure any Datakit or node processor. This also provides a simple mechanism for real-time load balancing, at the level of virtual machines, within a service node.

Global Messaging Architecture

Access Options

Users may access AT&T EasyLink Services from a variety of platforms, including

- PCs, including DOS, Windows, and Apple Macintosh
- Handheld mobile messaging mevices
- UNIX systems
- IBM AS/400 systems
- DEC minis
- Mainframes
- LAN email systems
- X.400-compatible systems

AT&T Mail has a wide range of other delivery options that are available to the user. Among these are telex, fax, U.S. mail, courier services, and MailTALK (the ability to access a message from a touch-tone telephone).

AT&T EasyLink Services is provided through deployed nodal processing sites or by strategic alliances with value-added resellers that provide local access to AT&T EasyLink Services' network, sales, and support functions.

The following summary provides the names and country locations of these processing centers:

- AT&T EasyLink Services Asia/Pacific
- AT&T EasyLink Services Australia Ltd., Australia
- AT&T EasyLink Services Ltd., United Kingdom
- AT&T JENS, Japan
- GOLDNET, Israel

- Unitel Communications Inc., Canada

In the Americas, the AT&T Mail service consists of two physical node sites located in Missouri and Virginia. These two sites, each consisting of multiple physical nodes, are currently interconnected with ACCUNET T1.5 facilities, and the nodes at each site are fully interconnected with fiber optics.

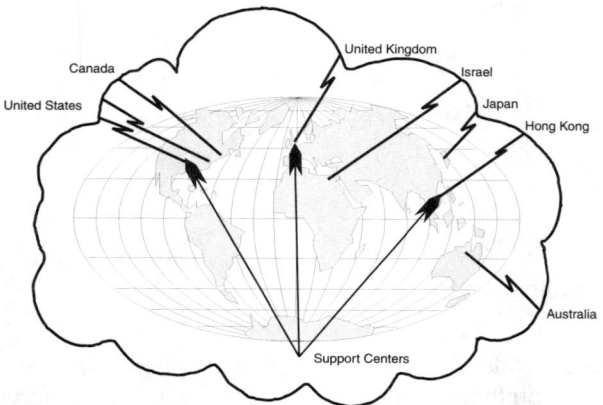

Figure 6-3 **Node Interconnections** AT&T EasyLink Services has local processing and support distributed internationally.

Each physical node consists of multiple UNIX system processors known as node processors, a storage coupling device, disk storage facilities, and a Datakit Virtual Circuit Switch (VCS). The physical processors are logically redundant, and storage is mirrored, providing levels of backup within each node site. Datakit establishes virtual circuit connections within and between nodes as data traveling on the backplane are packetized. This includes the host processor interfaces, customer access using 800 access within the United States, customer access using ACCUNET Packet Services (APS), and outbound connections to satellite processors and customer systems or devices. Plans also call for AT&T SDN customers to connect to AT&T EasyLink Services through SDN and for frame relay support for AT&T NetWare connectivity.

The network architecture uses a UNIX system file system to implement "virtual" machines which can reside on any processor in the node. This

Global Messaging Architecture

approach allows for timely recovery of all services on the remaining node processors without re-configuration of any Datakit node processor information when a given processor is unavailable.

Availability — AT&T's Global Messaging Service network computing platform is available on a 24-hour-per-day, 7-days-per-week basis. AT&T has designed the network to meet its high standards of network reliability and performance. This reliability is accomplished through redundancy and disk mirroring in the nodal processors. The network is maintained in accordance with AT&T network reliability standards for mission-critical operations.

Contingency Plans — Provisions exist for the loss of service on any level. Because of the service design as described above, the loss of any one node processor within a multi-node complex can be corrected by remounting the file systems of the failed processor on the other two processors of the node. With this concept, the loss of any one processor affects only a fraction of users with accounts at that node complex, and the outage duration is typically corrected within minutes. Information is backed up daily for each node processor at every node complex without service interruption during backup and is stored both at the node site and at an off-premises location. If necessary, off-premises data can be transported to other node complexes and customer accounts restored. AT&T does not warrant that the operation of AT&T EasyLink Services will be uninterrupted or error free and will provide a refund or credit for any messaging charges paid to AT&T EasyLink Services for services or associated support facilities which fail to perform as described in the applicable documentation.

Network Access	Subscribers can access the network through 800 numbers in the United States, local asynchronous and synchronous dial-up, UNIX communication protocols, software defined network (SDN), ACCUNET packet service, leased lines, frame relay, or any other locally available access method including telex, fax, and PTT services. Access methods may be restricted by local conditions such as government regulation or other telecommunications limitations, and may vary between the United States and other countries.
User Validation	The customer's identity is validated by a distributed authorization server that also offers the customer a menu of authorized services. The core store-and-forward network is linked to centralized operations, billing, and customer assistance systems that support all network services and provide a single point of support and a consolidated bill for all services. Customers use a single account and access arrangement to access AT&T Mail–based services and interactive services.

The AT&T security organization administers security practices in the same manner in which AT&T protects the privacy of telephone traffic carried over AT&T facilities. The AT&T Unified Messaging Architecture, by separating the envelope addressing from its contents, permits user-determined encryption limited only by governmental restrictions at the sending or receiving locations. The user is responsible for ensuring that security measures are adequate for the user's purposes, as AT&T provides message transport without assuming responsibility for the contents.

AT&T network services have a history of being designed to offer a high degree of security to their users. The AT&T Mail network provides multiple security levels. The first level of security is provided by requiring all customer access to be verified by an "authorization machine" before any

Global Messaging Architecture

inbound call is routed to a network application. Since the user interface program is selected by the authorization machine, inbound dial access to the core network can never result in access to the operating system.

Backup
: Sent or received messages are retained, by default, in the AT&T Mail service for 24 hours. Messages are deleted from the In folder 24 hours after they are read by the receiver, and are automatically deleted from the Out folder 24 hours after being sent. Users can modify their profile and set message storage time to up to 6 days. Daily backup tapes are retained for a period of 4 weeks. System-generated daily backup tapes for the past 30 days may be used for recovery on customer request.

Access Control
: All access to the AT&T Mail Service is controlled by user ID and password. Customer user IDs and passwords are established during the account registration process. All user IDs are unique and can have a syntax similar to that of a business name (i.e., XYZ Freight - user ID = !xyz) or a human name such as John Doe - user ID = !jdoe. For systems such as mainframe/midrange computers, node names can correspond to type of system and/or location, with the individual user ID indicated after the exclamation sign, such as s36egypt!jdoe.

Users who require additional access security may set a secondary password in their profiles to supplement the AT&T-assigned primary password. The user can change the secondary password as required. Since this secondary password is assigned by the user, only the user will know it. Most AT&T Mail asynchronous access packages scripting capabilities support the use of secondary passwords. Access PLUS supports the secondary password capability.

The AT&T EasyLink Services Customer Service and Support Center will relay password information only to individuals who know the security word associated with the account. Users who employ a second private password cannot have that password compromised, since it is encrypted prior to storage. AT&T can reset the password but cannot learn it. This limitation maintains the integrity of the password usage audit trail. AT&T Mail Access PLUS users will be prompted for the password each time service access is requested if they choose not to enter it in the software.

Password Changes

Password and user ID administration is typically performed by the AT&T EasyLink Services Customer Service and Support Centers. User password inquiries must be verified by the individual's security word. Large corporate users may perform self-administration by using the Remote Customer Support Module (RCSM). A corporate administrator can perform user management and control from an on-premises asynchronous terminal. The administrator must know user security words to make account changes. Secondary password users cannot receive Support Center password assistance, as secondary passwords are encrypted. However, at user request, the Support Center may delete secondary passwords to perform profile administration.

Message Protection

AT&T Mail uses multiple protocols to provide the user with error-correcting network connections for message upload or download sessions. Only the part of the message transmission is re-sent to correct transmission errors. Three log-on attempts are permitted prior to disconnection.

After the third failed log-on attempt, the caller is disconnected and the network logs the occurrence to alert network staff of a possible unauthorized access attempt. Information on unauthorized access (hacker) monitoring capabilities and detection methods is not disclosed by AT&T to maintain network security.

AT&T EasyLink Services programmatically reads message envelopes to determine message routing. Message content is not programmatically examined other than when agreed to for some EDI message classes or when media conversion has been requested.

AT&T EasyLink Services can perform most service-related special handling, like message repair, with message envelope access only. Troubleshooting of certain problems may require operations to examine customer message contents.

AT&T EasyLink Services employees may examine messages under strict procedural control when this is essential to maintain the quality and integrity of the network service. In this regard, AT&T EasyLink Services complies with the U.S. Electronic Communications Privacy Act of 1986.

AT&T Mail, at this writing, supports the transfer of text and binary electronic messages with a 10-Mb file size limit for any one email message, or 3-Mb for fax. There is no restriction on the number of messages sent or received within any one communications session. These size restrictions will be changed as customer message size requirements expand to support video and sound. Access methods, such as slow-speed modems, may also limit file size.

Software Architecture

AT&T Mail is media independent, allowing the transfer of voice, text, or any other binary content. Message Transfer Architecture is an ITU's Message Handling System (MHS) X.400 functional superset. X.400 is the globally accepted standard for messaging movement and management.

Conceptually, X.400 uses postal mail terminology and a client/server organization. A message is defined as an envelope, which contains addressing information, and contents. Messages are stored in post office boxes until they are read by the recipient.

User agents begin and end mail transfer, while message transfer agents move mail from post office to post office. These agents are implemented as client/server processes. Since these elements are common to all message types, the same network can be used to transport any envelope content: email, fax, video, EDI, telex, and other text or binary data.

The AT&T UMA envelope provides functions equal to those of an X.400 envelope containing address and audit trail information This allows the network to identify the sender and the receiver, and provides message date/time-stamp information. Other fields contain audit trail data which track the message's passage through the network. AT&T also supports non-X.400 (synchronous) network interconnections between other value-added networks to meet customer needs.

AT&T Unified Messaging Architecture's purpose is to ensure that all AT&T messaging products and services are interconnected. This is achieved through a common underlying architecture implemented in each product and service. An example is AT&T's Global Messaging Service, which consists of two primary elements: the user interface and the service and communications architecture. The user interface permits many industry-standard email and EDI user interfaces to be used for access. One user interface, MailTALK, provides a text-to-voice service for touch-tone phone email access.

Global Messaging Architecture

The UMA infrastructure provides for messages and other information types, such as spreadsheets, graphs, voice objects, voice-annotated text, image, and other complex types of information. UMA also provides for connectivity to international services and other vendors' products and services. Global Messaging and Information Systems, built according to UMA standards, therefore supports multifunction multimedia mailboxes. The Unified Mailbox allows a user to retrieve AT&T Mail and AT&T Enhanced FAX messages using a single subscriber ID from a single mailbox during one session.

AT&T EasyLink Standards Support

A partial list of the standards supported by AT&T Mail includes the following:

OSI Reference Model	The AT&T Mail and AT&T EDI service components are OSI standards–based and follow the seven-layer data communications OSI Reference Model. Client processes, which function as user agents, have a common look and feel for access by PC, data terminal, or voice terminal (telephone). The architecture is mainly at the OSI model application (7) and presentation (6) layers and therefore is independent of the network below server processes (applications).
ITU X.400	AT&T EasyLink Services uses the ITU X.400 Message Handling Systems (MHS) 1984, 1988, or 1993 interface standards, as appropriate, with systems that comply with the International Telecommunications Union's MHS recommendations. The X.400 standards define protocols and message formats for message exchange between dissimilar systems and for unaltered relay of message traffic by the AT&T Mail 400 Service.

AT&T Mail is a registered, recognized Administration Management Domain (ADMD) providing routing and service to other AT&T Mail/EasyLink users, other host systems, ADMDs and Private Management Domains (PRMDs), EDI, and the Internet, as well as telex, fax, remote printers, and U.S. postal delivery. AT&T Mail 400 Service provides two basic functions: the message transport function, which provides a general, application-independent, store-and-forward message transfer service, and the translation function necessary to move AT&T Mail messages from the AT&T Mail network for delivery to X.400-compliant systems. AT&T Mail 400 handles text messages as well as binary files.

Since the AT&T Mail 400 Service is resident on the AT&T Mail network, all AT&T Mail users can direct messages to the AT&T Mail 400 Service, including those on PCs, UNIX systems, or other host machines. No additional software or hardware is required for X.400 messaging. Installations using X.400 software can register as PRMDs and exchange messages with AT&T Mail/EasyLink users and all users of other systems or networks connected to AT&T Mail. PRMD users can also use the AT&T Mail facsimile, telex, remote printer, and postal delivery facilities.

PRMDs access AT&T Mail 400 Service through AT&T's X.25 network, ACCUNET Packet Service (APS). Conformance testing is scheduled with AT&T's X.400 Customer Implementation Group when the customer registers as a PRMD. The tests prepare customers for movement to production X.400 use. Billing starts after the customer is completely satisfied and in

Global Messaging Architecture 133

production.

AT&T Mail 400 Service supports the Organization Name (O) and Organizational Unit (OU) addressing attributes, which allow users to uniquely identify their enterprise by registering an Organization Name and up to four Organizational Units with AT&T Mail.

Interoperability Testing

AT&T has a comprehensive X.400 interoperability test program which all vendors must complete prior to commercial availability. The AT&T Mail PRMD Software Vendor (PRMDSV) program provides an X.400 testing environment to ensure interoperability between vendor products and AT&T Mail 400 Service. X.400 vendors that have successfully completed testing with AT&T Mail 400 Service are:

Company	X.400 Product
CDC	Mail/VE, OSIWare
DEC	All-in-1, VMS, MRXII
Retix	Open Server 400. This product is also guaranteed by the vendor to work with AT&T Mail 400 Service in the following environments: cc:Mail Link to X.400, DaVinci email, Higgins to: X.400 Gateway (ProtoComm), mbp Fax 400, MHS Novell, MHS to X.400, Microsoft Mail, OfficeWorks 400, OpenMail, Oracle*mail 400 Gateway/UNIX, Personal Office 400, Poste, QuickMail, SMTP to X.400 Gateway, The Notework, and WordPerfect Office Connection.
Hewlett-Packard	HP DESK 3000, OpenMail 9000
Tandem	Transfer
IBM	OSME, PROFS

Toshiba	MHS/Motis
IS Technologies Touch Comm.	Worldtalk 400
ISOCOR	ISOPLEX Ver. 2.3.1
Unisys	Unisys MHS X.400, OSI-MHS
Lotus	Totally Automated Office, Soft*Switch Central
Marben	AXESS X400
Wang	Wang Office
Microsoft	MS Mail
NCR	Message Center 400

Administration Management Domain (ADMD)

AT&T Mail 400 was one of the world's first public X.400 implementations. AT&T is registered as "attmail." and provides routing and service to AT&T EasyLink Services users; LAN, midrange, mainframe, and UNIX email systems; other ADMDS, Private Management Domains (PRMDs), EDI, the Internet; telex; fax; remote printers; and U.S. postal delivery. AT&T also offers private X.400 system connectivity for AT&T Mail 400 Service using PRMDs. AT&T's X.400 support conforms to the NIST email and EDI agreements for the United States and to the European implementation agreements (A/311). At this writing, AT&T Mail 400 Service has 52 interconnections in 29 different countries.

Country	Company	Email Service
Australia	OTC	OTC
Australia	Telecom-Australia	TELEMEMO

Global Messaging Architecture

Country	Company	Email Service
Austria	Plus Communications	UMI-AT
Austria	Radio-Austria A.G.	ADA
Belgium	BELGACOM	RTT
Brazil	EMBRATEL	EMBRATEL.INTL
Canada	STENTOR	TELECOM.CANADA
Canada	Canada Post Corporation	CPCMHS
Canada	Government of Canada	GOVMT. CAN ADA
China	Directorate General of Telecommunications	PIPMAIL
Costa Rica	Radiografica Costarricenese S.A	RASCAMAILI
Denmark	Telecom-Denmark	TELDK
Finland	Helsinki Telephone Co.	ELISA
Finland	PTT Finland	MAILNET
France	Transpac	ATLAS
Germany	Deutsche Bundespost	TELEKOM DBP
Germany	LION	LION

Country	Company	Email Service
India	Videsh Sanchar Nigram Ltd	VSNB
Ireland	EIRTRADE, Ltd	EIRMAIL 400
Italy	Italcable	OMEGA
Italy	Teleo S.p.A.	MASTER400T
Japan	ACE Telemail	ATI
Japan	KDD	KDD
Japan	NTT PC Communications, Inc.	NTTPC
Korea	DACOM	DACOMMHS
Netherlands	#Unisource Business Networks	400NET
Norway	Telepost Communications	TELEMAX
Russia	Sprint Networks USSR	SOVMAIL
Singapore	Singapore Telecom	SGMHS
Spain	Telefonica Servicios, S.A	MENSATEX
Sweden	Swedish Telecom Int'l	TEDE
Sweden	Scandinavian Info Link	SIL

Global Messaging Architecture

Country	Company	Email Service
Switzerland	Swiss PTT	ARCOM
Taiwan	Directorate General of Telecommunications	PIPMAIL
UA Emirates	Emirates Telecom	EMNET
UK	British Telecom	GOLD 400
UK	#Mercury Comm	CWMAIL
UK	Sprint International	TMAILUK
USA	#Advantis	IBMX400
USA	AT&T EasyLink Services	WESTERN UNION
USA	BellSouth Adv.Netwks,Inc.	BELLSOUTH
USA	BT Tymnet	DIALCOM
USA	CompuServe	COMPUSERVE
USA	#GEIS	MARK400
USA	Graphnet	GRAPHNET
USA	#INFONET	INFONET
USA	MCI	MCI
USA	Motorola	EMBARC
USA	Pacific Bell	PACBELL

Country	Company	Email Service
USA	US Sprint	TELEMAIL

Note: "#" includes interconnections in various countries.

AT&T Mail X.400 Service is Government OSI Protocol (GOSIP) compliant at the MHS layer.

Basic Messaging Functions

The message transport function provides a general, application-independent, store-and-forward message transfer service, while the message translation function provides the translation necessary to move AT&T Mail network messages to X.400-compliant systems. AT&T Mail 400 Service resides on the AT&T Mail network and accepts messages from all AT&T Mail users, including those on PCs, UNIX systems, or other hosts.

AT&T Mail subscribers' access to the network is dependent upon the application, the user location, and the telecommunications capability. Subscribers may chose from many alternative speeds and protocols based on the access point of origin.

The access options that are available for local network access are based on the country point of origin. They include

- Local dial (provided via AT&T facilities in Japan, the U.K., Canada, Australia, Hong Kong, Israel, and the United States; via Unitel facilities in Canada)
- Green Phone (800-type service) dialing (covers much of the Europe mainland)

Global Messaging Architecture 139

| Zone | User Type ||||
| | Synchronous || Asynchronous ||
	Access Type	Host Location	Access Type	Host Location
1. Europe	Dial/Ded.	UK	Dial/X.25	UK
1. United Kingdom	Dial/Ded.	UK	Dial/X.25	UK
2. Asia	Dial	U.S.	X.25	Japan
2. Japan	Dial	Japan.	Dial	Japan
2. Hong Kong	Dial/Ded.	Hong Kong	Dial/X.25	Hong Kong
3. South America	Dial	U.S.	X.25	U.S.
4. United States	Dial/Ded.	U.S.	800#	U.S.

Figure 6-4 **Access Types** Access varies by user location and local conditions.

- Packet access (AT&T ACCUNET Packet and Worldnet in the United States; PTT packet networks in international locations; other carrier or VAR networks throughout the globe)
- Synchronous dial or dedicated private access lines
- Asynchronous dedicated access lines
- Toll-free 1-800 service (limited to the United States and Canada)
- 950-1ATT (AT&T Interspan Access Service — IAS)

The normal international access options available for travelers, regional multinational corporate offices, and AT&T Mail end users include

- European Access Service: EAS (Austria, Belgium, Denmark, Luxembourg, Finland, France, Germany, Italy, Netherlands, Norway, Portugal, Spain, Sweden, and Switzerland)
- LA Access: Argentina, Austria, Belgium, Brazil, Denmark, France, Germany, Indonesia, Ireland, Italy, Korea, Luxembourg, Malaysia, Mexico, Netherlands, New Zealand, Norway, Philippines, Portugal, Russia, Singapore, Spain, Sweden, Switzerland, Taiwan, United States
- Connectivity with international electronic mail services

- Connectivity with international value-added networks (VANs) deployed globally
- Local dial to the in-country AT&T Mail nodal site (U.K., Canada, Australia, Hong Kong, Japan, Israel)
- International DDD connectivity

		\multicolumn{5}{c}{Line Speeds}
Mode		1200	2400	4800	9600	19200
Dial	Async.	X	X		X	
	Sync.		X	X	X	
Dedicated Line	Async.				X	
	Sync.			X	X	X

Figure 6-5 **Access Speeds by Area** 14,400 async is supported at some locations.

SDN Connectivity

SDN is a software-defined virtual network within the public switched network which allows customers to configure private networking functionality within the AT&T World Wide Intelligent Network.

The software defined network (SDN) Enhanced FAX service provides secure store-and-forward delivery of fax transmissions worldwide by coupling AT&T Enhanced FAX to the transport capabilities of SDN. SDN's rates are tariffed and usage-based. Adding AT&T Enhanced FAX applications can therefore potentially lower overall SDN transport costs by adding fax to voice and data usage to achieve usage levels. Transport charges incurred for access to and egress from the SDN network appear on the customer's monthly SDN bill. All fax messaging charges will be charged by and appear on the AT&T EasyLink Services invoice.

SDN Enhanced FAX users are charged only for delivered pages, eliminating resend costs. SDN customers can access the fax service from on-network and, by using SDN Network Remote Access (NRA), from off-network sites using existing equipment such as Group III fax machines and touch-tone keypads (telephone or autodialer). This feature allows authorized users to simply dial into their SDN network, provide their ID and password, and then dial other locations.

AT&T EasyLink Services adds two more levels of security, individually assigned IDs and passwords, to the SDN network access authorization process. Additional security, especially for fax receptions, is provided to the SDN customer who uses the features of Fax Mailbox. SDN Enhanced FAX also provides added administrative convenience. Large corporations can have all their subscribers' accounts consolidated for easy processing, yet still maintain subscriber-specific detail for fax usage tracking.

AT&T and the Internet

The AT&T EasyLink Services platform allows messaging interchange with proprietary mail systems, public mail systems, and non-commercial email systems such as the Internet, BITNET, and UUNET. The Internet is a worldwide TCP/IP interconnected family of commercial, educational, and research networks developed without centralized management or control. UUNET connects UUCP mail services and is part of the Internet. BITNET, a university/college network, is also part of the Internet. AT&T Mail can transfer mail to and from the Internet.

AT&T EasyLink Services enables users on corporate enterprise networks to send and receive Internet mail from the system of approximately 14,000 interconnected data networks, reaching more than 100 countries and serving commercial organizations, governments, and universities. Direct connection to the Internet is provided through the AT&T InterSpan group. The method of interconnection is flexible, supporting both frame relay and dial-up technology. While interconnection is desirable, companies are increasingly trying to establish "firewall protection" for their host resources by restricting access to intended users rather than the general population. The architecture AT&T supports enables the customer to take advantage of the wide resources and connectivity available through the Internet while permitting AT&T to serve as a management and security buffer between the Internet and the enterprise's resources.

In addition, AT&T EasyLink Services provides connectivity to its value-added messaging services via Simple Mail Transfer Protocol (SMTP) over TCP/IP in response to frequent customer requests. This expands the reach of Internet users and gives them the ability to use additional delivery options, such as telex, and fax.

In Figure 6-6, Customer A connects to AT&T EasyLink Services using a UUCP connection and the AT&T EasyLink Services gateway. Customer B uses TCP/IP and the AT&T EasyLink Services Gateway. Customer C connects through AT&T InterSpan Frame Relay Services for full Internet connectivity services with its own Internet identity and with the AT&T EasyLink value-added services. Customer D is directly connected to the Internet and accesses AT&T EasyLink Services to extend its reach to the non-Internet world.

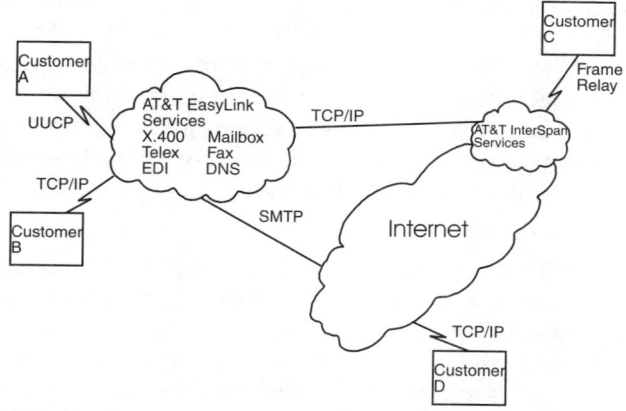

Figure 6-6 **Internet Access Methods** AT&T EasyLink Services supports multiple methods for subscriber access to the Internet.

Global Messaging Architecture

AT&T provides its customers with one-stop shopping for their Internet connectivity needs, with InterSpan providing access and AT&T EasyLink Services providing an extended set of value-added messaging services.

AT&T EasyLink Services has a frame relay connection to InterSpan, and through InterSpan to the Internet. AT&T InterSpan Services has a frame relay gateway to the Internet through the Advanced Network and Services (ANS) CO+RE Systems, Inc. backbone network. ANS provides a direct Internet interface. AT&T, to diversify connections, may in the future interconnect with other direct Internet providers.

InterSpan Internet Access

InterSpan frame relay service customers have two access methods to the Internet:

Direct InterSpan Frame Relay Service	A permanent virtual circuit (PVC) from a customer's premises to AT&T's Internet gateway
InterSpan Access Service	Dial-up access to AT&T's Internet gateway

InterSpan Frame Relay Service is part of a set of innovative data connectivity solutions which simplify enterprise distributed computing through customized data services that evolve to support changing data connection needs. The supported InterSpan Internet protocols and applications are, at present, TCP/IP networking and TCP/IP applications such as Telnet and FTP. InterSpan Information Access Service (IAS) provides Telnet and SLIP applications with dial access. IAS users may dial in from an asynchronous PC or terminal and access the Internet via an AT&T network Telnet server or may use a PC's SLIP communications software package for full TCP/IP connectivity. These Internet services are in addition to X.25, SDLC, TCP/IP LANs, X.75, and InterSpan Frame Relay Services. All IAS services are accessed through a single, 7-digit nationwide toll-free number (950-1ATT) and a uniform user interface supporting access speeds to 14.4 kbps.

InterSpan Services users have access to AT&T EasyLink Services messaging services as well as access to Internet's mailing lists, Usenet news groups, and bulletin boards. Users will be able to use standardized large files transport mechanisms for access to advanced online information services.

AT&T MAIL Internet Direction

AT&T EasyLink Services offers Simple Mail Transfer Protocol (SMTP) support, the prevalent Internet message exchange method, providing TCP/IP access to the full range of messaging services, including mailbox, text-to-fax, and telex delivery, as well as message exchange with subscribers of other commercial messaging services worldwide via X.400.

AT&T EasyLink Services supports the Domain Name Service (DNS) for AT&T EasyLink Services and InterSpan Services customers. The Internet domain style address has become a defacto standard for email addresses. Subscribers to AT&T Mail UUCP, X.400, and SMTP services will be able to register their own Internet domain name and to use that name for Internet addressing. AT&T provides the necessary DNS service for customers who wish to register their own domain name for use by the AT&T EasyLink Services Internet email gateway. This service eliminates the need for a customer to manage its own Internet name server and the associated costs. Customers who have non-Internet-compliant remote systems connected to AT&T Mail can have the appearance of being on the Internet with a company.com address.

The AT&T EasyLink Services Internet email gateway provides Internet messaging interoperability for AT&T EasyLink Services customers who subscribe to AT&T EasyLink Services message store (mailbox) services or who use other messaging protocols. This email gateway provides a method of exchanging messages with the Internet without the security risks of direct connection. The email gateway is also available to InterSpan Services customers who wish to use TCP/IP access to AT&T EasyLink Services.

Global Messaging Architecture

AT&T EasyLink Services also provides access to its messaging services to users of the Internet. These services include mailbox, text-to-fax delivery, telex, and message exchange with subscribers of other commercial messaging services worldwide via X.400.

InterNIC Directory and Database Services

These directory and database services are the pointers to the Internet's resources. These services include

InterNIC Directory of Directories	This directory of directories allows location of Internet resources through keyword searches and includes site lists, lists of various types of servers available on the Internet, lists of white and yellow pages directories, library catalogs, and data archives.
InterNIC Directory Services	This telephone directory equivalent for the Internet provides both white and yellow pages type services, allowing easy access to and communication with people and organizations, as well as making large volumes of information available to users. Users of InterNIC Directory Services using Netfind and X.500 will be able to locate individual Internet users and organizations.
InterNIC Database Services	These services provide access to a wide variety of databases, documents, and other information available on the Internet.

The Internet services currently available to AT&T EasyLink subscribers are SMTP-based and do not include some Internet functions such as FTP (file transfer protocol), Telnet, and Multipurpose Internet Mail Extensions (MIME). InterNIC services are available to anyone on the global Internet.

Sales and Support Structure

AT&T EasyLink Services are provided in the United States through a combination of direct sales and resellers (agents, value-added resellers, etc.). Internationally, sales are made through a combination of direct sales and Global Alliance Program members. Global Alliance Program members are entities that have agreed to join with AT&T EasyLink Services to sell and support messaging services within a defined territory. There are three different types of alliance members:

Network Program Members (NPM)	This group provide sales, marketing, billing, and technical support in a country or region. These members also have a share in the investment in the node in their country. The NPMs are AT&T EasyLink Services U.K. Ltd.; AT&T EasyLink Services Asia/Pacific (in Hong Kong, supporting Hong Kong, PRC, and Macao); AT&T-Jens in Tokyo, supporting Japan; Unitel (Canada); Goldnet (Israel); and AT&T EasyLink Services Australia Ltd. (Australia).
Value-Added Reseller Program Members (VARPM)	This group provide sales, marketing, billing, and technical support in their country and includes Cable & Wireless (Bermuda), EasyMail Chile S.A. (Chile) Codetel (Dominican Republic), Nilenet (Egypt), AT&T EasyLink Services—France (France), AT&T EasyLink Services—Germany (Germany), ISYS (Hungary), Pars Supala (Iran), New Southern Engineering Co. Ltd (Taiwan), and SEVA (Italy).
Sales Program Members (SPM)	This group supports sales in a country or vertical market. While there may not always be an obligation to provide support, some SPMs are stepping up to the support function. SPMs are located in Argentina, Brazil, Colombia, Korea, Paraguay, Peru, Philippines, Russia, Taiwan, Thailand, Uruguay, and Venezuela.

Global Messaging Architecture

Regional Support Centers

AT&T EasyLink Services provides global customer support through its headquarters location, Regional Support Centers, and Alliance Program members. The Regional Support Centers provide day-to-day sales and technical support to customers and alliances within their geographic region.

Americas
Regional
Support Center
(ARSC)

New Jersey
Attmail!arschelp
Tel. 201-331-4165
Fax 201-331-4513

European
Regional
Support Center
(ERSC)

Brussels
Attmail!erschelp
Tel. 322-676-3737
Fax 322-676-3810

Asia/Pacific
Regional
Support Center
(PRSC)

Hong Kong
attmail!prschelp
Tel. 852-846-2800
Fax 852-840-1068

U.S. Regional
Support Center
(USRSC)

Missouri
attmail!atthelp
Tel. 800-624-5672

Chapter 7

AT&T Mail

Overview

AT&T's public email network adds location independence to existing networks, allowing cost-effective deployment and operation of mobile messaging and telecommuting across corporate and country borders. AT&T Mail provides the tools and services needed to combine private and public email networks which integrate LANs, host computers, stand-alone personal computers, dumb terminals, telephones, facsimile machines, telex, express mail, and the postman into a single unified communication system extending messaging to anyone, anywhere, at any time.

AT&T Mail, the company's public messaging service, lets the enterprise interconnect industry-standard email systems hosted on LANs, mainframes, midrange systems, minicomputers, and PCs into a globally, universally connective email network. The reach and scope of existing networks is extended by AT&T Mail's services. These services add the capability to connect to X.400 public and private networks through use of AT&T Mail gateways and interconnections. The combined system functions in a manner similar to a private branch exchange (PBX), which permits cost-free usage between stations within an organization and also extends access to telephones worldwide at standard telephone rates.

Similarly, AT&T Mail adds the ability to connect outside the company's locations over the public network. This adds location independence to existing LAN and WAN email while maintaining the cost-effectiveness of internal email systems. Email messages can be sent from the internal network using the AT&T Mail service to email users not on the enterprise network and to non-email users. Messages to non-email users can be delivered to a receiver's fax machine, converted to paper copy for delivery through the U.S. Postal Service or courier service, or delivered via telex. AT&T Mail is GOSIP-compliant and includes 1984 X.400 standard features. Other AT&T Mail features include

Fax Capabilities	AT&T Mail users may send text-to-fax or graphic-to-fax messages. Users with AT&T Enhanced FAX accounts may select a combined mailbox which allows sending and receipt of fax and email in a single email session using Access PLUS for Windows software. Access PLUS for Windows software users also may send messages to fax machines by creating and printing the message, which can contain graphics, from any Windows application using a supplied print driver.
Online Directory	AT&T Mail users have an easy-to-use, flexible directory service. This integrated capability provides alphabetic and phonetic look-up, and the ability to cut and paste the address directly into the body of a message using appropriate software.
Online Help Capability	AT&T Mail provides clear, context-sensitive help screens. The user can also send messages requesting help with the service to a special electronic mailbox. These messages are not charged to the subscriber requesting assistance.

AT&T Mail

Binary File Transfer	Users may send binary program files or binary character output produced by a word processor, spreadsheet, database, or other application to AT&T EasyLink Services' subscribers and to recipients on interconnected X.400 networks.
Broadcasting	Users may send one message to many predetermined locations in a single session. Messages can be broadcast to preset distribution lists. Mailing lists can be created, modified, shared, and nested. A nested mailing list is created by including the name of one mailing list in another mailing list. These easily modified mailing lists also may be shared economically with other users, as only one person is charged for the list storage.
Other Networks	Messages can be transferred to or from users on any interconnected X.400 network, the Internet, or any other system connected through an AT&T Mail gateway.
Online Storage	Users may establish online folders for storing messages, mailing lists, and forms on the network.
Closed User Groups	Selected users may be assigned to closed user groups, which constitute virtual private networks for customers selecting private email services.
Reverse Billing	This service permits clients or trading partners to send messages to a subscriber with the recipient paying for the message transmission. If the recipient rejects the message, the sender is notified. This is similar to the reverse billing of a United States 800 number.
User-Defined Configurations and User-Controlled Administration	Subscribers can control their own environments by changing their profile information. This determines the configuration of the online user interface. The profile command is used to set a network mailbox to user preferences for page widths and lengths, time zones, mail forwarding

instructions, secondary service passwords, extended answering services, and command prompts. The configuration range includes the following features. The Profile command may be used to change account information permanently or only for the duration of the current session. Some information, however, such as the AT&T Mail secondary password, can only be changed permanently. Other settings, such as the names of logos and signatures, can be changed only by sending a free message to !atthelp or by calling Customer Service and Support. Since the profile supports multiple AT&T EasyLink Services, some profile commands apply to services other than AT&T Mail.

PostScript Printing	Integrated text and graphics printing is supported for messages targeted for paper delivery. The documents can be generated on a UNIX system, on an Apple Macintosh, or with word processing and desktop publishing software that uses PostScript.
MailTALK	AT&T Mail also supports message retrieval using touch-tone phones. Messages are retrieved by responses to a voice menu and are read to the subscriber by a synthesized voice.
Customer Service and Support	Subscribers have 24-hour-a-day access to support provided by globally distributed Customer Service Centers.

AT&T Mail User Environment

The AT&T Mail user environment is conceptually similar to an office, with a desk, an in box and out box for mail, and a wastebasket. All AT&T Mail subscribers' offices support four functions:

Desk	Temporary storage provided for message preparation.
In box	Storage for messages sent to the subscriber.

AT&T Mail

Out box — Storage for messages sent by the subscriber.

Wastebasket — Temporary storage for messages the subscriber wishes to have deleted. Messages are held in the wastebasket for retrieval during the current session. The wastebasket is automatically emptied when the subscriber logs off.

AT&T Mail automatically places a copy of the message in the subscriber's out box (sent folder), and a copy is retained for one to six days based on the subscriber's preference. Additional message storage folders, beyond the basic four, may be created by users who subscribe to the Forms/Files option.

AT&T Mail User Classes

There are two types of AT&T Mail Accounts. These are Basic and Forms/Files. Basic subscribers are provided with an in and out mailbox on the network and the capability to create, edit, read, delete, and send messages. Basic subscribers can use shared lists and shared folders. However, they do not have the authority to create their own folders. Basic subscribers may also search the online directory for addressing information. The Basic user has all the functionality associated with message creation, editing, reading, and sending/receiving. Forms/Files users are provided with additional capabilities. These include form creation, the ability to use additional network file storage, and the ability to create shared folders and authorize their use.

PC users who use certain agent programs such as Access PLUS have forms and file storage functionality provided by the software and message storage on their local system. These users may, at their option, subscribe to the Forms/Files option to obtain its other benefits. Mobile and telecommuting users may use the Forms/Files storage for key files and for off-site backup. Files may be uploaded and retrieved at any time from anywhere in the world, making this an effective method of storing and retrieving centrally stored and maintained information. Mobile and remote users can use network folders to store backup data on AT&T Mail. Backup files can be retrieved from the network using AT&T Mail. This backup method is exceptionally useful to mobile users who need easily accessible backup file storage and retrieval.

The Forms/Files user may create shared folders and use online storage and is charged for use of these options. Forms/Files subscribers have these added capabilities:

Create network folders	The Forms/Files user can create additional network folders for longer message storage or improved organization. These are in addition to the basic in, out, and wastebasket folders.
Create and store forms on the network	The Forms/Files subscriber can create customized electronic text message forms which can be shared among other AT&T Mail subscribers.
Create and share mailing lists	The Forms/Files subscriber can create address lists and share them with other subscribers.
Create and populate network shared folders	The Forms/Files subscriber can create network folders and share them with other subscribers.
Create an Autoresponse folder	A folder can be created with messages that the AT&T Mail service matches to terms in the subject line of received email messages. This capability provides an automatic response to incoming messages.

Mailbox Capabilities

Mailboxes can be used for email, AT&T Enhanced FAX, or EDI only or in any combination. Telex is an optional service which complements email. Mailboxes can be provided for individual users or systems. Individual email users normally use local storage to retain and organize their messages on their user workstation, but they have network storage as an option.

AT&T Mail

A subscriber to both AT&T Enhanced FAX and AT&T Mail may select a Combined Mailbox. The subscriber, using appropriate software, can use a single access, user ID, and password to obtain both email and fax messages in the network in box. The Combined Mailbox allows email and fax messages to be sent or received in a single connection and is more efficient and economical for both mobile and office users.

Access Methods

Users may access their mailbox in two ways and alternate between options as needed. The options are

Interactive mode (online) using a terminal or terminal emulator

Batch mode (offline) using agent software

AT&T Mail services can be used in either online or offline mode. In online mode, the AT&T Mail service is used interactively to create, retrieve, and administer messages. Online access requires either a terminal and modem, a communicating word processor, or a PC acting as a terminal with a modem. While online, the user can create, send, and receive mail, manage address lists, and perform administrative functions. The major functions which must be performed online include searches of information services databases, directory searches, and personal profile management.

AT&T Mail MailTALK is an online method which uses a touch-tone telephone to retrieve but not create messages. MailTALK users hear their messages read by a synthesized voice.

Message creation, sending, and response may be performed either online or offline. The offline mode is preferred for message operations. In off-line operations, the user creates and retrieves messages using programs which interact with AT&T Mail. These include general-purpose communications programs using scripts, the Access PLUS family of agent or client programs, and LAN, mainframe, and midrange computer email systems with gateways to AT&T Mail. Many of these programs permit offline creation and batch input of message operations, often in the background. This is a more efficient method of messaging than the online message mode and is lower in cost, as online message creation on AT&T Mail incurs a online message creation charge.

The preferred method for use of AT&T Mail is an offline user interface designed to interface with AT&T EasyLink Services. An example of such software is the Access PLUS software family. These cost-saving interfaces use the local system's intelligence for message creation and storage, with network access needed only for sending and receiving messages.

AT&T Mail Directory Services

The Customer Directory Service allows users to interactively search, in online mode, for other registered subscribers. These registered subscribers may be individual users or users located on LAN, mainframe, midrange, UNIX, and X.400 customer premises systems who choose to be listed in the public directory. The Customer Directory contains customer name, location, phone number, messaging addresses, and services.

Directory searches may use any permitted messaging addressing format, such as user name, customer name, and system or gateway name. Searches are not case-sensitive and adapt to spelling variations. The search results can be a single item or a list of possible matches for user selection.

A directory search for a unique registered user would contain the following information:

Username: !fpublic
NumericID: !1234567
Name: Francis Lee Public
Company: AT&T
Address: Lincroft, NJ 07738 USA
Phone: +1 908 555 9999
Fax: +1 908 555 0000
ELN: 62123456

AT&T Mail

Telex: 12345678

Directory: AT&T Mail

Services: MAIL, EDI, E-Fax, TELEX

AT&T Mail users may retrieve their own X.400 addresses in the directory to assist their correspondents on other systems.

Users on private email networks connected to AT&T Mail can register with the public AT&T Mail service to have messages forwarded to their systems and can have their electronic mail IDs listed in the AT&T Mail service directory.

AT&T Mail users in closed user groups are not listed in and do not have access to the general directory. They are limited to the directory provided for their private group.

AT&T EasyLink Services is a founding member of the North American Directory Forum (NADF). The NADF is an association of member companies, including AT&T EasyLink Services, Advantis, Canada Post Corporation, GEIS, MCI, Rapport, and others. The organization represents users and providers of directory services and software whose objective is to speed development of interoperable X.500-based distributed directory services. These services are not yet commercially available. NADF has a pilot project underway.

Addressing Messages

Messages can be addressed to single or multiple recipients, using a variety of delivery methods, including email. The header of an AT&T Mail message contains the list of recipients for which the message is intended. The service allows the user to distinguish between primary and secondary recipients by providing To: and CC: fields within the header. BCC:, for blind courtesy copy, allows the user to send a copy of the message to a recipient without disclosing that recipient to other message recipients. Messages can be sent to multiple addresses by adding multiple To, CC, and BCC lines to a message or through the use of a distribution list. Users can use private lists or shared lists, which can be public or restricted to a group.

Email messages can be sent to other AT&T Mail subscribers, other email service subscribers, and recipients using private email systems. AT&T Mail IDs are customer selectable and are usually a person's surname preceded by the first initial of his or her given name. X.400 IDs conform to the standard X.400 addressing algorithm. Messages can also be addressed to a recipient's fax machine, telex machine, or U.S. postal address. The following address types can be used individually or in combination in an AT&T Mail message.

- AT&T Mail subscribers
- Distribution lists
- Private email systems
- X.400 addresses
- Fax addresses
- Telex addresses
- Postal addresses (United States and Canada only)
- Courier services (United States only)
- Remote printers
- LANs, mainframes, and midrange computers (including UNIX systems)
- Mobile devices (such as pagers or personal communicators)

Replying to Messages

Users may reply to messages by using the Answer command, which automatically creates a message envelope listing the message originator as the recipient and the subject of the original message preceded by Re:. The user can elect to reply to the author only or to all the recipients of the message.

The AT&T Mail form allows a Forms/Files subscriber to create a fill-in-the-blanks email message. When replying to a AT&T Mail form, the service will display the text of the form and pause where a response is required from the user. Once the user has completed filling in the form, the user sends the completed form back to the originator as a message.

AT&T Mail

AT&T Mail Basic Features

Commands

Online (interactive) users have a user-friendly command-line interface. The primary commands used for online messaging are

Read	Command used to read messages
Create	Command used to compose messages
Send	Command used to instruct AT&T EasyLink Services to deliver messages
Answer	Command used to respond to the current message
Forward	Command used to forward the current message
Profile	Command used to display and change the account information in the AT&T EasyLink user profile
Move	Command used to move the message to a user-defined network folder
Edit	Command used to revise any message
Directory	Command used to access the online customer directory to obtain information about any registered AT&T mail user or registered UNIX or LAN system

Message Delivery

AT&T Mail message transfer is on a near real-time basis — generally under a minute, regardless of system traffic or uploaded message volume. The AT&T Mail system is provisioned (designed, maintained, and staffed) to minimize traffic-related delays and to provide stable, predictable performance under all normal and most abnormal conditions. Subscribers can request receipts which show when the sent message was retrieved from the recipient's AT&T Mail mailbox or was transferred to the recipient's destination network. The message transfer time, for messages destined for recipients on X.400 or UNIX systems, includes any additional time required to establish contact with the receiving system. The sender may mark a message for special attention, request a message delivery receipt, or send the message COD.

Individual User Administration

Each AT&T Mail user has an individual user profile. In an online session, users can access their profile and perform such activities as modifying message retention (1 to 6 days), setting a second password, using the auto-answer or auto-response feature, or changing their time zone. Some additional profile settings are

- Level of detail displayed in online menus
- Terminal line length and page length
- Printer page length
- Message retention period
- Time zone information, used for message datestamping
- Secondary password, used for additional security
- Activation of one of the Auto answer, Auto forward, or Auto response extended message answering services
- Default logo for paper and fax messages
- AT&T Mail folder to be displayed on login
- Inclusion of subscriber's phone number in messages

AT&T Enhanced FAX account subscribers' profiles have additional profile options, which are

- Confirmation Option for AT&T Enhanced FAX messages submitted using the AT&T Enhanced FAX touch-tone interface
- Coversheet Generation Option for AT&T Enhanced FAX messages submitted using the AT&T Enhanced FAX touch-tone interface
- Disclose Recipients Option for AT&T Enhanced FAX messages
- Download AT&T Enhanced FAX messages to PC
- Latest Delivery Time Option for AT&T Enhanced FAX messages

AT&T Mail

- Consolidated Reports Option for AT&T Enhanced FAX messages
- Daily Reports Option for AT&T Enhanced FAX messages

Users can have directory entries modified by request to the AT&T Customer Service and Support Center. A Remote Customer Support Module (RCSM) capability allows large corporate clients to perform self-administration, with changes, deletions, additions, and password administration performed by a corporate messaging administrator.

Distribution lists can be created by the user or with the assistance of the AT&T Customer Service and Support Center. Users typically administer their own private and/or public distribution lists.

Online Storage

All AT&T Mail users have an in folder to collect incoming messages (in box) and a sent folder for outgoing messages (out box). The in folder has a theoretically unlimited message capacity, with unread messages stored, without charge, on the network until they are read. Read messages are retained in the in folder for 24 hours, and users may increase retention of read messages to up to 6 days by online profile modification. A Forms/Files user may copy read messages from the In folder to another network folder for permanent retention. AT&T Mail retains copies of outgoing messages in the Sent folder as specified in the user's profile.

Service Reporting and Notifications

AT&T Mail, in keeping with its role as a commercial mission-critical messaging service, provides multiple progress reports and notifications to keep end users aware of message delivery progress. These audit trail reports include Receipt Acknowledgment, Delivery Notification, Offline Notification, Arrival Message Notification, and MailFAX Delivery Notification.

Audit Trail	A unique message identification number supports message auditing/tracking and is a required AT&T Message Transfer Architecture (MTA) addressing field. The MTS-MESSAGE-ID is generated when a message is submitted to the service, and it replaces all existing information except for

messages submitted by X.400 systems, where the MTS-MESSAGE-ID is preserved intact. Premises-based tracking is supported by the UA-CONTENT-ID field. The DATE line in the header identifies the date (month, day, year, time, and time zone) when a message was created by the originator. AT&T EasyLink Services will automatically add this line if it is not present on messages sent to the service. The service will preserve the DATE line from messages created on off-premises systems, but will then add a RECEIVED line which indicates the date and time the message was submitted to the network. This capability thus corrects any instances when off-net systems may have incorrect date and time stamps. The internal system time is Greenwich Mean Time (GMT).

Receipt

Receipt acknowledgment is a user option that results in an electronic confirmation (status message) that is sent by AT&T Mail to the originator of a message when any of the following occur:
The recipient reads an electronic mail message.
The recipient signs for a same-day or overnight printed message delivered by courier.
An unread message is deleted by the recipient.
A receipt-requested message is delivered to a premises-based system (IBM, DEC, HP, LAN, UNIX system).
An electronic mail message is delivered to a fax machine, telex, or remote printer.

Delivery Notifications

The message sender may request a delivery notification when he or she creates the message. The requested delivery notification is sent back to the sender when the message is transferred to the recipient's mailbox or transferred to the off-network system. Delivery notification does not confirm that the message has been read.

AT&T Mail

Offline Notification	In the United States, AT&T Mail sends a printed notification through the mail to any user whose mailbox has mail unread for two weeks.
Arrival Message Notification	Some software, including the AT&T Mail Access series, provides the user with selectable visual and/or audible notification of new mail arrival.
MailFAX Delivery Notification	For fax messages, an email message from the network informs the sender of a connection problem. The entire message is returned to the sender via email with a delivery failure notice if it is not delivered within 6 hours and delivery efforts by the network terminate.

AT&T Mail Advanced Features

AT&T Mail provides many advanced facilities for users to share information with other subscribers. These are

Large-Scale Broadcast	The stored address list capability allows users to create address lists and store them on the network. Lists can be created interactively or managed with software such as Access PLUS. These address lists can be shared with other network users. Large-scale broadcasts require only the list name as the address, reducing the chance of errors and omissions and the time needed to transmit addresses to the network.
Shared Folders	A Forms/Files subscriber can post information to an online folder, which can then be shared with or made accessible to other users. Other AT&T Mail users may subscribe to these shared folders, and the information owner who posts messages may authorize read-only or read-and-write access to subscribers. Shared folder content can include standard text or binary content.

Shared Folder Autodelivery	Subscribers to Shared Folder Autodelivery have AT&T Mail automatically deliver messages placed in a shared folder to the address or shared address list specified by the subscriber to receive the Autodelivery. This feature expands the number of recipients who can receive shared folder messages, since endpoints may now include UNIX systems, LANs, X.400 systems, fax machines, remote printers, paper addresses, on-network mailboxes, and other shared folders. Telex addresses are not delivery endpoints for Shared Folder Autodelivery. Some possible applications include newsletters and employee communications, product bulletins, pricing bulletins, and course catalogs and other educational needs.
AT&T Mail Catalog	AT&T Catalog is a form of extended answering available only to Forms/Files account subscribers. These users can create a folder of messages that the AT&T Mail service automatically matches to incoming request messages. Matching messages are sent the appropriate reply. Incoming messages must start with REQUEST: in the Subject: line. Possible applications include technical support areas where specific scripts or files can be provided on demand. Examples include pricing folders, competitive folders, promotional program listings, job postings, product information, training information, technical documentation, and indexes of available information.
FYI Info Boards	Corporate customers may choose to post information on any topics they desire, with access through an online interactive process using layered menus. These bulletin boards may be public or private, restricting access to those authorized by the corporate customer. Information is updated by a customer administrator on a customer-determined schedule.

AT&T Mail 165

Menu Prompt	Users may select a menu prompt which allows the user to access AT&T Mail and AT&T Information Services in interactive mode. These Information Services include InfoMaster, Investment ANALY$T, PUBCITE, FYI NewsAlert, and others. See Chapter 13, "AT&T Information Services."
Forms Creation and Storage	Forms/Files subscribers can create electronic forms with blank fields. Recipients electronically complete these forms and return them. Basic users may reply to forms but not create them. An example would be a survey of a subscriber group. A form has questions and response areas and is preaddressed to the author. It is sent via email to the survey group, who answer the inquiry and return the response.
Autoforward	Incoming messages can be automatically forwarded to any device or location supported by the network, such as a mailbox, fax machine, or remote system. Subscribers may have AT&T Mail messages and confirmations autoforwarded to another address. When this option is selected, the AT&T Mail system places a copy of each autoforwarded message in the subscriber's Autoforward folder if it has been created or, otherwise, places it in the subscriber's Sent folder. This is useful while the subscriber is on vacation or if the subscriber wants mail sent to an external UNIX system. The forwarding electronic address is interactively entered in the profile by the subscriber.
Autoanswer	Subscribers may have the AT&T Mail service send a standard response to all incoming messages. The reply message contains the text and message-handling options specified by the subscriber activating the Autoanswer service. The reply is sent to the message author and the message retained in the subscriber's In folder.

Only one Autoanswer response per week is sent to an author regardless of the number of messages received from that author. After activating the feature, the subscriber specifies the message to send when answering incoming messages. To activate this service, either DESK or the folder name and sequence number of a message in one of your folders must be entered.

Autoresponse Subscribers may have the AT&T Mail service automatically answer all incoming messages with a subject field having Request: as the first word. AT&T Mail will select and send one or more response messages located in a response folder specified when the Autoresponse feature is activated. The message returned will be the message or messages in the response folder whose subject matches the subject requested. The subjects match if the request contains the same first word or words as the response message. A response has the handling options of the response folder message. If the response folder contains a message whose subject is Default, then that message will be sent when a request message has no match. This is useful for sending a catalog of response messages. A matching request message will be saved only if the subscriber creates a folder named Autoin. In that case, all matched requests will be saved. Response envelopes can be saved if a folder named Autosent is created.

Project and Hierarchical Billing Subscribers may select individual billing by client or project or billing as sub-accounts under a supermaster account. Project codes allow subscribers to allocate service charges among projects or clients. Bills then have service charges sorted and subtotaled by project code. Project codes, assigned by the subscriber, can be any alphanumeric characters with a fifteen-character limit.

AT&T Mail

Logos and Signatures	Subscribers can register graphics such as company logos or individual signatures and have them appear on U.S. mail, overnight courier deliveries, and AT&T MailFAX. Each AT&T Mail account can register up to three logos and three signatures. X.400, UNIX, midrange, and LAN accounts may register up to three logos for messages to be delivered by U.S. Mail or overnight courier.
Gatename Format Addressing	This feature provides gatename surrogate abbreviations for simplified addressing of messages to connected networks. Gatenames may be viewed online using the help X.400 command.
Large File Transfer Feature	Large file transfer is particularly useful to customers who send and receive fax, CAD/CAM, or EDI files of from 2 to 10 Mbytes. Both the submitter and the recipient must register with the AT&T Mail Customer Support Center as large file users and use access speeds over 4,800 kbps. Most popular user interfaces are supported.
File Attachments	In online mode, only normal message files may be attached to one another. Some software, including the AT&T Access PLUS family, allows users to attach binary files to a message for detachment as individual files by the recipient. These attached files can be word processor or spreadsheet documents, forms, or other binary files. The number of messages attachable is unlimited, but the total message size must fall within the registration limit for both the subscriber and the recipient.
Uploading and Downloading Files and Messages	While in interactive mode, users have access to all online AT&T Mail service capabilities, including 8-bit data transfer between PCs and the network. Messages can be transferred between AT&T Mail and the PC using AT&T Mail Access PLUS software's upload and download commands. The

software provides error-free transmission of both text and binary files as well as flow control. AT&T EasyLink Services supports protocols to overcome most line noise that may be encountered when data are transferred over standard voice-grade lines or wireless communications.

For asynchronous connectivity, AT&T messaging services and associated software support error detection/correction through the use of FMODEM, YMODEM, YMODEM251, XMODEM, and UUCP protocols. ZMODEM support is planned for the near future. For synchronous connectivity, error detection and correction is supported through the 3780/3770 protocols. The AT&T Mail service supports XON/XOFF flow control.

Message Bundling and Multi-Part Messages	Users may send or receive single or multiple messages during a single communication session when using an agent program. Any single message may be made up of text, binary, or combined text and binary (multi-mode) information.
Binary File Transfer	AT&T Mail messages have two parts, the header or envelope and its contents. Information movement is based on header data only, eliminating the need to parse or process information contents. The envelope contents can be pure text, binary, or any combination of data types. AT&T's Message Transfer Architecture (MTA) places all transport data in the envelope, eliminating any need to process the contents of the message. This also applies to files sent through X.400 interface gateways.

Users can transfer text and/or binary files as multi-part messages using appropriate agent software. These files retain their individual identities and can be detached, using appropriate software, by the recipient. The attached files can

AT&T Mail   169

Encryption	be of any or all types, including spreadsheets, word processing documents, or executable program code. This feature is exceptionally useful for supporting remote or mobile non-technical users, as the instructions and software files can be combined in the same message.
Encryption	When encryption is desired, it must be performed by the customer using its own software, as the AT&T Mail service does not provide network-based encryption services. AT&T Mail supports the transfer of encrypted files, since binary message contents are not parsed and all transport is based on the header.
AT&T Mail Delivery Options	The sender's mail delivery options include the recipient device type, message format, and special delivery options. These options are selectable within the message header during addressing or during the creation of distribution lists. The Send command allows users to send messages to one or more recipients listed in the message envelope. The same message can be sent to one or more of the following device types simultaneously.

Messages can be electronically delivered to the user's electronic in box. The in box may be associated with a UNIX system, LAN, mainframe, mid-range system, X.400 system gateway, or AT&T Mail subscriber. Messages can be sent using a distribution list, a shared folder posting, or the AT&T Mail Catalog. Some delivery types are

Telex	Messages can be sent, by subscribers who have requested telex service, to any telex subscriber through the AT&T Mail telex link. The recipient can respond directly to the sender's electronic mailbox.
MailFAX	Messages can be sent directly to a fax machine. The user addresses the message to Fax! and enters the destination fax telephone number and

	an identifier. The identifier, commonly a telephone number, allows the recipient to be easily identified when the message is sent to a shared fax machine.
MailPRINT	AT&T Mail messages can be delivered to and printed on a modem-equipped printer which can automatically answer AT&T Mail telephone calls.
Postal Service	Paper copy messages can be sent anywhere in the United States through the mails.
Courier Delivery	Paper copy messages can be sent by overnight delivery throughout the contiguous United States. Same-day delivery is available in 50 major metropolitan areas.
Mobile Devices	Messages can be sent to pagers, personal digital assistants, or personal communicators using paging or packet radio service.

Message and Format Options

AT&T Mail provides format, delivery, grade of service and confirmation options which can be combined as needed. These options can be specified in the message envelope or the Create or Send command lines. Message specified options override options specified as general options or at the Send command line.

Format Options

The available format options vary with the delivery method selected. Some format options include

Memo	This option is for messages delivered on paper. This format places the From:, Phone:, Date:, Message ID:, To:, and Subject: information at the top of the page in memo format.
Business	This option is for messages delivered on paper. This format places Date, and To: information at

AT&T Mail   171

	the page top and the return address and delivery address at the bottom in letter format.
Free format	This option is for messages delivered on paper. This format does not place a return address or To: information on the message.
Logo	This option can be selected or deselected for messages delivered on paper or by fax. Subscribers may use registered private logos, override the default logo specified in their profile, specify blank lines instead of a logo, or specify a public logo.
Signature	Subscribers may select from their preregistered, scanned signatures.
Landscape	This option can be selected for messages delivered by fax. The message is delivered in 132-column width. Logos and signatures cannot be used with the Landscape option.

Delivery Options

Delivery options control the way a message is delivered to the recipient and control whether the message is sent by electronic or paper mail. The delivery options include

Project	This optional entry, consisting of a maximum of 15 alphanumeric characters, is used to track service charges relating to specific customers or projects. The code entered appears on the AT&T Mail subscriber's invoice.
Electronic	This is the AT&T Mail system default; it sends a standard electronic message.
U.S. mail or paper	This option instructs the system to deliver the message on paper. It is used with a service-grade option, such as urgent for overnight delivery by courier.
Address	This option specifies the recipient's paper mail delivery address.

COD   This option instructs the system to bill the
                        recipient for the message charge.

No COD   This option instructs the system to bill the sender
                        for the message charge and is the system default.

Grade of Service Options

The grade of service options specify the form of delivery and the speed of delivery desired.

Paper priority   This option specifies overnight courier service for
or overnight   paper messages in supported areas. Messages
                        are delivered on Monday through Friday
                        excluding holidays.

Urgent   This option specifies same-day courier service for
                        paper messages in supported areas. Messages
                        are delivered on Monday through Friday
                        excluding holidays.

Nonurgent   This option is for messages sent to a fax
                        machine. It instructs the system to deliver the
                        message at an off-peak time and is billed at a
                        discounted rate.

Standard   This option specifies standard electronic delivery
                        and is the AT&T EasyLink Services default.

Confirmation Options

Confirmation options are used to have AT&T EasyLink Services report message status to the sender. Some options include

Delivery   This option instructs the system to send a
                        message to the sender when the message is
                        delivered to the recipient's In folder, fax machine,
                        or any gateway. The message does not confirm
                        that the message was read by the recipient.

No Delivery   This option instructs the system not to send a
                        message to the sender when the message is
                        delivered to the recipient's In folder, fax machine,

AT&T Mail

or any gateway. This is the AT&T EasyLink Services default.

Receipt
This option instructs the system to send a message to the sender when the message is read by the recipient. AT&T EasyLink Services sends a receipt message when the recipient reads an electronic message or an unread message is deleted by the recipient; a paper message delivered by mail is printed; a recipient signs for an urgent or overnight message; or a message is delivered to a UNIX system, telex, fax, or remote printer.

Noreceipt
This option instructs the system not to send a message to the sender when the message is read by the recipient. This is the AT&T EasyLink Services default.

Report
This option instructs the system not to include the message content when a nondelivery report is returned by AT&T EasyLink Services. The nondelivery report contains the original message header.

Return
This option instructs the system to include the message content when a nondelivery report is returned by AT&T EasyLink Services. The nondelivery report contains both the original message header and message content.

Ignore
This option instructs the system to suppress nondelivery messages, including expiration notices. It is used only with fax and remote printer messages.

Shared Folders

Shared Folders provide user-controlled bulletin board capabilities for the AT&T Mail user community that are fully integrated with AT&T Mail. Forms/Files subscribers can post information to an online folder, which can then be shared with or made accessible to other users, providing bulletin board functionality without the costs for computers, software, or administration present in premises-based bulletin board systems. The integration with AT&T Mail provides access to these information resources through the common access methods. AT&T Mail users may subscribe to these shared folders, and the information owner who posts messages may authorize read-only or read-and-write access for subscribers. Shared Folder content can include standard text or binary content. A subscriber locates Shared Folders using interactive commands in online mode. Information may be retrieved from a Shared Folder interactively, by use of a client program such as Access PLUS, or by Autodelivery. Subscribers to Shared Folders can have AT&T Mail automatically deliver messages placed in the shared folder to the address or shared address list specified by the subscriber to receive the Autodelivery.

Both Basic and Forms/Files accounts can access messages from authorized Shared Folders using AT&T Mail online commands or software agents such as the Access Family. Basic account subscribers can perform read-only operations on messages within a Shared Folder. Commands to use and manage Shared Folders support the following activities:

- Display subscriber's own Shared Folders.
- Display another user's Shared Folders.
- Display a list of the user's Shared Folder subscriptions.
- Display a list of Shared Folder Autodelivery subscriptions.
- Share subscriber's own folders.
- Unshare a subscriber's folder.
- Subscribe to a Shared Folder.
- Cancel Shared Folder subscription.
- Create Autodelivery subscription to a Shared Folder.
- Cancel an Autodelivery subscription to a Shared Folder.

AT&T Mail

Shared Lists

A shared list is an address list that has been made available to other users. These lists may be created interactively or with the use of client software such as Access PLUS. They reduce the chance of error in entering addresses repeatedly and ensure that all users mail to the full set of addresses. This feature, which establishes enterprise mailing lists usable from anywhere at any time, is useful for mobile and remote workers.

Commands for use and management of shared lists support the following activities:

- Make lists available to other AT&T Mail subscribers.
- Display a list of subscriber's shared lists.
- Create a shared list interactively.
- View subscriber's own lists.

AT&T Mail Billing

Monthly billing for the AT&T Mail service contains summarized usage information for each account. During account registration, various billing options are available. A single account is registered as the master or billing account and receives the bill. A group of accounts can be hierarchically arranged into master and supermaster levels by AT&T EasyLink Services. The billing options allow the corporate user to have the bill and detailed usage data sent to separate, appropriate destinations within the organization. Billing data can also be grouped by category to allow account tracking within groups by using project codes to define each account or activity requiring separate tracking.

Pricing

With AT&T Mail, the subscriber pays only for messages sent. Receipt and reading of mail are not charged for unless the subscriber chooses to read a COD message, use AT&T MailTALK, read messages from Shared Folders that charge for access, or receive messages from non-subscribers on the public Internet. The sender is billed for the message if the recipient deletes a COD message without reading it.

Group Partitions

A virtual private email network operating as a closed subset of the public AT&T Mail offering is called a closed user group. Option selections restrict messaging to members of the closed user group domain. Users not in the closed user group cannot send messages to members of the group. These users can be partitioned into their own private subdirectory and not be listed or have access to the public AT&T Mail Customer Directory Service listings. Closed user group members can be restricted to the sub-directory list of their own group's members. See Chapter 2, page 41.

Chapter 8

Personal Computer Software

The growing strategic importance of email and mail-enabled applications makes the selection of messaging networks and software major decisions for the organization with complex on- and off-campus messaging needs.

The solutions provided by AT&T EasyLink Services alliances offer enhanced messaging capabilities which extend customers' reach globally to business and trading partners. This is particularly true for documents which need review by business partners such as law firms, where ease of use and reach extension can provide major economic and time-to-market advantages. Such inter-company solutions require compatible software, adequate hardware capacity for all users, and compatibility with existing in-house messaging systems.

Subscribers may use a variety of systems to connect to AT&T Mail. Software designed to interface tightly with AT&T EasyLink Services provides superior functionality and easier use than general-purpose communication packages. AT&T EasyLink Services provides its own software packages and has worked with other companies to produce or extend their email packages to work with AT&T Mail. These companies are platform communication software specialists. The alliances and software products currently available are described below:

Microsoft	Microsoft Mail for PC Networks is a leading email package for local area networks. Each Microsoft Mail for PC Networks package includes a gateway to AT&T Mail. Microsoft's stand-alone messaging software product, Microsoft Mail Remote for Windows, also includes an AT&T Mail driver.
Instant Information Inc.	Instant Information Inc.'s InstantCom messaging software connects to AT&T EasyLink Services. InstantCom software is available for stand-alone users on a personal computer, or in a LAN version. Customers who are not currently using any other LAN messaging product may purchase the multi-user version of InstantCom, since it provides both the post office and user agent software for local messaging, as well as connectivity to AT&T Mail. This software is sold by AT&T EasyLink Services sales, and is supported by the AT&T EasyLink Services' Customer Service and Support Center.

Stand-alone PC Connectivity

The desktop or mobile environment commonly uses personal computers and stand-alone applications programs. Examples of the types of application programs that can be used with AT&T Mail are general-purpose communications software, AT&T Mail Access PLUS software family, Microsoft Mail Remote for Windows, and InstantCom//MS software. See Chapter 10, page 219 for descriptions of LAN connectivity products.

General-Purpose Communications Software

The use of general-purpose communications or terminal emulator software packages to access AT&T Mail is not a good technical or economical approach, although AT&T Mail can be used with almost any communications or terminal emulation package. Some of these packages provide scripts for logging on to the service, but, as of this writing,

Personal Computer Software 179

no such script supports the offline creation of messages, message management, file transfer using the optimum FMODEM protocol, integrated local directories, or the low resource utilization provided by specialized access software. Online or interactive message preparation carries a premium charge on AT&T Mail, and significant savings can be realized by offline message preparation using appropriate agent software.

It is possible to write scripts using the languages which are part of many general-purpose communication packages. However, the preparation of scripts to perform the same agent functions as the specialized agent programs is time-consuming and difficult. The enterprise will have to provide ongoing training and support for multiple users and will be responsible for developing enhancements to the script.

Another consideration is resource demand on the desktop or mobile PC. Hybrid designs, such as Access PLUS for Windows, which use a terminate and stay resident (TSR) background communications program and Windows-based software for local message management, are more efficient designs for AT&T EasyLink Services agent programs. The hybrid design can run effectively on older machines and uses less Windows resources. This permits the software to remain loaded in the background without limiting the use of other Windows software. Elimination of Windows overhead also provides dramatic speed improvements in certain processes, such as sending a graphic-to-fax message using Fax Sender, where the end user will see faster rendering and lower connection times.

AT&T Mail Access PLUS Software Family

The most efficient way to access the AT&T Mail service is through an offline user interface, such as the AT&T Mail Access PLUS software family. Access PLUS software is designed to take advantage of PC intelligence by allowing users to manage their electronic message creation and storage offline. Access to the network service is required only to send previously created messages or receive new ones. Online or interactive access capabilities are provided to allow the subscriber to access interactive offerings. These interactive operations include functions such as directory searches or Information Services database searches.

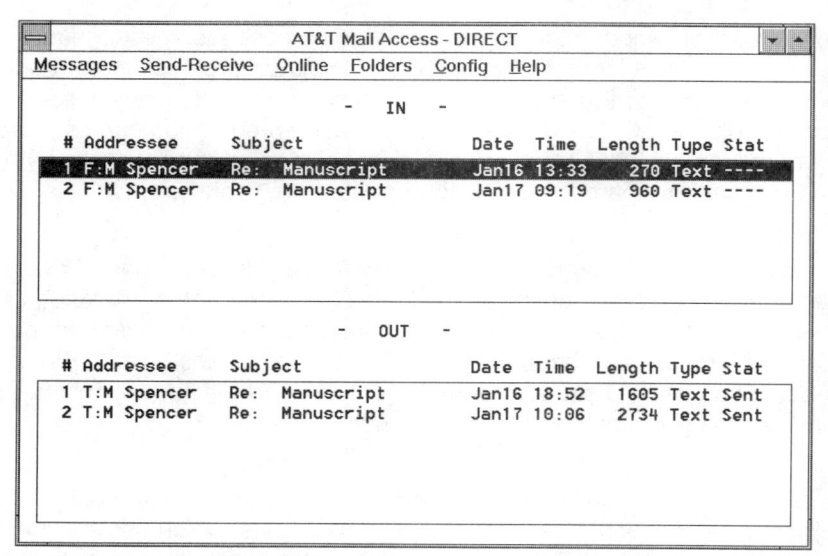

```
┌─────────────────────────────────────────────────────────┐
│ ═                  AT&T Mail Access - DIRECT        ▼ ▲ │
│ Messages  Send-Receive  Online  Folders  Config  Help   │
│                         -  IN  -                        │
│ # Addressee     Subject          Date   Time  Length Type Stat │
│ 1 F:M Spencer   Re: Manuscript   Jan16 13:33    270 Text ---- │
│ 2 F:M Spencer   Re: Manuscript   Jan17 09:19    960 Text ---- │
│                                                         │
│                         - OUT -                         │
│ # Addressee     Subject          Date   Time  Length Type Stat │
│ 1 T:M Spencer   Re: Manuscript   Jan16 18:52   1605 Text Sent │
│ 2 T:M Spencer   Re: Manuscript   Jan17 10:06   2734 Text Sent │
└─────────────────────────────────────────────────────────┘
```

Figure 8-1 **Access PLUS** This screen shows messages in the local PC folder.

AT&T Mail Access PLUS software provides an attractive, function key-driven interface for DOS use and graphical interfaces for Windows or Macintosh. The AT&T Mail family of software products provides the end user with features to simplify message management. The In box, Out box and Wastebasket are automatically created to store messages. Users can create additional message storage folders as desired without incurring online storage costs. The online message creation surcharge is not applied to messages created offline using Access PLUS software. Background message sending and receipt allows the enduser to continue work during transmissions which require little or no user monitoring. The background mailer feature also allows automatic creation and dispatch of application-to-application messages, allowing simple creation of mail-enabled systems with low system overhead.

AT&T Mail Access PLUS Application Support

Access PLUS software supports development of mail-enabled applications using Access PLUS as the AT&T Mail software interface. Functionally, the mail package manages the message transmission while the

Personal Computer Software 181

application creates messages for sending and processes received messages. These mail-enabled applications create and process messages sent and received through AT&T Mail. Access PLUS software includes documentation on using the software's features in both DOS and Windows applications. Windows applications can use Windows Dynamic Data Exchange (DDE) protocol and the Access PLUS for Windows Mailer program. The Access PLUS for Windows Background Mailer, a terminate and stay resident (TSR) module, allows a PC to send or receive mail on demand, on a schedule, or at fixed intervals.

AT&T Mail provides a simple, documented interface for the development of AT&T Mail-enabled applications. Applications can create and process mail messages using software components to control messaging functions. These components are packaged with Access PLUS but can be used without loading the full Access PLUS software package. The developer can also use Access PLUS software as the software message transfer component. These mail-enabled applications require that the PC and Access PLUS for Windows software be properly configured prior to application use and that the PC be able to send and receive AT&T mail.

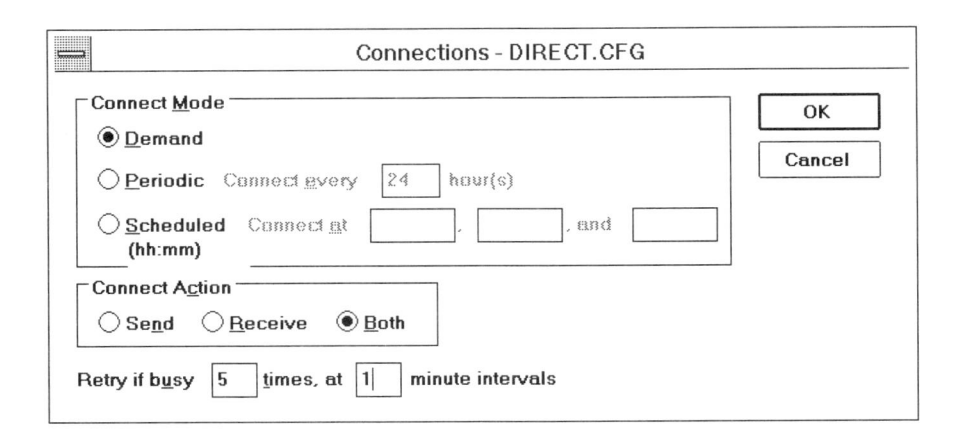

Figure 8-2 **Multiple Configurations** Access PLUS supports on demand, periodic, and scheduled connections as part of each configuration to simplify use in changing environments.

An example of its use would be a user application which created a message, placed it in the local Access PLUS Out folder, and wanted the message sent at once. The user application would instruct the Background Mailer to "Send" and follow it with a "Now" command. The command combination would immediately send all queued messages. The application would enable the Background Mailer, and the Background Mailer would then dial out to the AT&T Mail service and send the queued messages. The application could monitor the Out folder or poll it, using a function code, to determine if the message was sent successfully.

The application may process received messages using a tag analyzing process. The application can specify an optional application tag for searching so that only messages of interest are processed. When a message contains the requested application tag, the application can then read all the message headers and/or copy the message contents (parts) to specific files for application processing. If the message is a status message, a delivery notification, or a non-delivery notification, the application may examine the results. The application may delete these messages. The application can scan for messages successfully sent by the application and procede to delete these messages. The Access PLUS for Windows software also allows the application to scan for messages rejected and use the rejection reasons as the basis for further action.

Application developers may communicate with the Access PLUS for Windows Background Mailer from DOS programs, from batch files, or by calling the DOS INT 21h 5769h API from within a program. A sample DOS C language program demonstrating the call of BGMAIL using the DOS INT 21h API is included in the Access PLUS for Windows documentation. AT&T EasyLink Services may develop additional mail-enabled development tools in response to customer requirements.

Access PLUS for MS-DOS

AT&T Mail Access PLUS software is available in a character-based DOS version. This version provides a character-based, user-friendly, function key-driven user interface for the mail service. Users can perform basic mail functions such as creating, reading, sending, and deleting messages with a single keystroke. Advanced messaging functions can

Personal Computer Software 183

also be performed with a single keystroke or by use of a "hot key." Access PLUS for MS-DOS Personal Computers features include

User-Friendly Interface	All messaging functions are performed by selecting program function keys for character-based Access PLUS for DOS. These functions include creating, editing, sending, receiving, reading, and printing messages.
Offline Message Creation	Access PLUS for DOS allows users to create messages offline, eliminating online message creation surcharges. Users can create simple text messages, forms, or multi-part messages. Multi-part messages can consist of text and binary files.
Integral Editor	Access PLUS for DOS provides users with a full-screen editor for easy message creation and revision. The maximum file size that can be created is 400 lines. An external editor can be used to create larger files, and the information can be imported into the document or sent as an attachment.
Personal Directory Features	Access PLUS for DOS provides a personal address book that the user can create and maintain. Users can create one or more directories, each containing up to 32,000 entries, for convenient storage of personal and professional contacts. Fields are provided for name, address, telephone number, electronic mail address, fax, and other information. Personal directories are maintained and accessed only by the user. The software provides hot key access to personal directories from within any non-graphical MS-DOS application or at the operating system prompt. The Access PLUS for DOS software also provides the user with the ability to cut and paste names and electronic mail addresses from the Personal Directory into a mail message. In addition, Access PLUS allows users to go online to the mail service to take advantage of the

Chapter Eight

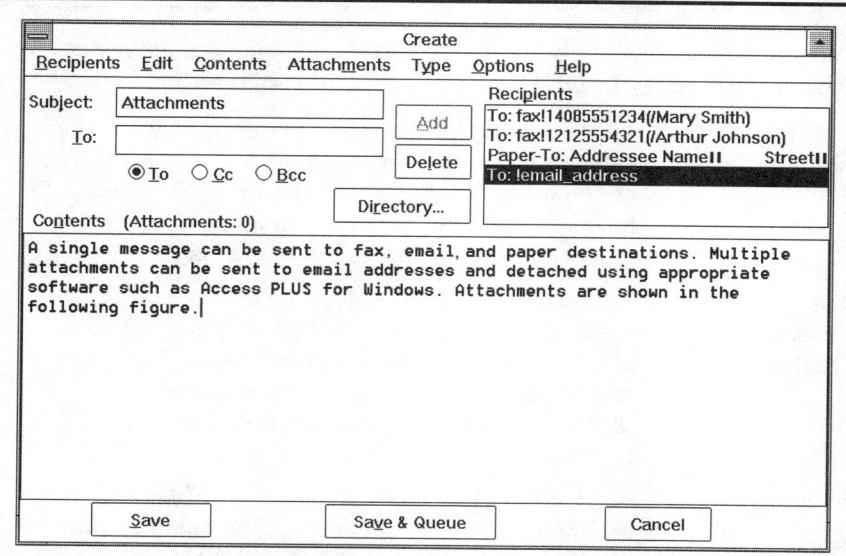

```
┌─────────────────────────── Create ───────────────────────────┐
│ Recipients  Edit  Contents  Attachments  Type  Options  Help │
│ Subject: [Attachments                    ]  ┌─────┐  Recipients                              │
│                                             │ Add │  To: fax!14085551234(/Mary Smith)        │
│ To:      [                               ]  └─────┘  To: fax!12125554321(/Arthur Johnson)   │
│                                             ┌──────┐ Paper-To: Addressee Name❚❚   Street❚❚ │
│            ⦿ To   ○ Cc   ○ Bcc              │Delete│ To: !email_address                     │
│                                             └──────┘                                         │
│                                             ┌──────────┐                                     │
│ Contents  (Attachments: 0)                  │Directory…│                                     │
│ A single message can be sent to fax, email, and paper destinations. Multiple                 │
│ attachments can be sent to email addresses and detached using appropriate                    │
│ software such as Access PLUS for Windows. Attachments are shown in the                       │
│ following figure.|                                                                           │
│                                                                                              │
│                                                                                              │
│                                                                                              │
│                                                                                              │
│       ┌──────┐              ┌───────────────┐              ┌────────┐                        │
│       │ Save │              │ Save & Queue  │              │ Cancel │                        │
│       └──────┘              └───────────────┘              └────────┘                        │
└──────────────────────────────────────────────────────────────┘
```

Figure 8-3 **Message Creation** A single message can be easily sent to multiple delivery points using Access PLUS.

	Directory Lookup capabilities of the AT&T Mail service.
List Management	Address lists can be created for email and fax broadcasts with fax telephone numbers, Enhanced FAX IDs, or other address lists. Lists can be nested. Lists can be maintained offline, and uploaded and downloaded as needed.
Transmission Protocol Support	Access PLUS for DOS supports the XMODEM, YMODEM 251, and FMODEM transmission protocols.
Binary File Transmission	Access PLUS for DOS transmits text, binary, and image files using error-correcting protocols. This allows graphics, spreadsheets, and word processing documents to be transferred without modification. Executable programs can be transferred between subscribers, thereby eliminating the need for re-keying or photocopying information. This process requires

Personal Computer Software

	little training or PC knowledge, making it suitable for novice PC users. A menu selection allows incoming binary files to be autotyped and read by the corresponding program.
Search Capabilities	Users can enter a string of characters as a search key and the system will automatically find the mail items matching the key. Users may search by information found in the message header or the message body.
Message Marking	Users can mark or unmark selected messages for processing. The Send, Move, Copy, Delete, and Print commands can be performed on all marked messages. This feature can also be used in conjunction with the search capability described above.
Background Mode Operation	Access PLUS for DOS provides the user with the option of operating in background mode. Users set up to operate in the background mode can: Set up the system to periodically log on to the mail service to check for messages. Receive mail even if using another MS-DOS application. Be instantly notified audibly and visually when a new message has arrived. Hot-key into a terminate and stay resident program (TSR) which allows the user to pop up a mail window and read and reply to his or her messages without exiting the current application.
Attachments	Messages created in a word processor or spreadsheet program can be sent as an attachment to a message. There is no limit on the number of attachments that can be sent. Attachments can be text (ASCII) or binary files such as spreadsheets or word processing files. Messages can also be imported into a message, and will appear as message content when the message is opened. Access PLUS for DOS

provides a single function key look-up to select files for attachment.

Application Mapping	Applications such as spreadsheets can be executed from the Attachment field automatically for instant access and easy file revision through the use of file extensions mapped to applications using the application mapping file. This feature allows users who receive binary files such as Lotus or MS-Word files to have these attachments automatically opened by the program when they open the mail messages. Attachments can also be detached to a user-specified file for later use.
Printing Options	The user has the ability to print a message either from the main menu or while reading the message. The user can print the message header, the message body, or both. Several print options are available, including print current mail item only, print all mail items in the current folder, print all new mail items, or print all marked messages.
Special Attention Messages	Messages can be flagged as "Special Attention" and/or "RSVP." These options alert the recipient that the message requires urgent or special attention or that a response is requested. If the receiver is using appropriate software and the message is marked "Special Attention", then the message is marked "Attention" and a Special Attention icon flashes in the status field of the main menu to let the receiver know that an urgent message has arrived.
Security Features	Passwords entered as part of the auto-logon process are scrambled in the configuration (MAIL.CFG) files, enhancing end-user security. Software hooks are provided to run a user-supplied encryption program to encrypt a message and/or attachments.

Personal Computer Software

![Attachments dialog box]

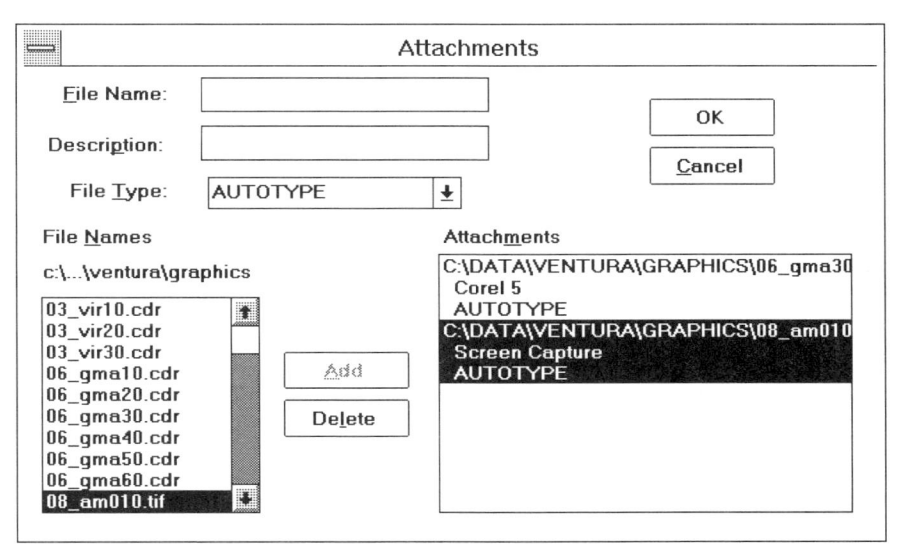

Figure 8-4 **Attachments** Multiple files, text and binary, can be attached to and detached from a mail message.

Online Capabilities	An online function is available which allows the user to log on to AT&T EasyLink Services to perform profile management and use interactive services.
Integrated Access to Information Services	Access PLUS for DOS allows users to access information services on AT&T Mail and to capture these sessions to a folder or to a file. Captured sessions are managed in the same manner and with the same tools as message management. Access to information services is accomplished via VT100 terminal emulation.
Session Capture	Users can store an online Session in a folder for later retrieval. A Session folder is created to store messages saved to a folder. All or part of the session can be stored.
Folders	The user can create multiple folders or subdirectories for message management. Messages in each folder are identified by date,

subject, and length. Access PLUS for DOS automatically creates the local In folder (for new messages), the Out folder (for messages that the user wishes to send), the Waste folder (a temporary depository for all deleted messages until the user logs off Access PLUS), and the Sessions folder (to store data captured online).

Forms Creation and Fill-in — Access PLUS for DOS provides tools for designing and sending a mail form message. Recipients with the same software have an easy-to-use forms fill-in capability that enables them to automatically have the cursor stop at the proper field for fill-in. Access PLUS for DOS provides simple forms capability.

New Mail Notification — Access PLUS for DOS notifies a user of incoming mail while working in an MS-DOS application with the background mailer activated.

ACCESSory — A hot key is used to access a mail window called ACCESSory. This allows the review, creation, and sending of mail from within any MS-DOS application without exiting the application and without having to load Access PLUS for DOS. This saves the time otherwise needed to exit from the application and access electronic mail.

Expanded Memory Support — Portions of Access PLUS for DOS can be loaded into Expanded Memory through the use of an expansion memory board and corresponding drivers adhering to the LIM EMS 4.0 specifications. This increases the user's personal processing power by letting the user run more, or larger, applications in main memory while Access PLUS for DOS runs in Expanded Memory, ready for immediate use when needed.

Other Access PLUS for DOS capabilities include

- Background Mailer status display
- VT100 Terminal emulation

Personal Computer Software 189

- Keyboard macros
- Logon scripts
- Links to other applications

Access PLUS for Windows

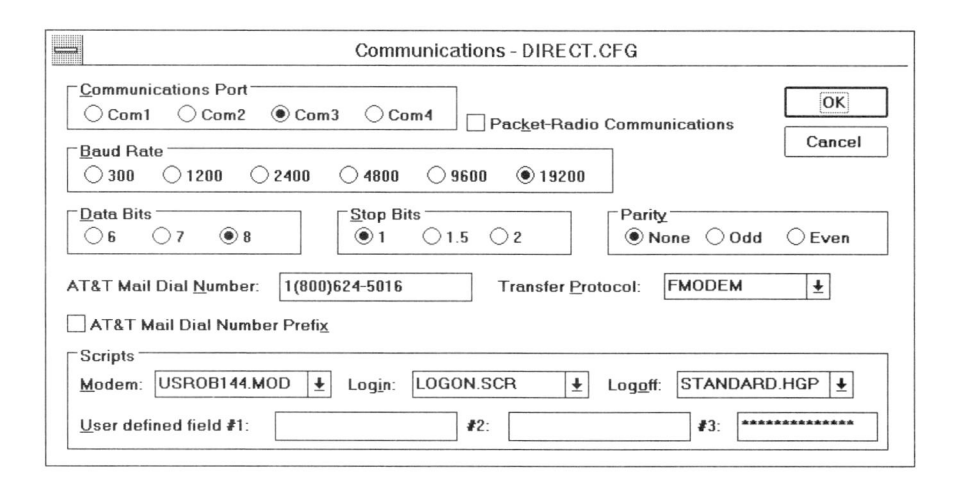

```
Communications - DIRECT.CFG
Communications Port
 ○ Com1   ○ Com2   ⦿ Com3   ○ Com4     □ Packet-Radio Communications     [ OK ]
Baud Rate                                                                 [Cancel]
 ○ 300   ○ 1200   ○ 2400   ○ 4800   ○ 9600   ⦿ 19200
Data Bits              Stop Bits              Parity
 ○ 6   ○ 7   ⦿ 8       ⦿ 1   ○ 1.5   ○ 2      ⦿ None   ○ Odd   ○ Even
AT&T Mail Dial Number: [1(800)624-5016]     Transfer Protocol: [FMODEM  ↓]
□ AT&T Mail Dial Number Prefix
Scripts
 Modem: [USROB144.MOD ↓]   Login: [LOGON.SCR ↓]   Logoff: [STANDARD.HGP ↓]
 User defined field #1: [          ]   #2: [          ]   #3: [**************]
```

Figure 8-5 **Configuration Support** Access PLUS supports a wide variety of modems, LANs, ISDN, and other scripts for AT&T Mail connection.

Access PLUS for Windows uses the Microsoft Windows graphical interface. It provides support for wireless network access using both cellular and radio frequency modems. The software also supports Microsoft's Dynamic Data Exchange (DDE) protocol to allow information to be exchanged between Access PLUS for Windows and other DDE-compliant applications such as Word for Windows 6 and Excel. The software also provides its users with features and functionality equivalent to Access PLUS for DOS while taking advantage of the multitasking possible under Windows.

The Access PLUS for Windows software supports radio packet access to AT&T Mail using wireless modems. The wireless support features include wireless modem logon scripts and the Preview Mail feature. Access PLUS, in its Receive mode, downloads all messages to the PC.

The Preview Mail feature allows a user to review messages and select the ones to be downloaded to the local computer during the session. In Preview mode, the user can scan subject and sender information and determine which messages should be downloaded. This feature can be used to manage connect time when using time-charged wireless networks.

Access PLUS for Windows contains features called Fax Viewer and Fax Sender. These features allow fax messages to be viewed and sent, respectively.

Wireless Access	Access PLUS for Windows supports wireless access to AT&T EasyLink Services through RAM Mobile Data Network using a wireless modem.
User-Friendly Interface	All messaging functions can be performed with point-and-click mouse commands for Access PLUS for Windows. These include creating, editing, sending, receiving, reading, and printing messages.
Offline Message Creation	Access PLUS for Windows allows users to create messages offline, eliminating online message creation surcharges. Users can create simple text messages, forms, or multi-part messages. Multi-part messages can consist of either text or binary files.
List Management	Address lists can be created for email and fax broadcasts with fax telephone numbers, Enhanced FAX IDs, or other address lists. Lists can be nested. Lists can be maintained offline, and uploaded and downloaded as needed.
Integral Editor	Access PLUS for Windows provides users with a full-screen editor for easy message creation and revision. The maximum file size that can be created is 400 lines. An external editor can be used to create larger files, and the information can be imported into the document or sent as an attachment.

Personal Computer Software

Personal Directory Features	Access PLUS for Windows provides a personal address book that the user can create and maintain. Users can create one or more directories, each containing up to 32,000 entries, for convenient storage of personal and professional contacts. Fields are provided for name, address, telephone number, electronic mail address, fax, and other information. Personal directories are maintained and accessed only by the user. Users can cut and paste names and electronic mail addresses from the personal directory into a mail message or any MS-DOS application by mouse operations.
Transmission Protocol Support	Access PLUS for Windows supports the XMODEM, YMODEM 251, and FMODEM transmission protocols. ZMODEM support is planned for near-term release.
Binary File Transmission	Access PLUS for Windows transmits text, binary, and image files using error-correcting protocols. This allows graphics, spreadsheets, and word processing documents to be transferred without modification. Executable programs can be transferred between subscribers, thereby eliminating the need for re-keying or photocopying information. This process requires little training or PC knowledge, making it suitable for novice PC users. The user can read incoming binary files by clicking on a menu selection. The file is autotyped and displayed by the corresponding program.
Search Capabilities	Users can enter a string of characters as a search key and the system will automatically find the mail items matching the key. Users may search by information found in the message header or the message body.
Message Marking	Users can mark or unmark messages for processing. The Send, Move, Copy, Delete, and

	Print commands can be performed on all marked messages. This feature can also be used in conjunction with the search capability described above.
Background Mode Operation	Access PLUS for Windows can operate in background mode. In background mode, the software can: Periodically log on to the mail service to check for messages. Receive mail even if using another MS-DOS or Windows application. Be instantly notified (audibly and visually) when a new message has arrived. Click on a flashing icon to display mail window and read and reply to mail messages without exiting other applications.
Attachments	Messages created in a word processor or spreadsheet program can be sent as an attachment to a message. There is no limit on the number of attachments that can be sent. Attachments can be text (ASCII) or binary files such as spreadsheets or word processing files. Messages can also be imported into a message, and will appear as message content when the message is opened. Files to be attached are selected by mouse commands.
Application Mapping	Applications such as spreadsheets can be executed from the Attachment field. This allows rapid content access and easy file revision in the application used to create the file. The access is accomplished through the use of file extensions mapped to applications using the application mapping file. This feature allows users who receive binary files such as Lotus 123 spreadsheets or MS-Word files to have these attachments automatically opened by the program when they open the mail messages.

Personal Computer Software

Attachments can also be detached to a user-specified file for later use.

Printing Options	The user has the ability to print a message from the main menu or while reading the message. The user can print the message header, the message body, or both. Several print options are available, including print current mail item only, print all mail items in the current folder, print all new mail items, or print all marked messages.
Special Attention Messages	Messages can be flagged as "Special Attention" and/or "RSVP." These options alert the recipient that the message requires urgent or special attention or that a response is requested. If the receiver is using appropriate software and the message is marked "Special Attention," then the message is marked "Attention" and a Special Attention icon flashes in the status field of the main menu to let the receiver know that an urgent message has arrived.
Security Features	Passwords entered as part of the auto-logon process are scrambled in the configuration (MAIL.CFG) files, enhancing end-user security. Software hooks are provided to run a user-supplied encryption program to encrypt a message and/or attachments.
Online Capabilities	Access PLUS for Windows online function allows the user to log onto AT&T EasyLink Services to perform profile management and use interactive services.
Integrated Access to Information Services	Access PLUS allows users to access information services on or off AT&T EasyLink Services and to capture these sessions to a folder or to a file. Access to information services is accomplished using VT100 terminal emulation.
Session Capture	Users can store an online session in a folder for later retrieval. A Session folder is automatically created to store sessions as messages. All or part

of the session can be stored. Session captures are managed identically and in a fully integrated manner with mail messages.

Folders	The user can create up to 199 local folders or subdirectories with 199 messages in each folder or subdirectory for message management. Messages in each folder are identified by date, subject, and length. Access PLUS for Windows automatically creates the In folder (for new messages), the Out folder (for messages that the user wishes to send), the Waste folder (a temporary depository for all deleted messages until the user logs off Access PLUS for Windows), and the Sessions folder (to store AT&T Information Services sessions after using online capture). Other local folders are created by the user as desired.

Preview Mail	This Access PLUS for Windows feature facilitates radio packet access to AT&T Mail. This feature shows message headers in a network AT&T Mail folder and allows easy selection of those to be downloaded. The user can view new mail headers and download important messages. The information shown is subject, addressee, date, content type, length, and comments (e.g., ATTN).

Forms Creation and Fill-in	Access PLUS for Windows provides tools for designing and sending a mail form message. Recipients with Access PLUS software have an easy-to-use forms fill-in capability that enables them to automatically have the cursor stop at the proper field for fill-in. Access PLUS provides simple forms capability.

New Mail Notification	Access PLUS notifies a user about new incoming mail with a flashing icon and an audible tone when working with the background mailer activated.

Personal Computer Software

Dynamic Data Exchange (DDE)	Access PLUS in Windows versions provides Microsoft DDE protocol support to allow users to send mail messages from DDE-compliant applications, such as MS-Word and Excel.
Combined Mailbox Support	AT&T Enhanced FAX and AT&T Mail subscribers, using Access PLUS for Windows, can request a combined mailbox for email and fax messages. Access PLUS for Windows Fax Viewer can be used to view and print messages with fax content. Fax messages are managed as email messages and appear as email messages with fax content. Both email and fax messages are downloaded in a single session using the same logon ID and password.
Fax Viewer	Access PLUS for Windows includes a feature which displays fax messages for AT&T Mail subscribers who also have AT&T Enhanced FAX accounts. Access PLUS for Windows can be used to access the user's AT&T Enhanced FAX mailbox, or, if the user has Combined Mailbox support, download received faxes together with email messages. The Fax Viewer commands allow a subscriber to view the image at various scales and to print all or any pages of the received fax.
Fax Sender	The Fax Sender functions within Windows as an additional printer called Fax Sender on EasyLink. The Fax Sender converts the application's print output directly into a fax message, complete with the recipient address list, and stores it in the Access PLUS Out folder. A fax message is created, addressed, scheduled, and sent by printing from within the application to the Fax Sender on EasyLink printer. The Fax Sender printer driver then converts the application print output into a high-quality fax message and retains all application formatting, including fonts, graphics, and images. The fax message, created

using the Fax Sender, is directly generated from the application without printing to paper or scanning and the resulting fax is of very high quality.

Other Access PLUS for Windows features include

- Background Mailer Status
- VT100 terminal emulation
- Multi-tasking

AT&T Mail Access PLUS for Apple Macintosh Computers

AT&T Mail offers a software product for Apple Macintosh computers which provides these computers with easy access to AT&T Mail functions. AT&T Mail Access PLUS for Macintosh has the ability to send multiple attachments in a single message, text, binary, or combined. It also can perform the unattended scheduled transfer of mail in the background and has a quick message feature which allows mail transfer while in an application. Access PLUS for Macintosh also supports forms integrated with messaging, an unlimited number of directories with groups, a customizable display, and individual delivery preferences. Access PLUS for Apple Macintosh provides Macintosh users with many of the features described above for Access PLUS for DOS and Access PLUS for Windows. Access PLUS for Apple Macintosh capabilities include

Icon-based Interface	Screens comply with Macintosh user interface guidelines. All messaging functions are performed by point-and-click mouse commands for Access PLUS for Apple Macintosh. These include creating, editing, sending, receiving, reading, and printing messages.
Offline Message Creation	Access PLUS for Apple Macintosh allows users to create messages offline, eliminating online message creation surcharges. Users can create simple text messages, forms, or multi-part messages. Multi-part messages can consist of either text or binary files.

Screen Editor	Access PLUS for Apple Macintosh provides users with a full-screen editor for easy message creation and revision.
Personal Directory	Access PLUS for Apple Macintosh provides an integrated personal address book that the user can create and maintain. Users can create personal directories for convenient storage of personal and professional contacts. Fields are provided for name, address, telephone number, electronic mail address, and other information. Personal directories are maintained and accessed only by the user.
Address Cut and Paste	Access PLUS for Macintosh can cut and paste names and electronic mail addresses from the personal directory into a mail message. Access PLUS for Apple Macintosh allows users to go online to the AT&T Mail service for directory searches, using the directory lookup capabilities of the mail service.
Transmission Protocol Support	Access PLUS for Apple Macintosh supports the XMODEM, YMODEM 251, and FMODEM transmission protocols.
Binary File Transmission	Access PLUS for Apple Macintosh transmits text, binary, and image files using error-correcting protocols. This allows graphics, spreadsheets, and word processing documents to be transferred without modification. Executable programs can be transferred between subscribers, making the process suitable for novice PC users with limited PC knowledge.
Search Capabilities	Users can enter a string of characters as a search key and the system will automatically find the mail items matching the key. Users may search by information found in the message network header or the message body.
Mark Capabilities	Users can mark or unmark selected messages for processing. The Send, Move, Copy, Delete, and

	Print commands can be performed on all marked messages. This feature can also be used in conjunction with the search capability described above.
Background Mode Operation	Access PLUS for Apple Macintosh provides the user with the option of operating in background mode. Users set up to operate in the background mode can: Set up the system to periodically log on to the mail service to check for messages. Receive mail even if using another application. Be instantly notified (audibly and visually) when a new message has arrived.
Attachments	Messages created in a word processor or spreadsheet program can be sent as an attachment to a message. There is no limit on the number of attachments that can be sent. Attachments can be text (ASCII) or binary files such as spreadsheets or word processing files. Messages can also be imported into a message, and will appear as message content when the message is opened.
Attachment Execution	Applications such as spreadsheets can be executed from the Attachment field automatically for instant access and easy file revision using the Apple Macintosh file naming conventions. This allows users who receive binary files, such as Lotus or MS-Word files, to have these attachments automatically opened by the program when they open the mail messages. Attachments can also be detached to a user-specified file for later use.
Printing Options	The user has the ability to print a message from the main menu or while reading the message. The user can print the message header, the message body, or both. Several print options are available, including print current mail item only,

Personal Computer Software

	print all mail items in the current folder, print all new mail items, or print all marked mail.
Security Features	Passwords entered as part of the auto-logon process are scrambled in the configuration files, enhancing end-user security.
Terminal Emulation	A terminal emulation function allows the user to log on to the AT&T EasyLink Service, perform profile management, and use interactive services.
Access to Information Services	Access PLUS for Apple Macintosh allows users to access information services on AT&T Mail and capture these sessions to a folder or to a file. Access to information services is accomplished using VT100 terminal emulation.
Session Capture	Users can store an Information Services session in a folder for later retrieval. A Session folder is created to store messages saved to a folder. All or part of the session can be stored.
Folders	The user can create folders for message management limited only by memory on the local computer. Messages in each folder are identified by date, subject, and length. Access PLUS for Apple Macintosh automatically creates the In folder (for new messages) and the Out folder (for messages that the user wishes to send). Other folders are created by the user as desired.
Forms Creation and Fill-in	Access PLUS for Apple Macintosh provides tools for designing and sending forms. Recipients with the same software have an easy-to-use forms fill-in capability that enables them to automatically have the cursor stop at the proper field for fill-in. Access PLUS for Apple Macintosh provides simple forms capability.

Microsoft Mail Remote for Windows

AT&T EasyLink Services has a strategic relationship with Microsoft Corporation, and an AT&T Mail driver is bundled with Microsoft Mail Remote for Windows software. The Microsoft Mail PC remote package can serve as a full-featured interface to AT&T Mail. U.S. versions of Microsoft Mail Remote for Windows come with two drivers: a driver to access a Microsoft Mail LAN remotely, and a driver to access AT&T Mail directly. In other countries, the Microsoft Mail Remote AT&T Mail access driver is available from AT&T EasyLink Services. Microsoft Mail PC Remote for Windows is a product primarily for mobile workers or stand-alone PC users who need the ability to communicate with people back in the office, their customers, or their vendors either by dialing into a LAN or through the AT&T Mail public network. Mobile or remote workers can communicate with people back in the office, their customers, or their vendors using this product.

Microsoft Mail PC Remote for Windows is a stand-alone PC messaging software package that provides stand-alone users with many of the messaging capabilities that are available in the Microsoft Mail LAN version. Microsoft Mail PC Remote for Windows users may send and receive electronic mail messages from remote locations, set up a schedule for sending and receiving mail, and access messages on their LAN or on the AT&T Mail service. Most of the Microsoft Mail features described earlier apply to the PC Remote product.

At installation, users have the option of installing a driver to AT&T Mail, to their MS Mail LAN, or to both systems, but only one driver can be active at any one time. Users can change the selected driver using the Microsoft Mail System Selector installed with the product.

Users who install both drivers will have access to two different mailboxes. One is their LAN mailbox, and the other, on their PC, contains AT&T Mail messages. These two mailboxes are not integrated, and messages created and received while using the LAN driver and associated

Personal Computer Software

LAN mailbox are not stored with messages created and received while using the AT&T Mail driver.

A registered AT&T Mail service user with an active AT&T Mail driver has access to all store-and-forward messaging features, including access to online functions. The combination of the driver and Microsoft Mail PC Remote for Windows software turns the stand-alone PC into a powerful electronic messaging tool with extensive message storage, background send and receive capabilities, directory features, connectivity options, and information services access. Users create messages offline and access the AT&T Mail service to send and receive mail or to access interactive services.

Microsoft Mail PC Remote for Windows includes a terminal emulator which allows users to access all AT&T Mail interactive capabilities, such as Information Services access and online directory and capture sessions, as a file on the user's personal computer.

Microsoft Mail PC Remote for Windows includes extensive addressing screens and templates that are not present in the LAN product. An example is a pop-up screen which simplifies X.400 addressing.

Microsoft/AT&T Mail Benefits

Many Microsoft Mail LAN users purchase Microsoft Mail Remote for Windows as their mobile or stand-alone PC access solution. These Microsoft Mail Remote for Windows users may connect to their office LANs or connect using AT&T Mail as the store-and-forward messaging transport service. In many cases, the use of AT&T Mail and the AT&T Mail driver is a superior solution. Some features available to AT&T Mail users are

- Access through AT&T Mail makes better use of ports and LAN resources. Costs and port requirements are lower.
- Long distance and international phone charges are reduced.
- All AT&T Mail delivery options, such as fax, X.400, telex, and paper-based options, are available to remote and stand-alone users.

- Driver users have access to AT&T Mail online features, such as information services and the online directory.

- Support of wireless users is technically simpler and more cost-effective than trying to develop services in-house, with end-user support provided by AT&T Mail customer service 24 hours per day, 7 days per week worldwide.

Selection Criteria

Access PLUS for DOS is for PC users who do not run Microsoft Windows. Microsoft Mail Remote for Windows does not, at this time, support multiple configurations, such as a telephone and wireless connection, and cannot have two drivers active at the same time. The software is not available in a DOS version. Access PLUS for Windows provides comprehensive AT&T Mail functionality and low hardware requirements. Its use of a TSR for background operations keeps Windows resources available for other applications. It can maintain an unlimited number of configurations and comes with scripts for wireless and cellular modems, ISDN, and X.25 access methods.

Chapter 9

AT&T FORMsolutions

AT&T FORMsolutions is the umbrella term used for intelligent electronic forms produced by electronic forms packages to enhance and replace paper forms. An electronic form (eform) is a solution which allows the design, completion, transmission, and storage of forms to take place electronically. Electronic form intelligence allows the designer to apply rules and intelligence to the forms data fields to eliminate errors during the completion process. The form software can check the field entries to make sure that the user has provided the right type of information. Alphabetic data can be blocked from numeric fields, formats such as dates and social security numbers can be checked for validity, and items can be restricted to a predetermined set. Automatic mathematical calculations can be performed on specified data fields. Electronic forms can provide additional benefits depending on the design tools used.

A traditional business form is paper-based and is used to collect, store, and distribute information. The use of paper forms for business transactions is a labor-, resource-, and capital-intensive process. Recent estimates are that over $360 billion annually is spent on paper form distribution, storage, and updating; about $8 billion annually is spent on preprinting paper forms, and an additional $2 billion annually is lost through waste and obsolescence in the United States alone. Estimates for form processing costs are that $30 to $60 are spent for each dollar

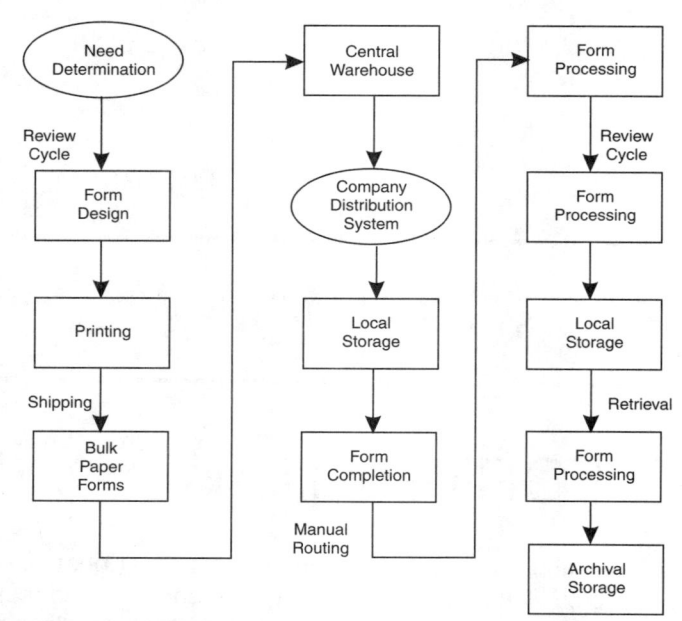

```
Need              Central          Form
Determination     Warehouse        Processing
      |               |                |
 Review|               |                |Review
 Cycle |               |                |Cycle
      v               v                v
   Form           Company            Form
   Design        Distribution      Processing
                   System
      |               |                |
      v               v                v
   Printing         Local            Local
                   Storage          Storage
      |               |                |
Shipping|               |            Retrieval
      v               v                v
   Bulk            Form              Form
   Paper         Completion        Processing
   Forms
                    |                 |
                 Manual               v
                 Routing          Archival
                                  Storage
```

Figure 9-1 **Paper Form Cycle** Paper forms are subject to shipping and processing delays.

spent to create or purchase forms. Mail-enabled electronic forms reduce costs while enhancing productivity by automating the form process.

An example would be a purchase order, where the software can automatically calculate the price for multiple items and add tax and shipping charges. The software can complete data fields by drawing information from a database based on entries by the operator. Data can be automatically uploaded to a database. Some eform packages provide a signature capability by use of a password which locks access to selected form fields. The combination of electronic forms and AT&T Mail allows forms to be delivered and processed automatically with fewer errors. The added intelligence found in electronic forms can eliminate wasted time associated with rejection of a form and the need to re-enter information.

The paper form development cycle is slow and complex. The process begins when the need for structured data collection is confirmed. The form

AT&T FORMsolutions

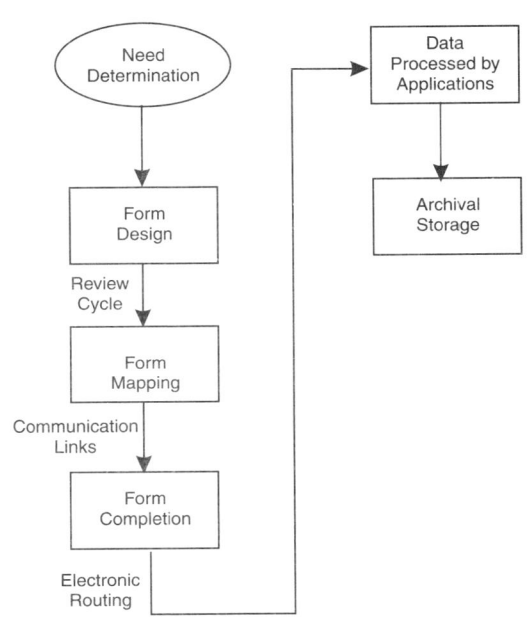

Figure 9-2 **Electronic Form Cycle** Electronic forms move over communication links and are stored on computers. Processing of completed forms does not require manual operations.

is then designed, often by an outside graphics designer, and a form master is created. The form is then reviewed and revised by the people who will enter or process the information. The master is printed, often in quantities which ensure economies of scale, which exceed estimated demand. The print order is packaged and stored centrally. Forms are ordered by end users and distributed. Local inventory is stored on-site, and users retrieve forms from their local file cabinet. The end user completes the paper form, and the form is then routed, either through the company mail system, U.S. mail, or overnight mail, for required reviews and approvals. Several cycles of review and approval may be required as part of the form process. Actual paper form processing may involve multiple additional steps for data capture before the form is routed to archival storage. The form is then routed again or the data are rekeyed for final archival storage.

The electronic form development cycle is fast and relatively simple. The process begins when the need for structured data collection is confirmed. The form is then designed, reviewed, and mapped in an electronic format. This is often done by existing staff. The electronic form is stored on the network or local machines, updated at will, and distributed over communication links. Users store forms on PCs and load the appropriate form as needed. The completed electronic form is sent for review and ap-

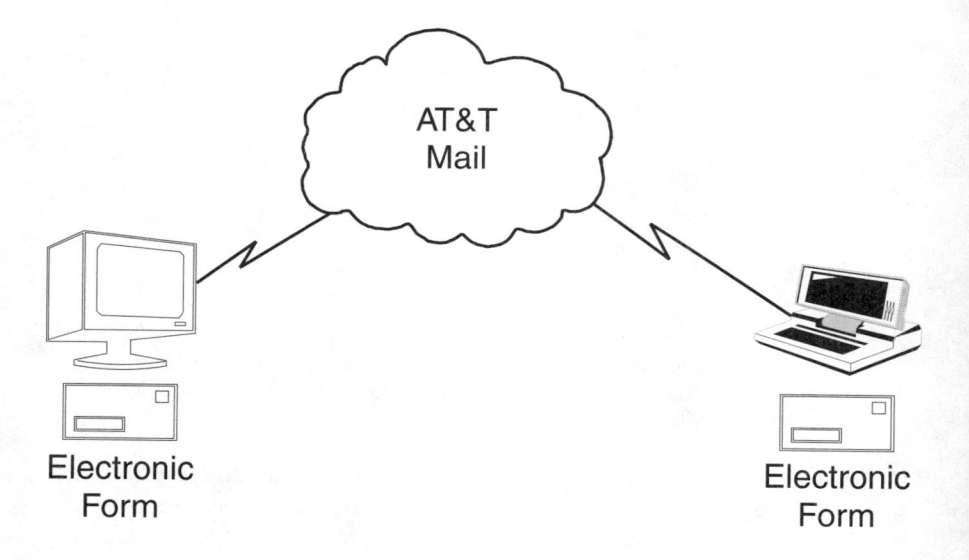

Figure 9-3 **Form Transmission** AT&T Mail allows forms to be transmitted over the public network to remote offices.

proval over communication links, with immediate distribution and faster turnaround. Data are automatically integrated into the host application or system, processed, and automatically archived.

Third-party software vendors provide the intelligent forms development tools which extend the use of form-based applications to external electronic commerce. Form examples include customer orders, expense reports, insurance forms, salesperson management reports, personnel forms, and other documents. FORMsolutions supports error trapping,

AT&T FORMsolutions

routing, calculation, and other functions which provide more functionality than text-based message processing applications can. AT&T EasyLink Services has alliances supporting mail-enabled intelligent electronic forms and markets these capabilities under the umbrella name of FORMsolutions.

These applications, and their development, completion and routing, use AT&T Mail to extend their reach to remote offices and business partners. The use of AT&T Mail as the external messaging transport allows mail-enabled form applications to be used outside the enterprise campus. Mail-enabled form applications can be used in any process where an AT&T Mail message can be created or processed by an application without human action. Forms, unlike messages, contain substantial intelligence provided by the forms software. An intelligent electronic form software package usually consists of two major functions. These are

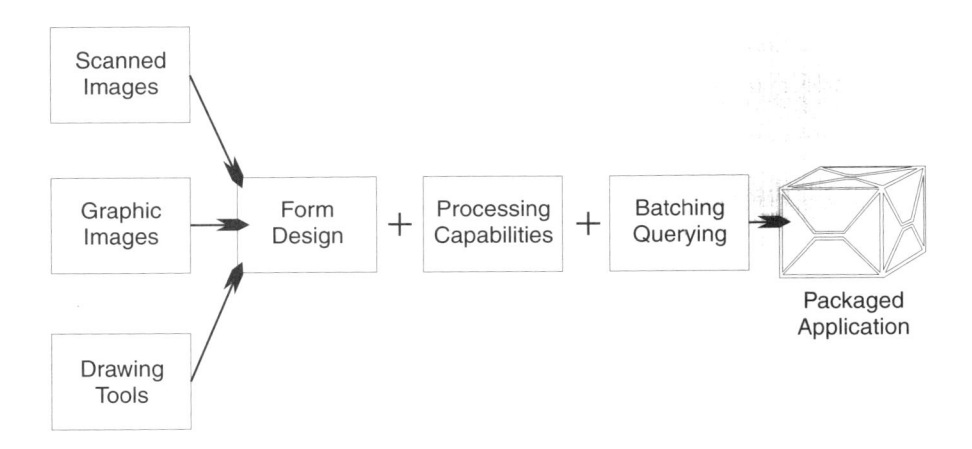

Figure 9-4 **Packaged Applications** Form software allows non-technical staff to develop packaged applications.

Designer Package	The designer package is the form developer's interface and uses graphical interfaces, typically Microsoft Windows, for the form design, artwork, and intelligence-building capabilities. Designer packages are end-user tools and do not require programming skills or extensive training.
Forms Filler	The forms filler package is the user interface to the forms. It is used for viewing, completion, printing, saving, and form transaction transmission.

AT&T EasyLink Services FORMsolutions uses the AT&T Mail network to provide value-added communication services. At the design stages, form processes usually require data obtained from multiple sources, locations, and people. There often are several development cycles, such as a submittal cycle, a review cycle, and a final approval cycle. AT&T Mail is used to transmit form information for the design, storage, and distribution of completed forms and supports the full communication cycle of the intelli-

Form Transport
  Email
  Fax
  Telex
  Paper
  Shared Folders
  Information Services
  Other AT&T EasyLink Services

AT&T EasyLink Services

Form Transport Only

Filler used with AT&T Mail

Standalone Filler

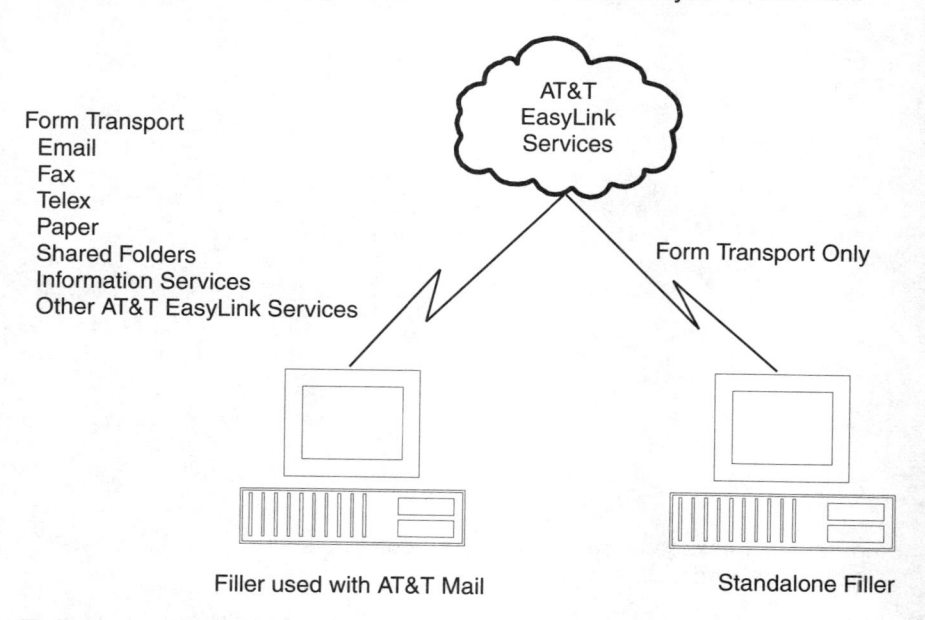

Figure 9-5 **Alternative Delivery Points** Form applications using AT&T EasyLink Services can use most AT&T Mail delivery options.

AT&T FORMsolutions

gent form from design to completion. One benefit of intelligent electronic forms is the reduction of the form transit time. AT&T EasyLink Services integration allows this benefit to extend from the local workgroup to other locations or companies, or to mobile workers using all AT&T Mail connectivity options which support anywhere, any time communications.

AT&T FORMsolutions supports two transmission options for intelligent electronic forms. One type is called stand-alone filler software and enables its user to send form data directly to the AT&T Mail network from the stand-alone filler software. The other is used in combination with Access PLUS. Access PLUS is AT&T EasyLink Services' PC-based email management software and is discussed in Chapter 7. Electronic form filler software used with Access PLUS provides a more powerful and fully functional communications tool which provides the user with access to a broad spectrum of services offered through AT&T Mail, such as shared folders or bulletin boards. These AT&T Mail features can be used to distribute and update forms. The combination also supports the full range of AT&T Mail delivery options, including telex, fax, paper, and other delivery modes.

Mail-enabled form-based applications have the ability to

- Perform calculations based upon specific input of data into certain fields.
- Interact with databases to receive automatic input of information to data input fields.
- Restrict the data fields to receive only specific types of data input.

AT&T works with third-party forms suppliers as an open system provider. The AT&T Mail integration support services are non-exclusive arrangements, and AT&T EasyLink Services is actively seeking relationships with additional suppliers of intelligent electronic forms in accordance with its position as an open system provider supporting market-leading forms vendors. AT&T's third-party relationships include

- AT&T Global Information Solutions/Delrina (Liberty)
- FormLink
- Microsoft Corporation

Inter-enterprise use of electronic forms has been limited, as standardization on proprietary solutions is difficult across enterprise boundaries. Electronic form software is often proprietary, and both the sender of a form and the receiver of the form must use compatible products on a form designed with a specific form package. Electronic forms work best when a company can standardize on a common application forms package for use throughout the enterprise. Forms products developed with a specific form-design package are used with processing software which is often available only from a single vendor. Mail-enabled applications which are not form based can work with any email message in a standardized format.

FORMsolutions Options

Liberty

Liberty is an enhanced version of Delrina's FormFlow product line. Liberty's key enhancement is its tight integration with AT&T Mail. It was developed for AT&T Global Information Solutions Electronic Forms and is exceptionally scalable. The Liberty software supports multiple automation levels ranging from simple to complex, making it suitable for either beginning or advanced users of intelligent electronic forms. Increasing the scale of implementation from simple to complex does not require significant redevelopment or redesign work. AT&T Global Information Solutions provides a one-stop solution for electronic forms, including hardware and software components, education, professional services, and communications. AT&T EasyLink Services supports the integration effort.

AT&T Global Information Solutions is a leading provider of paper forms. In 1990, the company analyzed available electronic forms software and entered into a joint marketing and development effort with Delrina Technology, an industry leader in the Windows and DOS electronic forms market. AT&T Global Information Solutions' Liberty is the result of a joint effort between AT&T Global Information Solutions' Business Forms Division, Delrina Technologies, and AT&T EasyLink Services. Delrina is a recognized technical and market leader in PC forms and fax software and a

AT&T FORMsolutions

leading publisher of content software. The Liberty product is a mail-enabled intelligent electronic forms application which uses AT&T Mail as its value-added communications network.

AT&T Global Information Solutions Electronic Forms Division works with Delrina Technologies and AT&T EasyLink Services to develop and add value to the Liberty product offering. AT&T Global Information Solutions commissioned Delrina Technology to perform the technical work needed to mail-enable the AT&T Global Information Solutions Liberty software using the AT&T EasyLink Services network. The product is composed of two modules:

Liberty Designer	The designer package is the form application development tool built on Delrina's state-of-the-art Perform Pro Plus product. It allows the corporate customer or software developer to create or edit a graphic form on a PC and to build intelligence into the electronic form fields.
Liberty Filler	The filler package is the user interface. It is used to load, store, complete, and route the form and allows the user to fill out, print, and electronically mail the form. The filler package also supports a signature capability essential to proof of authorization in form processing. AT&T Global Information Solutions' Liberty automatically extracts information contained on electronic forms so that it can become part of a company's database.

AT&T Global Information Solutions markets a full line of filler products that will work on a variety of hardware platforms and environments, including Microsoft Windows. The filler product allows a user to electronically transmit form data through the AT&T Mail network and have the form re-created at the receiving end. After retrieval of the information from an AT&T Mail mailbox, the data within the fields are an exact replica of the original form data.

AT&T Mail provides support for Liberty's wide-area networking capabilities, permitting forms to be routed outside the campus environment and processed using Liberty client software. Liberty forms can be routed in a campus environment using LAN email systems such as Microsoft Mail and cc:Mail.

AT&T Global Information Solutions offers a single supplier solution — application software, hardware platforms, worldwide communications, business forms expertise, forms engineering, and customer support. As a part of the Liberty product offering, AT&T Global Information Solutions offers electronic forms consulting to its customers. AT&T EasyLink Services provides the global communications network and support structure for the AT&T Global Information Solutions Liberty product. The product is marketed by AT&T Global Information Solutions. AT&T Global Information Solutions, assisted by AT&T EasyLink Services, markets the software in the United States and Canada. International distribution is being developed.

FormLink

Axint Technologies' FormLink was developed from the unique perspective of a transaction processing-oriented software developer. Other form software companies began by automating the development of forms. Axint's goal was enhancing the collecting and moving of data entered on electronic forms. FormLink is exceptionally strong where workflows are well established and automated transaction processing is the automation objective.

FormLink provides flexible forms design supporting the import of scanned or graphic images and image enhancement with a full-featured drawing tool. Processing and batching/queuing capabilities can be added to designed forms. The result is run-time versions of complete and packaged applications that are ideal for high-volume transactions. FormLink is a Microsoft Windows–based application that allows developers to build intelligent electronic forms.

AT&T FORMsolutions

AT&T EasyLink Services has a co-marketing agreement with Axint Technologies and Fame Computer to market and resell FormLink as part of its FORMsolutions line of AT&T Mail-enabled intelligent electronic forms capabilities. Axint Technologies Corporation has teamed with AT&T EasyLink Services to mail-enable the product and provide an efficient way for companies to quickly automate their traditional forms processing. The FormLink development team has extensive experience with Microsoft Windows design and programming. There are two parts that compose the FormLink product. These are the

- FormLink Development System
- FormLink Transaction System

FormLink Development System

The development system employs scanning technology to convert paper forms and has a drawing capability to design and create new forms. The development system consists of five components, which are

FormDictionary — This component allows the developer to define the data field elements within a form. A data field element can be used repeatedly and in multiple forms. FormDictionary provides standard edit functions, including required field designation, range of acceptable values, calculations, cross-field checking, and table validation. External processing programs, such as database applications, can be linked to individual data fields by specifying the program name in the FormDictionary.

Formation — This component is a full-featured drawing tool with a WYSIWYG (What You See Is What You Get) Windows interface used to create and draw forms.

FormEdit — This component is used to define the position of data fields and relate the field positions to the element names in FormDictionary. It is also used to enhance scanned image quality.

FormTable	This component is a table-building utility used to prefill fields on a form.
FormCompile	This component completes the application by assembling all the results of the Development System.

FormLink Transaction System

FormLink Transaction System is the run-time or filler version of the FormLink software application that users load to fill and store electronic forms. The Transaction System has three components, which are

FormView	This component manages the image of a form on a screen. Forms can be scrolled or positioned on a screen using a mouse or a keyboard. FormView automatically positions the entry point at the correct input field and displays appropriate error and help messages. Information can be imported from a database and merged into a form, and form information can be exported to a database. FormView can also copy information from one form to another. FormView is custom-tailored for AT&T EasyLink Services and can use either AT&T Access PLUS or Axint's FormConnect to queue and manage the transmission of FormLink applications over AT&T Mail.
FormPrint	This component is a print management facility which allows the user to print the entire form or to fill in data in a preprinted form.
FormConnect	This component directly connects a FormLink forms application to AT&T EasyLink Services and provides transmission and management capabilities for the FormConnect queue. A menu option within FormView sends a transaction to FormConnect. FormConnect users can designate applications to be sent and where to send them. FormConnect also provides return receipts and

notification of whether transactions were accepted or rejected by the receiving party.

FormLink is designed to convert paper forms into screen images, making the conversion from paper transactions to electronic transactions easier. FormLink gets electronic forms on-line quickly, as scanning technology reduces the time needed for form design. Axint Technologies, the developer of FormLink, has mail-enabled its product using AT&T Mail as the value-added communications network.

Axint Technologies was founded in 1987 to provide form transaction solutions for the insurance industry and currently is the leading supplier of insurance industry forms-based transaction processing software products. Axint Technologies is a current member of the ACORD insurance industry standards organization and has compiled an extensive library of electronic industry standard ACORD forms. Axint Technologies is expanding from its insurance industry knowledge base and applying its knowledge of forms technology, developed in that forms-intensive industry, to other business functions.

Fame Computer is a software developer and service provider. Its market focus has been on the financial services industry, and, in 1992, it helped form the United Kingdom electronic trading initiative. The initiative is a consortium of 20 leading United Kingdom life insurance companies developing advanced electronic commerce techniques.

The FormLink product was integrated into AT&T Mail according to AT&T EasyLink Services specifications and is sold by AT&T EasyLink Services representatives. The full-featured product is supported by AT&T EasyLink Services Professional Services. These group services include form scanning, development and design, and other support of a company's database integration needs. Axint offers FormLink customization for those enterprises with requirements beyond the standard solution. Axint can and will customize FormLink for customers that have such needs. AT&T EasyLink Services and Fame Computer offer the product globally. AT&T EasyLink Services sells the product in the United States, and Canada. Axint provides support in the United States, Canada and Mexico. Fame Computer sells and supports FormLink in other countries.

Microsoft Electronic Forms Designer

Electronic forms built with Microsoft Electronic Forms Designer are presented as easy-to-use structured email messages. They are designed to ensure effective person-to-person and person-to-process communications. Electronic forms use Microsoft Mail and a variety of access options. AT&T Mail can route data throughout an organization, across the office, or around the world. The Electronic Forms Designer helps customers create workgroup solutions by leveraging their Visual Basic knowledge and investment.

The Electronic Forms Designer comes with a generic template and three predesigned customizable electronic forms. The predesigned eforms are fully operational as is and can also be customized to meet specific business needs. The predesigned forms are

Generic Eform	The generic form template provides standard mail functions such as address, send and reply buttons, and standard mail controls such as recipients, subject, and comments.
Routing Eform	The routing slip form allows any file attachment to be routed serially to a list of users. This form can be used out of the box for elementary workflow processes, and allows users to route documents and spreadsheets directly from applications like Microsoft Excel and Word for Windows.
Telephone Note Eform	The telephone note form displays while-you-were-out information and includes a recipient's auto-dial button as a demonstration of the form's extended power and functionality.

The Electronic Forms Designer leverages the customer's investment in Microsoft Mail, Visual Basic, and AT&T EasyLink Services capabilities to create, send, and receive structured information. Forms created using the Electronic Forms Designer are easy to use.

AT&T FORMsolutions

Forms are tightly integrated with Microsoft Mail. Users compose, read, and address electronic forms just as they would standard mail messages. Users can distribute forms from either the Mail client or the program manager, allowing forms to serve as the front end for sophisticated applications that use Microsoft Mail to transport structured data. Forms can be installed on a user's local machine for offline reading or composing or can be shared among a workgroup to allow centralized administration. Developers can use the Visual Basic Professional Edition to develop standard Windows 3.1 help files.

Microsoft Electronic Forms Designer allows development of routing-based applications where either AT&T EasyLink Services, MS Mail, or both are the transports for the form. These applications include

- Customized phone message forms with autodialing capabilities
- Purchase request forms requiring signature approval
- Travel request forms
- Expense reporting
- Document routing forms for sending attachments on a prescribed routing sequence

Chapter 10

AT&T Mail Connectivity

AT&T Mail supports connectivity from almost all major email packages running on LANs, mainframes, and midrange systems. AT&T Mail allows users to retain and build upon their investments in legacy systems by adding the reach, scope, and flexibility of public service connectivity to their existing email operations. Users continue to use familiar packages, enhanced by access to AT&T Mail. The functionality of these packages varies by platform and email system in use.

The architecture of email is shifting from complete but stand alone proprietary systems to standards-based systems which accommodate modularized front-end clients and back-end services. Operating systems, such as Windows 95, will incorporate basic email services. Application programming interfaces (APIs) such as MAPI (Microsoft), VIM (Lotus), and OCE (Apple) are simplifying the task of creating value-added mail-enabled applications which often require off-enterprise connectivity. Open X.400 back-end messaging services are beginning to emerge, and client/server architectures and users are replacing multi-user host-based email. This, in turn, is resulting in the expansion of corporate workflow and groupware applications, which also must cross network boundaries for maximum benefits.

```
            1960-1980s                           1990s

       Host        Mini                       LAN-based

       IBM         DEC         Messaging   Microsoft Mail   On-Technology
       Profs       All-in-1    Direction
                                           DaVinci E-mail   Banyan
       HP          IBM                                      VINES
       New Wave    DISOSS                   Lotus
       Office                               cc:Mail         WordPerfect
       D-G         Wang                                     Office
       CEO         Office
```

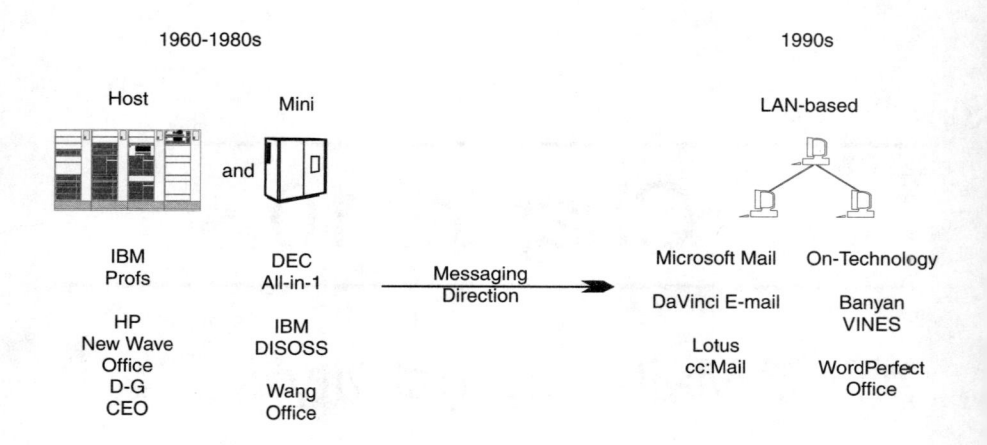

Figure 10-1 **Messaging's Changing Direction** Email is rapidly shifting from legacy systems to LAN-based email.

AT&T EasyLink offers multiple methods for connecting LANs to one another, and LANs to legacy WANs and to legacy mainframe and midrange systems. This provides investment protection for existing hardware, software, and user skills.

LAN Email Package Support

AT&T EasyLink Services makes it possible to connect approximately 90 percent of the LAN email packages on the market today to AT&T Mail. Connectivity options for LAN email products include but are not limited to

- Microsoft Mail
- Lotus (cc:Mail and Notes)
- WordPerfect Office
- DaVinci E-mail & Coordinator

AT&T Mail Connectivity

- CE Software & Inbox
- Banyan Network Mail
- On Technology/Notework
- Futur-us Team
- Beyond Mail
- StarGROUP Services for Microsoft Mail
- Higgins Group

Email System Interconnections

LAN email is an efficient, cost-effective way to interconnect people in a campus environment, but LAN users frequently must communicate with users of other electronic messaging systems. Some estimates are that about 20 percent of all messages created and sent from LAN clients must be sent to people off-LAN. These messages need to be sent to people using other LAN email products, mainframe systems, stand-alone PC software, or fax machines. The recipients could be people on another email system within the same company, business partners, or customers.

Network email users are now shifting to LAN email for economic reasons but still need to communicate with off-LAN users who may be on public, host, or mini systems. The AT&T Mail interconnection facilities are a cost-effective method for maintaining and extending connectivity to fixed and mobile users on public, host, mini, and non-standard systems. AT&T Mail therefore provides value-added gateway services for LAN email.

LAN interconnection solutions usually use gateways to connect LANs to other LANs or messaging systems. Gateways allow message exchange between heterogeneous electronic messaging systems, and the gateway software is responsible for transferring messages from the local messaging application to the foreign mail system. There are two major classes of gateways:

X.400 Gateways	Most computing and network platforms support X.400 connectivity between homogenous and heterogeneous systems to comply with open

systems standards. X.400 gateways are somewhat expensive, typically running about $3,000 per LAN in addition to leased line costs, and are complex to administer. Some messaging vendors, such as Microsoft, are incorporating X.400 as part of their LAN messaging applications, lowering the cost per LAN.

Native Bridges and Gateways Native bridges support communications between homogenous systems. For heterogeneous systems, a gateway that supports communications only between those two specified systems would be needed. A unique gateway would be required to enable a Type A system to communicate with a Type B system. A different gateway would be required to enable a Type A system to communicate with a Type C system, driving up costs and complexity as the number of types of systems increases. Each gateway is purchased and installed separately. The need for multiple gateways and connections, each tailored to the destination system, increases gateway cost and complexity.

Each gateway supports different capabilities; compatibility is limited, and functionality is often compromised to the level of the lowest common denominator. The reliability of the system depends on the gateways and the administrator's skills.

The AT&T EasyLink Services' value-added network solution provides the tools to allow users on multiple LANs to communicate not only with one another but with users connected through other types of systems, such as hosts, minis, or mobile devices, or residents on other ADMDs. AT&T Mail provides a set of standard gateways which are designed, installed, and maintained centrally and which support interconnection without the capital costs, ongoing administrative problems, or line costs associated with local gateways. Capacity planning and new technology are performed by the public network, and the AT&T Mail network is provisioned to maintain service levels regardless of message traffic or maintenance

AT&T Mail Connectivity

Capabilities	LAN-to-LAN AT&T Mail	LAN-to-LAN Gateway
Basic Connectivity	X	X
Availability/Reliability	X	X
Content Integrity	X	X
Familiar Interfaces	X	X
Easy Addressing	X	X
Full Functionality	X	X
Easy Administration	X	
Worldwide Access	X	
High Volume Distribution	X	

Figure 10-2 **LAN Gateway Alternatives** The use of AT&T Mail adds functionality unobtainable with direct LAN-to-LAN email gateways.

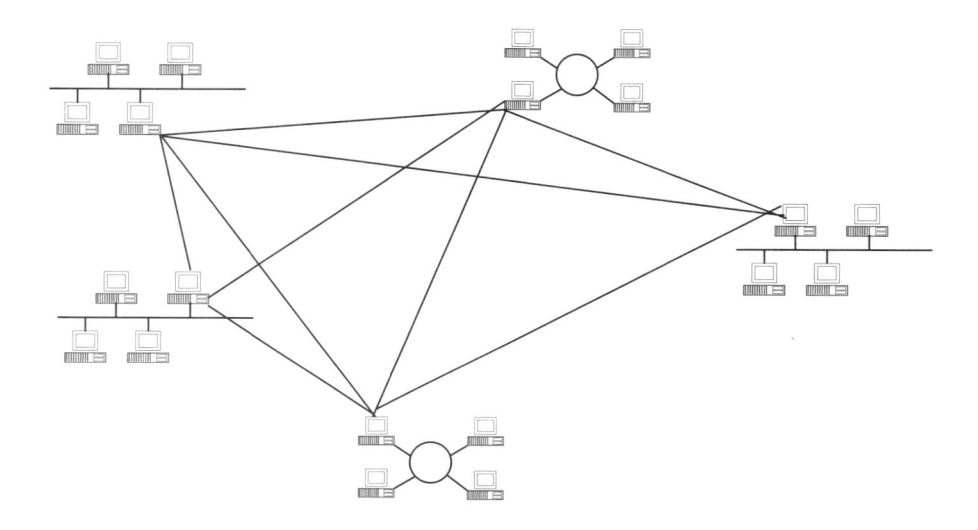

Figure 10-3 **LAN-to-LAN Gateways** This approach requires multiple gateways and links and does not provide messaging outside the enterprise.

requirements. Equivalent services are difficult and expensive to provide with local gateways. A VAN provides a messaging infrastructure that extends the communications reach of LAN users, while preserving their current investments, environments, and familiar interfaces.

AT&T Mail also extends location-dependent networks to mobile and remote users by extending email reach through mobile messaging and interconnections that are difficult to implement for a single corporation. The AT&T Mail service provides port availability to remote users, since it maintains the capacity to service both current and anticipated traffic and acts as a consolidator for the LAN. This eliminates the need for the LAN administrator to adjust ports and lines to traffic variations. The remote

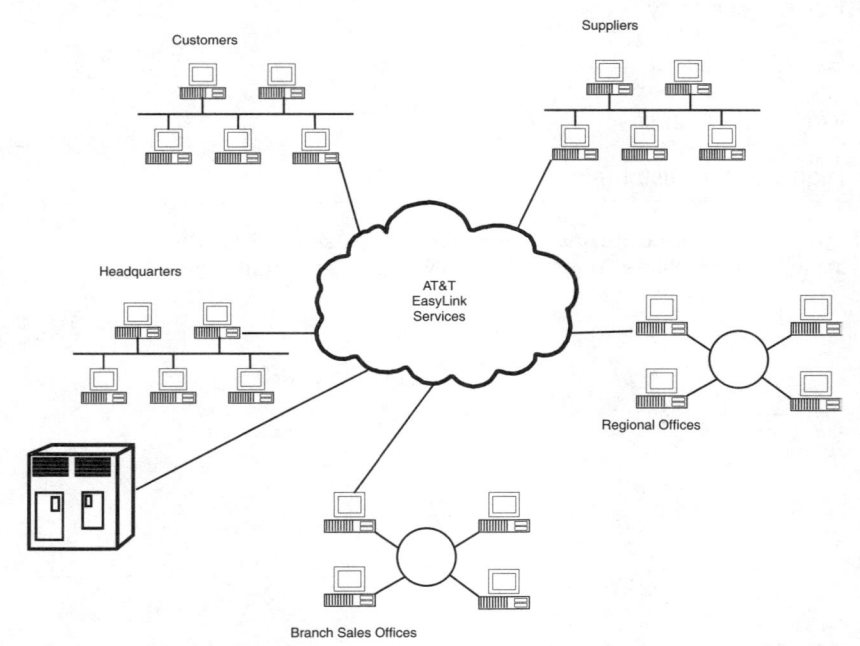

Figure 10-4 **LAN Connectivity** LAN connectivity through AT&T EasyLink Services provides messaging beyond the enterprise.

user, wired or wireless, accesses the public port, and the LAN software collects and sends messages periodically.

Other services, such as wireless, require external off-LAN connectivity if they are to be provided at a reasonable cost per user. Here, AT&T Mail acts as the link between the wireless provider and the LAN, again isolating the LAN administrator from the cost and complexity of gateway management. The administrator is concerned only with a single connection, and costs are usage-based, making the AT&T Mail solution practical for both large and small users. Support of remote users can also be minimized, as the Customer Support Centers, located worldwide, provide support to endusers on messaging questions, reducing the need for the LAN staff to provide this service.

Microsoft-AT&T Strategic Relationship

AT&T EasyLink Services and Microsoft have joined in a strategic relationship which capitalizes on the strengths of both companies. Microsoft is strong in LAN messaging, and AT&T EasyLink Services is strong in public messaging and connectivity. This powerful combination provides customers with simple, low-cost solutions for connectivity to others in their corporation, their customers and vendors, and those outside their companies. This relationship has enhanced the functionality of the products of the companies.

This strategic relationship has produced an integrated set of products which provides customers who purchase the Microsoft Mail software with the software needed for access to AT&T Mail at no additional cost. A gateway to AT&T Mail is included in every Microsoft Mail for PC Networks package, and a driver to AT&T Mail is included in every Microsoft Mail PC Remote for Windows package. The free gateway for access to a public network as part of a LAN messaging product is unique. MS Mail users and AT&T Mail customers can easily communicate with one another, as the software products maintain full compatibility.

Microsoft is bundling access to the AT&T Mail service with two primary messaging software products:

Microsoft Mail for PC Networks version 3.2	This product is bundled with a gateway to the AT&T Mail service. This DOS LAN server product supports DOS, Windows, OS/2, and Macintosh clients. Customers who purchase the LAN product can install the included gateway

	software, register their LAN with AT&T Mail, and administer the gateway to allow LAN user access to AT&T Mail.
Microsoft Mail Remote for Windows version 3.2	This product is bundled with a driver for the AT&T Mail Service. This MS Windows-based product is for stand-alone PCs or laptop computers. Customers install the included driver and register with AT&T Mail to use the service.

Both Microsoft Mail products comply with Windows interface standards and integrate with other applications using MAPI. The following discussion covers Word for Windows 6.0 integration with Microsoft Mail as an example. These features extend over the AT&T Mail network.

The benefits of integration are shown by the following example. Microsoft Mail automatically mail-enables Word for Windows by adding two items to Word's file menu. These are Send and Add Routing Slip. A Word document may be sent as an OLE encapsulated attachment by selecting Send. The normal Microsoft Mail screen appears with the document shown as an icon; it may be sent to any addressee who has the ability to read a Word file. Routing allows a document to be sent to multiple reviewers, and AT&T Mail integration adds the ability to include reviewers off the LAN and outside the enterprise. This may be either simultaneous or sequential. AT&T Mail extends the reach of such mail-enabled applications by implementation of the gateway to AT&T Mail.

Application Integration

Microsoft has announced products which will provide connectivity to the AT&T Mail service. One of these announced products is Exchange, which is Microsoft's N/T-based messaging server. This messaging server uses X.400 as the messaging backbone, and provides X.500-based directory services and other advanced messaging features. AT&T EasyLink Services will certify Exchange to be interoperable with AT&T Mail.

Microsoft Mail for PC Networks

The gateway to AT&T Mail extends the reach of MS Mail users to any AT&T Mail user, connected system, mobile device, or delivery option available on the AT&T Mail service. Once the gateway PC is installed and administered by the system administrator, local Microsoft Mail users can use all AT&T Mail delivery options with their existing, familiar Microsoft Mail interface. The AT&T Mail gateway does not modify or change any local Microsoft Mail messaging capabilities but extends the messaging reach of users by allowing them to communicate globally through AT&T Mail.

Many Microsoft Mail for PC Networks installations use the software to communicate with others on their LAN and have not considered the advantages of connections using AT&T Mail. AT&T Mail removes communication barriers, and extends LAN messaging beyond the local LAN environment without the need for the system administrator to purchase and install multiple gateway packages, such as one for X.400 and another for fax. The administrator installs the AT&T Mail gateway software and registers the gateway with AT&T Mail. Users of the local area network can then begin to send messages to virtually anyone, anywhere via email, fax, X.400, telex, or paper copy.

Microsoft Mail users are uniquely positioned to expand communications beyond their LAN environment and obtain the location-independent connectivity and economic benefits of AT&T Mail's public network services without the need to buy or integrate multiple gateways by using the software included with Microsoft Mail, version 3.0 and higher, in the United States and Canada. This includes

- Sending email messages to others not on their local area network
- Communicating with their remote workers using Microsoft Mail Remote for Windows
- Sending messages to users of other systems compliant with X.400
- Communicating with their trading partners, suppliers, customers, and alliance partners
- Sending fax, paper, or telex messages

AT&T Mail's gateway is free in North America and available at little or no cost internationally. Many other gateways have list prices over $695. AT&T Mail's gateway is packaged with Microsoft Mail for PC Networks in the United States and Canada. The user does not have to order the software, or request it from Microsoft.

AT&T Mail Gateway Features and Operation

The gateway to AT&T Mail supports all store-and-forward AT&T Mail features, but not interactive ones. End users do not have access to any AT&T Mail interactive services using this LAN-based gateway and are not issued individual AT&T Mail IDs unless they are personally registered with AT&T Mail. The server is registered with the AT&T Mail network, and the system administrator assigns user IDs to the gateway clients.

After the system administrator has registered the gateway server with AT&T Mail and completed initial administration of the gateway, the MS Mail LAN users can send messages using all AT&T Mail delivery options, including the sending and receipt of binary and OLE files through the AT&T Mail network. The gateway supports the store-and-forward AT&T Mail delivery options, including

- Fax delivery
- X.400 delivery
- Telex
- Paper delivery

Microsoft Mail supports an unlimited number of message attachments, which can include text, binary, and OLE objects. The gateway supports delivery of these attachments. AT&T Mail can transport messages up to 10 Mb in size. If the message size exceeds the limit, then a non-delivery notice is sent by AT&T Mail to the sender. An original message copy is not attached to this class of non-delivery notice.

Encapsulated messages sent across the AT&T Mail backbone maintain the integrity of the message contents when sent to another MS Mail user. Therefore, a message sent across the AT&T Mail backbone is identical to a message sent across a LAN, and the same message may be sent to addressees on both systems. All text, multimedia objects, schedule mes-

AT&T Mail Connectivity

sages, binary files, and directories appear in the format in which they were sent. For example, a message containing OLE objects sent from an MS Mail user to another MS Mail user would be received with the OLE object in the body of the message. However, If the same message was sent to an Access PLUS user, it would appear in non-encapsulated form, as the OLE object would appear as an attachment and would not appear in the message body.

Wide-Area Network Connectivity (Backbone)

MS Mail LANs can be interconnected using connectivity options available on the AT&T Mail network for mail and mail-enabled application exchange and operation, especially when connecting disparate mail systems and mail-enabled applications. This approach lowers hardware, software, training, administrative, and maintenance costs when compared to direct gateway connections between LANs.

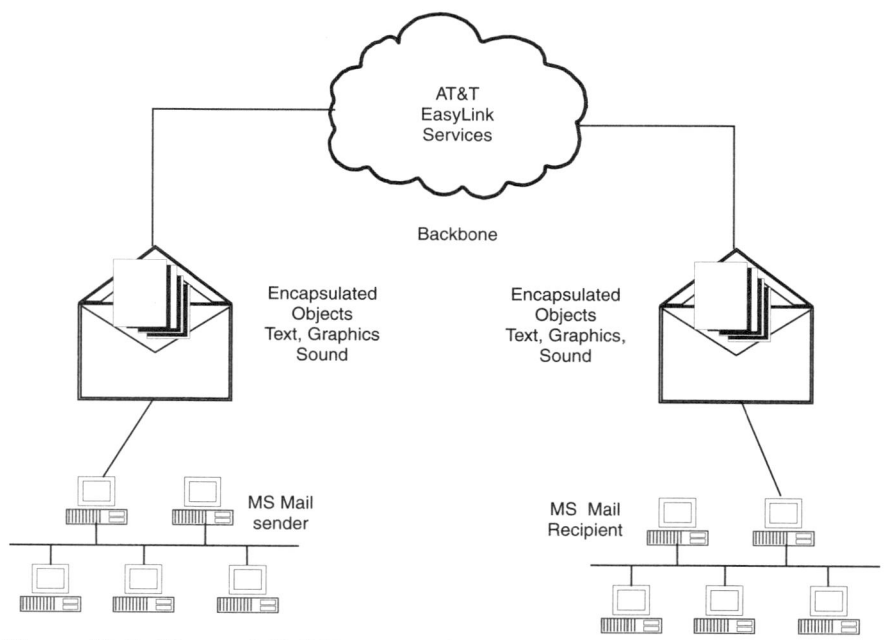

Figure 10-5 **Microsoft Mail Encapsulation** Encapsulated objects can be sent over AT&T Mail with Microsoft Mail for PC Networks.

An example of a Microsoft Mail over AT&T Mail application is the use of message encapsulation in Microsoft's directory synchronization function. This feature allows a LAN administrator to synchronize mail directories using AT&T Mail as the transport mechanism. Microsoft Mail provides robust directory synchronization capabilities which provide for directory up-

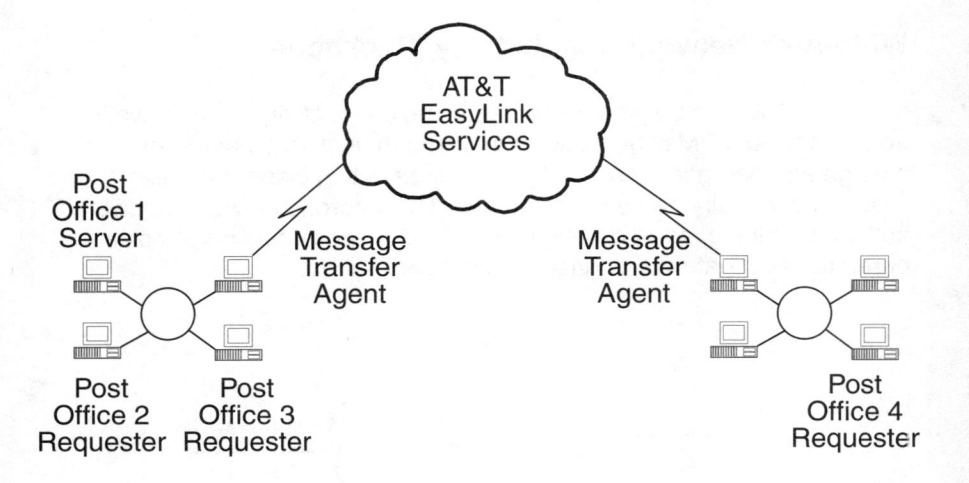

Figure 10-6 **Microsoft Mail Transient Connections** Post offices can connect, using AT&T Mail, for applications such as directory synchronization.

dates of any MS Mail address lists, including gateway lists and global address lists. The AT&T Mail network is a cost-effective communications link for directory synchronization across globally distributed LANs.

The addressing scheme to and from AT&T Mail conforms to the MS Mail LAN addressing scheme. The addressing uses a three-level addressing scheme:

< Network > / < Postoffice > / < Mailbox >

An MS Mail user is addressed through AT&T Mail as follows:

<Msmailgate> ! <Network> ! <Postoffice> ! <Mailbox>

Each address component may be a maximum of 10 characters.

AT&T Mail Connectivity

An AT&T Mail user is addressed through MS Mail either by identifying the user name from the address lists maintained by the MS Mail user or administrator or by using the SMTP (freeform) template to add the address.

ON-Technology Corporation's A-GATE Software

ON-Technology Corporation (formerly Noteworks Corporation), with AT&T EasyLink Services support, has designed an MHS-compliant AT&T Mail gateway product. Leading LAN email packages can connect to AT&T Mail using A-GATE. Some LAN email packages supported include

- cc:Mail
- Lotus Notes
- DaVinci E-Mail
- Noteworks Electronic Mail
- Banyan VINES Mail
- GroupWise 4.1
- Express-it!
- Coordinator

ON-Technology gateways are available in three versions. These are A-GATE for MHS, A-GATE for cc:Mail, and A-GATE for Noteworks Electronic Mail. Novell's MHS (V1.5) is bundled with A-GATE for MHS to simplify connecting to AT&T Mail.

LAN users connected through A-GATE have the off-LAN reach and delivery options available to AT&T Mail users, including email, telex, fax, X.400, U.S. Postal Service, and courier. A-GATE supports binary file transfer, multi-file attachments, and multiple addressing.

A-GATE software is installed on a gateway PC by the LAN system administrator. After the A-GATE gateway is set up and registered, LAN clients can send and receive messages using AT&T Mail through their existing, familiar user interface. Client software and LAN mail operations are unchanged by the gateway. The A-GATE gateway does not modify or change any of the local messaging capabilities but extends the messaging capabilities of the users to remote, mobile, and business partners, allowing communication using all the store-and-forward AT&T Mail delivery options to reach anyone on a connected VAN, LAN, UNIX, mini, or host email system as well as through paper and telex. The A-GATE software versions are:

A-GATE MHS/AT&T Mail Gateway	This gateway uses Novell MHS V1.5 to connect LAN-based email systems to AT&T Mail. This package provides connectivity for LAN email packages such as DaVinci Mail, WordPerfect, Notework, Lotus Notes, and Coordinator. The A-GATE MHS/AT&T Mail gateway connects to AT&T Mail once during each MHS cycle to send and receive AT&T Mail messages.
A-GATE for cc:Mail Users	This gateway allows Lotus cc:Mail LAN users to connect to AT&T Mail. Lotus Notes users require the A-GATE for MHS version.
A-GATE for Notework	This gateway allows Noteworks Electronic Mail users to connect directly to AT&T Mail without MHS installation.

The gateway to AT&T Mail supports all store-and-forward AT&T Mail features. End users do not have access to any AT&T Mail interactive services using this LAN-based gateway and are not issued individual AT&T Mail IDs unless they are personally registered with AT&T Mail. The server is registered with the AT&T Mail network, and the system administrator assigns user IDs to the local clients.

LANs can be interconnected using transient connections to the AT&T Mail network for mail and mail-enabled application exchange and operation. This approach lowers hardware, software, training, administrative, and maintenance costs when compared to direct gateway connections between LANs.

Addressing Scheme	The addressing scheme is dependent upon the LAN messaging application. A-GATE software provides gateway functionality without modifying the existing address scheme.

AT&T Mail Connectivity 233

Addressing/ Message Delivery Support	The A-GATE software does not make any changes to the LAN messaging application end-user interface or functionality. For this reason, there may be differences in the addressing capabilities of the gateway and of the AT&T Mail services. Examples of limitations include support for "BCC," receipts, and project codes.
Design Restrictions	The AT&T Mail gateway was designed to maintain unaltered LAN email operation and does not affect LAN email features, user interface, and functionality. For this reason, some AT&T Mail features are not available using A-GATE gateways.

Many LAN users will consider AT&T Mail as the store-and-forward messaging service to connect multiple LANs and off-LAN users such as business partners and mobile users. In many cases, the use of AT&T Mail is preferred for the following reasons:

- Access through AT&T Mail makes better use of ports and LAN resources. Costs and port requirements are lower.
- AT&T Mail acts as a security firewall or barrier, protecting the LAN and simplifying security.
- Long distance and international phone charges are reduced or eliminated if both sides use the 800 number service.
- All AT&T Mail delivery options, such as fax, X.400, Internet mail, telex, and paper-based options, are available to remote and stand-alone users.
- Support of wireless users is technically simpler and more cost-effective than trying to develop services in-house, with end-user support provided by AT&T Mail customer service 24 hours per day, 7 days per week worldwide.

StarGROUP Services for MS MAIL

AT&T Global Information Solutions' Software Products Division (SPD) offers value-added enterprise messaging solutions that leverage the combined communications strengths of AT&T and AT&T Global Information Solutions to provide customers with the hardware and software products for integrated premises-based multimedia messaging systems. AT&T Global Informations Solutions was formerly NCR.

AT&T Global Information Solutions provides products for two distinct user classes:

- Enterprise messaging
- Personal productivity messaging

Enterprise messaging is targeted at centralized business operations with messaging requirements using X.400 and X.500 backbones. These environments often include multiple replicated sites, such as banking or retail, and highly structured communications. StarPRO Enterprise Messaging addresses these environments.

Personal productivity messaging targets individual messaging as a productivity tool. Server-based communications are common in this environment class.

StarGROUP Gateway for Microsoft Mail integrates the functionality of Microsoft Mail with UNIX SMTP and UUCP on StarGROUP LAN Manager, and provides messaging support for the personal productivity market. Customers with the StarGROUP Gateway for Microsoft Mail product will be able to upgrade to the StarPRO (X.400, X.500) Enterprise Messaging features when full MAPI support is available. AT&T Global Information Solutions' Software Products Division (SPD) provides StarGROUP Services for Microsoft Mail.

This software allows customers using the StarGROUP LAN Manager operating system to use Microsoft Mail for messaging using StarGROUP clients and UNIX clients. It also enables connectivity to AT&T Mail. The StarGROUP LAN Manager operating system is AT&T Global Information

AT&T Mail Connectivity 235

Solutions' UNIX version of Microsoft's LAN Manager operating system. StarGROUP Services for Microsoft Mail is based on Microsoft's SMTP gateway and provides both LAN messaging and AT&T Mail connectivity using the Microsoft Mail client interface. However, Microsoft Mail Remote for Windows is not supported in this environment.

StarGROUP Services for Microsoft Mail is composed of a core product. The core product, StarGROUP Gateway for Microsoft Mail, combines Microsoft Mail with UNIX SMTP and UUCP under StarGROUP LAN Manager. The StarGROUP Gateway for Microsoft Mail is responsible for performing the following functions:

- Translation of messages from Microsoft Mail format to SMTP message format.
- Transport of messages between the gateway and AT&T Mail or any other UNIX SMTP and/or UUCP subsystem.
- Configuration of multiple SMTP gateway post offices. The StarGROUP server post office is a gateway post office supporting downstream post offices without change.

The Microsoft Post Office (MSPO) is made up of shared file server files used to store email messages. Mail manipulation procedures and processes are stored on the post offices as executables which send or receive messages from AT&T Mail over an SMTP network. The standard Microsoft Mail configuration permits multiple post offices on the same server.

Microsoft Mail clients are connected to the post offices as virtual drives accessed over the LAN. DOS and Windows clients can connect to the same StarGROUP server post offices. User programs include the following functions:

- Receive, read, write, attach files to, and send mail messages.
- Create a personal address list for subsequent use in addressing mail messages.
- Create personal folders for filing mail messages.
- Delete, save, and manage received and filed mail messages.

The administrator programs provide the following functionality:

- Add/remove users from the local post offices and define user privileges.
- Specify and configure external post offices/gateway communication, track inter-post offices communication costs, and constrain inter-post office periods.
- Track post offices' disk storage consumption, both total and per user, and delete old mail messages to recover disk space.
- Configure the post offices to participate in automatic directory synchronization.

StarGROUP Services for Microsoft Mail integrates Microsoft Mail functionality with UNIX SMTP and UUCP for StarGROUP LAN Manager running on a multi-threaded UNIX server. This gateway was created to operate in the UNIX LAN environment and communicate with AT&T Mail. StarGROUP Services for Microsoft Mail has several advantages when compared to Microsoft's DOS server SMTP gateway

StarGROUP gateway for Microsoft Mail eliminates the need for dedicated gateway computers required by the DOS-based Microsoft Mail to SMTP gateway. The StarGROUP gateway provides all functions running on a more reliable and scalable multi-threaded UNIX platform with StarGROUP LAN Manager for UNIX. StarGROUP network clients can use AT&T Mail when the system administrator registers the server with the AT&T Mail network. Users may then take advantage of all the AT&T Mail delivery options.

StarGROUP Gateway for Microsoft Mail provides binary compatibility with Microsoft Mail text message exchange for existing PMX/StarMAIL installations. The StarGROUP PMX to Microsoft Mail Migration Utility allows exchange of binary attachments for compatibility between the two environments.

StarGROUP Gateway for Microsoft Mail is scalable as to the number of email users. Customers are not restricted to a single gateway MSPO (Microsoft Post Office). Up to four MSPOs, each supporting up to 500 users, can be configured on the StarGROUP LAN Manager server. Multiple UNIX systems can communicate via UUCP.

AT&T Mail Connectivity

The StarGROUP server for NetWare clients allows workstations running either Microsoft LAN Manager or Novell NetWware to access a common Microsoft Mail to UNIX gateway.

StarGROUP Gateway for Microsoft Mail

The gateway to AT&T Mail supports all store-and-forward AT&T Mail features, but not interactive ones. End users do not have access to any AT&T Mail interactive services using this LAN-based gateway and are not issued individual AT&T Mail IDs unless they are personally registered with AT&T Mail. The server is registered with the AT&T Mail network, and the system administrator assigns user IDs to the gateway clients.

LANs can be interconnected using transient connections to the AT&T Mail network for mail and mail-enabled application exchange and operation. This approach lowers hardware, software, training, administrative, and maintenance costs when compared to direct gateway connections between LANs.

Many LAN users will consider AT&T Mail as the store-and-forward messaging service to connect multiple LANs and off-LAN users such as business partners and mobile users. In many cases, the use of AT&T Mail is preferred for the following reasons:

- Access through AT&T Mail makes better use of ports and LAN resources. Costs and port requirements are lower.
- AT&T Mail acts as a security firewall or barrier, protecting the LAN and simplifying security.
- Long distance and international phone charges are reduced.
- All AT&T Mail delivery options, such as fax, X.400, telex, and paper-based options, are available to remote and stand-alone users.
- Support of wireless users is technically simpler and more cost-effective than trying to develop services in-house, with end-user support provided by AT&T Mail customer service 24 hours per day, 7 days per week worldwide.

After the system administrator has registered the gateway server with AT&T Mail and completed initial administration of the gateway, the MS

Mail LAN users can send messages using all AT&T Mail delivery options, including the sending and receipt of binary and OLE files through the AT&T Mail network. The gateway supports the store-and-forward AT&T Mail delivery options, including

- Fax delivery
- X.400 delivery
- Internet mail transfer
- Telex
- Paper delivery

StarGROUP Services for Microsoft Mail is sold internationally by Global Information Solutions. Registration of the LAN with AT&T Mail is through AT&T EasyLink Services.

InstantCom//MS for LAN

InstantCom//MS software has been developed by Instant Information Inc. with full participation by AT&T EasyLink Services. This product is available for domestic and international sale. InstantCom//MS offers full support of all AT&T Mail message types, including email, fax, and telex. In addition, there is an optional Bank Testkey Interface Module fully integrated with Leeson Howe Associates' Telextester software to support the "testing" of both sent and received messages. This feature is used in telex financial transactions.

InstantCom//MS for LAN supports up to 999 users and includes the InstantCom//CS (Communications Server) software, which can control a "LAN modem pool." Using X.PC, each modem can support up to four simultaneous AT&T Mail service sessions. The InstantCom//IS module is also bundled with the software to allow the package to function as a MHS gateway to AT&T Mail. This module will work with email applications that support MHS, such as DaVinci, Noteworks, cc:Mail, and Microsoft Mail. InstantCom//MS also comes in a stand-alone PC version.

AT&T Mail Connectivity

InstantCom//MS software is messaging software that provides customers with the ability to send and receive mail using AT&T EasyLink Services. This software is available in both stand-alone and LAN versions and comes with server and user agent (client) software. InstantCom//MS was developed to support the AT&T EasyLink Services Telex group's interactive telex requirements. It provides AT&T Mail connectivity and is a full-featured LAN or stand-alone PC solution for AT&T Mail users. The current version of InstantCom//MS also serves as a gateway for any MHS messaging application.

InstantCom//MS offers full support for AT&T Mail delivery options, including email, fax, and telex, and

- Binary file transfer
- Full-featured word processor
- Full telex support
- AT&T EasyLink Services Virtual Telex
- On-line conversation
- Store and forward
- Address books
- Forms module
- X.400 message delivery
- EDI file transfer
- Optional encryption and file compression
- Inbound and outbound message
- Private and public subject files
- Internal email between network users
- Password security
- Archiving, printing, and journaling of all sent and received messages
- Background communications
- Parallel and serial printer support

- Programming interface for integration with other applications
- Optional interface module to Leeson Howe Associates Telextester software

LAN Email Interface Considerations

Clients do not have direct access to AT&T Mail from most LAN email packages registered with AT&T Mail. The email server is registered with the AT&T Mail network, and all clients receive a user ID defined by the system administrator. The limitation exists because the end users do not have a separate ID on AT&T Mail. They also do not have the ability to access AT&T Mail services directly, as the email gateway acts as a store-and-forward post office, forwarding email to and from AT&T Mail. End users do not have integrated access to any of the on-line capabilities of AT&T Mail. Therefore, gateway users cannot access on-line information services such as FYI or the AT&T Mail on-line directory unless they are individually registered with AT&T Mail and use a terminal emulation program.

Midrange Systems

Midrange systems are defined as non-UNIX computers whose capabilities fall between those of mainframes and desktop PCs. AT&T EasyLink Services gateway software includes OfficeAccess for DEC VAX and OfficeAccess for IBM AS/400.

AT&T EasyLink Services offers electronic mail gateway software for the midrange DEC VAX computer environment. OfficeAccess extends the functionality and reach of DEC VAX email beyond the network to anyone, anywhere, at any time. Messages may be sent globally, using any of the AT&T Mail delivery options from a VAX workstation in the same manner in which messages are sent over VMS Mail or through All-in-1 systems.

OfficeAccess is a true gateway that allows messages to be transferred between DEC VMS systems and the AT&T EasyLink Services mail network. Messages are sent and received directly by individual VMS Mail or

AT&T Mail Connectivity

DEC All-in-1 system users in the same manner used for internal mail messaging.

The OfficeAccess and VMS Mail combination provides major additional messaging capabilities without requiring that users learn any special or new procedures. Message delivery options include electronic mail, X.400, telex, fax, and paper. These additional options are accessed using standard VMS Mail and All-in-1 screens and commands.

Off-network recipients' names are added to the VMS Mail directory to simplify external message addressing. Incoming messages are delivered immediately and directly to the user over VMS Mail.

OfficeAccess implementations for DEC VAX support the following:

- Senders' personal names, as defined in the VMS Mail utility, will be automatically incorporated into the outgoing message.
- Multipart messages are subdivided into submessages, and the user will receive each of these messages as a separate message.
- The VMS Mail and All-in-1 CC: feature is supported by OfficeAccess.

OfficeAccess is fully integrated into VMS Mail and follows standard VMS conventions for storage into folders of new mail and sent, accepted, rejected, and received messages. OfficeAccess also provides additional message management features including the following:

- Log files provide a record of every communication session. In case of transmission failure, the system manager is immediately notified.
- A billing and project code feature is available to track specific usage either by defined defaults or on a per message basis.

AT&T EasyLink Services provides the enterprise with secure communications off its private network. OfficeAccess software also provides additional security options controlled by the system administrator, such as

- Limiting users to those who should have access to OfficeAccess and AT&T EasyLink Services
- Designating specific users who may either receive-only or send over the network

- Preventing end users from accessing one another's files

OfficeAccess has been developed for networked VAX clusters. A system can be designated as a hub (VAX node) for communications while remote systems retain control of users, messages, and administration. OfficeAccess provides remote systems with automatic message formatting for AT&T EasyLink Services through the hub system. Incoming messages and disposition notices are automatically routed to the remote system and appropriate users. This OfficeAccess feature reduces telecommunications and software costs by taking advantage of networked VAX clusters.

OfficeAccess for IBM AS/400

OfficeAccess for IBM AS/400 systems is an applications program which provides connectivity between an IBM minicomputer and AT&T Mail messaging services. OfficeAccess is tightly integrated with the AS/400 system, allowing network users to send and receive messages using AT&T Mail store-and-forward services. Office Access seamlessly supports both IBM AS/400 Office users and non-Office users. Sending and receiving email or telex or sending fax messages is accomplished using standard IBM directory entries, screens, functions, and menus.

OfficeAccess for IBM AS/400 Release 2.0 is an applications program developed for AT&T EasyLink Services to connect the AS/400 system to the AT&T Mail service and provide messaging to anyone, anywhere, at any time. Users on the AS/400 can exchange messages easily with any other user system linked with AT&T Mail. OfficeAccess offers versions supporting systems equipped with IBM's office automation software package with or without Office Vision/400.

The messaging process using AT&T Mail is the same as sending and receiving messages from other AS/400 users. OfficeAccess lets users of an AS/400 workstation send to those business partners or co-workers who may be linked to the same IBM network. OfficeAccess connects users to AT&T Mail, and they then can send mail to almost anyone, anywhere in the world. Users can send an email, fax an order, telex a confirmation, and send paper copies by postal delivery.

AT&T Mail Connectivity

OfficeAccess can transparently support IBM OfficeVision/400 users by running in the background of the existing office mail. Integration of OfficeAccess and the IBM AS/400 system provides users with a wide range of messaging capabilities. OfficeAccess provides its own user interface consistent with IBM AS/400 standards for those IBM AS/400 users who have not implemented OfficeVision.

The messaging screens are familiar to OfficeVision users, and users need only learn simple AT&T Mail addressing to extend the reach and scope of recipients from only local users to anyone reachable by AT&T EasyLink Services' robust set of worldwide delivery options, making messaging outside of the internal network as easy as sending a message to a neighbor's desktop on the local mail system. This seamless connectivity extends to most common LANs, mainframes, other midrange and UNIX systems, DOS PCs, or Apple Macintoshes.

The software automatically dials into the AT&T EasyLink Services network for mail transfer at specified intervals, using the auto-dialer and scheduler to make the entire system self-managing. Message queues permit the tracking of all incoming and outgoing messages. Log files provide a constant update of network status. The system administrator is immediately alerted about transmission problems. Message status reports track delivery or non-delivery of all messages. Delivery notices are automatically appended to each message.

Some OfficeAccess implementations include a single gateway, user agent, and communications module for both Office and non-Office environments. This provides a common look and feel for both IBM Office and non-Office versions. Common screens and user and administration guides are used for both Office and non-Office users and administrators. Some OfficeAccess features include

- Binary file transfer support is provided for PC Support users.
- Extensions to the Database API are provided for EDI capabilities.
- Users can use the existing OS/400 directory or create custom personal directories.
- Inbound messages received from AT&T EasyLink Services are routed directly to users by using the "To:" field information.

- From line information is used for the reply feature.
- Office and non-Office users can use the same OS/400 system directory for storing addresses, including X.400 recipients.
- The delivery notification option will notify the sender that the message has been placed in the receiver's message queue.
- Ability to mail-enable existing applications.

In addition, some implementations can support the following:

- Binary file transfer is supported for PC Support users.
- Applications can be interfaced to EDI systems.

AT&T EasyLink Services' field Technical Support Specialists are trained in the IBM Office environment and can provide field support during implementation or upgrades. Call-in support to the Customer Service and Support Center is also available.

Mainframes

Mainframes are considered to be IBM synchronous and compatible computers. Many mainframe computer manufacturers emulate IBM communications, and this is the defacto standard for mainframe computing. This type of connectivity is often essential in any medium to large company for enterprise-wide messaging requirements. Users whose messaging is with either a synchronous or PROFS interface can use the full range of AT&T Mail delivery options, including type of delivery, receipt requested, and COD.

The AT&T Synchronous Gateway, also referred to as the AT&T EasyLink Services Sync FEPS, offers synchronous mainframe users the speed and convenience of direct host access to the AT&T Mail, AT&T EDI, fax, telex, X.400, and paper delivery functions. With the AT&T Synchronous Gateway, messages can be exchanged between registered mainframes using the AT&T Mail service as the transport.

The AT&T Synchronous Gateway supports communications with mainframes supporting 3780 Binary Synchronous Communications (BSC),

AT&T Mail Connectivity

3770 Systems Network Architecture (SNA), Remote Job Entry (RJE) workstations, and the LU6.2 (SNA) protocol. The gateway enables users to take advantage of the AT&T Mail service and AT&T EDI service by emulating the functions of a 3780 or 3770 RJE workstation. AT&T Mail supports LU6.2 connectivity using the XCOM6.2 transaction program.

The AT&T Synchronous Gateway is compatible with many mainframe communications systems without additional software. A simple header providing network address information is required to exchange email messages with the AT&T Mail service. AT&T EasyLink Services offers a 3780 dialer utility for JES hosts without such dialing capability. Users have two port type choices, which are

Shared Ports	A shared port is an entry channel that may be shared by many customers. Only dial access is supported on shared ports. Shared ports are recommended if only low-volume message traffic is expected. Appropriate speeds up to 9,600 bps are allowed.
Dedicated Ports	A dedicated port is an entry channel reserved for just that user or application. It is for high-volume message traffic. The port can be associated with either a dial-up or a private line facility. Speeds may range up to 56,000 bps.

The synchronous communication characteristics supported include

Protocol	Workstation emulation — 3780 BSC/RJE, 3770 SNA protocol supported by emulating the IBM 3776 or IBM 3777 model 3 and 4 workstations. LU6.2 using the Spectrum Concept product. XCOM6.2 supporting AS/400 and MVS IBM systems.
Speeds	4800 bps, 9600 bps, and 56 kbps.
Modems (standard)	4800 bps — 801/208 modems. 9600 bps — 2296A modem or V.32 compatible. 56 kbps — AT&T Paradyne 2656 dial-in. 56 kbps — AT&T Paradyne 3610 DSU dedicated circuit.

Certified modems	AT&T Paradyne.
Dial/Dedicated	Dial and dedicated supported switched 56 kbps (Domestic United States only, 3770 SNA including XCOM LU6.2).

IBM PROFS/DISOSS

The AT&T EasyLink Services PROFS/DISOSS interface provides a transparent communication link between AT&T's EasyLink Services and any users of IBM's PROFS/DISOSS system. This gives PROFS users the capability to communicate to virtually anyone in the world. AT&T EasyLink Services appears as a node on the PROFS network, allowing use of standard PROFS/DISOSS addressing.

AT&T EasyLink Services SNADS

The AT&T EasyLink Services SNADS connection offers a native interface from the IBM Office systems or SNADS network to the AT&T EasyLink Services network. The AT&T EasyLink Services SNADS connection has been developed to allow expansion of the communication capabilities of an IBM network to an off-network environment using the standard IBM SNADS protocol. AT&T EasyLink Services' modern communications technology will allow an IBM system to communicate with dissimilar, incompatible systems without having to worry about protocol conversions. The AT&T EasyLink Services network provides the gateway to AT&T's IBM mainframe processor.

Document Assembler Disassembler

AT&T EasyLink Services has a Document Assembler Disassembler (DAD) interface that communicates with Soft*Switch's Central product using native protocols.

Protocol Format Converter (PFC)

The PFC (Protocol Format Converter) is a set of fully redundant and fault-tolerant Tandem Cyclone computers operating as a front end to AT&T EasyLink Services. The PFC provides customers with the capability to

AT&T Mail Connectivity

access AT&T EasyLink Services using synchronous protocols and/or nonstandard formats. The PFC is designed to provide synchronous access to AT&T EasyLink Services from a customer's computer system and is able to handle a wide variety of protocols, such as 2780, 3780, and 3270 Bisync and 3270, 3770, 3776, and 3284 SNA, as well as a number of custom protocols. A computer system using one of these protocols can be connected through the PFC to AT&T EasyLink Services and from there to the world. Standard AT&T EasyLink Services message formats are preferred, but the PFC is also capable of handling special customer formatting requirements. IATA, 201A SAFE, and a variety of custom formats are currently being handled for customers. The following list shows some of the special protocol and format interfaces available.

- PFC interfaces (dial-up and dedicated)
- 2780/3780 bisynchronous
- 3270 BSC & SNA/SDLC
- 2780/3780 Wang (OIS)
- IATA interface
- 201A Safe

UNIX

The UNIX operating system is used universally and is a popular operating system at the midrange level. UNIX, developed by AT&T in 1969, comes bundled with its own limited internal email system. Several versions are common. These versions include "mail" and "mailx." UNIX is also rich in communications capability, including the UNIX to UNIX COPY (UUCP) program. UNIX computers communicate with one another using UUCP. AT&T EasyLink Services provides UUCP support, and UNIX systems are therefore easily connected to AT&T Mail without additional software.

An enterprise that registers for UNIX Connectivity to AT&T Mail receives an Administrator's and a User's Guide. The administrator's questionnaire requires information such as UNIX machine names, modem information, and UNIX administrator information. The AT&T Mail on-line command

"HELP UNIX", used without a qualifier, displays all connected UNIX systems and should be used with care, as the list contains thousands of systems.

AT&T Mail Gateway400 Service

AT&T Mail Gateway400 Service is AT&T's interface with other systems that have implemented the ITU-T X.400 recommendations for message handling systems (MHS). These recommendations define the standardized protocols and message formats for allowing dissimilar systems to exchange messages. AT&T Mail is a registered and recognized Administration Management Domain (ADMD) and is capable of providing routing and service to other AT&T EasyLink Services users, other host systems, ADMSs and PRMDs, EDI, and the Internet, as well as telex, fax, remote printers, and U.S. postal delivery. AT&T Mail Gateway400 Service provides two basic functions: the message transport function, which provides a general, application-independent, store-and-forward message transfer service, and the translation necessary to move AT&T Mail messages from the AT&T Mail network for delivery to X.400-compliant systems. AT&T Mail Gateway400 handles text messages as well as binary files.

Since the AT&T Mail Gateway400 Service is resident on the AT&T Mail network, all AT&T Mail users can direct messages to the X.400 gateway, including those on PCs, UNIX systems, or other host machines. There is no additional hardware or software required to accomplish X.400 messaging. Installations with X.400 software can register as PRMDs and exchange messages with AT&T EasyLink Services users, as well as users of other systems or networks that are also connected to AT&T Mail. PRMD users can also take advantage of the fax, telex, remote printer, and postal delivery facilities that are available to AT&T Mail users.

PRMDs will access AT&T Mail Gateway400 Service over AT&T's X.25 network, the (APS). Upon receipt of registration information, testing is scheduled with AT&T's X.400 Customer Implementation Group. The tests performed during this period are intended to prepare customers for

AT&T Mail Connectivity 249

movement to the production environment. There is no billing until the customer is completely satisfied and is in production.

AT&T Mail Gateway400 Service supports the Organization Name (O) and Organizational Unit (OU) addressing attributes that allow users to more uniquely identify themselves by registering an Organization Name and up to four Organizational Units with AT&T Mail.

AT&T has a comprehensive X.400 interoperability test program which all vendors must complete prior to commercial availability. The AT&T Mail PRMD Software Vendor (PRMDSV) program provides an X.400 testing environment to ensure interoperability between vendor products and AT&T Mail Gateway400 Service.

Chapter 11

AT&T EDI

EDI is the electronic replacement of paper documents, such as trading or transaction documents, that "trading partners" exchange frequently. Data interchange standards are essential to make EDI work, and industry groups and countries have established dissimilar standards whose use limited EDI development and use. Today, these standards are being consolidated, and the present growth of EDI is based on widely accepted international standards.

AT&T EasyLink Services supports ITU X.400 MHS (Message Handling System) and ASC X12 Mailbag protocol interchange standards for message interchange between networks and provides compatibility with older non-conforming value-added networks (VANs). The network upon which AT&T EDI resides is modeled on ITU MHS X.400 — the internationally accepted standard for messaging, which offers greater security and reliability for message transmissions.

AT&T EasyLink Services supports international EDI message content standards, including EDI for Administration, Commerce, and Transport (EDIFACT), UN/Trade Data Interchange (UN/TDI), GTDI, Odette, Tradacoms, and industry standards approved by the American National Standards Institute (ASC X12) and Transportation Data Coordinating Committee (TDCC) Uniform Commercial Standard (UCS).

AT&T EDI is part of the AT&T EasyLink Services Messaging Network, provided on the AT&T messaging service public value-added store-and-forward network. This strategic decision is based on the conclusion that the future of EDI is with X.400-based networks. The AT&T EasyLink Messaging Network is separate from the AT&T Public Switched Network, which provides voice services such as long distance, 800 number service, and WATS.

The network uses a layered architecture that conforms to the Unified Messaging Architecture (UMA). The core network validates the recipient, transports the message, and either stores the message for retrieval by the recipient's system or starts automatic post-delivery processing. Messaging services are added as server applications on the core store-and-forward network and supply the functions and capabilities to the subscriber. Gateways and interfaces to subscriber systems and public networks are also implemented as server applications.

AT&T is a pioneer in the development of X.400. Its network is modeled on the ITU X.400 standard. It is committed to ongoing support of the X.400 standard — including X.435, the protocol for EDI. In 1993, in partnership with ISOCOR, a California corporation that provides state-of-the-art application solutions for electronic messaging and EDI, AT&T successfully tested the transport of an EDI document using X.435 Relay.

AT&T Unified Messaging Architecture or Message Transfer Architecture (MTA) is a patented, unified messaging network architecture which is a functional superset of ITU's Message Handling System (MHS) X.400 standard. The use of UMA, a superset of the MHS X.400 messaging structure, positions AT&T and its clients for a smooth transition into the international EDI marketplace. In Europe, most EDI VANs are interconnected through MHS X.400, while in the United States, most EDI VAN interconnects are based on older, less reliable, and less secure synchronous technology.

Subscribers connect to the network through dial-up, ACCUNET Packet Service, or private lines. The subscriber's identity is validated by a distributed authorization service. The core store-and-forward network is linked to centralized AT&T EasyLink Services operations, billing, and customer assistance systems that support all network services.

X.400 is based on the concept of inter-personal messaging, or electronic mail, which is modeled after the postal system. The paper mail model is the basis for moving electronic messages over computer networks and includes

Messages	Messages consist of an envelope and its contents.
Mailboxes	Mailboxes are used for the storage of unread mail.
User agents	Processes are invoked by the sender or receiver of mail to initiate or terminate the mail's movement.
Message transfer agents	Processes move the mail from post office to post office.

AT&T EDI is X.400-based, and AT&T recommends use of X.400 network interconnections. AT&T provides non-X.400 (synchronous) network interconnections to other value-added networks to support customer connection requirements.

International EDI Services

AT&T offers in-country support services worldwide, including design and implementation of software, standards support, and network connections. AT&T offers international EDI capabilities that expand domestic EDI applications to trading partners and subsidiaries overseas and provide access to EDI service from over 100 countries through AT&T International ACCUNET Packet Service Network. Connections are available to more than 150 countries and territories throughout the world using AT&T's Worldwide Intelligent Network. AT&T provides EDI interoperation with other EDI networks around the world through X.400 interconnects and synchronous gateways and provides direct EDI messaging services with the United Kingdom, Japan, Canada, Hong Kong, Australia, and Israel.

In the United Kingdom, AT&T EasyLink Services, UK operates EDICT. This fully integrated messaging system is part of the AT&T Global Messaging network. This advanced service automatically performs translations to, from, and between the North American ASC X12 standard, the European GTDI standards, and the UN/EDIFACT and UN/Trade Data Interchange (TDI) standards. EDICT also supports standards compliance checking and provides network security. AT&T EDI is also available in the United Kingdom.

Transaction Types

The types of documents which can be exchanged in an EDI system include but are not limited to

- Invoices
- Purchase orders
- Purchase order acknowledgments
- Shipping notices
- Payments notices
- Credit instructions
- Credit notifications
- Electronic remittances
- Other types of business transactions

Standard data formats allow companies to transmit documents using EDI. Today's typical EDI usage is as follows:

An application data file, such as purchase orders, is processed by EDI translation software to generate industry-standard electronic documents.

A communications module selects these documents and sends them to a value-added network.

AT&T EDI 255

The network reads the address information contained in the transmitted documents, and places each transaction in the proper mailbox.

Gourmet, Inc. Purchase Order

ID99901   Purchase Order

1000 Park Avenue   N01001

New York, NY 1001   Date 10/1/95

To: Worldwide Suppliers   Ship to: Warehouse 19

ID0000   ID00001

123 Main Avenue   Route 17

Keasby NJ 98765   Scottsdale, MN 11332

Figure 11-1 **Paper Purchase Order** The paper purchase order requires extensive manual processing, unlike the EDI equivalent.

The recipient calls the network or is called by the network, picks up all new messages, and, when appropriate, drops off outgoing EDI messages. The recipient, through its EDI translation software, converts the standard-format messages to the recipient's internal format for application program processing.

Purchase Order Example

An example of the flow of EDI information between trading partners is the transmission of a purchase order from subscriber to supplier through the AT&T EDI network.

EDI transactions are sent from one business partner's application system to the other business partner's application system. Before the trading partners can begin exchanging EDI documents, they need to agree on standards, which vary by country and industry. Some U.S. industries, such as automotive, retail, and transportation, use industry standards. Most other U.S. industries use the ASC X12 standards.

An effective EDI implementation effort requires that existing applications, such as purchasing, be integrated with the EDI system to maximize EDI benefits and value. When Company A orders a product from Company B, its purchasing application generates a purchase order and transmits it to the EDI translation system.

This process translates the purchase order data into a standard format such as X12. This translation can be performed on a PC, midrange computer, or mainframe computer running translation software, or less efficiently and at greater cost on a public EDI network offering the service. AT&T does not provide network translation between standards, as customer-premises methods are more efficient and less costly.

```
ISA*00* *00* *ZZ*CUST0MER *ZZ*DEM0
*120195*1555*X*00200*000D000008*0*T*GS*PO*CUS-
TOMER*DEMO*890811*1555*1*X*002001.ST*850*001
.BEG*00*SA*IIIIIIIII*IIIIIIIII**210193**NEW ORDER.NTE*GEN*SPECIAL OR-
DER FOR EDI SHOW.PER*BD*123456789.FOB*DF*ZZ*FACT0RY LESS
10.NI*SE*WORLDWIDE SUPPLIERS* 92*00001.N3*123 MAIN
AVENUEN4*SCOTSDALE*MN*11332.PER*SR*S SELLER.NI*BY*GOUR-
MET SPECIALTIES INC*91*99901.N3*1000 PARK AVENUE.N4*NEW
YORK*NY*10011.PER*BD*B BUYER .NI*ST***WARE-
HOUSE19*92**0001.N3*ROUT17.N4*KEAS-
BEY*NJ*98765.ITD*0I.ZZ*10**30.SHH
*SD*010*121193.SHH*DD*002*121293.TD5*0*ZZ***TRUCK.P01*1*
120*EA*225*WE*VN*0IIII1S *IN*0221119.PID*F*****P0INSETTIAS
SCH*120*EA****002***121593 CTT*I.SE*28*14001.SE*
1*1.IEA*1*000000008.AT&T EDI
```

Figure 11-2 **ASCX12 Purchase Order — 850 EDI Format** This is a rendition of the sample purchase order in EDI format.

AT&T EDI

After the translation, the EDI transaction is submitted to the AT&T EDI network. The EDI transaction contains the mailbox address of Company B, and the AT&T EDI network delivers it to Company B's mailbox. Company B connects to the EDI network periodically and downloads messages to its EDI translation system. At Company B's location, the EDI translation software converts Company A's EDI transaction into a form compatible with Company B's order entry system and transmits it to that system. There are no transit delays or human handling of paper in the process.

EDI Information Flow (Purchase Order)

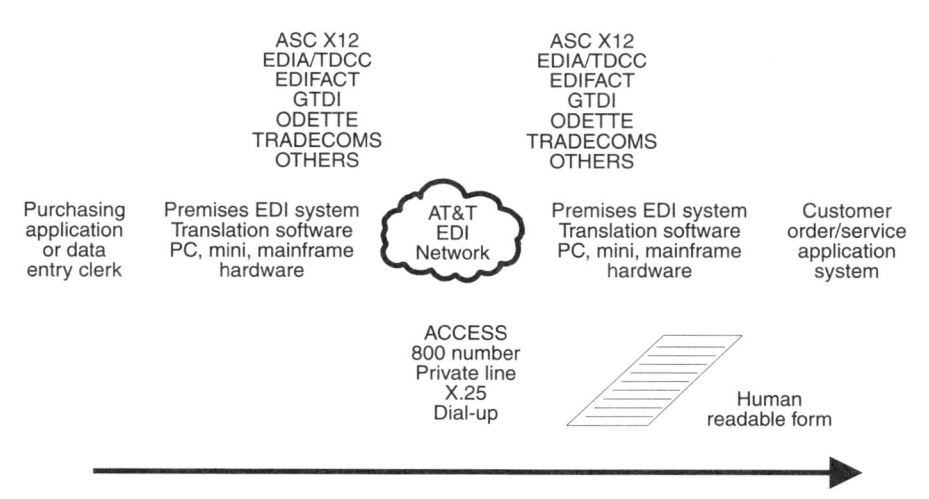

```
                        ASC X12                        ASC X12
                        EDIA/TDCC                      EDIA/TDCC
                        EDIFACT                        EDIFACT
                        GTDI                           GTDI
                        ODETTE                         ODETTE
                        TRADECOMS                      TRADECOMS
                        OTHERS                         OTHERS

Purchasing        Premises EDI system     AT&T    Premises EDI system     Customer
application       Translation software    EDI     Translation software    order/service
or data           PC, mini, mainframe   Network    PC, mini, mainframe    application
entry clerk       hardware                         hardware               system

                                        ACCESS
                                        800 number
                                        Private line
                                        X.25
                                        Dial-up                    Human
                                                                readable form
```

Figure 11-3 **AT&T EDI** AT&T provides a full range of standards-based EDI services supporting all common platforms and human-readable forms.

From Company B's system, a standard EDI functional acknowledgment is generated acknowledging receipt and acceptance of the Company A purchase order. This transaction loop occurs in minutes, not the days or weeks it often takes to exchange paper documents. No human processing is needed, and the timing is independent of distance, countries, or time zones.

Company B also generates shipping documents and transmits the invoice to Company A, decreasing its float on the transaction while providing Company A with more detailed information on the product's shipment status, arrival, and billing. The financial settlement can also be done electronically, eliminating check writing and the related costs.

This is a basic description of EDI document flow using value-added networks. A VAN, such as AT&T EDI, provides the public network and public server functions such as standards-based conversion and transmission. These services connect trading partners who may have incompatible systems and who may subscribe to dissimilar EDI systems. The development and maintenance costs of these shared services are usage-based, and the subscriber benefits from greater reach, lower capital costs, and lower operating costs.

EDI Standards

Document standards are essential for exchanging business documents electronically. EDI standards development began in the 1960s as industry groups began to develop industry-specific EDI standards for purchasing, transportation, and financial applications. Most such standards supported intra-industry trading; others, such as bills of lading and freight invoices, were suitable for cross-industry use. Over time, national and international standards for cross-industry use developed, and today there are hundreds of accepted EDI standards in use.

AT&T EDI supports all of the major EDI standards, including ASC X12, TDCC, UCS, WINS, UN/EDIFACT, and UNG/TMI. ASC X12 is the most widely used standard in North America. The TDCC, UCS, and WINS standards are industry standards that pre-date the X12 standard. X12, which is a national, cross-industry standard, evolved from these three industry standards, and the four of them are similar in syntax. TDCC is used in the transportation industry, UCS is used in the retail and grocery industries, and WINS is used in the warehouse industry. Recently, TDCC, UCS, and WINS were merged into X12.

AT&T EDI

EDIFACT is the international EDI standard that evolved from X12 and the European EDI standard, UNG/TMI. Eventually, X12 will be merged into EDIFACT.

As a global EDI provider, AT&T EasyLink Services supports all accepted EDI industry standards and proprietary standards that are established in the global marketplace. AT&T, as a corporation, is committed to standards, and an AT&T organization is dedicated to data communications and telecommunications standards support. AT&T EasyLink Services staff are active on standards groups worldwide and on the ASC X12 committee. An AT&T executive is on the ASC board of directors.

AT&T EDI Architecture

The AT&T EasyLink Services network uses a common architecture for its current and future services. AT&T EDI, AT&T Mail, and AT&T Enhanced FAX use Message Transfer Architecture. AT&T's intent is to have all AT&T EasyLink Services use a single network interface, a single network account, and a single network session. Many of these capabilities exist today.

The AT&T EDI network provides the reliable features essential for successful EDI implementation. Trading partners all over the world can exchange EDI documents with the benefits of globally distributed processing nodes, support, and sales.

Investment Protection

AT&T EDI supports most common platforms and offers multiple software options to protect existing systems investment. The enterprise's current investment in hardware, software, and systems is protected and leveraged through the wide range of EDI integration options provided.

AT&T EDI interface software modules allow subscribers to use most common translation software and interfaces with the AT&T EDI network.

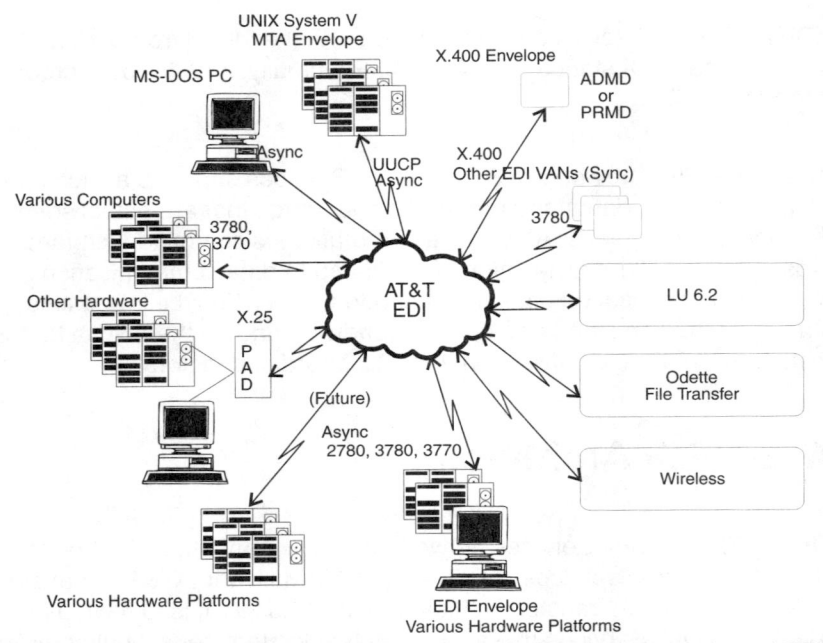

Figure 11-4 **Investment Protection** The combination of standards-based EDI and EDI interfaces to standard platforms and translation software protects existing investments.

These modules are supported and sold by AT&T. AT&T EasyLink Services has agreements with leading EDI software suppliers to provide high-quality EDI translation software for PC and midrange and mainframe computer platforms. The Value-Added Software Supplier and Certification (VASS) programs, in conjunction with translation software companies, provide subscribers with maximum software choice flexibility. Subscribers select software and the software vendor based on their requirements while being assured that these AT&T EDI business partners have been carefully evaluated and selected. The qualification process criteria include product quality, company financial viability, and subscriber support quality. These software packages are the strongest EDI translation packages available with extensive application integration features and are AT&T certified as fully AT&T EDI service integrated.

Under the EDI Software Certification Program, AT&T works with virtually all commercially offered translation software vendors to test and certify their software. AT&T EasyLink Services provides three levels of certifica-

AT&T EDI

tion, beginning with basic connectivity through full EDI and email integration.

International Access

A subscriber has worldwide access to AT&T's EDI service using international packet service. AT&T is connected to over 100 local packet services around the world via AT&T ACCUNET Packet Service, AT&T Istel's INFOTRAC network, and AT&T Jens Jensnet.

Local telephone numbers may be used to either pass through a local access node in the AT&T network or reach a third-party VAN interconnected to AT&T's network. The third-party network then delivers the message to the closest AT&T EasyLink Services network node.

The subscriber can direct dial the closest AT&T EasyLink Services network node via a long distance number. AT&T bills for all AT&T EasyLink Services messaging services, but access charges are billed by the local service provider. High-volume users can establish a private line between their system and the closest AT&T EasyLink Services network node.

Connectivity

AT&T EDI asynchronous support is provided for low- to moderate-volume applications using low- and high-speed asynchronous modems. High-speed modems' error correction and data compression features are supported. Protocols supported include X, Y, and F Modem. AT&T EDI is one of the few EDI VANs supporting UNIX UUCP protocols, a benefit to the downsizing company. The modem standards supported are

Speeds	V.32 (9600); V.32bis (14,400 bps).
Error Correction	V.42; MNP 4.
Data Compression	V.42bis; MNP 5.

Private Line	Private lines support speeds up to 19.2 kbps.
X.25	ACCUNET Packet Service provides the X.25 interface through 9.6-kbps ports using DataKit X.25 interface cards. Each port can support a maximum of 36 virtual calls. X.25 must be used in order to interface to the X.400 gateway available on the network.
Synchronous	Synchronous interfaces are available using U.S. AT&T 800 number service.
Bisynchronous	3780 RJE: 9600 bps.
SNA	3770 RJE: 4800 bps (AT&T 208 modem and compatibles). 9600 bps (AT&T 2296 modem and compatibles). 9.6 kbps dial/private line. 19.2 kbps/56 kbps/private line. 56 kbps switched. SNA LU6.2 provides an efficient, high-throughput data link protocol which is implemented in a wide variety of environments from PCs to midrange computers (AS400) to mainframes (i.e., MVS).
Network Dial-Out	The network can dial out on a timed or message count basis to 3780 RJE (Remote Job Entry) (BSC) and 3770 RJE (SNA) devices to deliver and pick up EDI transactions. A subscriber may want the network to automatically deliver its messages when its mailbox fills to a predetermined level. Other subscribers may want the network to poll for messages at fixed intervals.
Open Mailbox (Public Networking)	This service allows AT&T EDI service subscribers to send or receive transactions from non-subscribers. The AT&T EDI subscriber is billed for send and receive charges plus an off-net surcharge. This feature allows non-subscribers to send or receive transactions to or from AT&T EDI subscribers. An AT&T EDI subscriber sends messages to non-subscriber

AT&T EDI

trading partners through the open mailbox. The network's open mailbox then dials out to the non-subscriber and delivers the message. The non-subscriber can dial into the open mailbox, which delivers the message to the AT&T EDI subscribing trading partner. The AT&T EDI subscriber pays all charges for both sent and received messages.

Large File Transfer — Users with appropriate high-speed connections, 4800 bps or higher, may currently send files up to 10 Mb in size.

Binary File Transfer — AT&T EDI support for binary file transfer supports exchange of CAD/CAM information, databases, spreadsheets, etc., as EDI documents.

VAN Interconnections

AT&T EDI has interconnections to all major value-added networks to allow its subscribers to reach all of their trading partners.

The following is a list of current AT&T EDI VAN synchronous interconnections.

- Advantis (IBM & Sears)
- MCI/BT
- Commerce Network (Ordernet)
- GE Information Services (GEIS)
- GM/EDS
- Harbinger
- Kleinschmidt
- Sprint International
- Transettlements

True X.400 gateways are available for connection to private and public administrative management domains. The movement of EDI over the X.400 gateway to other domains must be negotiated, in advance, between the parties. Some X.400 gateways are

- Telecom Canada (TradeRoute and Envoy 100)
- MCI

ASC X12 Mailbag

Most EDI VANs have not reached a state of X.400 readiness but are planning to support X.400. The X12 Mailbag standard overcomes bisynchronous interconnect problems between all VANs. An example would be one VAN sending a batch of messages to another VAN in a "mailbag" which includes a control number identifier in the mailbag envelope (i.e., the header and trailer pair) and a message count in the mailbag trailer. This count must match the number of messages within the mailbag. When the mailbag arrives at the receiving VAN, an acknowledgment of "safe storage" or rejection, based on a count of messages in the mailbag, is sent to the sending VAN. If the receiving VAN accepts the mailbag, the messages are parsed and sent to the correct mailboxes on the network. A mailbag database on the network keeps track of messages and provides daily reports and real-time alarms for rejections.

EDI Message Enveloping

The AT&T EDI Premises Platform Architecture consists of the hardware and software products set which simplifies AT&T EDI. The architecture supports four hardware platforms which support EDI translations, network connectivity, X.400-like enveloping, and EDI file management.

The EDI translator and the MTA wrapper (enveloping software) are the two key components of each platform. Synchronous, PC, or UNIX system users may, at their option, elect to interface with the network in native EDI protocol, but the PC platform requires a minimal MTA header. The four hardware architectures are

- Mainframe
- Personal computer
- UNIX System V
- IBM System 36/38 and AS/400

Network Interface and Translation Software

The network interface software (UMA or MTA enveloping) provides the messaging structure or X.400-based envelope which contains the addressing information. The translation software converts a data file containing the subscriber's internally formatted business transactions into the EDI standard format.

AT&T EDI network interface software can be purchased as a stand-alone option or as part of the translation software incorporated into some EDI software packages from vendors such as Supply Tech, APL, and EDI, Inc. The network interface modules (NIMs) can also be purchased separately for subscriber integration into an EDI premises system. Two types of premises software are available:

- Network interface software (UMA or MTA enveloping software)
- Translation with network interface modules software

EDI Software Certification Program

The EDI Software Certification Program provides AT&T EDI subscribers with maximum flexibility in translation software package choice. AT&T EDI works with the translation software that subscribers select to suit their operating requirements and is another example of AT&T EasyLink Services' commitment to open systems. The software certification program ensures that software meets the AT&T EDI network service interface requirements and is supported by AT&T's Service and Support

Center. Uncertified translation software is not supported by AT&T's Service and Support Center.

There are three levels of certification:

Connectivity Testing for EDI	Vendor software is certified at level 1 when testing confirms that the software can send and receive AT&T network EDI messages. This testing level is normally used for connectivity software only, and level 1 software is recommended for use with EDI-only mailboxes.
Full Feature Testing for EDI	Vendor software is certified at level 2 when testing confirms that the software can send and receive AT&T network EDI messages, and process network-generated status, notification, and error reports.
Full Feature Testing for EDI and Email Integration	Vendor software is certified at level 3 when testing confirms that the software can send and receive AT&T network EDI messages, process network-generated status, notification, and error reports, and support email integration.

Value-Added Software Supplier Program (VASS)

AT&T has agreements with selected EDI companies to ensure that translation software is made available and supported on PC, mini, and mainframe platforms. These business partners are evaluated and selected based on overall product quality, company financial viability, and support quality. Levels 2 and 3 certified software vendors are eligible for VASS program participation and the vendor's translation software is certified to work on the AT&T EDI network.

UMA Envelopes and EDI Interchange

The UMA header (envelope) is the functional equivalent of an X.400 envelope containing sender and receiver address, date/time stamp, and other audit trail information. The majority of third-party network EDI traffic is processed using EDI interchange envelopes. These envelopes contain information about the sender and the receiver and audit trail tracking numbers. Their role is to provide routing information.

Asynchronous and X.400 subscribers may submit single and multiple interchanges with a minimal MTA envelope using native EDI. The bundles will be delivered as native EDI messages, with each interchange parsed and individually processed. Network interface software is required for protected protocols if subscribers elect interchange wrapping on the premises. This software is available from AT&T or is included in the Value-Added Software Sales program packages.

The process of enveloping an EDI interchange in UMA is one of correlating addressing and copying the EDI audit data. The sender and receiver IDs from the EDI interchange, along with the unique number, are extracted from the EDI envelope and mapped into corresponding fields in the UMA envelope. On the AT&T EDI network, an X.400 envelope is used to wrap and move an EDI interchange envelope. The envelope is then appended to the EDI interchange. This envelope is a header preceding the EDI interchange; there is no UMA trailer. The Interchange Control Number (ICN) of the EDI interchange is placed in an audit field in the UMA. The EDI interchange is not altered. One EDI interchange is wrapped in each UMA envelope. This one-to-one mapping complies with the National Institute of Standards (NIST) recommendations for using X.400 for EDI transport. AT&T EDI supports all market-accepted enveloping standards in addition to some proprietary standards.

The mapping of the sender and receiver IDs may involve an address translation table. For each EDI interchange address, the table contains the corresponding AT&T network ID in a one-to-one fashion. The correct UMA ID for the receiver, as specified in the EDI envelope, is put into the UMA envelope. This address translation occurs during the wrapping process (i.e., sending to the UMA network) only. It is not necessary on the strip side (i.e., receiving from the UMA network), as the EDI interchange is still present to identify both the sender and receiver to the EDI application.

The maintenance of this address translation table varies with the operating environment. There are two general locations where UMA enveloping can occur: on the premises or on the network.

Premises-based Enveloping	Premises-based enveloping of EDI data occurs before the message enters the network and is accomplished by software on the sender's premises. Network interface modules (NIMs) are integrated into EDI translation/communication packages to execute the wrapping and unwrapping function of the UMA X.400 envelope. This follows the overall structure of the X.400 model, extending the benefits directly to the subscriber's premises. On the receiver's side, similar software "strips" away the UMA header, leaving the original EDI interchange as it was before it was "wrapped." This "stripping" is also run on the premises. Premises enveloping is available to subscribers who purchase AT&T EDI NIMs or vendor software packages and is generally more economical.
Network-based Enveloping	Network-based UMA enveloping/stripping is available for asynchronous and synchronous interfaces. In network-based UMA wrapping, the user sends the pure EDI stream, also known as native EDI, and the network begins by building the corresponding MTA (UMA) envelope. The address translation function is performed by means of an Address Translation Table (AXT) maintained by the subscriber through the EDI administrative interface.

One user can choose to envelope wrap and strip on the network while the trading partner can choose to envelope wrap and strip on its premises. The network tracks such differences, and the subscribers need not coordinate their decisions. AT&T EDI also provides full X12 compliance

AT&T EDI

for EDI acknowledgments and delivery notifications. Some network communications interface setup is required. Subscribers who choose the network-based enveloping option incur additional charges.

FreeForm Conversion Service

AT&T EDI offers a network-based human-readable format conversion service for subscribers who may have some trading partners lacking EDI or computer capabilities. Through the FreeForm Conversion Service, an EDI document can be converted and sent to a fax machine, electronic mailbox, or telex to communicate EDI formatted information to a non-automated trading partner.

The FreeForm Conversion Service converts encoded EDI transaction sets into human-readable message formats, extending the benefits of Electronic Data Interchange to key business partners requiring paper-based documents. It is fully compatible with ASC X12, UCS, and EDIA/TDCC standards. It also supports the EDIFACT standard. A typical use would be for a subscriber to generate an EDI ASC X12, 850 purchase order and send it over the AT&T EDI network. The network receives the document, converts the document to human-readable form, and delivers it in the pre-specified manner, i.e., fax, telex, or email. The network sends a Functional Acknowledgment to the subscriber. Special implementation procedures are required to set up the FreeForm Conversion Service. Additional setup and usage charges also exist.

The FreeForm Conversion Service provides maximum flexibility and allows expansion of the trading partner universe to non-automated trading partners or special applications such as advising sales offices or production or inventory departments of orders being sent or status notifications.

Hardware and Software Platforms

Mainframe Platform
: The AT&T EDI mainframe platform for the IBM/MVS/JES operating environment consists of

the AT&T certified mainframe software for EDI translation and the UMA wrapping/unwrapping facility for X.400-like enveloping of EDI messages. Components required for a given configuration may be purchased through AT&T or from a third party. Data typically flow from an application database to the EDI translator. After translation to EDI format, the UMA wrapper places a UMA header on a message and queues it for submission. The dial-out utility is invoked, at user-determined intervals, to establish a session for UMA-wrapped transactions to be delivered to the AT&T EDI service, which delivers them to the recipient.

Personal Computer (LAN and Stand-alone) Platform

The AT&T EDI platform for the personal computer MS-DOS operating environment consists of the certified personal computer software for EDI translation and EDI file management, the optional UMA wrapping/unwrapping facility for X.400-like enveloping of EDI messages, and the background mailing facility for establishing connectivity into the AT&T EDI service.

PC translation software is purchased directly from software vendors. Data typically are entered from the EDI translator, which acts as a business application. After translation to EDI format, the UMA wrapper places a UMA header on a message and queues it for submission. The background mailer utility is invoked, at user-determined intervals, to establish a session between the host and the service for delivery of UMA-wrapped transactions to the AT&T EDI service, which delivers them to the recipients. The inbound process requires the PC to dial in and pick up messages using the background mailer. The PC EDI translator removes the UMA header and translates EDI format data into the format needed for the customer's database system or into human-readable format for end users.

AT&T EDI

PCs may be used as host EDI front ends. Application files are downloaded from the host to the PC. The EDI translator converts these flat files into a standard EDI format and prepares the files for transmission to the AT&T EDI service. The PC also translates messages being received from AT&T EDI to host format. PC translator packages can use "native EDI" submissions which eliminate the EDI translator's MTA enveloping for each submitted EDI interchange. Typical outbound data flow begins with data entry into the PC EDI translator. The data are translated into an EDI format and stored for batch submission to the AT&T EDI network service. At user- or translator-set intervals, the EDI translator software front-ends the EDI batch with MTA envelope header information and submits it to the AT&T EDI Network Service using a file transfer protocol such as XMODEM. On receipt, the AT&T EDI network separates each interchange found and uses the Address Translation Table to determine interchange recipient MTA envelope information. The MTA envelope then transports the interchange to the recipient.

Inbound data flow starts with a message originator, and the data are transported across the AT&T EDI network service, where they are queued for PC delivery.

On downloads, the EDI translator removes the MTA envelope and translates the message content from an EDI format into either a file for the user application system or a human-readable format.

System 36/38 and AS/400 Platforms	The AT&T EDI System 36/38 and AS/400 platforms consist of the certified software for EDI translation and EDI file management and optional built-in UMA wrapping and unwrapping facilities. Typical outbound data flow begins with data from an application database sent to the EDI translator. The data are translated into an EDI

format, and the UMA wrapper places an MTA header on each message and queues them for AT&T EDI network submission. At intervals, a 3780 dial-out utility establishes a session between the host and the AT&T EDI service where messages wrapped in MTA are submitted and delivered to the recipients.

Inbound data flow begins with a message originator, and the data are transmitted across the AT&T EDI network, where the data are queued for recipient host delivery. A 3780 dialer is invoked, and messages are delivered to the recipient host. On downloads, the UMA unwrapper removes the UMA header, writes status information to the appropriate log files in the UMA wrapper module, and passes the EDI data to the EDI translator. The message content is converted from the EDI format into a file for the user application system.

Messages submitted in native mode are network wrapped. If a non-MTA interface is used, then an MTA header is not used. AT&T uses administrative files to associate recipient names and addresses with the EDI address information found in the EDI interchanges. These files are maintained online within the AT&T network and are accessed through an asynchronous administrative login.

UNIX Platform

The AT&T EDI UNIX System V/386 and System V/3B2 platform consists of the certified UNIX system software that performs EDI translation and EDI data management and the AT&T EDI network interface module/UNIX (NIM/UNIX) software that performs MTA wrapping/unwrapping of EDI interchanges and management of network notifications.

The UNIX operating system's subsystem UNIX-to-UNIX Copy Program (UUCP) transports messages to the AT&T EDI service. Certified

UNIX translation software, purchased from a software vendor, is integrated with AT&T's NIM/UNIX software, which can also be used via the UNIX command-line prompt. The AT&T software uses UNIX Basic Network Utilities to send and retrieve messages.

Typical outbound data flow begins with data from an application database being sent to the EDI translator. An application file (in flat file format) is passed to a UNIX EDI translator for EDI translation. The business application process may be co-located on the same UNIX processor as the EDI translator, or on a different platform. In the second case, the application file is downloaded to the UNIX platform with the EDI translator.

A user application may alternatively create an EDI format file. The EDI translator or end user uses the AT&T EDI NIM/UNIX-provided utility to wrap the message in an MTA envelope and place the message into an "outbound" queue. At intervals, another NIM/UNIX utility submits queued messages to the UNIX UUCP subsystem, which establishes a network session with the AT&T EDI network service.

Inbound data flow begins with a message originator, and the data are transmitted across the AT&T EDI network, where they are placed in the recipient's UNIX gateway network mailbox. The network may "call" the recipient's computer, or wait until the computer initiates a communication session. The choice is determined on account setup. AT&T EDI messages move to the recipient's UNIX platform through UUCP. Software instructs Enhanced UNIX Mail (EUM) to identify EDI messages and then use a NIM/UNIX utility which removes the MTA envelope and places the file in an inbound queue. EDI status reports or notifications are appended to a global UNIX system EDI log file.

An alternative approach is native or non-MTA submission. In that case, UNIX native EDI translation software is purchased from a third party. Native EDI submission uses UNIX mail capabilities. In the native mode, the user must administer the Address Translation Table (AXT) and create entries that map EDI address information contained in the interchange to an AT&T EDI network address prior to submitting EDI interchanges without an MTA envelope.

Online Administration

The online administrative interface gives subscribers the ability to manage their own account. Through this interface, such functions as adding or updating trading partner information, message screening, split billing, logging, tracking, and reporting can be easily administered by the user. Users can administer their personal profile through this interface, which is basically the same for AT&T Mail, AT&T EDI, and AT&T Enhanced FAX. With the online administrative interface, users can have direct control of their account activities. There is no need to log off AT&T Mail to go into a separate EDI account to administer EDI activities. The Profile command is common across all services and allows users to set up their own profile.

The Administer command is unique for EDI users. This command allows users to manage adding, changing, or modifying their trading partner listings. In the Options table, users can define split billing parameters and administer screening of messages. The administrative interface is designed for asynchronous access and is available to non-X.400 and X.400 users. The administrative interface is primarily intended for setup/initiation operation. The interface is normally used only for changes, such as adding a trading partner or changing a split bill percentage. A need to track message movement through log review may require frequent administrative interface operations. All tracking and reporting can be administered through administrative logging. Users can administer their account anytime as needed to add trading partners, or make changes to their account without waiting for someone else to update it. Some administrative functions are:

Re-queue	This function allows the user to download retained messages and transactions again.
Message Screening	This function allows a subscriber, on a trading-partner-by-trading-partner and transaction-by-transaction basis, to set a network flag that controls traffic from that trading partner. Message screening can be positive or negative and accept or reject messages from a specific trading partner. This feature allows users to reject messages from unauthorized or incorrect trading partners. The appropriate flag can be set online by the subscriber or by request to AT&T Customer Service and Support.
Directory Services	There is a common directory for all services, including AT&T Mail, AT&T Enhanced FAX, and AT&T EDI. The directory provides easy access to information on users of all its services.
Profile	From the administrative interface, users have easy access to review their current profile and make changes on the spot. Users can administer a variety of values, such as the number of days to retain messages, and, for added security, users can set a secondary password.
Selective Download	The Selective Download feature allows synchronous users to receive messages sorted in categories specified at the time of registration. Documents such as purchase orders, ship notices, and invoices can be sorted and prioritized for delivery as required. This feature allows users to prioritize and manage messages they receive. With Selective Download, messages are sorted into categories, and users can download only the

messages they want to receive at a given time. Form types can be ordered by priority, and a list of messages in form type requested; and documents that are most critical to users' business can be downloaded frequently. Purchase orders may be scheduled for downloading several times during the day, while invoices are scheduled for downloading daily or weekly. A threshold may be set by message category to trigger downloading when the mailbox level is reached.

Selective Download allows subscribers to prioritize the downloading of their EDI messages according to their specific needs. Messages can be sorted based on sender, type of content (binary or text), EDI document type (P.O., Invoice, Ship Notice), or any other MTA header element. Currently, EDICT users (both PC and host) use Selective Download to sort their EDI documents by type (i.e., purchase order, invoice, etc.). The messages then arrive on the subscriber's system sorted into files containing a single EDI document type.

Audit Trails

The need to maintain audit trails is as critical in the electronic environment as it was with paper-based processes. AT&T EDI provides a substantial electronic document logging and tracking system. Detailed information about every message a user sends and receives is posted in the user's network log and is available to the user, who may monitor and track message network progress.

AT&T provides customers with multiple tracking and reporting capabilities to create a detailed record of the progress of their messages.

AT&T EDI

Companies using EDI must maintain an audit trail of their electronic documents, just as they did in their previous paper-based environment. AT&T EDI provides a strong EDI document audit trail. The user's network log compiles detailed information about every message sent or received. Access to the log through the administrative interface allows selection from various tracking and reporting options. Message tracking can be on demand or by scheduled adaptable reports defined by the user through the administrative interface. Reports can be specified in either machine- or human-readable format.

EDI Reports, human- or machine-readable, are available to users on demand or scheduled by users using the administrative interface. The reports can be full or exception. The full report displays each message sent or received during a given time range. Exception reports show information on messages with errors or still pending. Users can define 10 different reports. The reports can be sent to an AT&T Mail ID or a list of mail IDs, fax machines, or printers. Information about messages users send and receive are tracked across the network and placed in their user log. Information logged includes trading partner IDs, interchange numbers, and date and time stamps that allow users to know the progress of their messages. Users can get online, machine-readable, and human-readable reports, all providing a valuable audit trail of business documents.

Message tracking can be in the form of daily reports, online queries, or premises-based reports. The user can direct the network to automatically generate a report each night that summarizes the network activity for that day. These reports contain data extracted from the EDI interchanges to assist in tracking. In addition, time stamps are provided for each interchange indicating the date/time submitted, delivered, and picked up. The user can access logged information by performing an online query at any time through the online administrative interface. Once the logging feature is enabled by the user, the network begins to compile information about every message a user sends and receives. This record is available to the user to monitor and track the progress of messages through the network for ten days. Once a logged entry exceeds the interval, it is automatically deleted from the log.

Notifications are generated by the network and are returned to the user's electronic mailbox in the form of an electronic mail message. A notification must be requested by the user. There are two types of notifications:

- Delivery Notification indicates if a message was delivered to the recipient's mailbox.
- EDI Notification indicates if a message was picked up by the recipient. Currently, when a user on the AT&T network sends a message to a trading partner on another network, the AT&T user will receive notice only that the message was delivered to the trading partner's network. With the implementation of ASC X12 Mailbag standards, the synchronous gateway provides a control structure and an audit mechanism to facilitate the exchange of EDI data between interconnected users. When messages are sent to an EDI VAN or a user, the VAN or user will return an acknowledgment to indicate whether or not the "sent" mailbag has been "safe stored."

X12 Mailbag/TA3 Acknowledgment

AT&T supports the X12 Mailbag standard, which allows EDI value-added networks to exchange EDI messages using this standard. It facilitates the movement of EDI documents over differing networks. Recently announced support for the standard TA3 Acknowledgment provides greatly improved tracking across cooperating networks that support TA3 Acknowledgment. An audit trail of messages sent to and received from those trading partners on cooperating TA3 networks is available.

Security

AT&T EDI provides encryption support for the protection of EDI system electronic information. Security is also provided through login IDs and passwords and secondary passwords.

Pricing

Pricing is based on usage without hidden costs or embedded support fees. List, or published usage, prices for EDI network service are simpler than for other EDI VANs, allowing subscribers to easily plan their budgets. AT&T EDI pricing is based on the message's character count, allowing subscribers to project costs by volume.

An example would be if a trading partner were to send twenty purchase orders to another trading partner on the AT&T EDI network in twenty separate envelopes. Users can clearly see the savings when the trading partner sends all twenty 631-character purchase orders in one envelope.

The examples are based on the sender paying to send and the receiver paying to receive if both trading partners are on the AT&T EDI network. If the sender's trading partner is on another VAN, the receiver will pay whatever that VAN charges. The AT&T subscriber will pay the default 50 percent send and receive charge plus the $0.00010 off-net surcharge. Interconnects are one of the off-net activities. The off-net surcharge applies to non-subscribers or for dialout delivery. Most major networks have similar off-network surcharges, which may be hidden in standard pricing.

Billing

AT&T EDI offers subscribers two types of billing reports. The summary reports, which all subscribers receive, provide an itemized list of all messages — similar to a telephone bill summary of calls. The subscriber receives a sender summary and a receiver summary. In this report, all usage elements associated with a message are summarized together. The optional detailed billing reports provide users with detailed information on all messages sent to and received from each trading partner. Usage element charges are individually identified for each trading partner. With their monthly invoice, users will automatically receive a summary of their EDI transactions by trading partner. Users can also request detailed billing reports that itemize billing information, trading partner by trading partner.

Billing for the AT&T EDI service is monthly and contains summarized usage information for each account, including UNIX system and other remote system users. A single account is registered as a master account and receives the bill. A group of accounts can be hierarchically arranged into master and supermaster levels. The billing options allow flexibility in determining which levels receive the actual bill versus billing reporting data. The AT&T EDI service also supports split billing under the direct control of the EDI user. Through the EDI administrative interface, a user can set either global or trading partner-specific split billing percentages. In this way the cost of the movement of one interchange can be divided between the sender and the receiver. Split billing is optional. Billing data can also be categorized to provide individual account tracking within a group. This can be accomplished by using project codes to define each account or activity requiring separate tracking. Billing via EDI is currently planned for deployment.

The split billing feature of AT&T EDI allows trading partners to share the cost of transporting messages. The flexibility of this feature goes beyond a basic 50/50 split. It allows users to set either global or trading partner specific percentages, such as 40%/60% or 30%/70%.

Hierarchical billing allows the subscriber to maintain categorized records and provide individual account tracking within a group. Billing can be set up by project codes, or in the hierarchical billing form that allows users to maintain an organized tracking system. Billing data can be categorized to provide individual account tracking within a group.

Subscribers receive monthly summaries that itemize messages categorized by "sender" and "receiver" and may request reports that provide detailed information on messages sent to and received from each trading partner, categorized by trading partner.

Support

A basic set of standard support functions is provided to subscribers and covered in the network usage charge and is available from the AT&T EasyLink Services Customer Service and Support Center. This includes

AT&T EDI 281

- Establishment of connectivity to and from the AT&T EDI Network
- Problem resolution via telephone for network interface/connectivity problems
- Support services

The Regional Customer Service and Support Centers provide hotline support by knowledgeable EDI service representatives to ensure that EDI implementation continues to work for users. This is available 7 days a week, 24 hours a day. Specific escalation procedures, which include the expertise of Bell Labs support, are in place and operational. AT&T EDI philosophy ensures that migration to new enhancements is easy and seamless for the subscriber. The AT&T EDI architecture and its support services provide effective service upgrades and enhancements to connected EDI subscriber systems. Customer Service and Support Centers provide direct support to AT&T EasyLink Services' subscribers located in their respective areas. They also serve as support centers to value-added reseller (VAR) organizations requiring assistance and or product technical support. AT&T EasyLink Services has increased its global presence through global alliances, international value-added reseller programs, and expanded direct field sales offices.

Special subscriber support options range from marketing support teams to service implementation teams, from tiered technical support to executive partnership programs. Training for administrators, users, and business partners is available. User forums include the customer advisory council, as well as customer newsletters. Development resources, supported by Bell Labs, with its inherent reputation for innovation, quality, and superior execution, provide carefully crafted enhancements.

AT&T EasyLink Services helps users compete more effectively by providing a wide range of flexible professional services and options. During the design stage of a project, consulting is available to help users study and formulate solutions for their re-engineering endeavors. During installation and implementation, users can obtain assistance through the critical early stages that often determine the long-term viability of new systems. During the ramping to production of EDI applications, Professional Services team services are available to guide users through the coordination, resource management, training, and documentation. Experts in various stages of design and implementation professionally manage these programs for users to ensure successful implementation.

Professional Services Support Programs

The AT&T Professional Services Organization offers fee-based custom and structured implementation support options for EDI planning, development, and implementation. The programs are customized to fit the needs of the subscriber. The Explorer Program is a consulting program for companies learning about EDI. The Explorer Program provides consulting for companies studying how EDI (or other messaging services) can be used within their organization or company. The program's objectives are the development of approaches to the re-engineering of existing current business processes for electronic commerce and the development of system specifications for system implementation. The Target Program provides consulting designed to assist a company in the installation of EDI or other messaging services and the initial implementation stages of an EDI program. The program's objectives are to get software and hardware operational and to establish electronic commerce with a small number of users or trading partners. The Champion Program provides consulting to assist a company in gaining the most efficient use of its EDI (or other messaging application) program. Program managers can build a communications plan for program expansion, negotiate and implement communications with trading partners, and provide end-to-end testing with trading partners prior to ramp-up to full electronic commerce.

Global Subscriber Support Services

AT&T's EasyLink Messaging Services provides global customer support through its headquarters location, Regional Support Centers, Network program and retail channels.

Regional Support Center locations and AT&T EasyLink Services Offices include the Hong Kong Regional Support Center (Pacific Rim), Belgium Regional Support Center (Europe), Parsippany N.J. (Americas), AT&T EasyLink Services Germany, and AT&T EasyLink Services, France.

Network Program members include Unitel, AT&T EasyLink Services U.K. Ltd., AT&T EasyLink Services Asia Pacific, AT&T JENS, AT&T EasyLink Services Australia, and Goldnet.

Retail channels include VARs and sales agency members located in Argentina, Bermuda, Brazil, Chile, Colombia, Dominican Republic, Egypt, Hungary, Iran, Italy, Korea, Lebanon, Mexico, Paraguay, Peru, Philippines, Russia, Taiwan, Thailand, Uruguay, and Venezuela.

Chapter 12

AT&T FAXsolutions

AT&T FAXsolutions is a family of solutions designed to work with and enhance the capabilities of conventional fax equipment. These offerings provide users with network-based services which enhance existing systems. AT&T FAXsolutions adds functionality to fax operations which improves delivery of fast, accurate, economical, and reliable hard copy to one or a thousand locations, domestically or internationally. The network-based handling of busy signals and unavailable fax machines lowers the costs and effort required to transact business.

The term AT&T FAXsolutions refers to the entire range of AT&T EasyLink Services' globally available fax services. AT&T FAXsolutions are designed for users or applications that generate high message volumes. AT&T FAXsolutions' pricing and features are most attractive to medium and large enterprises with numerous customers, vendors, employees, prospects, and field sales staff with associated high-volume communication requirements. The services are designed for large enterprises but are equally well suited to smaller users with high-volume fax requirements. These smaller high-volume fax users, such as travel and marketing communications companies, find AT&T FAXsolutions to be a highly productive, cost-effective method which enhances the scope, reach, and functionality of their fax-based marketing programs and operations. AT&T FAXsolutions allows both large and small enterprise users to

AT&T FAXsolutions

AT&T Enhanced Fax	Network enhancements for standard fax
AT&T FAXAFORM	Text and network-stored fax merge and broadcast
AT&T FAX Catalog	On-demand network-based fax response
AT&T Mail	Combined email and fax mailbox
Access Plus for Windows FAX Viewer/Sender	PC-based fax software using data modems
FreeForm Conversion	EDI to human-readable fax
AT&T EasyLink FAX AT&T MailFAX	Data and Graphic Fax Conversion

Figure 12-1 **AT&T FAXsolutions** The AT&T FAXsolutions range includes enhancements to standard fax machines, fax services, fax software for PCs, and conversion of computer-generated data to fax.

- Enhance the power of existing fax hardware and staff.
- Furnish universally available fax service to their enterprise with multiple input and output options.
- Ensure global message transmission and receipt.
- Protect message confidentiality and integrity.
- Integrate fax, voice, email, and future technologies.
- Provide sophisticated tracking, reporting, and archiving features.
- Make fax operations a centrally managed service with extensive reporting features and controls.

AT&T FAXsolutions includes a wide range of globally-available services. These services are maintained, provisioned, and staffed at a level which is designed to handle peaks in fax network traffic.

AT&T FAXsolutions 287

A subscriber, therefore, may execute large-volume operations without prior arrangement and without the need to provide hardware and phone lines for what may be infrequent but high-volume use. AT&T EasyLink Services' FAXsolutions uses the AT&T Worldwide Intelligent Network to enhance the productivity, reach, and scope of fax operations by providing a variety of fax offerings which address high-volume, high-productivity fax requirements. The range of AT&T FAXsolutions' services includes

- AT&T Enhanced FAX for broadcasting, auto-retry, and reliable, inexpensive, and fast international communications using standard fax machines
- Fax Mailbox for mobility and security
- AT&T FAX Catalog for network-based fax-on-demand response systems
- AT&T EasyLink FAX for graphic-to-text services originating from the AT&T EasyLink Services platform
- AT&T FAXAFORM for merging data into network-resident forms and sending the combined document by fax
- AT&T Mail combined email and fax mailbox providing common message storage and retrieval with a single access, ID, and password
- AT&T MailFAX for text-to-fax services originating from the AT&T EasyLink platform
- Access PLUS for Windows FAX Viewer/Sender for fax-on-PC viewing and email-based graphic-to-fax applications for both stationary and mobile users (see Chapter 8, page 195).
- FreeForm Conversion Service for EDI-to-fax transmission of data in human-readable format (see Chapter 11, page 268).

AT&T FAXsolutions' services are designed to eliminate the problems found with conventional fax in high-volume commercial environments. Conventional fax, although an essential business tool, has many defects which limit its effectiveness in large-scale use. Some problems often found with high-volume use of conventional fax are:

- Recurring busy signals are frequent, frustrating, and disruptive of workflow.
- Fax broadcasting to multiple locations is time-consuming, machine-intensive, line-intensive, labor-intensive, and monotonous.
- Faxes are often garbled or incomplete, and the sender is charged for the unusable transmission, required to resend the defective fax, and charged for the retransmission.
- Computer-generated fax broadcasting requires multiple modems and phone lines for very large broadcasts.
- The use of AT&T FAXsolutions may permit PBX blocking of international calls, providing added protection against toll fraud and international call misuse.
- Faxes are difficult to forward to business travelers, often arriving too early, so that the fax is lost, or too late to trigger the desired business function.
- Accounting for fax by department, project, or client is difficult, and charge-back is therefore often impractical for most companies.
- Conventional faxes are sent to machines which may or may not be secure.

These improvements in business productivity are found in both domestic and international operations. Network-based fax enhancements provide significant improvements in both security and confidentiality while providing better fax access for traveling executives, salespeople, and telecommuters. The use of network-based services releases existing fax machines for other uses, such as receipt of incoming messages. The AT&T FAXsolutions services also allow customers to use existing and/or less expensive facsimile equipment while obtaining the benefits of the most sophisticated equipment available. The network service supports fax transmissions 24 hours a day, 7 days a week domestically and internationally and provides continuous customer support worldwide, as well.

AT&T Enhanced FAX

The AT&T Enhanced FAX service allows a subscriber to send a fax message, using a standard Group III fax, to AT&T's store-and-forward network. User access to AT&T Enhanced FAX is through domestic and international telephone networks. The network then stores the fax and forwards it to its destination as specified by the subscriber. The fax destination may be any Group III fax machine reachable by direct-dial telephone service or an AT&T Enhanced FAX subscriber's Fax Mailbox.

The AT&T Enhanced FAX service is designed for large-volume fax users and is especially useful in international operations. The store-and-forward messaging network's auto-retry and non-urgent/economy delivery can be used to reduce the need for staff to work odd hours to make an international fax connection. The network auto-retry capability reduces the cost and effort of repeated manual fax retries over poor-quality phone lines. Extensive consolidated reports keep sender management aware of fax results and are available in multiple languages.

High-volume users who originate faxes in areas, such as the Pacific Rim, which have relatively high telephone rates may find that the AT&T Enhanced FAX service is a more cost-effective replacement for point-to-point fax over International Long Distance (ILD). In North America, AT&T Enhanced FAX is primarily used for broadcast faxing and the benefits provided by its mailbox functions. Large-scale recurring broadcasts of multiple pages to hundreds of locations or faxes of many documents from many locations back to a central location are common applications.

Faxes can be delivered to a fax machine or to a network-based Fax Mailbox, if the recipient is a AT&T Enhanced FAX subscriber. AT&T Enhanced FAX transmissions can be sent to all direct dial countries. The Guest Submission feature allows AT&T Enhanced FAX subscribers to permit non-subscribers to send fax messages to their mailbox with charges paid by the mailbox owner, allowing the subscriber to provide toll-free faxing to selected correspondents.

AT&T Enhanced FAX utilizes the AT&T Worldwide Intelligent Network and shares the same messaging platform as AT&T Mail. AT&T Enhanced FAX uses the AT&T Unified Messaging Architecture (UMA) common envelope structure. This envelope structure permits integration of fax with other AT&T EasyLink Services.

The messaging network's store-and-forward design supports features which add capability to stand-alone fax machines. These fax features are differentiated data communications services which apply the intelligence built into the messaging network to fax operations. The network intelligence makes better use of existing equipment and allows simpler, less expensive equipment to be used in high-volume operations. Existing Group III fax machines may, therefore, be released for other use and the purchase of more expensive fax equipment avoided. The AT&T Enhanced FAX service provides enhanced network-based services to existing fax machines, which include:

- Electronic mailbox capability for inbound faxes
- Store-and-forward capability for outbound faxes
- Auto-retry for outbound faxes
- Broadcast capability to transmit a single fax message to multiple delivery locations with a single command
- User-generated broadcast list creation
- Automatic retry of undelivered faxes
- User specification of latest fax delivery time
- Customer selected delivery confirmation options
- Non-urgent/economy delivery options
- Flexible billing for management control and chargeback
- Customer use of simpler, less costly facsimile machines

AT&T Enhanced FAX provides its subscribers with the added functionality provided by the store-and-forward AT&T Enhanced FAX network for standard Group III fax machines. These features are available to sub-

AT&T FAXsolutions

scribers as required. Security is provided by individually assigned IDs and passwords. The Fax Mailbox feature provides additional security for fax receipt. AT&T Enhanced FAX processors are distributed throughout the world, with local processing and customer support. The AT&T Enhanced FAX service provides support to its users through its touch-tone voice prompts, optional auto-dialer provisions, and subscriber control of profile management. The increased functionality of AT&T Enhanced FAX provides benefits for fax users unavailable with the use of the telephone dial-up network. Examples of this enhanced functionality include

Broadcast	The subscriber can send a single fax message to the network and have it sent to up to 1,000 locations using a mailing list and AT&T Mail Enhanced FAX.
Fax Mailbox	The subscriber has a private network-based Fax Mailbox, which buffers fax forwarding and delivery, providing both enhanced security and the ability to retrieve faxes from remote locations.
Guest Access	The subscriber may permit non-subscribers to send toll-free faxes to the subscriber's private mailbox.
Auto-Retry	The network automatically resends undelivered faxes using a preprogrammed progression that automatically attempts to redeliver the fax if the network encounters busy signals or no answers or disconnects, a common problem in "high-blockage" countries. The time allowance for retries may be controlled by the subscriber's setting for latest delivery time. A warning notice is sent to the user if a fax is not delivered within 1 hour after submission. A non-delivery notice is sent after 2 hours or after the specified latest delivery time if the fax is still not delivered.
Latest Delivery Time	The subscriber may either limit the latest delivery time for time-dependent materials or extend the period for delivery retries.

Non-Urgent Delivery	This feature holds messages on the network until off-peak hours to take advantage of lower rates.
Delivery Reports	These AT&T FAXsolutions reports can be provided individually or in a consolidated form to verify fax receipt. Kanji reports, as well as English, are available in Japan.
Toll-Free (800) Access	Reduces phone charges.
Auto-Forward	The subscriber can have received faxes automatically forwarded to a specified fax machine or another AT&T Enhanced FAX account.

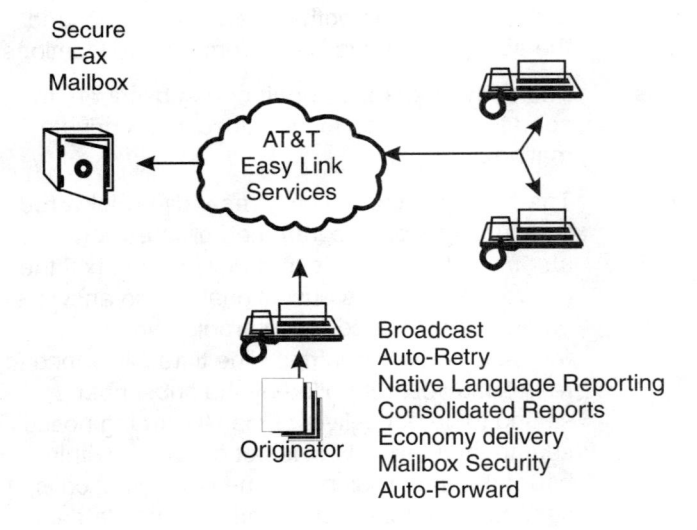

Figure 12-2 **Store-and-Forward Fax** AT&T Enhanced Fax adds a secure mailbox and reporting and broadcast capabilities to standard Group III fax equipment.

AT&T FAXsolutions 293

Comprehensive Monthly Reports — These AT&T FAXsolutions reports provide the subscriber with the tools which permit control and management of previously unmanageable fax communication costs by department or other code.

Detailed Billing — The subscriber can request billing breakdowns by user-specified IDs, which allows a company to bill back charges to specific accounts and departments.

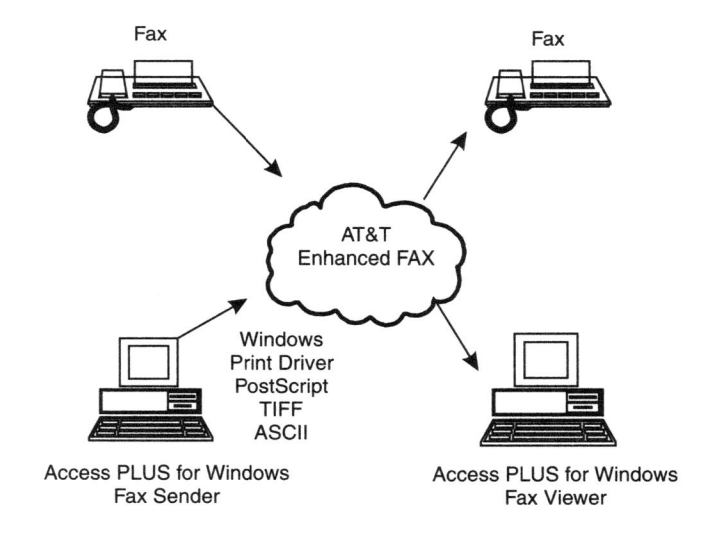

Figure 12-3 **AT&T Enhanced FAX** AT&T Enhanced FAX adds advanced fax capabilities to Group III fax machines and AT&T EasyLink Services.

Fax Sender/Viewer — These Access PLUS for Windows software features allow print and graphic faxes to be sent directly from any Windows application. AT&T

	Enhanced FAX subscribers may also download and view faxes on their PCs.
Combined Mailbox	Subscribers to both AT&T Enhanced FAX and AT&T Mail may elect to have email and faxes stored in a single mailbox for combined up and downloading and retrieval of both email and fax messages in a single session.
Continuous Access	24 hours per day 7 days per week access to the service.
Continuous Support	24 hours per day 7 days per week support by Customer Service and Support Representatives.

Subscribers are billed monthly for services used. The AT&T Enhanced FAX service can be used with any Group III fax machine that has a touch-tone keypad, with a separate touch-tone phone, or with an auto-dialer. Group III fax is the international standard for the most widely used fax machine type, which operates at transmission speeds up to 9600 baud and is the most common type of fax in use. In the United States, 98 percent of all fax machines in use are Group III fax machines. The AT&T Enhanced FAX service can be used with a PC equipped with a Group III–compatible fax board.

A subscriber is notified, on login, when received faxes are in his or her AT&T Enhanced FAX Mailbox. This notification is by the voice prompt feature when a touch-tone pad is used. This series of human prompts, designed for ease of use, assists the subscriber in using the AT&T Enhanced FAX service to send or receive faxes. The voice prompt interface also provides assistance in creating short distribution lists for broadcast fax use. Longer lists can be created by faxing the list to the Customer Service Center, which creates the list and sends a copy back to the subscriber for verification. Lists may be stored and named with a numeric code for future use. Users may also create and edit broadcast lists using a computer in either online mode using terminal emulation or offline mode using a PC with AT&T Access PLUS communication software.

AT&T FAXsolutions

The AT&T Enhanced FAX service is accessed from a touch-tone keypad connected to or part of a Group III facsimile machine or through an auto-dialer, by dialing a local number in most other countries or by dialing a toll-free number in North America. The service provides voice prompting through the call setup process, and provides the ability to send or receive messages or obtain help during the call. This call, from a standard fax machine, is answered with a voice menu which requests the caller to enter his or her personal ID and password and delivery instructions for faxes. AT&T Enhanced FAX then executes the instructions and provides

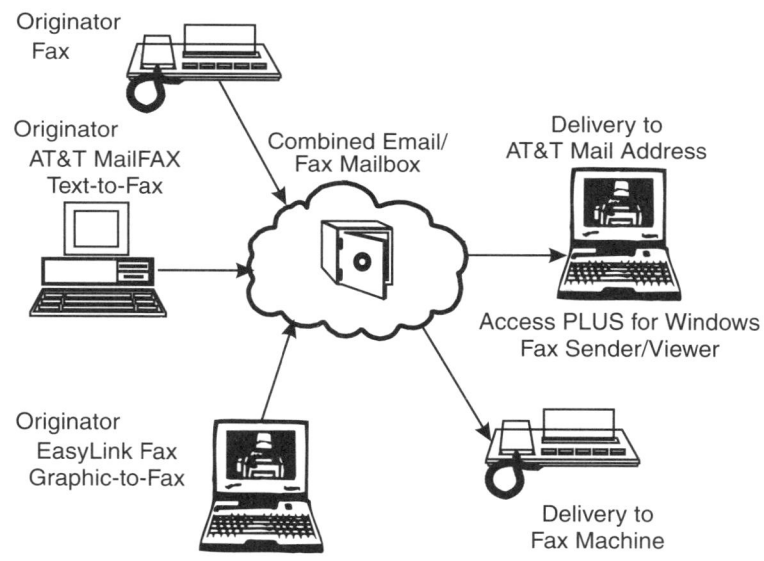

Figure 12-4 **Multiple Fax Input and Delivery Options** The AT&T Enhanced FAX service provides the ability to create and deliver faxes using computers and fax machines.

retries, confirmations, and consolidated reports. Mailing lists can be used to send the same fax to many locations worldwide, releasing fax equipment and staff for other functions.

The use of AT&T Enhanced FAX releases staff from routine and repetitive functions, reduces the need for fax machines and telephone lines, and isolates the sender from problems at the receiving fax machine. With AT&T Enhanced FAX, one copy of a fax can be uploaded to the network using any fax-capable device. Mailing lists, managed from a PC or touch-tone telephone, can trigger multiple sends or take advantage of lower-cost delayed sending or perform extremely large broadcasts. The AT&T Intelligent Network then performs the tasks, which otherwise would be fax machine-, telephone line-, and staff-intensive.

AT&T Enhanced FAX provides the additional benefits inherent in its store-

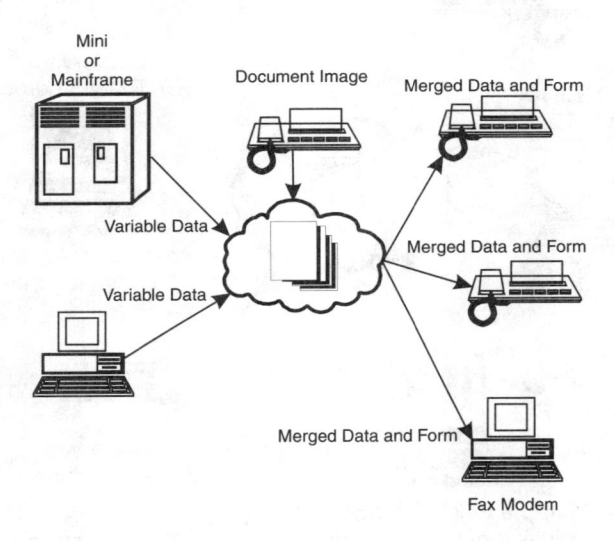

Figure 12-5 **Broadcast Fax** Mailing lists and network-stored form images can be combined and transmitted to any Group III fax device.

and-forward architecture. These benefits include a reduction in the number of fax machines and telephone lines required for support of peak fax traffic, as the AT&T Enhanced FAX network is designed and provi-

AT&T FAXsolutions 297

sioned to support high-volume operations. The automatic retry feature eliminates the need to have the recipient's machine available at the fax send time. The enterprise equipment is freed as soon as the fax is transmitted to the AT&T Enhanced FAX network. The network then handles retries. Extensive delivery reports and consolidated reports confirm fax delivery or report non-delivery.

The AT&T Enhanced FAX service is the foundation for other AT&T FAXsolutions, including

| AT&T FAX Catalog | A service providing on-demand fax transmission of stored documents to end users |
| AT&T FAXAFORM | A service for merging data with network-stored fax forms and sending the combined document to a fax machine |

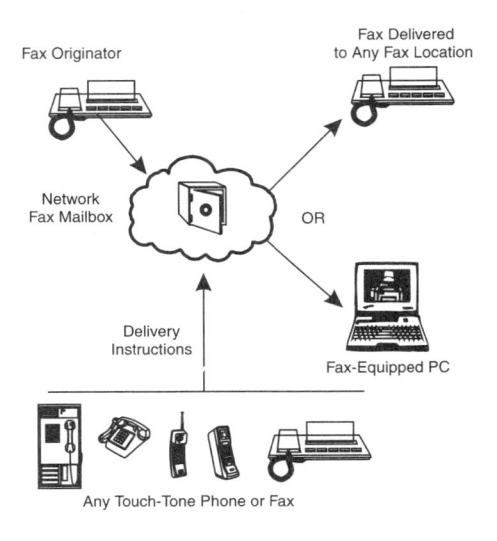

Figure 12-6 **Secure Fax Mailbox** The Fax Mailbox provides a higher degree of security for received faxes, as the subscriber can determine the time and place of final delivery.

AT&T FAX Viewer/Sender — Software support for integrated viewing, deleting or printing of faxes using AT&T Access PLUS for Windows. See Chapter 8, page 195.

Fax Mailbox

An individual Fax Mailbox is automatically assigned to each AT&T Enhanced FAX subscriber. The subscriber can use the Fax Mailbox by entering his or her assigned user ID and password. Subscribers dial into the network to send and retrieve fax messages at their convenience, 24 hours a day, 7 days a week from any Group III fax with touch-tone phone capability. The security of faxes in the mailbox, which are retrievable only with the correct user ID and password combination, is superior to the security of typical fax transmissions. Commonly, faxes are sent to a fax machine whose security is unknown by the sender. The fax machine may be in a public area where faxes can be viewed by unauthorized readers. With the Fax Mailbox, the recipient can control the location and time of delivery to ensure that the receiving fax machine is secure when the message is received.

AT&T Enhanced FAX subscribers may have faxes in their mailbox delivered to any Group III fax machine at any location at any time. The auto-forward feature allows AT&T Enhanced FAX account subscribers to have their fax messages automatically forwarded to a Group III fax location of their choice in a "follow-me" mode operation. AT&T Mail subscribers who also have AT&T Enhanced FAX accounts can request a combined mailbox. Fax messages are combined and managed in the same manner as email messages and read using the Access PLUS for Windows Fax Viewer display and print capabilities.

Users may manage profiles and fax delivery lists either through the phone or by use of a PC. Subscribers to this service can use either fax machines, AT&T Access PLUS for Windows' Fax Sender, or PCs with fax modems to access the service. AT&T Enhanced FAX billing is based on usage. Transmission costs are page- and location-dependent. Users are not billed for transmission time and, therefore, are not charged for re-

AT&T FAXsolutions 299

tries, busy signals, line impairments, or slow fax machine speeds. Fax security is enhanced by providing users with a private mailbox and individually assigned IDs and passwords.

The AT&T Enhanced FAX service provides an advanced feature set to its subscribers. These features are:

Authorization — Each individual account is assigned a network-determined unique user ID and password. AT&T Enhanced FAX requires that the user respond to network voice prompts with the matching user identification and password to establish authorization. The AT&T Enhanced FAX call is terminated by the network if the user ID/password match fails validation after three attempts during a single call attempt. This feature provides subscribers with access control over their account usage. If the Fax Mailbox is used for fax receipt, then the user controls access to received faxes and the points to which these faxes can be delivered or forwarded.

Submission — The user accesses the service using a touch-tone phone, auto-dialer, or Group III fax machine with a built-in keypad, has the user ID and password combination validated, and then uses the Group III fax machine to submit fax documents for transmission. The public switched network (PSN) is the access method. The AT&T Enhanced FAX service provides North American users with a toll-free 800 number, which reduces phone charges, can enhance security by allowing blocking of international calls, and simplifies use by mobile users.

Submissions from areas outside North America may use different access methods depending on local conditions. The network records the date, time, number of pages, originator ID, destinations, and transmission time for all submissions. This information is used for reporting and billing purposes. A single fax submission, which includes the fax image and system-generated data, can contain approximately thirty typed pages with standard fonts and margins. The file size limit is 3 Mb for fax.

Broadcast
The user may send a single fax to up to 1,000 destinations in each network submission. This feature may be used by entering either the fax telephone numbers or the numbers assigned to stored lists of fax numbers after network log-on. The network will then transmit the fax to each recipient without further action by the sender.

Address Lists
The user may store fax telephone number lists for repeated use to make broadcast faxing easier. Lists are used when there are many recipients for a single document or when faxes are sent to the same locations frequently. The subscriber's fax distribution lists may contain fax numbers, AT&T Enhanced FAX subscriber IDs, and/or AT&T Mail addresses for AT&T Enhanced FAX subscribers. The lists may be managed by touch-tone phone, terminal software, or Access PLUS for Windows, or by faxing the list to the AT&T EasyLink Customer Service and Support Center. The feature reduces the effort needed by subscribers to send one or more documents to many users in a single transmission session with the network. The use of stored lists reduces errors. List nesting supports large address requirements by allowing group lists.

Delivery Reports
The AT&T Enhanced FAX store-and-forward network provides a series of delivery reports

AT&T FAXsolutions 301

which give the subscriber timely information on the delivery status of any transmission. These reports allow the subscriber to efficiently track either single or broadcast fax transmissions and provide quick visibility into problems which result from equipment or line failure at the receiving fax. The reports include a warning notice which notifies the sender that a fax was not delivered within the first hour following submission and notice of non-delivery when a message is not delivered 2 hours after submission or after the subscriber's specified latest delivery time. The sender may request an optional confirmation notice which confirms delivery of the fax to specific locations. This feature provides the AT&T Enhanced FAX subscriber with message tracking information on message status after the fax is submitted and provides exception reports. Multiple fax machine logs do not have to be screened to identify problems. The messaging network tracks each message and reports problems in a consistent, timely manner to permit corrective action. The delivery confirmation report provides delivery information on subscriber requests for specified messages, eliminating the need to search through multiple machine logs.

Consolidated Reports

The AT&T Enhanced FAX service can, at subscriber request, provide a summary of all deliveries and warning messages by broadcast submission. The network provides an initial consolidated report 80 minutes following transmission and a second report following the fax expiration setting. This feature makes managing large fax operations easier and is especially useful in broadcast operations, as multiple delivery reports and warnings are summarized into a single message.

Auto-Retry	The AT&T Enhanced FAX network will resend an undelivered fax several times in a 2-hour delivery window. The 2-hour window can be increased by specifying a latest delivery time which is more than the standard 2 hours or decreased by setting the latest delivery time to less than the standard 2 hours. This feature helps ensure delivery and eliminates clerical time and costs of retries. It is especially useful in high volumes where tracking and resending messages manually is often impractical.
Master Account	The master account billing feature allows a large enterprise to have the administration and billing of its individual accounts consolidated while retaining the identity of charges incurred by each individual subscriber's account. This feature provides centralized management control of costs and provides the information needed to charge costs back to individual users. The AT&T Enhanced FAX service provides this information, which otherwise would be too costly, too time-consuming, and too difficult to accumulate and integrate into a chargeback system. This benefit is unique to network fax and is usually unavailable in typical Group III fax operations. Obtaining similar information would require manually matching fax machine logs against telephone records and then producing a report.
Fax Mailbox	Subscribers can have their incoming faxes held in their AT&T Enhanced FAX secure network mailbox. Faxes are held until the subscriber accesses the AT&T Enhanced FAX network and provides a valid ID and password combination. After access is authorized, the subscriber may direct the AT&T Enhanced FAX network to forward the stored fax to any Group III fax,

AT&T FAXsolutions 303

anywhere at any time. Faxes which are not retrieved are held indefinitely on the network without charge. Retrieved faxes are deleted after receipt by the designated Group III fax or pick-up by a PC with Fax Sender/Viewer. This feature provides the subscriber with the ability to control when a received fax will be delivered and the ability to determine the location of that delivery. This AT&T Enhanced FAX feature therefore provides confidential delivery and security for sensitive documents while retaining the ability to use standard fax equipment. Mobile executives or salespersons can pick up faxes from anywhere, at any time using a local touch-tone Group III fax. This eliminates the need for home office staff to track fax phone numbers where the traveler may be reached and reduces problems with lost or misdirected faxes.

Auto-Forward This AT&T Enhanced FAX service allows subscribers to automatically forward faxes received in their Fax Mailbox to a specified Group III fax machine or other AT&T Enhanced FAX user's mailbox. This service is provided without charge in the United States and is available at low cost elsewhere. This feature allows a subscriber to control the delivery point of forwarded faxes in advance and ensures that the user always has faxed information sent to his or her current location, while traveling or working at a distant site.

Resolution The AT&T Enhanced FAX network supports standard and fine resolution. This support is transparent to the subscriber and requires no network settings or action. The resolution is controlled by the resolution used to upload the fax to the network. The receiving fax machine must support the selected resolution. This feature provides the benefits of high resolution as required. These include improved sharpness of graphics and easier-to-read documents and can eliminate resends requested by the recipient.

Cover Sheet — Subscribers may have the AT&T Enhanced FAX network generate a cover sheet for each fax message at no cost. The AT&T Enhanced FAX standard cover sheet contains the AT&T Enhanced FAX logo, identifies the fax sender, and contains service-related information. Subscribers have the option to specify a custom sheet utilizing a pre-registered logo, if desired. Logo registration has a one-time setup charge. This feature enhances corporate identification and image. The cover sheet improves the chances of getting the received fax to the desired recipient. Network generation eliminates the need for the subscriber to transmit the cover sheet, an important consideration in broadcast or large-scale operations.

Disclose Recipients — The subscriber controls the display of recipients on the cover sheet and may direct the service to suppress or enable display of all recipients on the fax cover sheet. The feature can be used to keep the fax mailing list confidential by not allowing individual recipients to receive the list of other recipients.

Guest Access — The subscribers can elect to receive fax messages from non-subscribers or "guests" in their AT&T Enhanced FAX Mailboxes. The faxes are paid for on a COD (reverse charge) basis by the subscriber. This feature provides the equivalent of toll-free fax service and can be used by providing the fax sender with the account user ID. The guest has no access to other faxes in the

AT&T FAXsolutions

	destination mailbox but can only transmit faxes to it.
Non-Urgent Economy Delivery	The AT&T Enhanced FAX service provides users with the option to have faxes sent to their destination at AT&T's off-peak times in order to receive a discount for such off-peak deliveries. This feature is intended for non-urgent messages where next day delivery is acceptable. The feature provides a more economical fax transmission charge by using off-peak delivery scheduling. The network-based Non-Urgent/Economy Delivery simplifies the process of scheduling faxes for off-peak delivery and provides management reports which permit enforcement of off-peak fax delivery policy.
Latest Delivery Time	Subscribers can specify a delivery expiration time from 1 to 72 hours after AT&T Enhanced FAX submittal. The fax delivery is canceled and the subscriber is notified if the delivery is not completed within the specified time. This feature is especially useful when a message is sent to a "high-blockage" country where disconnected calls are common. Specification of an extended latest delivery time expands the number of retries attempted by the network. The feature improves the chances of delivery completion and provides better control of transmission, including the ability to cancel faxes that are not delivered within the desired time frame.
Mobility	Computer users can receive, view, print, and manage faxes that they receive on their PCs or laptop computers. AT&T Access PLUS for Windows provides a Fax Viewer feature which can be used with a standard data modem. Other computer users equipped with a fax modem can have faxes delivered to their computer. This

feature allows computer users to view faxes on their computer from anywhere, at any time.

AT&T SDN Enhanced FAX

AT&T SDN is a software-defined virtual network within the AT&T public switched network which allows customers to configure private networking functionality within the AT&T Worldwide Intelligent Network. The AT&T Software Defined Network (AT&T SDN) Enhanced FAX service provides secure store-and-forward delivery of fax transmissions worldwide by coupling AT&T Enhanced FAX to the transport capabilities of AT&T SDN. Because AT&T SDN's rates are tariffed and usage-based, adding AT&T Enhanced FAX applications could potentially lower overall AT&T SDN transport costs by adding fax to voice and data usage to reach commitment levels.

AT&T SDN Enhanced FAX users are charged only for delivered pages, eliminating resend costs. AT&T SDN customers can access the fax service from the SDN network, or by using remote access methods such as 800 numbers and SDN card access, in addition to Group III fax machines, touch-tone keypads (telephone or autodialer), direct access, and other methods. This feature allows authorized users to simply dial into their AT&T SDN network, provide their ID and password, and then dial other locations.

Additional security, especially for fax receptions, is provided to the AT&T SDN customer who uses the features of Fax Mailbox. AT&T EasyLink Services adds two more levels of security, individually assigned IDs and passwords, to the AT&T SDN network access authorization process. AT&T SDN Enhanced FAX also provides added administrative convenience. Large corporations can have all their subscribers' accounts consolidated for easy processing, yet still maintain subscriber-specific detail for fax usage tracking, delivery and non-delivery reports, list management, and other functions. AT&T EasyLink Services provides global single-vendor service with local sales and support. Large users often prefer to consolidate communications with one primary vendor whose communication pricing, service, and support are price-competitive. AT&T SDN users can include fax volume to reach AT&T SDN commitment levels, thereby lowering overall AT&T SDN costs. The use of one vendor also lowers user purchasing costs and simplifies troubleshooting efforts by eliminating finger-pointing between vendors.

AT&T FAX Catalog

AT&T FAX Catalog Is a fax-on-demand application which supplies information providers with the use of a unique 800 number, voice prompting support using touch-tone telephones, and the AT&T Enhanced FAX network. The service delivers documents requested by a caller to a designated Group III fax machine. Callers request documents by calling an 800 number, listening to voice menu prompts, and requesting documents using a touch-tone keypad. Documents are sent to the fax telephone number entered with the keypad and usually arrive within an hour of the request.

AT&T FAX Catalog uses its own unique voice front-end platform with delivery of selected documents through the AT&T Enhanced FAX delivery network. This means that features such as the retry algorithm, non-delivery reports, and positive confirmation reports benefit all AT&T FAX Catalog customers. The major differences between AT&T FAX Catalog and AT&T Enhanced FAX are that AT&T FAX Catalog is used for distributing information requested by the receiver, while AT&T Enhanced FAX is used by the sender to distribute information, and the voice menu prompts are unique to and customizable for each AT&T FAX Catalog customer. Each AT&T FAX Catalog customer has a unique 800 number for callers and may use vanity numbers. Another feature, found only in AT&T FAX Catalog accounts, is the ability to create folders to manage images stored on the network. AT&T FAX Catalog subscribers may or may not be AT&T Enhanced FAX subscribers. The services are independent and support different functions.

The AT&T FAX Catalog service supplies a network-based fax-on-demand service to information providers who prepare and market documents. The information providers store fax documents on the AT&T Enhanced FAX network. The information provider's fax documents can be submitted for storage using any Group III fax machine, a PC that is equipped with a Group III fax board, or the Access PLUS for Windows Fax Sender feature. These documents are stored in folders within the information provider's mailbox on the AT&T FAX Catalog service.

Documents can then be retrieved by a caller, using a voice-prompted touch-tone phone interface. The caller instructs AT&T FAX Catalog to send selected documents, on demand, to the caller's fax machine. The AT&T FAX Catalog service uses AT&T Enhanced FAX as its delivery mechanism, and the full range of network-based fax enhancements is therefore incorporated in AT&T FAX Catalog. These include the advanced auto-retry and reporting capabilities. The auto-retry ensures delivery, while the reporting capabilities provide the information provider with advanced fax-on-demand management capabilities.

The network-based AT&T FAX Catalog service supplies its information providers with features and benefits which are direct results of its use of AT&T Enhanced FAX as the fax transport. These features are:

Worldwide Document Delivery	Requested documents, at the information provider's option, can be faxed to any Group III fax machine or PC with a fax board. The requesting call is restricted by the availability of international 800 service and is currently United States only.
Continuous Availability	AT&T FAX Catalog and the AT&T Enhanced FAX service are available 24 hours a day, 7 days a week, allowing document requests to be processed and delivered anywhere at any time.
System Flexibility	AT&T FAX Catalog supports instantaneous updates, additions, and deletions of documents and programs, which can easily be performed

AT&T FAXsolutions

remotely, at any time, using either a fax machine, a PC with a fax board, or a PC with the Access PLUS for Windows Fax Sender.

Voice Prompt Flexibility	The information provider selects the desired voice prompting and options for its customers and market conditions. The Information provider can use its own talent and record over the phone, or select a custom voice in any language.
Improved Conversion Rate	The use of AT&T FAX Catalog by an information provider can result in increased sales because a potential customer receives the information when interest is high, and the decision process takes less time.

AT&T provides the complete package, which includes voice prompts, 800 number, and automatic cover sheet, and optionally tracks caller information. All the information provider does is provide the fax documents and promote the availability of the service. The related benefits are:

- Telemarketing, clerical, communication, and material costs are reduced, as the customer initiates the information request using touch-tone menus.

- Information requests do not require information provider staff to interact with or spend time recording customer information for follow-up use.

- Response materials are kept up to date at lower cost. Information is sent only to individuals requesting it immediately upon request.

- Additional equipment, telephone lines, or staff is not needed.

- Printing and mailing costs are eliminated.

Information programs can be established with short lead times and modified to suit rapidly changing market conditions. Some examples are:

- Brokerage firms can provide time-dependent information to selected clients on an as-requested basis and can have the flexibility to instantaneously update materials to reflect changes.

- Manufacturing companies can provide product information, price lists, or other information to their sales force, distributors, customers, and prospects as requested, with delivery to any fax.

- Customer Service departments can provide technical specifications or repair instructions to technicians or customers on request and can charge for faxed documents as desired.

- Associations can provide membership forms, latest industry information, newsletters, and legislative information to members as requested and can charge for selected information.

The AT&T FAX Catalog service allows information providers to get their information products to market faster and provides a full range of support functions. The information provider supplies the fax documents and promotes their availability to the target market.

A toll-free 800 number, unique for each information provider, is established for the information provider by AT&T EasyLink Services. That information provider's unique toll-free number is advertised to the provider's target market and can be a vanity number. A caller who wants to obtain a document calls that number, which can be reached from within the United States and part of the Caribbean (809 area code). The caller indicates the documents desired using a touch-tone keypad. The caller does not have to call from the destination fax machine. After the documents are ordered, the caller is prompted to enter the fax telephone number for the fax machine that will receive the document. This can be any Group III fax reachable by direct dial service. The information provider can optionally request that information from the call, such as telephone number, name, company, or other data, be captured on tape. When the information request call is complete, the document is faxed to the fax machine entered by the caller, usually arriving within one hour after the call is completed. It is not necessary for the caller to place the request through the fax machine's telephone.

Some major AT&T FAX Catalog capabilities include:

AT&T FAXsolutions

800 Number Access	There is toll-free access from all 50 states and part of the 809 exchange (Puerto Rico and Virgin Islands).
Voice Prompting Control	Voice prompting menus are selectable by the information provider.
Single Item Retrieval	There is automatic selection of a predetermined document on access.
Pre-Arranged List Retrieval	Caller is guided to key document numbers when the index is large.
Multiple Item Menu-Based Retrieval	AT&T FAX Catalog prompts for and accepts requests for multiple documents.
Multiple Reports	Comprehensive reports assist the Information provider in monitoring the AT&T FAX Catalog program. They can be obtained at daily, weekly, and monthly intervals on magnetic tape, diskette, email, or paper.
Transcription	Caller voice or touch-tone phone input data can be recorded for the information provider.
Credit Card Verification	Information providers who charge for documents can have credit card numbers used by callers to pay for requested documents verified prior to document transmission. AT&T provides credit card verification under this option for the information provider, who then submits the charges against the verified card number but does not bill the caller. The information provider bills the cost of the information provided against the validated credit card number.

After a caller orders a document, the AT&T Enhanced FAX network creates a fax containing the document or documents and a cover sheet. The standard cover sheet identifies the sender (From) and recipient (To). Information providers can order a customized cover sheet with their logo, if desired, instead of the standard cover sheet. During the ordering process, an information provider can have the voice prompting request the caller's extension number to be added to the To field to allow the recipient to be easily identified.

Information providers can design their fax-on-demand voice prompts using AT&T FAX Catalog's three basic menu interface structures in their design. These voice prompt interfaces are designed for ease of design and use. The menu structures are:

Predetermined Document Retrieval	A unique 800 number is established for the program. A caller to that number automatically orders a predetermined document. The voice prompt instructs the caller to enter the fax telephone number, and the call is automatically terminated. The document is then sent to the designated fax machine using AT&T Enhanced FAX.
Single Document Retrieval from a Set of Documents	A unique 800 number is established for the program. A caller to that number hears a voice prompt requesting the document number or code number of the desired document. The information provider may also permit fax retrieval of an index of available documents. The voice prompt instructs the caller to enter the fax telephone number, and the call is automatically terminated. The document is then sent to the designated fax machine using AT&T Enhanced FAX. This voice prompt design is typically used for a program which sends all callers a single document per call selected from a large number of available documents. The document list is often provided in an advertisement or other information provider document.

AT&T FAXsolutions

Multiple Document Retrieval from a Set of Documents	A unique 800 number is established for the program. A caller to that number hears a voice menu of available documents. This menu may consist of one or more levels, and may include an option for fax retrieval of an index of available documents and/or voice prompts describing the document and its code number. The voice prompt instructs the caller to enter the fax telephone number, and the call is automatically terminated. The documents are then sent to the designated fax machine using AT&T Enhanced FAX. This voice prompt design is typically used for a program which provides a choice of documents and can send multiple documents per call. The document list can also be provided in an advertisement or other information provider document. This design is preferred when there are up to five or six document categories, each with its own distinct set of documents.

The AT&T FAX Catalog Service can also provide additional services which extend the functionality of the basic fax-on-demand service. Some services, such as voice data capture, may require prior authorization by AT&T FAX Catalog on a case-by-case basis. Examples of extended services available at additional costs are:

Transcription of Voice Data Captured during the Call	The information provider may request that data be captured during the inbound calling session. These data can be stored and sent to the information provider on a magnetic tape or transcribed into either hard copy or machine-readable format. The captured call content materials are sent to the information provider at agreed-upon intervals, at additional cost. This information often includes telephone number, name, company, address, or other information typically used by the information provider to build a marketing database. The voice

prompts can be expanded to request the customer to enter information in addition to the document number requested using the touch-tone keypad. These expanded data could include customer number, social security number, birth dates, or other useful information. The information provider benefits from improved tracking and control of caller information, which provides additional marketing and sales opportunities.

Credit Card Verification

Credit card verification services, at additional cost, can be used for information requests for chargeable documents. This service prompts the caller for a credit card number. Credit cards, at additional charge, can then be verified prior to the document delivery. If an entered card number fails validation, then a message can inform the caller that the request cannot be completed. This validation service is available for American Express, Discover, Visa, and MasterCard. The service can accept other card numbers but can only check the number of digits for correct length. The information provider benefits from the ability to charge callers for services by billing against credit cards and to block document delivery when an invalid card number is entered in order to control losses.

Call Limiting

This capability allows information providers to control the number of calls by a specified caller. The service supplies information providers with an automatically generated database which contains caller information to be used in AT&T FAX Catalog program management. This caller information can be used, in real time, to limit the number of times a specific caller can request documents. The identifying information may be a

AT&T FAXsolutions 315

	telephone number, a social security number, or other data provided by the caller, The maximum number of access times is determined by the information provider. The benefit to the information provider is that this service allows cost control by limiting an individual user's ability to excessively request documents.
Call Time Monitoring	This feature, requiring authorization by AT&T FAX Catalog, allows an information provider to control costs by limiting the length of time a call may take. The information provider can, optionally, incorporate a message into the script which informs the caller that the time available for the call has run out. However, a message informing the caller that time will run out cannot be generated before the call ends. The information provider benefits from the ability to control call length and costs.
Personal Identification Numbers (PIN)	Identification numbers can be automatically generated for each caller and stored in a database. The caller is provided with the assigned PIN, which is then validated on future calls. This feature allows the information provider to limit access to documents to authorized or need-to-know callers.
Call Transfer to Information Provider	Voice menu options can be used to allow customers to have their call transferred to an information provider's own representative. This menu option allows a dial-out to another location, such as one used by the information provider for telemarketing. The benefit to the information provider is reduction in caller confusion and a higher conversion rate of initially misdirected calls.

The information provider has multiple options for recording the voice menus. AT&T EasyLink Services can provide the customer with the necessary voice prompts based upon the script form completed by the customer. When this is complete, customers may

- Record the voice prompts using their own voice through the telephone.
- Have the voice prompts recorded at a qualified studio using the voice of their choice.
- Have AT&T EasyLink Services record the voice prompts, with a choice of voices.

The voice prompts must include a transaction number, assigned by the voice platform, for fax tracking and must end with "your fax will be delivered in approximately one hour." Other essential information includes the destination fax machine and the voice telephone number of the caller, essential for delivery to shared fax machines. Only numeric data can be captured using the touch-tone interface. Any other numeric information desired by the information provider can also be prompted for, captured, and transmitted to the information provider in a variety of formats.

The service requires the caller to use touch-tone phones. At the information provider's option, a voice prompt can instruct callers to dial another number if they are using a rotary phone or inform the caller that their call is being transferred and then provide dial-out to an operator.

Fax Services

AT&T EasyLink FAX is the computer- or terminal-to-fax service which provides text- or graphic-to-fax messaging. The fax contents can be created interactively or offline using supported AT&T EasyLink Services client software. This service supports PCs, Macintoshes, LANs, midrange computers, and other devices which can connect to AT&T EasyLink Services. The AT&T EasyLink FAX graphic-to-fax support can be used to send graphics, text, or combined graphics and text to a fax machine. The user does not need either a scanner or access to a fax machine to send formatted or graphic-based faxes. The specific features available vary with the connection mode and software capabilities.

AT&T FAXsolutions

AT&T Mail provides a complete, integrated fax solution for both the office worker and the mobile worker. This solution requires less hardware, lowers transmission time, and provides better-quality fax transmissions. Both text-to-fax and graphic-to-fax support is provided.

AT&T MailFAX provides text-to-fax support which sends a text mail message to a fax machine's telephone number. This provides the fax equivalent of a text message and is called AT&T MailFAX. Text-to-fax may be sent using any of the AT&T Mail access methods, including wired or wireless access from stand-alone, LAN, midrange, or UNIX systems. This text-to-fax support is very efficient for large-scale fax operations generated by computer. The text-based system provides subscribers with the tools to send large file transmissions to a large number of changing recipients. The options, which vary with subscription options, include the following:

Broadcasting	AT&T Mail subscribers can use up to 1,000 delivery addresses and AT&T EasyLink subscribers can used up to 30,000 delivery addresses in a single submission.
Logos and Signatures	Graphics can be scanned and stored at AT&T EasyLink Services and can be incorporated into fax messages at any location on the page.
Cover Sheets	Network-generated cover sheets may be generated on a permanent or per-message basis.
FAXAFORM	This AT&T EasyLink FAX service permits subscribers to store form images on the network. These form images can contain logos, graphics, signatures, text, and fonts of different sizes. The stored forms are used when the subscriber sends uniquely identified ASCII text messages into the network specifying a particular form. The text messages include the data, with line and character position identification for proper placement within the form. FAXAFORM allows

	merging of data and network-stored forms or letters for transmission to fax machines.
Access PLUS for Windows Fax Sender/Viewer	Access PLUS for Windows software allows subscribers with AT&T Enhanced FAX accounts to view faxes retrieved from their mailboxes on their PCs and to send faxes from any Windows program by selecting Fax Sender on EasyLink as the printer. The use of Access PLUS for Windows with AT&T Enhanced FAX accounts requires subscribers to use their AT&T Enhanced FAX access number, IDs, and password, not their AT&T Mail access number, ID, and password, to send and retrieve faxes using the AT&T Enhanced FAX service.
AT&T Enhanced FAX and AT&T Mail Combined Mailbox	This combined AT&T Enhanced Fax and AT&T Mail mailbox capability allows fax and email messages to be sent, received, managed, and read with a single network access, user ID, password, and Access PLUS for Windows software. This feature allows AT&T Mail subscribers with AT&T Enhanced FAX accounts who have combined mailboxes and Access PLUS for Windows Fax Viewer/Sender to send and retrieve faxes as part of their email operations. The combined mailbox is requested through the Customer Support Center. This feature does not require that a PC have a fax modem. The PC software also allows the user to send fax messages from any Windows application by selecting the Fax Sender on EasyLink printer driver and allows the sender to send a graphic-to-fax message directly from a Windows application. This is an ideal approach for the telecommuter or the mobile or remote worker.

Other AT&T EasyLink FAX functions include variable-length page, priority delivery, font size options, and alternate delivery modes.

FreeForm Conversion

FreeForm Conversion is an EDI delivery option that provides for delivery of data in readable format to a non-EDI recipient by converting it to a fax document and transmitting the information to Group III fax machines. This feature allows more participants into the user's EDI universe (see Chapter 11, page 268).

Chapter 13

AT&T Information Services

AT&T EasyLink Services provides a full range of information access and storage facilities known as AT&T Information Services. This group of information services supports access to and distribution of information. The services range from basic access to public research database collections to the creation of customized information storage, retrieval, or dissemination systems. Any privately owned business information or database can be made available to a broader audience using these AT&T Information Services. The information can be made publicly available, or access can be restricted to groups of authorized users. Public information available through AT&T Information Services can be merged with other information feeds and customized to create a virtual private information retrieval and dissemination network used to control and manage information flow. Custom information systems on AT&T Information Services distribute information owned, managed, and controlled by an information provider or information vendor.

Enterprise information requirements include either the need to locate information needed to operate a venture or the need to distribute information, either to enterprise employees or to business partners. The benefits include timely online access to the information collections created and marketed by information providers in all parts of the world. Examples of the information available include research reports, credit reports, international news updates, and stock analysis. Enterprises may need to ensure that the latest public industry information or specific news about the company and its products are sent to its customers, partners, or employees. Other data, such as confidential marketing data or calendars of events, require distribution to a selected group only. AT&T Information Services has a full range of such services which are tightly integrated with AT&T Mail. These services can be customized to meet specific information requirements. AT&T Information Services products and services include systems and tools to help access and distribute critical business information. AT&T Information Services allows information to be delivered

- When needed
- In the form needed
- To any device or system
- To any destination

AT&T EasyLink Information Services complement messaging services by providing information on demand, in easily accessible forms, whenever and wherever the user needs it. AT&T Mail users have simple, fast, and cost-effective access to one of the world's largest collection of online interactive databases, information services, online news, and flexible research services using a user-friendly online menuing system or email. Services are either usage-based or subscription services. AT&T Mail subscribers do not have to maintain separate subscriptions to each information service or learn individual database command structures. These services may be used anytime from anywhere over wired or wireless connections.

AT&T Information Services provides tools for satisfying business information needs. Increasingly, this type of information is essential to businesses and individuals that want to differentiate themselves in the market. Users have the advantage of getting their information and advanced messaging services from a single supplier. Both general and very specialized information can be obtained using AT&T Information Services. Information can be obtained without special training or online database experience, and most responses can be delivered to AT&T Mail addresses. Some responses require fax capabilities.

AT&T Information Services 323

Three unique services, PUBCITE, NEXIS EXPRESS, and ECLIPSE EXPRESS, can be activated by filling out an email form and including the question to be answered. PUBCITE provides the user with an expanded publication table of contents delivered to their mailbox. Subscribers can select articles from the table of contents for delivery by email or fax in full text. NEXIS EXPRESS allows the user to order a search performed by a professional researcher. A cost estimate can be obtained before a search is performed. ECLIPSE EXPRESS users can have a professional researcher create an precisely designed newsletter. These specialized newsletters can be delivered to the user on a scheduled basis. In all cases, the user pays only for the searches conducted or items requested.

AT&T Mail subscribers can obtain access to AT&T Information Services by email or telephone request to the Customer Service and Support Center. A complete set of database or information services is available to AT&T Mail users. They can communicate interactively with some AT&T Information Services information providers or use AT&T Mail to send research requests and to receive the results of information searches. These offerings span the gamut of complexity from summary information provided by news agencies to detailed information extracted from specialized databases by skilled researchers in response to email orders.

Users of Access PLUS can capture online sessions as mail files or hard copy. This simplifies the management of retrieved information. Information services, such as PUBCITE, NEXIS EXPRESS, and ECLIPSE EXPRESS, are ordered using AT&T Mail forms, and information is delivered as email or fax. Access PLUS provides a superior method of managing these information retrieval activities. Other communications packages providing terminal emulation and a session capture facility can be used with the interactive or mail-enabled services. These packages do not provide the message management or integrated management of session captures provided by the Access PLUS package.

Information retrieval is the location of relevant information from any combination of public or private sources. Subscribers who require information retrieval services have easy access from virtually any location and from any communicating device, using simple to learn and understand commands. AT&T Mail messaging features, such as store-and-forward, pri-

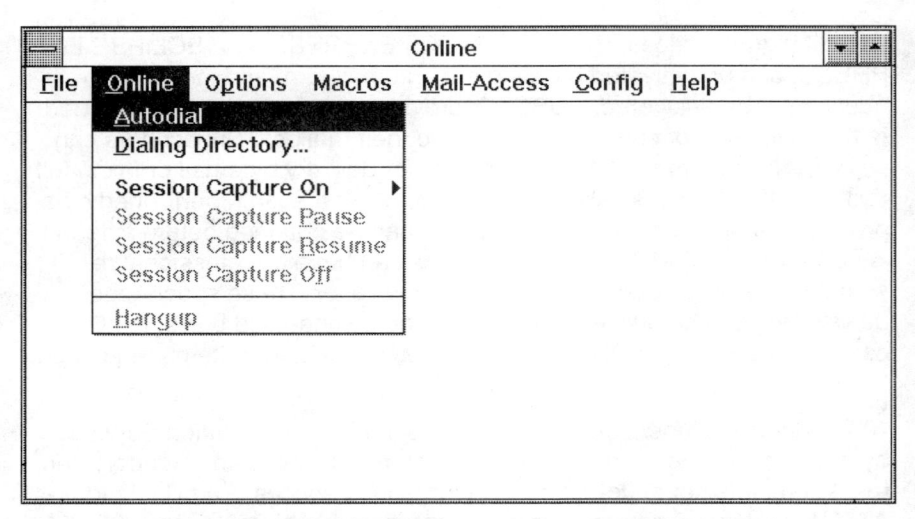

```
┌─────────────────────────────────────────────────────────────┐
│                          Online                      ▼  ▲   │
├─────────────────────────────────────────────────────────────┤
│ File  Online  Options  Macros  Mail-Access  Config  Help    │
│       ┌──────────────────────────────┐                      │
│       │ Autodial                     │                      │
│       │ Dialing Directory...         │                      │
│       │                              │                      │
│       │ Session Capture On        ▶  │                      │
│       │ Session Capture Pause        │                      │
│       │ Session Capture Resume       │                      │
│       │ Session Capture Off          │                      │
│       │                              │                      │
│       │ Hangup                       │                      │
│       └──────────────────────────────┘                      │
│                                                             │
└─────────────────────────────────────────────────────────────┘
```

Figure 13-1 **Access Plus for Windows Session Capture** Sessions may be capured and managed using the same commands and folders used for email.

vate mailbox, and multiple delivery alternatives, are fully integrated with AT&T Information Services. Some methods are:

Online Searches	Search one or multiple databases using menus or commands using InfoMaster.
Subscriptions	Have enhanced tables of contents for selected publications or custom newsletters deposited in the user's mailbox or on the user's fax on the same schedule as the printed publication, using PUBCITE.
Research on Demand	Arrange, over AT&T Mail, to have expert researchers execute detailed searches using NEXIS EXPRESS or LEXIS EXPRESS.

Information distribution is the selective distribution of information to those who should be aware of it. Subscribers who require information distribution services can use the full range of AT&T Mail delivery, storage, and retrieval techniques. Data can be delivered within a company or externally to business partners and customers. AT&T Information Services provides an efficient and flexible set of tools that can be customized to fit specific requirements. These tools include all AT&T Mail features and its flexible billing structure, multiple security levels, data management tools, data management services, and a variety of cost-effective delivery options. A company can, therefore, publish its information internally or publicly with security and without extensive setup and management effort.

AT&T Information Services offers a variety of information distribution tools or options designed to solve information delivery requirements for important messages and to convey general corporate news. These tools include:

- FYI InfoBoards (Bulletin Boards)
- Shared Folders
- FAX Catalog

Information Distribution

Information distribution tools can be used to deliver information to staff, customers, or business partners. AT&T Information Services provides the flexibility to implement an information distribution system which fits the way in which the information is gathered and presented to its intended audience. There are several approaches:

FYI InfoBoards Data can be loaded by either a user or an information provider and presented as a bulletin board of topics and categories known as an AT&T FYI InfoBoard. InfoBoards are non-subscription, and the user interactively selects the InfoBoard and reads the information. The InfoBoard owner can restrict access to specific InfoBoards as desired. InfoBoard owners can make product catalogs available to customers electronically, including product descriptions, prices, and promotional news.
The menu layering structure can be used to categorize products. This makes finding information fast and efficient for customers and distributors. As an example, a famous auto maker has created and maintains a menu of press releases, general product news, and price

promotion information categories for each of its automobile models. This application uses a separate menu for each model. Access to the information is limited to the manufacturer's dealers and trade journals.

Shared Folders Shared Folder subscribers have new information from the folder automatically delivered to their mailbox, where it is read together with other email to a particular folder. Messages in Shared Folders can either be retrieved by the recipients or automatically delivered to interested parties using the full range of AT&T EasyLink Services delivery options. Users can subscribe to the Shared Folder and either check for new messages or have new information periodically delivered to them.

Shared Folders are very versatile corporate information distribution tools providing electronic delivery to a wide range of systems and in various formats and media. Shared Folder information, either new or updated, can be automatically delivered to any device or system that connects to AT&T Mail. Formats and media include email, fax, remote printer, paper, and voice. Messages can also be delivered to other Shared Folders.

Shared Folders can be used to communicate company information. AT&T uses Shared Folders to distribute a daily company-wide newsletter containing policies and policy updates, industry and competitor information, and the company's current financial posture. It is delivered in many forms, including email, fax, and paper. Shared Folders are an extremely effective method for delivering this daily newsletter, which is distributed globally. Shared Folder costs can be billed to either the sender or the recipient. The Shared Folder owner can limit access to a specific group of AT&T EasyLink Services users or allow access to all network users.

AT&T Information Services

AT&T FAX Catalog	AT&T FAX Catalog is a fax-on-demand solution that provides a cost-effective, efficient way to provide customers, prospects, sales, and other staff with information that they need quickly. Callers request documents using a voice prompt menu, and the documents are faxed to the location they specify.
PUBCITE	To maintain current awareness of selected media.
NEXIS EXPRESS	For professional searches on specified topics.
ECLIPSE EXPRESS	For periodic searches on specified topics.
InfoMaster	An integrated front end to hundreds of publicly available databases.
Investment ANALY$T	An investment research service compiled from InfoMaster's finance and business databases.
AT&T FYI Service	AT&T FYI Service provides summaries of news and financial data. It supports the creation and use of private bulletin boards, known within FYI as InfoBoards, and also provides gateways to other information resources.

PUBCITE

PUBCITE provides a unique service which allows AT&T Mail subscribers to receive expanded tables of contents for a number of industry or general publications. These tables of contents are delivered as soon as the publication is available. Subscribers receive the expanded table of contents with their AT&T Mail messages and can scan the list for articles of interest. They can then order the full text of the desired articles by email. The full text is in their maibox or on their fax within 24 hours. PUBCITE is a current awareness message-based information service provided by Reed-Elsevier and AT&T EasyLink Services.

The PUBCITE service provides automatic delivery of enhanced tables of contents for publications selected by the user. The PUBCITE user can order full-text articles from the listings, which are also delivered by email or fax. Other research service types require the user to know what items they want to retrieve. The PUBCITE current awareness features are a browser's equivalent. The service allows AT&T Mail subscribers to have immediate, world-wide access to the table of contents of key business publications such as *Fortune*, *Forbes*, and *Communications Week* . The user can then scan the contents and order full-text business articles with delivery by fax or email within 24 hours anywhere in the world. PUBCITE allows executives to maintain current awareness of published business materials which affect their business or industry and to do so from anywhere at any time.

Other information services respond to questions. A question could be a request for information on multimedia messaging. PUBCITE, however, provides information on what topics are currently being written about in major general and industry publications. The benefits are that PUBCITE users can learn about topics in a browsing mode and keep abreast of the latest information about their business or industry appearing in major trade journals or magazines. PUBCITE delivers previews of articles published in these periodicals with the user's email. The user can therefore, for example, become aware that multimedia is being written about widely in both general and technical publications.

PUBCITE combines the global power and capabilities of AT&T EasyLink Services and Reed-Elsevier's NEXIS Electronic Information Services to deliver current awareness information. Some key features are:

- Simple, user-friendly electronic order form and easy retrieval of information
- Fast, 24-hour delivery of full-text articles
- Flexibility of fax or electronic mail delivery
- Delivery as frequent as the hardcopy edition of each publication
- Subscribers pay a fixed fee to receive indexes, and for articles they request

AT&T Information Services

PUBCITE, like a magazine subscription, delivers the requested tables of contents periodically and allows the user to browse and select articles to be read. Unlike a standard subscription, PUBCITE is delivered electronically and is available anywhere, at any time. Travelers or mobile workers can use the service from laptops or hand-held computers, over wired or wireless connections. PUBCITE is designed to provide busy people with an easy, flexible way to keep abreast of the latest information from leading publications. Users of AT&T Mail can obtain timely articles without having to sift through multiple screen menus, subscribe to specialized databases, or learn special search commands. PUBCITE streamlines information retrieval, providing the full text of selected articles directly in the user's mailbox. PUBCITE provides access to current publications quickly, easily, and cost-effectively, using email. Publications currently available include

- *American Demographics*
- *Business Week*
- *BYTE*
- *CommunicationsWeek*
- *Computerworld*
- *Corporate Legal Times*
- *Data Communications*
- *DM News* (formerly *Direct Marketing News*)
- *Forbes*
- *Fortune*
- *Harvard Business Review*
- *Industry Week*
- *Information Week*
- *Journal of Marketing*
- *Journal of Marketing Research*
- LAN Times
- Marketing Management

- Marketing News
- Marketing Research
- Network World
- Open Computing
- Time
- UNIX World
- U.S. News & World Report

The PUBCITE service allows AT&T Mail subscribers to:

- Keep ahead of industry trends and competitive products and services
- Track government activities and regulatory matters

PUBCITE provides additional value-added benefits and features as part of its service, such as

- Comprehensive, wide range of news from the business and trade press, regional publications, and international and financial data
- Easy to use, with requests made by pre-addressed email form
- Subscribe only to desired publications
- Access at the desktop or from a laptop computer
- Access to current information from any location, at any time
- Delivery options including the user's choice of email or fax

Executives in areas such as business planning, marketing, sales, finance, public relations, and advertising find PUBCITE to be a cost-effective means of staying current on the topics they need in order to be productive. PUBCITE provides a significant business advantage to staff in any function where being aware of current topics discussed in the media is important.

NEXIS EXPRESS

The NEXIS EXPRESS service provides on-demand access to an experienced team of researchers. The service finds information fast and deliv-

AT&T Information Services

ers answers to inquiries electronically, in as little as one business day. NEXIS EXPRESS is one of the mail-based online research services provided to AT&T Mail subscribers by Reed-Elsevier, a leading full-text electronic information services provider.

NEXIS EXPRESS is an AT&T Mail–based service. A request is sent using AT&T Mail, and the response is also received through AT&T Mail. The request is answered by an experienced team of professional researchers who find information fast, and deliver it when, where, and how a user wants it. NEXIS EXPRESS researchers have unlimited access to one of the world's largest full-text sources of news and critical business information. The services are accessed by retrieving a form from an AT&T Mail Shared Folder. The forms are pre-addressed AT&T Mail messages which are filled in with the desired information search by the user and sent.

Some of the features associated with these services are:

- Easy to use, with requests made by pre-addressed form
- Freedom from dependence on local information resources
- Cost estimates provided by email prior to search execution
- Speedy responses within one or two business days as desired
- Expert researchers do the searching
- Desktop access using equipment currently used for AT&T Mail
- Research can be ordered and results received from any location, at any time
- Results delivered through email or fax as specified by user

NEXIS EXPRESS provides the equivalent of a private research assistant on call 24 hours a day. This can be a significant competitive edge. The service uses the resources of Reed-Elsevier's LEXIS/NEXIS services, which are the world's largest source of full-text online news and business information. Searches commissioned through NEXIS EXPRESS provide current, comprehensive information for business use. The benefits of NEXIS EXPRESS include:

- Utilize professional researchers without the cost of hiring private consultants, librarians, and research assistants.

- Maintain confidentiality, as searches can be requested by, executed for, and delivered to an executive without the knowledge of other staff to keep search topics private.
- Increase productivity; spend less time researching a problem and more time analyzing results and making decisions.
- Secure more efficient utilization of limited resources.
- Enjoy customized research assistance, with targeted information results.

NEXIS EXPRESS researchers have unlimited access to the world's largest full-text source of news and business information and can find crucial financial information, the latest legal news, or even the latest experimental medical procedures. Some NEXIS EXPRESS service applications are:

- Planners can get up-to-date information on competitors, new products, market share data, regulations, and issues analysis.
- Marketing and sales representatives can check on prospects, potential clients, and key personnel before developing a market plan or making a sales call.
- Financial specialists can receive background or financial information on U.S. or multinational firms.

Pricing information is provided online in a Shared Folder with ordering information. The cost of NEXIS EXPRESS research varies with the breadth and complexity of the research. NEXIS EXPRESS is for one-time searches. If the search results are required on a scheduled basis to track a company or monitor a trend, then the search can be repeated automatically using the companion ECLIPSE EXPRESS service. ECLIPSE EXPRESS searches can be scheduled for daily, weekly, or monthly delivery and are otherwise identical to NEXIS EXPRESS searches.

NEXIS EXPRESS users use a pre-addressed form to request a search. Section I of the form is for billing information. Section II contains one multi-line field for the information request, which should be as specific as possible. The NEXIS EXPRESS service will send a message, or telephone if preferred, to clarify incomplete requests. Cost estimates are requested by checking the appropriate form field. Section III is the desired turnaround time, with one- and two-business day delivery options. Section IV is for the desired delivery method, which can be AT&T Mail or fax.

When NEXIS EXPRESS receives a completed order form for a research project, the Reed-Elsevier research specialists will first make sure they understand the request and contact the user with any questions. The research specialists will also send an estimate of the cost of the research project, if requested, for approval. After the estimate is accepted, they will perform the research and send a list of the articles they have located. The user selects the articles for which full text is desired and returns the form. The articles are then sent to the user's AT&T Mail address or fax, as specified

The response consists of a header line which identifies the search criteria and an article or cite list. This article list shows the identifying information for articles found in the search, such as the title, date, author, and publication the article appears in. The user selects the full-text articles desired and returns the article list, which is an email form, to NEXIS EXPRESS. This is more economical than the time and effort needed to perform the same search using manual methods. The return email would contain the article full text, which is the article contents without figures, tables, or pictures.

ECLIPSE EXPRESS

ECLIPSE EXPRESS is an electronic clipping service that has the same rich features as NEXIS EXPRESS. The difference, however, is that ECLIPSE performs daily, weekly, or monthly scheduled searches and delivers the results automatically on a subscription basis in what is essentially a custom search repeated on a scheduled basis. The ECLIPSE EXPRESS service provides as-needed access to an experienced team of researchers. ECLIPSE EXPRESS is one of the mail-based online research services provided to AT&T Mail subscribers by Reed-Elsevier.

ECLIPSE EXPRESS searches contain information specifically tailored for the user on any topics desired. The frequency of delivery is based on the user's needs. The custom searches allow the user to remain current on the status of a company, an industry, and competitors.

The ECLIPSE EXPRESS service offers access to an experienced team of researchers that provides information on subjects to be tracked on a daily, weekly, or monthly basis. The service uses the power of the NEXIS service to track a host of topics, from the competition's latest product announcement to the latest international news event.

ECLIPSE EXPRESS is an AT&T Mail–based service and is not used interactively. A request is sent using AT&T Mail, and the response is also received through AT&T Mail. The request is answered by an experienced team of professional researchers who design a search and deliver the search results when, where, and as often as the user wants it. ECLIPSE EXPRESS researchers have unlimited access to the world's largest full-text source of news and critical business information. The services are accessed by retrieving the form from an AT&T Mail Shared Folder. The forms are pre-addressed AT&T Mail messages and are filled in by the user and returned by AT&T Mail.

ECLIPSE EXPRESS creates custom searches and delivers NEXIS-like information on a regular or scheduled basis. Some of the features associated with these services are:

- Easy to use, with requests made by pre-addressed form
- Automatic execution and delivery of search results
- Daily, weekly, or monthly delivery of search results
- Cost estimates provided by email prior to search execution
- Speedy responses within one or two business days as desired
- Expert researchers do the searching
- Desktop access using equipment currently used for AT&T Mail
- Results delivered through email or fax as specified by user

ECLIPSE EXPRESS provides the equivalent of having a private research assistant scanning thousands of information sources and preparing reports of key information. This periodic update of key information provides an important business advantage. The service uses the resources of Reed-Elsevier's LEXIS/NEXIS services, which is one of the

AT&T Information Services

world's largest sources of full-text online news and business information. Searches commissioned through ECLIPSE EXPRESS provide current, comprehensive information for business use. The benefits of ECLIPSE EXPRESS include:

- Utilize professional researchers without the cost of hiring private consultants, librarians, and research assistants
- Freedom from dependence on local information resources
- Maintain confidentiality, as searches can be requested by, executed for and delivered to an executive without the knowledge of other staff to keep search topics private
- Increase productivity; spend less time researching a problem and more time analyzing results and making decisions
- Secure more efficient utilization of limited resources
- Monitor important issues by receiving scheduled up-to-date custom searches
- Enjoy customized research assistance, with targeted information results

ECLIPSE EXPRESS researchers have unlimited access to the world's largest full-text source of news and business information and can find crucial financial information, the latest legal news, or even the latest experimental medical procedures. Some ECLIPSE EXPRESS service applications are:

- Planners can get up-to-date information on competitors, new products, market share data, regulations, and issues analysis.
- Marketing and sales representatives can check on prospects, potential clients, and key personnel before developing a market plan or making a sales call.
- Financial specialists can receive fundamental financial information on U.S. or multinational firms.

Pricing information is provided online in a Shared Folder with ordering information. The cost of ECLIPSE EXPRESS research varies with the frequency, breadth, and complexity of the research. ECLIPSE EXPRESS is for periodic searches. If the search results are required one time, then the companion NEXIS EXPRESS service is used.

ECLIPSE EXPRESS users use a form downloaded from a Shared Folder. The form is sent, after completion, and is pre-addressed. Section I of the form is for billing information. Section II contains one multi-line field for the information request, which should be as specific as possible. The ECLIPSE EXPRESS service will send a message, or telephone if preferred, to clarify incomplete requests. Cost estimates are requested by checking the appropriate form blank. Section III is the desired execution schedule, with daily, weekly, or monthly delivery options. Section IV is for the desired delivery method, which can be the user's AT&T Mail address or fax.

When ECLIPSE EXPRESS receives a completed order form for a research project, the Reed-Elsevier research specialists will first make sure they understand the request and contact the user with any questions. The research specialists will also send an estimate of the cost of the research project, if requested, for approval. The results of the search are then sent by AT&T mail or fax, on the daily, weekly, or monthly schedule specified. Articles can then be ordered.

The user pays for the skilled researcher's time in setting up the initial search. Ongoing search charges are for information retrieval only.

Interactive Information Services

AT&T Information Services provides gateways to public database collections which are used interactively. Each gateway provides entry to an information provider's database collection. These services each have their own command structure, features, and pricing. Gateways, such as AT&T EasyLink FYI, may have gateways to other services. An example would be the Official Airline Guide Electronic Edition. These services also have their own command structure, features, and pricing.

Subscribers with access to interactive AT&T Information Services are presented with a menu when they access the service in terminal or online mode. The format of this menu varies depending on the services activated for the user and the user's membership, if any, in closed user groups. The AT&T EasyLink Services log on menu can be customized to

AT&T Information Services

support the requirements of user groups or associations. An example would be ABA/net, a closed user group, which uses custom login menus for its members.

A basic menu might contain the following five selections:

- Quit
- AT&T Mail
- InfoMaster
- Investment ANALY$T
- FYI NewsAlert

Entering the menu number associated with the item connects the user with the AT&T Mail, InfoMaster, Investment ANALY$T, or FYI services interactively. Each selection takes the user through the service gateway to the selected information service specific menu. Exiting from a service, using the appropriate menu selection or command, takes the subscriber

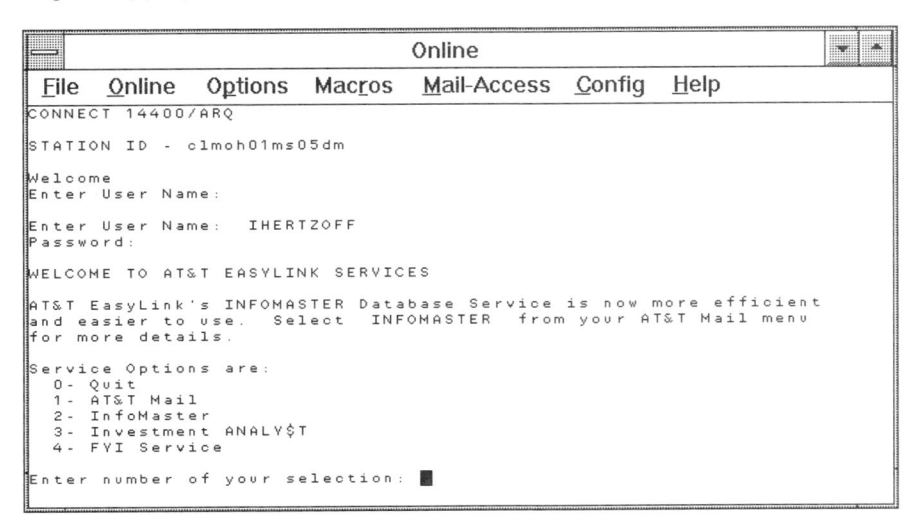

```
                            Online
 File  Online  Options  Macros  Mail-Access  Config  Help
CONNECT 14400/ARQ

STATION ID - clmoh01ms05dm

Welcome
Enter User Name:

Enter User Name:   IHERTZOFF
Password:

WELCOME TO AT&T EASYLINK SERVICES

AT&T EasyLink's INFOMASTER Database Service is now more efficient
and easier to use.  Select  INFOMASTER  from your AT&T Mail menu
for more details.

Service Options are:
  0- Quit
  1- AT&T Mail
  2- InfoMaster
  3- Investment ANALY$T
  4- FYI Service

Enter number of your selection: ▌
```

Figure 13-2 **Typical Interactive Menu** Menus seen by subscribers in terminal mode vary and can be customized for closed user groups.

back to the logon menu. Another service may be selected, or the online session may be terminated.

AT&T InfoMaster Service

AT&T InfoMaster provides access to databases located throughout the world under a common menu structure. This service gives users instant access to one of the world's largest collections of electronic information. Much of this information is professionally assembled, abstracted, indexed, and maintained to allow precision retrieval of search topics. The information in these databases is from leading publishers, universities, and government agencies worldwide. A free reference librarian service, provided by InfoMaster, is available and can be accessed using email, 800 numbers, or long distance. A user needing help can type SOS at InfoMaster prompts to start a conversational dialogue with a reference librarian who can assist in selecting the appropriate database and provide other search assistance.

A company can use InfoMaster databases to

- Conduct market research on a particular product or market group.
- Develop client or partner briefing packages for executives.

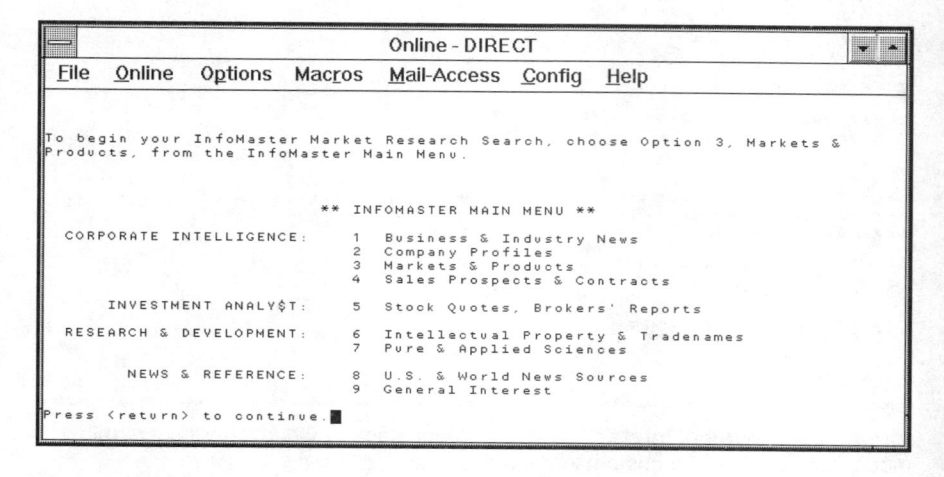

```
                        Online - DIRECT
 File   Online   Options   Macros   Mail-Access   Config   Help

To begin your InfoMaster Market Research Search, choose Option 3, Markets &
Products, from the InfoMaster Main Menu.

                      ** INFOMASTER MAIN MENU **

      CORPORATE INTELLIGENCE:    1   Business & Industry News
                                 2   Company Profiles
                                 3   Markets & Products
                                 4   Sales Prospects & Contracts

         INVESTMENT ANALYST:     5   Stock Quotes, Brokers' Reports
      RESEARCH & DEVELOPMENT:    6   Intellectual Property & Tradenames
                                 7   Pure & Applied Sciences

            NEWS & REFERENCE:    8   U.S. & World News Sources
                                 9   General Interest
Press <return> to continue.
```

Figure 13-3 **InfoMaster Main Menu** This menu allows selection of databases by subject type and provides access to sample searches, practice databases, and online assistence.

AT&T Information Services

- Compile better sales leads by obtaining specialized information on potential clients.
- Conduct preliminary searches for registered patents and trademarks, saving time and money on legal fees.
- Investigate industry trends, competitive products, and companies.
- Study technical innovations from around the world.
- Track government activities and regulatory matters.

InfoMaster offers a comprehensive range of online information, ranging from full-text articles to abstracts to reference sources designed to accommodate almost any information need.

InfoMaster is a collection of databases provided in conjunction with leading information suppliers. InfoMaster provides access to databases produced by information providers throughout the world without the subscription costs otherwise required to maintain accounts on each individual service or the requirement to learn multiple search languages.

The collection contains in-depth information for background study, research, competitive analysis, or other business information needs. It pro-

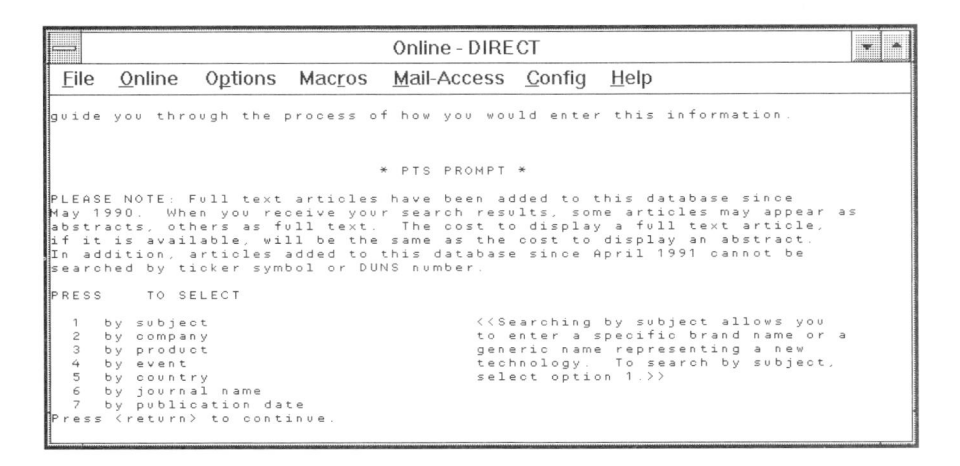

Figure 13-4 **Sample Database Search** The InfoMaster system provides annotated sample searches to demonstrate how a search is performed.

vides one of the broadest ranges of electronic information available today in one easily accessible service. The unique menuing system makes these resources available to unskilled users. The service does not charge for unsuccessful searches, other than connect time. Free online help with search techniques is provided. Advanced searchers can use InfoMaster to economically access database services for which they are untrained or on which they do not maintain accounts.

InfoMaster database classes include:

Directories   This type of database provides business and financial reports, listings, and specific factual data in standardized and concise formats.

Full-text   This type of database contains the full text of published articles. It usually does not provide the graphics or tables found in the original article.

Abstracts   This type of database contains summaries of articles that have appeared in periodicals, trade magazines, and journals. They contain the key elements of published articles in condensed format. Abstracts are a fast, effective way of

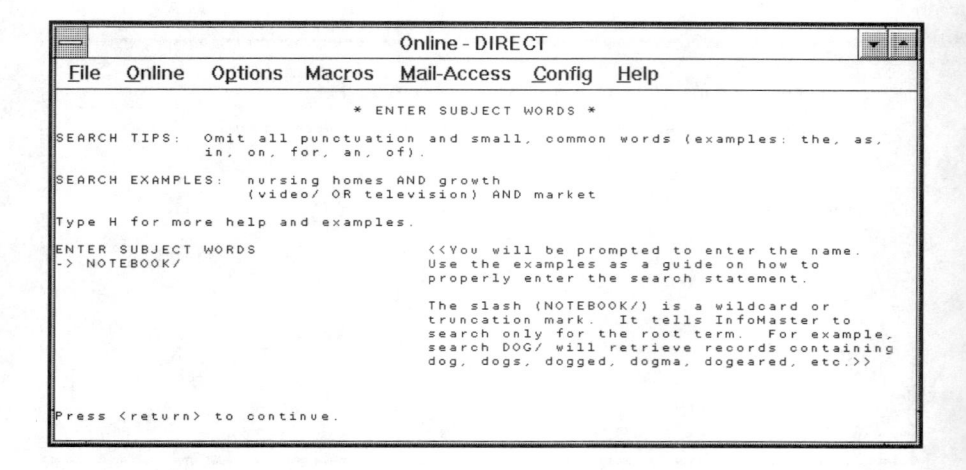

```
                          Online - DIRECT
File  Online  Options  Macros  Mail-Access  Config  Help
                    * ENTER SUBJECT WORDS *
SEARCH TIPS:    Omit all punctuation and small, common words (examples: the, as,
                in, on, for, an, of).
SEARCH EXAMPLES:    nursing homes AND growth
                    (video/ OR television) AND market
Type H for more help and examples.

ENTER SUBJECT WORDS                <<You will be prompted to enter the name.
-> NOTEBOOK/                       Use the examples as a guide on how to
                                   properly enter the search statement.

                                   The slash (NOTEBOOK/) is a wildcard or
                                   truncation mark.  It tells InfoMaster to
                                   search only for the root term.  For example,
                                   search DOG/ will retrieve records containing
                                   dog, dogs, dogged, dogma, dogeared, etc.>>

Press <return> to continue.
```

Figure 13-5 **Search Construction** This example shows how subject words are used to construct an InfoMaster search.

AT&T Information Services 341

obtaining the sense of an article without having to read the entire article.

InfoMaster provides a menu series which guides users through the process of selecting a database, entering search terms, and then executing the search. All items appear as textual information on the terminal, and the information obtained is displayed on the screen after the search is completed.

Since InfoMaster operates in terminal mode, the Capture or Log feature of the communications software should be used to keep a copy of the headings, articles, and other information retrieved. When this is activated, it will save a copy of everything that appears on screen to disk. Starting capture as soon as InfoMaster is used will allow the later evalu-

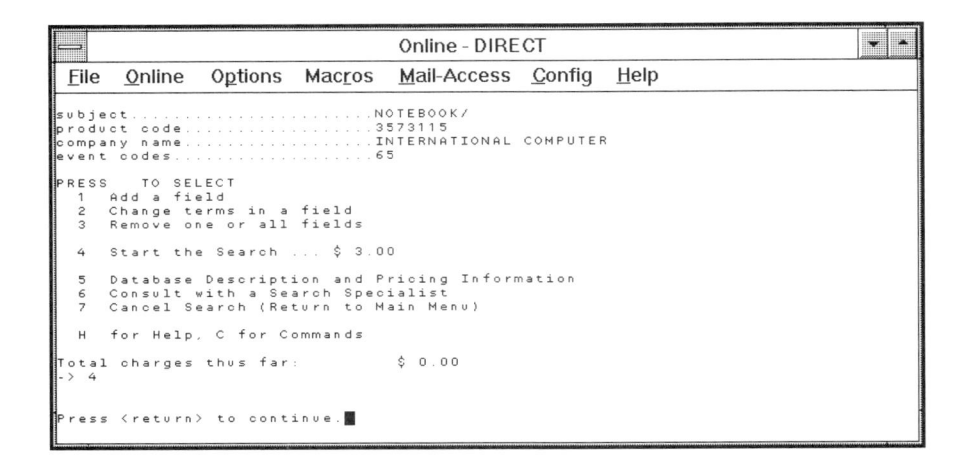

```
                         Online - DIRECT
 File   Online   Options   Macros   Mail-Access   Config   Help
subject.......................NOTEBOOK/
product code..................3573115
company name..................INTERNATIONAL COMPUTER
event codes...................65

PRESS   TO SELECT
  1   Add a field
  2   Change terms in a field
  3   Remove one or all fields

  4   Start the Search ... $ 3.00

  5   Database Description and Pricing Information
  6   Consult with a Search Specialist
  7   Cancel Search (Return to Main Menu)

  H   for Help, C for Commands

Total charges thus far:        $ 0.00
-> 4

Press <return> to continue.█
```

Figure 13-6 **Narrowing a Search** Searches are made more specific or narrrow by adding additional search terms such as product codes, company names, and event codes.

ation of the search strategy as well as the search results. The InfoMaster system does not keep a copy of the search results. This permits use of a word processor to review, edit, reformat, and print the search results.

Selecting an Infomaster Database

An InfoMaster database is selected from the InfoMaster main menu subject categories. Either a list of databases covering that area or one or two sub-menus to narrow your subject category will be displayed before a database list is displayed. Database descriptions can be displayed by entering DIR followed by the database name or number at any arrow prompt. An example is "DIR PHILADELPHIA INQUIRER or DIR 2734."

InfoMaster will display a database DIRectory entry including the database name and number, a brief description, the price for each searching transaction available in the database, and other relevant information, including start date, update frequency, output format, and reprint availability. Typing 'S' after viewing directory information starts a search in the previously displayed database.

In some cases, an option to scan databases is available. Selection of this option allows a search to be run against the indexes of the data-

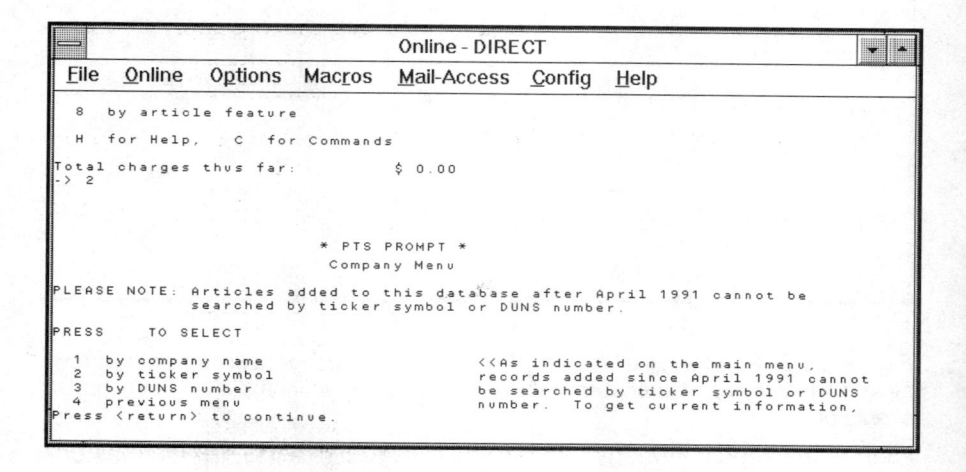

```
                          Online - DIRECT
 File   Online   Options   Macros   Mail-Access   Config   Help
   8   by article feature
   H   for Help,    C   for Commands
Total charges thus far:         $ 0.00
-> 2


                         * PTS PROMPT *
                          Company Menu
PLEASE NOTE:  Articles added to this database after April 1991 cannot be
              searched by ticker symbol or DUNS number.
PRESS    TO SELECT
   1   by company name               <<As indicated on the main menu,
   2   by ticker symbol              records added since April 1991 cannot
   3   by DUNS number                be searched by ticker symbol or DUNS
   4   previous menu                 number.  To get current information,
Press <return> to continue.
```

Figure 13-7 **Adding Fields** Company name is added to make the search for "Notebook" and the product code "3673116" more specific.

bases. The user can then select the database based on the number of

AT&T Information Services 343

occurances of the search found in each database. Otherwise, the database is selected and the search entered.

Search terms are constructed using key words. The system does not search common words such as "of," "the," "for," and "at" as part of the search term. For example, "King England" would be used rather than

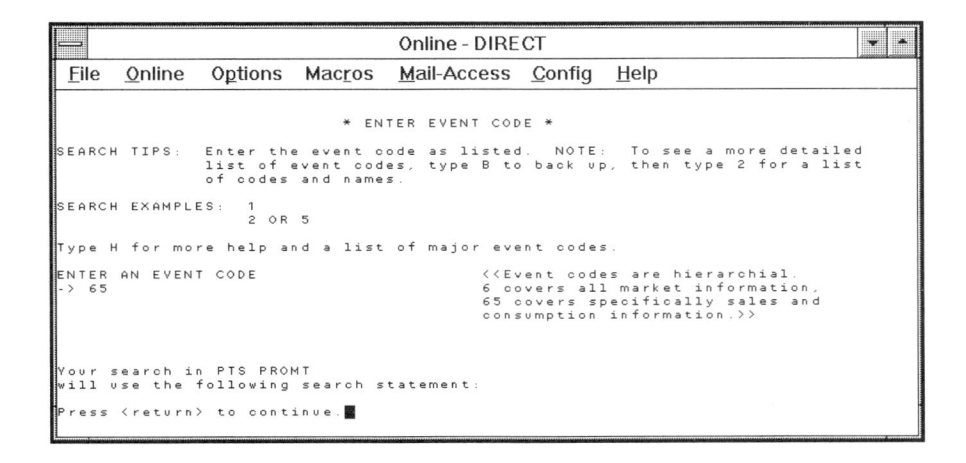

```
                              Online - DIRECT
 File   Online   Options   Macros   Mail-Access   Config   Help

                         * ENTER EVENT CODE *
SEARCH TIPS:   Enter the event code as listed.  NOTE:  To see a more detailed
               list of event codes, type B to back up, then type 2 for a list
               of codes and names.
SEARCH EXAMPLES:   1
                   2 OR 5

Type H for more help and a list of major event codes.

ENTER AN EVENT CODE                   <<Event codes are hierarchial.
-> 65                                    6 covers all market information.
                                        65 covers specifically sales and
                                        consumption information.>>

Your search in PTS PROMT
will use the following search statement:

Press <return> to continue.
```

Figure 13-8 **Event Codes** An event code restricts the search to a defined type of event. 65 is the code for Sales and Consumption. Codes are available online.

"King of England," as "of" cannot be part of the search term. Terms should be specific. An example would be the use of "wood" rather than "walnut" when "walnut" is the item desired. The use of "wood," a much more general term, would return many undesired references. Spelling variants can be retrieved by using "/" as a wild card. For example: Run/ retrieves Run, Runs, Runner, Running, and all other terms beginning with Run.

A search is narrowed or made more specific by combining search terms with the word "and." "And" requires that both search terms be present in the article and therefore restricts the search to articles in which both terms appear. It is used to combine two concepts as a search requirement.

A search is broadened or made less specific by combining search terms with the word "or." "Or" requires that only one of the terms be present in the article and therefore restricts the search to articles in which one or more of the terms appear. It is used to select alternatives such as "run/ or jog/." That would select any article with a term beginning with run or a term beginning with jog or both. It is used to search variant forms of the same concept.

Terms can be either phrases or single words. A phrase example would be "female runner." This phrase would result in the selection of articles where the two words appeared together and in the exact order specified. Phrases are enclosed in parentheses. "Female runner or male runner" can be ambiguous, and therefore the terms would be grouped using parentheses. "(Female Runner) or (Male Runner)" would select an article with either "female runner" or "male runner" as an article which satisfies the search criteria.

Investment ANALY$T

Investment ANALY$T is an information resource and stock analysis tool that helps users make sound strategic investment decisions. Investment ANALY$T can help users pinpoint the securities that best meet their investment goals. Its stock screening feature matches companies against the individual user's own selection criteria. This allows users to target companies on growth rate, dividend payment, price-to-earnings ratio, or other factors, alone or in combination. Additional factors can be based on comparison with industry ratios or on factors such as the amount and nature of insider activity.

With Investment ANALY$T, users have access to

- Stock quotes
- Latest company news
- Buy/sell indicators
- Insider trading data
- Broker evaluations
- Stock performance statistics

AT&T Information Services

- Company financial statements and forecasts
- Fundamentals and technical indicators

Investment ANALY$T provides menu-driven access to current price, earnings, volume, and trend information on more than 12,000 stocks and mutual funds from many financial services. It also includes the ability to produce a consolidated report from multiple sources with a single command. This consolidated report can be produced without the need for subscriptions to each source, the need to learn multiple search languages, or the time and cost of combining the individual results into a consolidated report. The Investment ANALY$T main menu includes information such as

- Current Stock & Mutual Fund Quotes
- Historical Stock & Mutual Fund Quotes
- Stock Charts, Indicators, Financials, News
- Brokers' Research Reports
- Stock Screening and Selection
- Ticker Symbol Look-Up
- Explanation of Options on This Menu
- Investment ANALY$T Service Disclaimer
- Leave Investment ANALY$T

AT&T FYI Service

AT&T FYI Service provides access to a variety of public information sources and the ability to publish private, corporate, or industry-specific information in bulletin board format without the provisioning or technical support requirements otherwise necessary. Corporate data can be published electronically both for customers and for internal use.

FYI NewsLink provides a broad range of late-breaking, worldwide news and economic business reports, including the most recent currency and metal prices and commodity and stock market news. The Official Airline Guide (OAG) Electronic Edition provides access to airline travel schedules, the ability to make a reservation directly from the schedule, and global hotel, city, and country information. News agencies, such as USA Today, provide direct feeds to the AT&T FYI Service containing general news, weather, and sports reports.

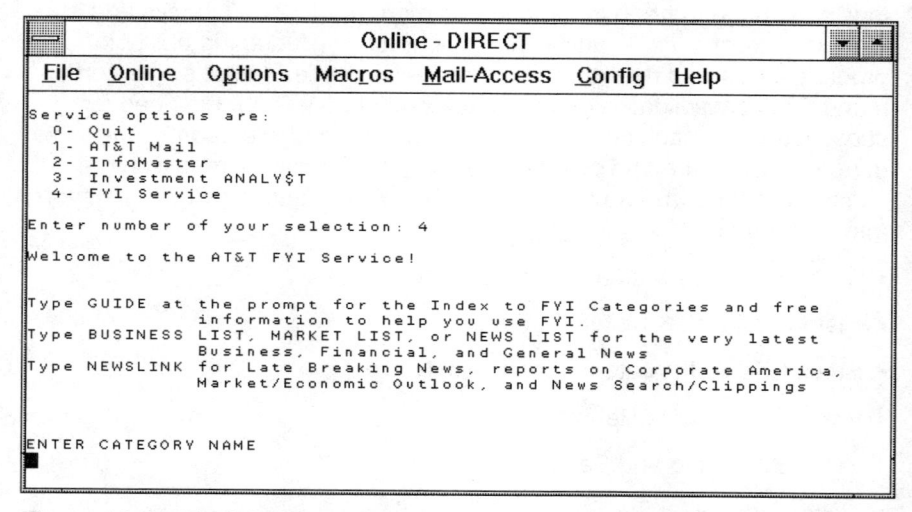

```
                          Online - DIRECT
 File   Online   Options   Macros   Mail-Access   Config   Help
Service options are:
  0 - Quit
  1 - AT&T Mail
  2 - InfoMaster
  3 - Investment ANALY$T
  4 - FYI Service

Enter number of your selection: 4

Welcome to the AT&T FYI Service!

Type GUIDE    at the prompt for the Index to FYI Categories and free
              information to help you use FYI.
Type BUSINESS LIST, MARKET LIST, or NEWS LIST for the very latest
              Business, Financial, and General News
Type NEWSLINK for Late Breaking News, reports on Corporate America,
              Market/Economic Outlook, and News Search/Clippings

ENTER CATEGORY NAME
```

Figure 13-9 **FYI Main Menu** This menu is the entry point for FYI and the starting point for all searches.

Mobile users and office users can review airline schedules, identify lowest fares, and check arrival and departure information at major U.S. airports. AT&T EasyLink Services subscribers can check current flight information, similar to that provided on airport monitors, for major U.S. cities, using a radio modem, while in a cab to the airport. International weather forecasts, including tropical storm warnings, and U.S. ski reports are available online.

FYI NewsLink provides reports on major world events and late-breaking news. These reports provide the information needed to make better-informed business decisions, develop sounder investment strategies, and be aware of current events. FYI NewsLink constantly monitors and gathers the news from major national and international news wires, specialized sources, the SEC, NASD, and important press releases. This information is often full-text. All FYI NewsLink reports are stored for rapid retrieval. These reports help track trends, chart changes, and evaluate

AT&T Information Services

emerging companies and evolving opportunities. FYI NewsLink provides the latest news and market information about NYSE, AMEX, NASDAQ, and pink sheet companies.

Users can obtain late-breaking summaries of world and local news, and financial and credit market information. Individual company activity can be tracked by simply entering a stock symbol or name at the appropriate prompt to receive a consolidated list of all news on that company.

AT&T FYI Service provides access to news, finance, markets, and other topics through a quick and easy interface. Many topics are stored directly in AT&T FYI topics on the FYI Service itself. Other topic areas, with more detailed or frequently changing information, are accessed through gateways out of the FYI Service. An example is AT&T FYI NewsLink. These gateways are smoothly integrated into FYI to allow easy movement between topics.

The AT&T FYI Service is used interactively. The service is arranged by topics and has an online topic guide. Topics are grouped into categories, and these category names can be public or private. Categories provide a fast way to move to the appropriate area. Menus can also be used to locate topics or categories.

The types of information features available include

- AT&T FYI NewsLink
- OAG for Travel
- FYI NewsAlert Subscription Option
- FYI InfoBoards for Corporations and Associations
- FYI Service Category Index

The AT&T FYI Service offers businesses an easy, electronically integrated way to stay ahead in today's competitive market.

FYI Service features include

Concise news summaries	Frequently updated world and local news located on public FYI InfoBoards, and a broad range of in-depth stories, which are updated throughout the day, in the FYI NewsLink gateway.
Market information	Easy access to the status of stock, credit, commodities, and currency markets. Mortgage rates and market indexes at the desktop.
Industry-specific news	Professionally prepared summaries of events in specific industries, including banking, business law, energy, real estate, travel, and telecommunications, presented in daily newsletters from the publishers of USA Today. Industry-specific reports are available through NewsLink.
International country data	Information needed by global business managers, including exchange rates, statistics on imports and exports, industrial production, unemployment, inflation rates, local customs, and local information such as ground transportation, hotels, and restaurants.
General news, market data	FYI NewsLink's extensive archives and stories can be searched using keywords to locate stories of interest.
Travel	Airline schedules and fares can be searched and flights booked interactively. Changes in travel plans can be made from anywhere, at any time from a laptop PC.
Weather	The FYI Service provides weather reports for major cities around the world.

FYI Services are priced on connect time. There are no monthly fees or subscription charges. Rate levels vary depending on the category or gateway used. Current prices are available online or in the AT&T EasyLink Services Pricing Guide.

FYI InfoBoards

FYI InfoBoards provide a fast, economical way to create business information applications such as online product catalogs or sales support systems. Configuration and security features permit groups to decide which information can be accessed, The creators of a private FYI environment can create their own menus. Authorized users who know what they want can go directly to that topic name. Users who need more information can use FYI online topic guides with a set of menus to guide them to the right topic. Users in corporate or association FYI environments can access both public and private data. Other users can access only public information.

The FYI Service offers corporations or associations the capability to electronically publish their information. Using the FYI InfoBoards, the lead time, complexities, and development costs of full-scale, traditional electronic publication are avoided. Uploading the information is done in a manner very similar to posting an AT&T EasyLink service message. Once uploaded, the material can be read by users just like the public FYI InfoBoard categories. The information provider determines whether the material is to be generally available to users of the FYI Service, or restricted to a specific group or groups.

FYI InfoBoards offer solutions for better communications with clients, suppliers, and business partners. For associations, this service can improve member services and allow for new association benefits in the form of electronic publications which can be more timely or cost-effective than traditional alternatives.

Information providers can

- Publish franchise policies, forms, and knowledge bases.
- Build an ordering or information request center without the need for full-scale systems development and without long lead times.
- Share the trade association knowledge with members.
- Provide an industry-specific classified advertisement service.
- Publish an industry or association calendar of events.

- Distribute proposal text.
- Provide online maintenance and support for products.
- Improve the timeliness and level of communications with suppliers by posting specifications, contract terms, and other data.
- Post contracts for electronic bidding to reduce expenses.

FYI InfoBoards providers pay modest setup, maintenance, and storage fees for each category. The connect-time charges for using the FYI InfoBoard are paid by the reader.

When multiple categories are posted, menu groupings into categories are recommended as a method of providing guidance to users.

FYI Interactive Forms Category

FYI supports the creation of categories which function as structured interactions between the user and the service. The FYI Interactive Forms Category allows the information provider to create a form for completion by the user which guides and structures responses. This category can be used for requests for additional information in which an address is requested for subsequent processing or for an order form for use with an on-line category. The creator of the form creates the questions and response fields, and the user responds to the prompts. These prompts are text-based.

FYI NewsAlert

This service is designed to provide informative summaries of news and financial data. With FYI NewsAlert, users get the latest available information on

- World and local news
- Data from financial, foreign currency, metal, and commodity markets
- Daily industry reports

FYI NewsAlert is invaluable for tracking down the latest stories on a particular issue or industry. Daily industry reports help users stay current with trends on important issues.

AT&T Information Services

Getting to the information desired by a user is simple. FYI NewsAlert is divided into preset categories. Users can use the online topic guide to select a category or enter the category name.

While news and data are major features, other FYI InfoBoard categories also provide access to travel, weather, and other timely information. The benefits of such services are:

- The AT&T FYI Service provides an online topic guide. When the topic name is known, the user can go directly to the information desired, bypassing the menus. Topics are organized and named as categories. Category names are the fastest way to get at what you want. There is a list of public category names at the end of this chapter.

- Full menus are are displayed by typing GUIDE. An FYI session takes place interactively. The steps are:

Connect to AT&T FYI Service interactively by selecting the FYI selection from the services menu displayed on interactive logon. This requires either a PC equipped with a terminal emulation package, a communicating terminal, or, in the case of Access PLUS software, connection in the online mode.

On entry to the FYI Service, a welcome screen provides information on FYI additions and special activities.

The FYI Service then requests the user to ENTER CATEGORY NAME.

The user can then type the category name desired, if known. If the user needs more information, then menus can be displayed by typing GUIDE. After the category has been typed and the return or enter key pressed, the report is displayed. Multiple reports can be selected at one time by entering the category names separated by commas. The multiple reports are displayed in the order entered.

FYI gateways are accessed by typing the name of the topic (gateway) you want. When the user passes through the gateway, the command interface and available topics are those established by the gateway service's information provider. When a gateway is exited, using the gateway exit command, the user is placed back at the FYI Service ENTER

CATEGORY NAME prompt and can either exit FYI, type another topic name, or type GUIDE to get the online user guide.

Communications software with a session capture capability allows the user to record all or part of the FYI Service session into a log file on a PC. This capability is described in the user documentation material for the software. Access PLUS captures log files as mail messages in a Sessions folder, allowing them to be managed as if they were mail messages.

FYI NewsLink

AT&T FYI NewsLink is entered by typing the keyword NEWSLINK at the ENTER CATEGORY NAME prompt in the FYI Service. Current major stories can be selected from the FYI NewsLink main menu, which is organized by topics.

A keyword is a single controlled vocabulary word or phrase that is used to index and retrieve stories on a particular subject or topic. A keyword search feature lets users search for stories using names of companies, countries, people, industries, ticker symbols, or phrases. Users can establish an FYI NewsLink clipping file. A clipping file will automatically re-

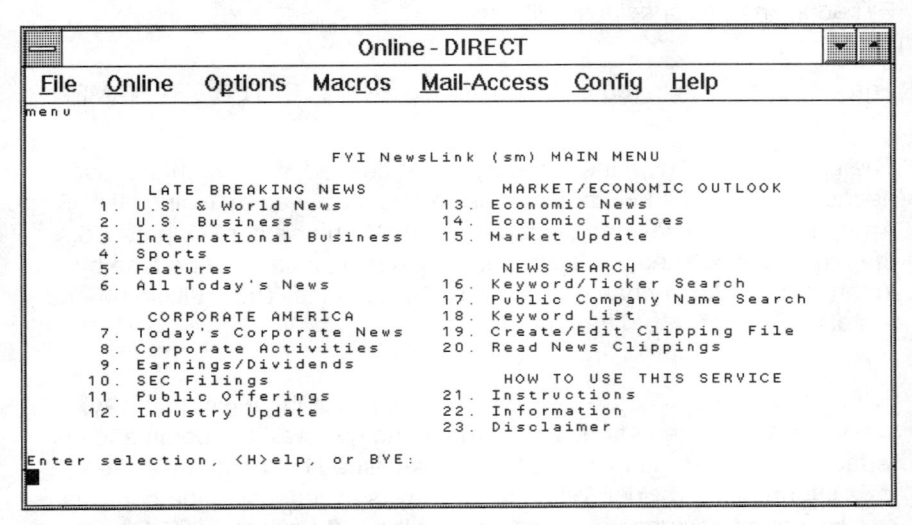

```
                       Online - DIRECT
 File    Online    Options   Macros   Mail-Access   Config   Help
menu

                      FYI NewsLink (sm) MAIN MENU

             LATE BREAKING NEWS            MARKET/ECONOMIC OUTLOOK
      1.  U.S. & World News           13.  Economic News
      2.  U.S. Business               14.  Economic Indices
      3.  International Business      15.  Market Update
      4.  Sports
      5.  Features                         NEWS SEARCH
      6.  All Today's News            16.  Keyword/Ticker Search
                                      17.  Public Company Name Search
             CORPORATE AMERICA        18.  Keyword List
      7.  Today's Corporate News      19.  Create/Edit Clipping File
      8.  Corporate Activities        20.  Read News Clippings
      9.  Earnings/Dividends
     10.  SEC Filings                      HOW TO USE THIS SERVICE
     11.  Public Offerings            21.  Instructions
     12.  Industry Update             22.  Information
                                      23.  Disclaimer

Enter selection, <H>elp, or BYE:
```

Figure 13-10 **FYI NewsLink** This menu provides a guide to FYI NewsLink services. Services may also be accessed using commands.

AT&T Information Services

trieve up to 15 stories on any subject and put them into an electronic file for the user.

A keyword search is performed by typing the word SEARCH and the keyword, such as SEARCH government. This search function allows you to review stories posted in the previous 30 days and can be performed from any menu level command line. Keywords can be the names of companies, sports, countries, people, industries or information classes. Ticker symbols can also be used but must be preceded by /, as in /T for AT&T.

Keywords are unique and must be spelled exactly as they appear in the NewsLink keyword list to maintain the precision of the FYI NewsLink search. Keywords which are phrases consisting of more than one word must have their parts joined by an underscore, as in prime_rate, or enclosed in quotes, as in "prime rate." Phrase keywords that are not linked by one of these methods are treated as separate search terms, so the search would retrieve any story containing the keyword prime or the keyword rate. This would be a less precise search.

FYI's advanced keyword search capability can be used for more precise document retrieval based on combinations of the keywords provided by the news service. This capability is intended for situations where you are looking for a very specific type of story. However, if the story was not coded with the keyword used, it will not be retrieved by this technique, although it might be retrieved by another search approach.

The search capability selects documents based on search expressions which may include multiple keywords, stock symbols, operators such as AND, OR, NOT, and parentheses in any combination needed to define the search.

Other options can be specified to limit the search. The user can specify how far back (in days) to search by adding #DAYS following the search string. Date ranges can be specified by using the #SINCE mm/dd and #BEFORE mm/dd dates following the search string. The results of an immediately preceding search can be used as a keyword with #PREVIOUS. These search options can also be entered in abbreviated form (#D, #S, #B, #P).

Asterisks function as wild cards, as in COMPUTER* or ACQUI*.

Underscores (_) present in some keywords and the slash (/) used with stock symbol keywords are required parts of keywords. A full keyword list is available online.

Examples:

COMPUTER* AND (NEW_PROD* OR ANNOUNCE*) #DAYS 5

(ACQUISITION* MERGER*) AND NOT OTC

/IBM AND NEW_PRODUCTS #SINCE 3/1

The FYI NewsLink system can automatically clip and save news items that match predetermined areas of interest. Clipping files are set up from the Create/Edit Clipping File selection on the Main Menu.

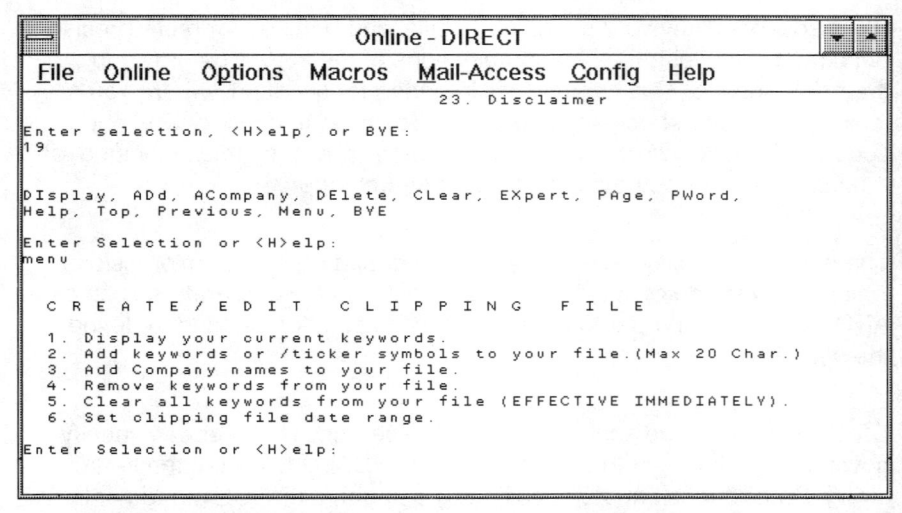

```
                         Online - DIRECT
  File   Online   Options   Macros   Mail-Access   Config   Help
                               23.  Disclaimer
Enter selection, <H>elp, or BYE:
19

DIsplay, ADd, ACompany, DElete, CLear, EXpert, PAge, PWord,
Help, Top, Previous, Menu, BYE
Enter Selection or <H>elp:
menu

    C R E A T E / E D I T   C L I P P I N G   F I L E

    1. Display your current keywords.
    2. Add keywords or /ticker symbols to your file.(Max 20 Char.)
    3. Add Company names to your file.
    4. Remove keywords from your file.
    5. Clear all keywords from your file (EFFECTIVE IMMEDIATELY).
    6. Set clipping file date range.
Enter Selection or <H>elp:
```

Figure 13-11 **FYI NewsLink Clipping Files** Keywords can be used to create a clipping file of matching articles which have appeared on the service in the preset time period.

AT&T Information Services

News clippings are read using the Read News Clippings selection from the Main Menu. Selecting this option displays up to 15 stories on each keyword that has appeared within the past 24 hours. The date range for retaining information in your clipping file and changes to keywords can be set from other menu options.

Official Airline Guide Electronic Edition

The Official Airline Guide Electronic Edition (OAGEE) gateway provides up-to-the minute information about airline flights, fares, lodging, and local information. It is one of the most comprehensive schedule, fare, and booking information sources. Its services include

- Up-to-date flight schedule and seat availability
- Airport arrival and departure times, delays, and gates at major United States airports
- Airport locator service to find the nearest airports to a city
- Fare quotes and booking capability
- Travel weather
- Hotels and restaurants, lists and reviews
- Worldwide travel facts

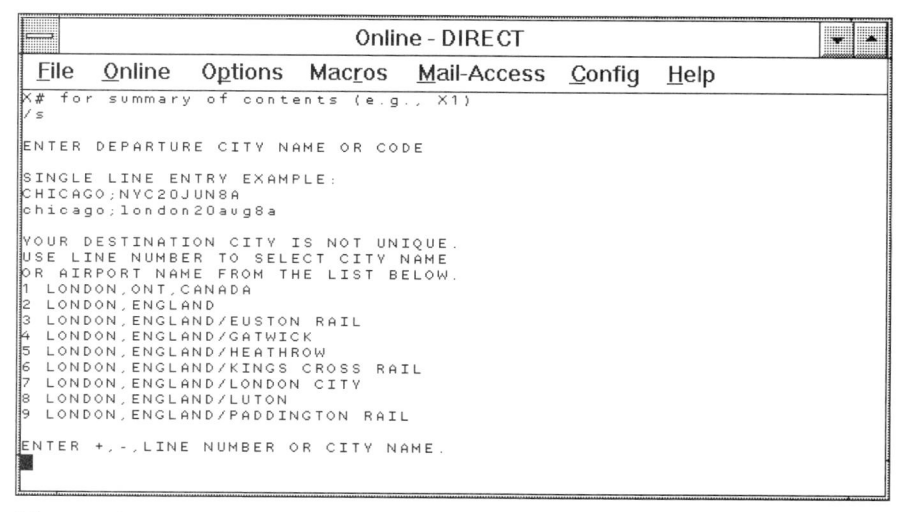

```
                        Online - DIRECT
 File   Online   Options   Macros   Mail-Access   Config   Help
X# for summary of contents (e.g., X1)
/s

ENTER DEPARTURE CITY NAME OR CODE

SINGLE LINE ENTRY EXAMPLE:
CHICAGO;NYC20JUN8A
chicago;london20aug8a

YOUR DESTINATION CITY IS NOT UNIQUE.
USE LINE NUMBER TO SELECT CITY NAME
OR AIRPORT NAME FROM THE LIST BELOW.
1  LONDON,ONT,CANADA
2  LONDON,ENGLAND
3  LONDON,ENGLAND/EUSTON RAIL
4  LONDON,ENGLAND/GATWICK
5  LONDON,ENGLAND/HEATHROW
6  LONDON,ENGLAND/KINGS CROSS RAIL
7  LONDON,ENGLAND/LONDON CITY
8  LONDON,ENGLAND/LUTON
9  LONDON,ENGLAND/PADDINGTON RAIL

ENTER +,-,LINE NUMBER OR CITY NAME.
```

Figure 13-12 **OAGEE Schedule Display** The system returns a menu of items when an entry is ambiguous. In this case, multiple cities match London.

- Travel industry news: promotional offers, etc.

The OAG Electronic Edition gateway is entered by typing OAG at the ENTER CATEGORY NAME prompt in the FYI Service. OAG can be used either in menu mode or, more efficiently, in command mode. In menu mode, a series of questions guides the user in building a query. The information required for either schedule or fare searches is the arrival and departure cities, date of departure, and approximate time desired. Airports close to a city can be located through another menu option. The OAG system session is ended by typing OFF to return to the FYI ENTER CATEGORY NAME Prompt. The options available at the OAG main

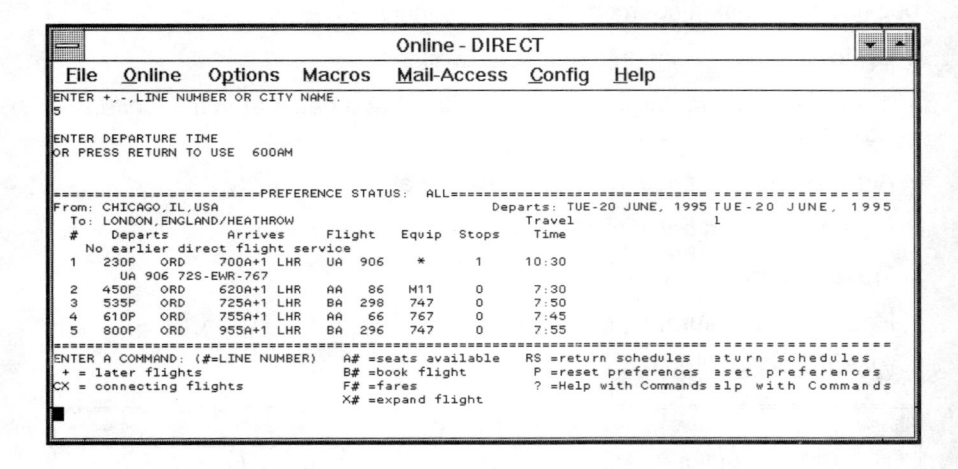

```
========================== Online - DIRECT ==========================
File  Online  Options  Macros  Mail-Access  Config  Help
ENTER +,-,LINE NUMBER OR CITY NAME.
5

ENTER DEPARTURE TIME
OR PRESS RETURN TO USE   600AM


==================PREFERENCE STATUS:  ALL========================= =================
From: CHICAGO,IL,USA                         Departs: TUE-20 JUNE, 1995 TUE-20 JUNE, 1995
   To: LONDON,ENGLAND/HEATHROW                        Travel             1
      #   Departs      Arrives    Flight  Equip  Stops   Time
      No earlier direct flight service
      1   230P    ORD    700A+1 LHR   UA   906    *       1    10:30
          UA 906 72S-EWR-767
      2   450P    ORD    620A+1 LHR   AA    86   M11      0     7:30
      3   535P    ORD    725A+1 LHR   BA   298   747      0     7:50
      4   610P    ORD    755A+1 LHR   AA    66   767      0     7:45
      5   800P    ORD    955A+1 LHR   BA   296   747      0     7:55
==================================================================== =================
ENTER A COMMAND: (#=LINE NUMBER)   A# =seats available  RS =return schedules  aturn schedules
 + = later flights                 B# =book flight       P =reset preferences  aset preferences
CX = connecting flights            F# =fares             ? =Help with Commands alp with Commands
                                   X# =expand flight
```

Figure 13-13 **Schedule Display** This screen shows flights from Chicago to London.

menu include

- Airport arrivals, departures and gate information
- Accu-Weather forecasts
- In-flight movies
- Lodging and dining
- Worldwide travel facts
- Travel industry news

AT&T Information Services

- Frequent traveler programs
- Leisure and discount travel
- All cruise travel
- What's new
- General and how-to-use
- User comments and suggestions

The OAG Electronic Edition airline schedules and fares database uses a set of commands or menus to

- Display flights between two points by time of departure.
- Display flights between two points in ascending fare order.
- Limit flight schedule or fare displays to selected airlines.
- Display hotel information.
- Display or cancel booked flights.

Arrivals, departures and gate information can be displayed from the menu or by command. This database contains current flight arrival and departure information for more than 17 major airports throughout the United States and is similar to the information displayed on the airport

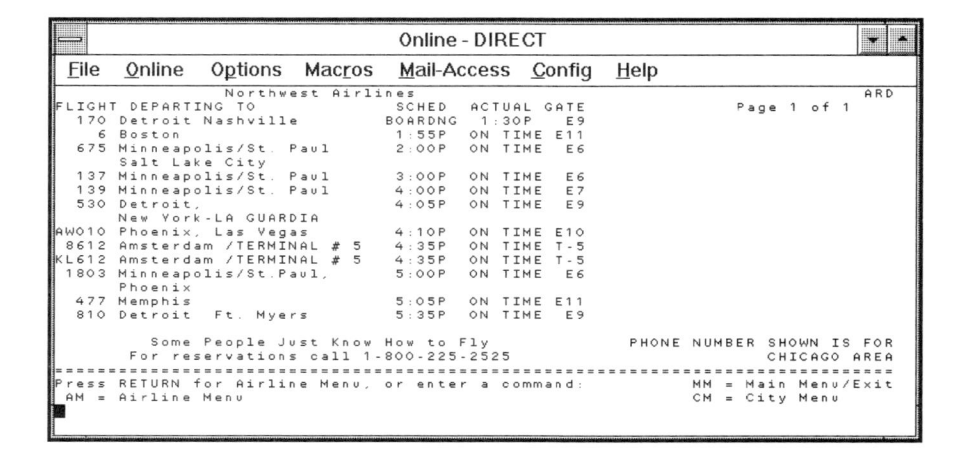

```
╔══════════════════════════════════════════════════════════════════════════╗
║                          Online - DIRECT                                 ║
╠══════════════════════════════════════════════════════════════════════════╣
║  File   Online   Options   Macros   Mail-Access   Config   Help          ║
║              Northwest Airlines                                       ARD║
║FLIGHT DEPARTING TO             SCHED   ACTUAL GATE      Page 1 of 1      ║
║  170  Detroit Nashville        BOARDNG  1:30P    E9                      ║
║    6  Boston                    1:55P  ON TIME  E11                      ║
║  675  Minneapolis/St. Paul      2:00P  ON TIME  E6                       ║
║       Salt Lake City                                                     ║
║  137  Minneapolis/St. Paul      3:00P  ON TIME  E6                       ║
║  139  Minneapolis/St. Paul      4:00P  ON TIME  E7                       ║
║  530  Detroit,                  4:05P  ON TIME  E9                       ║
║       New York-LA GUARDIA                                                ║
║AW010  Phoenix, Las Vegas        4:10P  ON TIME  E10                      ║
║ 8612  Amsterdam /TERMINAL # 5   4:35P  ON TIME  T-5                      ║
║KL612  Amsterdam /TERMINAL # 5   4:35P  ON TIME  T-5                      ║
║ 1803  Minneapolis/St.Paul,      5:00P  ON TIME  E6                       ║
║       Phoenix                                                            ║
║  477  Memphis                   5:05P  ON TIME  E11                      ║
║  810  Detroit   Ft. Myers       5:35P  ON TIME  E9                       ║
║                                                                          ║
║       Some People Just Know How to Fly       PHONE NUMBER SHOWN IS FOR   ║
║       For reservations call 1-800-225-2525              CHICAGO AREA     ║
║==========================================================================║
║Press RETURN for Airline Menu, or enter a command:   MM = Main Menu/Exit  ║
║ AM = Airline Menu                                   CM = City Menu       ║
╚══════════════════════════════════════════════════════════════════════════╝
```

Figure 13-14 **Airport Information** Arrival and departure information, in a form similar to that shown on airport monitors, is available for major U.S. cities.

monitors including gate, baggage claim area, and status (delayed, on time, canceled, etc.).

Arrival and departure times are updated as transmitted by the individual airports. The time and date of the last update is displayed on the Airline menu.

Another database example is the Frequent Flyer/Lodger award information, which is a summary of the Frequent Flyer and Frequent Lodger award programs offered by airlines and hotels. There are listings for major airlines and hotel chains. The Frequent Flyer Information includes

- Program name, address, and telephone number
- Participating airlines
- Participating hotels
- Participating car rental companies
- Participating bank card
- Minimum mileage awards
- Program awards

The Frequent Lodger information includes

- Program name, address, and telephone number
- Participating airlines
- Participating car rental companies
- Minimum award level
- Accrual of awards
- Program awards

FYI Categories and Topics

This is a listing, by category, of the FYI Services organized by descriptive headings. Each of the categories beneath the main descriptive heading describes the service name and the category name. For example, the descriptive heading General News lists the information service names

AT&T Information Services

under that grouping—TODAYS NEWS and DECISIONLINE, for example. Keyword names, such as NEWS, appear in bold. Category names, such as GL00, and secondary heading names, such as GL01 and GL02, are listed where appropriate.

General News	Today's News Enter NEWS for a concise summary of current, worldwide news stories and NEWSLINK for up-to-the-minute details.
DECISION LINE	USA TODAY or GL00 This is a daily series of 18 separate newsletters by industry or topic areas compiled by Gannett National Information Network. Typing USA TODAY or GL00 shows the main menu. Reports can be selected directly by entering the appropriate selection, such as GL12, or from the menu.
News	GL01
Weather	GL02
Personal Investing	GL03
Banking and Economy	GL05
Energy	GL06
Insurance	GL07
Business Law	GL08
Real Estate	GL09
Issues	GL10
Technology	GL11
Telecommunications	GL12
Travel	GL13
Trends and Marketing	GL14
Advertising	GL15

Health	GL16
Sports	GL17
Bonus	GL18
International News	GL40
Japan News	JAPAN Domestic and international news coverage affecting Japan and feature articles of Japanese interest.
Science and Health News	SCIENCE Shows a menu with ten categories of timely stories on medicine, high tech, environment, space, etc., by the American Chemical Society.
Sports News	NEWSLINK for both headlines and the full stories or GL17 for the Gannett Decisionline summary report.

Business and Finance News

U.S. Business News	BIZNEWS Summaries of the day's top business news stories for the United States.
International Business News	INTL BIZNEWS Summaries of the day's top business news stories around the world. Excludes the United States, which is provided in BIZNEWS. NewsLink provides current details.
Market Commentary	MARKET U.S. stock market commentary and latest market averages. Updated throughout the day when markets are open.
Economic Reports	ECONOMY Summary of current and upcoming statistical releases from United States and other governments. Updated weekly by News-a-tron.
Mortgage News	MORTGAGE Federal mortgage indications. Daily report by News-a-tron keeps you abreast of changing rates, FNMAs, FHLMC, GNMAs.

AT&T Information Services 361

Markets

Asian Stock Markets	ASIA STOCKS Asian stock market wrapup, provided each weekday morning (U.S.).

U.S. stock reports are grouped by area. The Dow Jones, NYSE, and SAP indexes are updated throughout the day; others are updated once per business day.

Closing Index for DJ, NYSE, AMEX	CLOSING INDEX
NYSE Index	NYSE INDEX
AMEX Index (Close)	AMEX
OTC Index (Close)	OTC
Dow Jones Averages	DJ INDEX or DJ AVERAGE
Standard & Poor's Index	SP INDEX
NYSE Closing: Active Stocks, Trends	NYSE CLOSE
AMEX Closing: Active Stocks, Trends	AMEX CLOSE
OTC Closing: Active Stocks, Trends	OTC CLOSE
Credit Report	CREDIT Daily report provides analytic coverage of the credit and cash markets. Also commentaries on interest rates internationally. By News-a-tron.
Credit Market Yields	YIELDS Summary of yields in the credit markets, posted each business day after the markets close.

Treasury Bill Auction	TBILLS The results of U.S. Treasury bill auctions, posted weekly on Monday after the close of the markets.
Foreign Exchange Commentary	COMMENTARY Twice daily foreign currency reports by News-a-tron. Rates for top currencies and survey of market sentiment.
Foreign Exchange	CURRENCY Foreign exchange interbank seller rates and foreign currency equivalents. Covers fifty countries. Updated daily.
Yen Exchange Rate	YEN RATE Currency exchange rate for yen, at Tokyo market close.
Money Report	MONEY Quick review of the U.S. dollar abroad, gold and silver prices. Updated once daily.
Precious Metals Quotes	PMETALS Precious metals quotes, worldwide; updated twice daily.
Coinquote Close	COIN QUOTE A daily update of gold and silver coin price quotes, representing wholesale selling prices as quoted by Manfra Tordella and Brookes.

Commodity Prices

This is a set of categories providing commodity price information in concise packages. Grain and fuel are updated twice daily; others are updated daily.

Cotton (NY Close)	COTTON
Grain (Various U.S. Markets)	GRAIN
Metals (London Close, Nonprecious)	METALS
Metals (NY Midday, Nonprecious)	NY METALS

AT&T Information Services

Petroleum Markets	FUEL
Sugar	SUGAR
Commodity Futures (Includes Cocoa, Coffee, Cotton, Gold, Silver, Copper, Platinum, Sugar, and Others)	COMMODITY FUTURES or CFUTURES

Research Services

NEXIS EXPRESS	NEXIS EXPRESS For more information on how to request research through FYI.
Barter	BARTER How your company can exchange goods or services for almost anything. International Business Clearinghouse negotiates direct trades.
Translations	TRANSLATION Have your correspondence translated into the language of your choice, many times in just hours (International Business Clearinghouse).

Travel

Official Airline Guides	OAGEE The electronic edition allows you to choose the best flights and fares, hotels, and restaurants.
Travel News	GL13 Travel information from Gannett National Information Network, covering tourism highlights. Updated daily.

Weather

Traveler's Forecast	CITIES Abbreviated 2-day forecast (National Weather Service) covering 30 U.S. cities.
Two-Day Detail by City	WEATHER Menu of U.S. cities to retreive a detailed 2-day forecast from the National Weather Service.
Weather Summary by Gannett	GL02 Weather conditions from Gannett National Information Network. Includes regional forecasts, world temperatures, and forecasts for 28 cities across the United States.
U.S. Summary	US WEATHER Current temperature and conditions around the United States.
International Summary	INTL WEATHER Current temperature and conditions around the globe.
Storm Warnings	HURRICANE Tropical storm updates for the Atlantic, Gulf of Mexico, and Caribbean Sea from the National Weather Service.
Ski Reports	SKIING Seasonal menu by states with instructions for accessing individual reports.

Consumer Information

Consumer Reports	CONSUMER Summaries from Consumer Reports magazine, updated weekly and presented in a topic menu.
Personal Investing	GL03 Daily summary of news affecting personal investments, compiled by Gannett.
Health	GL16 Daily summary of news affecting your health, compiled by Gannett.
Recipes	GOURMET Trendsetting, elegant, and easy recipes.

AT&T Information Services

Entertainment

Review Menu	REVIEWS Book, movie, video, and record reviews.
Bookshelf	BOOKS Best seller hardcovers and paperback compiled by Publishers Weekly (updated weekly). Capsule reviews of new books compiled by Kirkus Reviews, updated twice a month.
Home Video	VIDEO Weekly reports on movies and other VCR and cable programming.
Movie Briefs	MOVIES Mini-reviews and ratings for current showings, new releases, and coming attractions.
Soap Opera Summaries	SOAPS Menu of daily soap opera summaries, soap opera news, gossip, ratings, and puzzler.
Daily Trivia	TRIVIA Trivia contest.
Greeting Cards	GREETINGS List and description of greeting card designs.

Chapter 14

AT&T Global Telex Services

AT&T Global Telex Services provides its subscribers with a powerful communications tool which is fully integrated into the electronic workplace and which is an essential part of today's global electronic commerce. AT&T provides one of the most complete global telex networks. It combines universal reach and worldwide access, immense breadth and scope of products and services, comprehensive application integration features to promote business growth, and time- and cost-efficient telex enhancements.

Telex is one of the most reliable and universally available forms of electronic communication. Banks and other financial institutions rely on telex for electronic funds transfer because of its highly developed security features. These security features include automated machine-generated answerbacks that verify terminal ID and the almost universal use of test-key codes to authenticate the contents of telex messages. Multinational corporations use telex to send messages to remote subsidiaries or affiliates, especially in areas with underdeveloped communications. AT&T Global Telex Services continues to expand the reach and scope of its worldwide telex support and functionality. Today, telex retains its place, together with electronic mail and fax technology, as an essential element of international electronic commerce.

AT&T Global Telex Services' value-added features integrate telex into today's world of electronic commerce. With AT&T EasyLink Services, a subscriber can send a telex from a desktop computer, receive a telex in an electronic mailbox, or convert a telex message to a fax or electronic mail message for forwarding to non-telex delivery points. Telexes can be generated by applications running on mainframes, midrange systems, UNIX systems, or PCs. Subscribers can send telexes from either standalone or LAN-connected PCs and receive responses in their AT&T EasyLink Services' email mailbox. An application running on an IBM AS/400 and connected to AT&T Global Telex Services can therefore send telexes with automatic test-key authentication. With traditional telex, an employee would have to carry the application-generated output text which was to be sent by telex to the communications department. In the communications department, an operator would type the data again and add the required test-key codes. With AT&T Global Telex Services, the telex function is integrated into the network environment, with logging and text coding as automated, integrated application functions. The application can directly generate the telex output.

Global Access

AT&T Global Telex Services supplies subscribers with universal reach provided by a seamless network of services and products, which eliminates geographic, time, and technology boundaries and which can convert telex messages to use a wide variety of delivery options. AT&T Global Telex Services is the transport of choice for an extraordinary volume of time-critical, high-value messages each day to destinations that include hundreds of countries, islands, and territories throughout the world. These telexes move with the accuracy, reliability, and efficiency that is essential in financial operations. One of the key AT&T Global Telex Services' enhancements is full X.400 integration for sending and receiving messages, allowing businesses to incorporate this worldwide connectivity into existing and new applications. These enhancements are provided in addition to the traditional access to the entire universe of worldwide telex users that AT&T Global Telex Services users have had.

AT&T Global Telex Services provides direct international access to and from many countries, using its own facilities. It has connectivity arrange-

AT&T Global Telex

ments with all major telex vendors worldwide and high-speed, officially accredited communications to the worldwide base of telex subscribers. AT&T monitoring and tracking ensures that subscribers will have accurate, reliable messaging and immediate secure transmissions. AT&T Global Telex Services' computerized telex switching systems are monitored around the clock by a globally distributed expert technical staff.

AT&T Global Telex Services delivers the support needed for mission-critical applications with total responsiveness and single-source accountability. The single source provides a safety net of products, services, and technical support from the time the first keystroke is typed to the moment the message is received and confirmed. AT&T Global Telex Services provides network access 24 hours a day and uses fully integrated, redundant switches with dedicated emergency power stations designed to switch around problems without loss of data and without undue message delay.

Other enhanced telex features provide productivity and efficiency. These features include

- Two- or three-digit dialing
- Automatic busy number redialing
- Automatic answerback
- Multiple calls in a single connection
- Departmental billing

Message Security

Telex remains one of the most reliable, secure, and officially accredited forms of written communication. Banks, for example, depend on telex to deliver thousands of confidential payment transactions totaling billions of dollars each business day. With AT&T's mailbox delivery feature, access to confidential telex messages can be restricted to designated employees, using PCs from their desks with the use of full bank test-key coding applications.

AT&T Global Telex Services provides reliable, immediate message delivery with the ability to track messages using specialized report formats and the capability to request alternative routings for both incoming and outgoing messages.

Telex Modes

Telex traditionally operated in a real-time mode, where the sending and receiving machines were directly connected over a slow-speed circuit.

Real-time telex provides immediate online transmission between two telex terminals anywhere in the world in the same manner that a telephone does. A bank in Tokyo which needs an immediate answer from a correspondent international bank in the United States would use real-time telex. This is an interactive service which requires both sending and receiving terminals to be available at the same instant. It is primarily for one-to-one transmission.

Store-and-forward telex provides near real-time transmission between telex terminals or any other delivery point in the same manner that AT&T Mail does. A major oil company which needs to send price updates to 500 domestic and overseas locations immediately would use store-and-forward telex. This is a non-interactive service which does not require both sending and receiving terminals to be available at the same instant. AT&T EasyLink high-speed store-and-forward telex eliminates waiting and busy signals as problems with telex use.

Database Access

AT&T Global Telex terminals can access databases which contain up-to-the-minute news and business information, allowing users in remote areas with poor communications to keep up with events. Users have instant access to market news, commodity prices, currency exchange rates, and news flashes, and can make travel reservations.

Delivery Options

AT&T Global Telex users also have access to the family of AT&T EasyLink Services. This allows the subscriber to convert a telex mes-

AT&T Global Telex

sage to fax quickly, easily, and economically. The subscriber can also use other messaging options, including electronic mail, cablegram, and hard copy delivery. An inbound telex can be converted to fax or electronic mail and held in a password-secured computer mailbox to be delivered at the time and location desired with higher security than standard telex.

Value-Added Services

All telex terminals and most PCs, minicomputers, and mainframe computers have easy direct access to AT&T Global Telex Services in the United States. When telex terminals can be reached directly through AT&T Global Telex Services, the subscriber does not need to pay the added network interconnect cost that is applicable when the sending and receiving terminals are on different telex networks. Easy upgrades and growth products allow the subscriber to replace expensive dedicated telex lines with standard low-cost telephone lines or inexpensive packet network access.

High-volume users can use AT&T dial-in/dial-out service to supplement existing dedicated lines during busy periods. Low-volume users can enjoy significant cost savings while maintaining the quality and responsiveness of a worldwide telex network.

Chapter 15

AT&T Professional Services

AT&T Professional Services provides high-quality, customized support for companies that want to implement technically complex electronic messaging applications. AT&T EasyLink Services formed its Professional Services organization to support companies shifting from outmoded paper-based commercial practices to advanced information technologies such as electronic data interchange (EDI), electronic mail (email), computer-generated fax services, online bulletin boards, and other messaging-based systems. These consulting services are designed for enterprises that see electronic messaging as their best means for competing in the global economy.

The AT&T EasyLink Professional Services organization offers a series of programs which include consulting, design, and customized implementation support for message-enabled applications, and customized training and education to meet the needs of individual customers and applications. The organization also offers technical and strategic education in areas such as technical EDI issues and EDI/corporate email network design and implementation.

AT&T specializes in projects that have defined electronic commerce objectives. It provides support to a company on a short-term basis to meet the company's electronic commerce goal. The programs include staff training to equip a company to support its electronic commerce expansion plans and its operational use of electronic commerce.

AT&T Professional Services provides unique capabilities which are often unavailable within the company or its potential employee sources. These skills often make the task of implementing electronic commerce less costly and less time-consuming than an implementation handled solely by internal resources. Some of the benefits are:

- AT&T Professional Services provides its clients with access to the insights gained from implementing electronic messaging applications for many other companies.

- AT&T Professional Services' recommendations for re-engineering an enterprise's business processes are based on the broad range of perspectives gained in successful global internal and external applications.

- AT&T Professional Services provides training to ensure that employees are equipped to handle the technical requirements of electronic commerce.

- AT&T Professional Services' experienced consultants provide on-the-job training, which reduces the risk of costly mistakes and oversights.

- Documented roles and responsibilities provided are the basis for ongoing program management and for measuring the success of the electronic commerce program.

- AT&T Professional Services, as part of a full-service, global electronic messaging company, is uniquely able to recommend a complete range of related technologies, and provide support for a worldwide electronic messaging project. The time to internal implementation of the electronic commerce program and the ramping of trading partners to full participation are accelerated.

Client requirements are clearly defined and products customized to fit them during the AT&T EasyLink Professional Services product provisioning process. The customized product is described in a detailed Statement of Work which is part of AT&T EasyLink Services Professional Services' contract with the client. The agreed-upon Statement of Work is then executed by the consultants, with constant review of the client's satisfaction at every step. Project quality is ensured by AT&T EasyLink Professional Services' vigorous technical professional development program for its consultants, as the consultant's talent and skill is the product provided. These consultants are therefore supported with the best possible training, structured technical development, and career plans.

Program Design

AT&T EasyLink Services Professional Services has designed a three-step set of programs based on its extensive experience with implementing electronic commerce. These programs can be customized to solve unique business needs. The programs develop from the observation that businesses develop internal expertise over time and cannot simply jump into electronic commerce. These complex messaging applications affect all internal and external business relationships, and the internal expertise must be developed in stages if full benefits are to be achieved. The programs are designed to deal with companies at each level of expertise in electronic commerce and are structured to provide the technical and market competencies needed for the next level.

Consulting and Design

The Explorer Program is the appropriate choice for the enterprise just beginning to evaluate how electronic messaging can be used by the company, or for the enterprise re-evaluating its current position in electronic messaging.

The Explorer Program is the consulting and design stage of the growth model. It has two main objectives:

- To formulate solutions for re-engineering the enterprise's current business processes to accommodate electronic messaging
- To provide the system specifications needed to implement the solution the enterprise selects

The consultants achieve the Explorer Program's objectives by observing the operation of the business, interviewing the people involved, and developing a diagram of the business process. Regularly scheduled status reports keep the client up to date on the progress of the program, and documented findings are discussed in person with the client. A written report of recommendations for business is prepared based on the agreed-upon findings, which form the basis of a presentation made to the client, the steering committee, and/or upper management representatives.

Installation and Implementation

The Target Program guides the enterprise through the startup stages of an electronic messaging application and is the installation and initial implementation stage of AT&T EasyLink Services Professional Services' electronic messaging growth model. It provides expert assistance for

- Establishing an electronic messaging environment
- Enabling the first three external users to communicate with the company

This program pays careful attention to early identification and resolution of potential problems. The enterprise's goals are analyzed to determine the requirements for the electronic messaging application. These findings form the basis of the Hardware, Software, and Communications Recommendation(s) Report prepared by the consultants. After this report is acceped by the client, the AT&T EasyLink Professional Services staff installs and tests all aspects of the electronic commerce project at the client's location. The staff works from its own location to help the first application users communicate with the client.

The Target Program includes regularly scheduled status reports which keep the client informed of the program's progress. Clients also receive a report on the results of the communication connectivity and end-to-end application testing with the application users. At program completion, AT&T EasyLink Professional Services provides a no-charge teleconference to introduce the client and application to the AT&T EasyLink Services Customer Service and Support Center.

Ramping

Ramping is an expansion process that requires careful coordination and resource management. It takes the client's electronic commerce project from pilot to full implementation and includes the expert assistance needed to create a network of successful application users. The program provides the skills and services in application marketing which prepare the company to achieve the full benefits of its electronic messaging application.

A Communications Plan developed in initial planning sessions with the client establishes the most effective methods for increasing the number of application users. The AT&T EasyLink Professional Services organization then produces and distributes the materials required for communicating the client's electronic commerce program to its users. These products include:

- User documentation
- Correspondence with users
- Presentation materials
- Meeting/conference facilitation
- Project management

AT&T EasyLink Services Professional Services assumes responsibility, because of the program's scope and duration, for managing the communications plan which implements application marketing. It regularly distributes status reports to keep all participants up to date. The consultants communicate and negotiate with each user on the client's behalf and work one-on-one with the users to explain, install, and test the application. Upon completion, AT&T EasyLink Services Professional Services provides a report that analyzes program goals as related to program results. A no-charge teleconference is provided to introduce the client and its application to the AT&T EasyLink Services Customer Service and Support Center.

AT&T Organizational Units

AT&T Business Units

AT&T Consumer Communication Services	Provides services for U.S. and international long distance users.
AT&T Universal Card Services Corporation	Markets a consumer credit card for general purchases and long distance calling.
AT&T Business Communications Services	Provides over 80 U.S. and international long distance services to businesses.
AT&T Business Multimedia Services	Charged with delivering multimedia solutions to customers' business needs through access connectivity, integrated messaging, information hosting, and applications design, among others. This unit now includes AT&T EasyLink Services, which develops and markets global electronic messaging services for business customers worldwide.
AT&T Istel	This is a leading European information technology services company providing integrated computing and communications services to commerce, industry, and the public sector.
AT&T Paradyne	Develops, manufactures, and markets data communications equipment and technology for U.S. and international business.

AT&T Ventures	Invests in new businesses that are based on AT&T competencies or that enhance AT&T's business opportunities.
AT&T American Transtech	Provides telephone-based services to help large businesses acquire new customers and improve relationships with existing ones.
AT&T Consumer Products	Designs, manufactures, sells, and leases communications products globally for personal use within and outside the home, and in small businesses.
AT&T Global Business Communications Systems	Offers premises-based products and customer service to business.
AT&T Global Information Solutions	Formerly NCR, brings computing and communication solutions together to provide people easy access to information and to one another.
AT&T Network Systems	A leading manufacturer and marketer of network telecommunications products. The units within network systems are: Switching Systems—develops, manufactures, and markets digital switching systems and software for communications networks. Transmission Systems—designs, manufactures, and markets transmission equipment. Operations Systems—makes and markets software and hardware for telecommunications systems and networks. Network Cable Systems—is the world's largest supplier of fiber-optic and copper cable for communications providers and users worldwide. Network Wireless Systems—manufactures and markets radio and switching systems for the global wireless industry.
AT&T Capital Corporation	Provides leasing and financing services for AT&T products and systems, and for such non-AT&T

AT&T Organizational Units

	products as transportation, office, computer, manufacturing, and general business equipment.
AT&T Bell Laboratories	One of the world's foremost industrial research and development establishments. Its scientists invented the transistor, laser, solar cell, and communications satellite. It has won an average of a patent a day since it was established in 1925. Seven AT&T Bell Labs scientists have received the Nobel Prize, and it is the first institution to be awarded the National Medal of Technology.
Actuarial Sciences Associates, Inc.	An AT&T subsidiary that advises corporations in the design, maintenance, and financing of employee benefit programs of all types.
McCaw Cellular Communications, Inc.	The merger of AT&T and McCaw, America's largest cellular service provider, has been approved by the FCC.

AT&T's Joint Ventures and Alliances

AT&T has rapidly expanded its international marketing capability through joint ventures, alliances, and investments. A partial list follows:

Asia

AT&T of Beijing Fiber Optic Cable Co. Ltd.	AT&T Network Systems formed this joint venture with Beijing Optical Communications Co., Beijing Cable Works, and China National Posts and Telecommunications Industry Co. to produce fiber-optic cable for use in China.
AT&T of China Ltd.	Based in Shanghai, this venture manufactures, sells, and services subscriber loop carrier network access systems for use in the Chinese telecommunications network. AT&T and the

	Shanghai Telecommunications Equipment Factory each own 50 percent.
AT&T Japan Semiconductor Marketing Ltd.	AT&T holds 51 percent and NEC Corp. 49 percent of this venture that markets AT&T semiconductors in Japan.
AT&T JENS	AT&T owns 66.7 percent of this joint venture with 22 major Japanese firms to provide value-added network services in Japan.
AT&T Network Technologies (Thailand) Co. Ltd.	This joint venture of the Great Electronics (Thailand) Co. Ltd. (51 percent equity) and AT&T (49 percent equity), located south of Bangkok, manufactures devices for connecting copper and fiber-optic cable in telecommunications applications.
AT&T of Shanghai Ltd.	AT&T Network Systems International holds 50 percent of this venture with Shanghai Optical Fiber Communications Engineering and Shanghai Telecommunications Equipment Factory. It manufactures, sells, and services digital transmission equipment for public and private network customers in China.
AT&T Software Japan, Ltd.	AT&T is the majority owner, with Industrial Bank of Japan and Software Research Associates, of this company that offers UNIX and fault-tolerant software applications.
AT&T Switching Systems (India) Pvt. Ltd	In partnership with Tata Industries Ltd., this joint venture will manufacture and market state-of-the-art central office switching equipment for use in India's telecommunications network. AT&T owns 51 percent. The Trans-India Network Systems venture manufactures and markets transmission equipment to connect remote locations to central offices in India's major cities.
AT&T Taiwan Telecommunications Co. Ltd.	This joint venture with the Directorate General of Telecommunications of Taiwan, the Bank of Communications, United Fiber Optic Communication Inc., and the Yao Hua Glass

AT&T Organizational Units

	Company manufactures the 5ESS switch and transmission equipment for use in Taiwan. AT&T owns 60 percent.
AT&T Yazaki	AT&T is a 51 percent owner of this venture with Yazaki Electric Wire Co. Ltd. of Japan to manufacture and sell fiber-optic cable in Japan.
AT&T EasyLink Services Asia/Pacific	This venture provides value-added networking services in Hong Kong and the Pacific region.
PT AT&T Network Systems Indonesia	This joint venture between AT&T Network Systems and PT Citra Telekomunikasi manufactures, installs, and services AT&T's 5ESS digital switches. AT&T holds a 75 percent share.
United Fiber Optic Communication Inc.	AT&T owns 15 percent of this Taiwanese company which manufactures fiber cable and transmission products.
Western Electric Saudi Arabia, Ltd.	With A.S. Bugshan Brothers, AT&T provides installation, operation, and maintenance services in Saudi Arabia, Jordan, Dubai, and Sudan. AT&T owns 40 percent.

Europe

AT&T Network Systems España	AT&T Network Systems International owns this Spanish subsidiary that develops, markets, and manufactures 5ESS digital switching systems and transmission equipment for the Spanish market.
AT&T Network Systems International B.V.	Based in the Netherlands, this joint venture company with Spain's Telefonica (6 percent) is AT&T's holding and management company for marketing, development, manufacturing, and sales of all network communications products, primarily for public telecommunications

	companies in Europe, the Middle East, Africa, countries of the CIS, and other nations.
AT&T Prague S.R.O.	AT&T Network Systems International owns 70 percent of this venture with Czech Telecommunications Tesla a.s. of Prague. Initially the company will sell AT&T's digital transmission equipment to the Czech market.
AT&T of St. Petersburg	AT&T Network Systems International owns 68 percent of this joint venture with Dalnya Sviaz (DALS), a Russian telecommunications company. The venture sells and provisions AT&T digital transmission equipment in Russia.
AT&T Telfa S.A	AT&T Network Systems International owns 80 percent of this Polish company, located in Bydgoszoz, that develops and manufactures telephone switches, relays, and connectors for public telecommunications.
Lycom A/S	AT&T owns 51 percent of this joint venture with Nordic Cable and Wire Works to make and market optical fiber for sale primarily in Scandinavia.
Telmos	This equal equity joint venture between AT&T Network Systems International and Moscow City Telephone Company (MGTS) will offer local, long distance, and international telephone services to business and residential customers in Moscow.
UTEL	A joint venture, in which AT&T and Deutsche Bundespost each own 19.5 percent, PTT Telecom of the Netherlands owns 10 percent, and Ukraine State Committee of Communications owns 51 percent, to modernize and operate Ukraine's international and domestic long distance communications networks.

Mexico/South America/Caribbean

AT&T Grupo Itsa — AT&T Global Business Communications Systems owns a majority interest in this Mexico City–based supplier of integrated voice, data, and video communications systems to businesses in Mexico.

AT&T Network Systems Do Brasil — This venture will manufacture and market the 5ESS switch in Brazil. Equity is split between AT&T (47 percent), SID Telecon of Brazil (51 percent), and MARCEP (2 percent).

Jamaica Digiport International, Ltd — This joint venture with Cable and Wireless Ltd. and Telecommunications of Jamaica provides telecommunications services to and from free trade zones in Jamaica. AT&T owns 35 percent.

Venezuela — AT&T has a 5 percent stake in a GTE-led consortium with Telefonica International de España, CIMA, and Electricidad de Caracas, which owns 40 percent of the Venezuelan telephone company CANTV. AT&T manages CANTV's international operations.

United States/Canada

AG Communication Systems Corporation — AT&T has a joint venture with GTE in Phoenix, Arizona, to develop, manufacture, install, and maintain computerized switching systems for telephone central offices. AT&T owns 49 percent.

AT&T Fitel Co. — AT&T Network Systems owns 51 percent of this venture in Georgia with The Furukawa Electric Co. Ltd. of Japan.

General Magic — AT&T joins Apple, Matsushita, Motorola, Philips, Sony, and other major corporations in an equity alliance backing General Magic's development of the Telescript communications language, a standard that enables different brands of personal communicators and computers to exchange

	messages. AT&T has introduced AT&T PersonaLink communicators offerings based on Telescript.
The Imagination Network, Inc.	AT&T has an equity position in this online computer service, formerly named The Sierra Network, that provides networked interactive multimedia entertainment over regular telephone lines.
Litespec Inc.	AT&T owns 51 percent of this Research Triangle, N.C., venture with Sumitomo Electric Industries Ltd. to produce and sell specialty optical fibers in the United States and elsewhere.
Micro-electronics and Computer Technology Corporation	AT&T Global Information Solutions is a shareholder-participant in this Austin, Texas, consortium engaging in long-term research and development in microelectronics and computer technologies.
Telehouse International Corp. of America	With 20 Japanese companies, AT&T owns 12 percent of this New York–based real estate, site management, data processing, and telecommunications consulting service company.
Unitel Communications Inc	AT&T is a 20 percent owner of this Canadian long distance company, also owned by Canadian Pacific Limited (48 percent) and Rogers Communications Inc. (32 percent).

Glossary

Accredited Standards Committee (ASC X12)	A committee chartered by ANSI in 1979 to develop uniform document standards for electronic interchange of business transactions.
Addressee	The person to whom an AT&T Mail message is addressed.
American National Standards Institute (ANSI)	Parent organization of ASC X12. A government/industry/user organization which adopts standards for many data processing functions (languages, protocols, character sets, etc.). The standards are not legally binding but are adopted by different vendors to allow products to communicate with one another.
Answer	An AT&T Mail command used to reply to messages.
Application Interface	The software component that transfers electronic transactions between application systems.
Application Program	A customized software program written to handle specific functions unique to an application.
ASCII	American Standard Code for Information Interchange (ASCII). A standard code that uses numbers to represent characters and control instructions.
AT&T EasyLink FAX	An AT&T Mail feature that permits the transmission of text or graphics documents, with or without logos or signatures, over telephone lines to any Group III fax machine.

AT&T MailFAX	An AT&T Mail feature that permits the transmission of text documents, with or without logos or signatures, over telephone lines, to any Group III fax machine.
Authentication	A mechanism that allows the receiver of an electronic transmission to verify the sender as well as the integrity of a transmission's content through the use of an electronic "key" or algorithm shared by the trading partners. This is sometimes referred to as an electronic signature.
Author	The person who creates a message.
Blind Courtesy Copy Recipient	A person whose identity is not shown to other recipients of a message.
Character	A letter, digit, or other graphic symbol.
Command	An instruction entered using the keyboard of a communications terminal that controls the activity of the AT&T Mail service.
Confirmation Options	Options which allow the sender to request notification of the delivery progress of a sent message.
Courtesy Copy Recipient	A person designated to receive a copy of a message addressed to another recipient. This recipient's name is displayed to other recipients.
Create	An AT&T Mail service command used to create messages.
Cross-Industry Standards	Data standards that apply to and are adopted by several industries. ASC X12 document standards are cross-industry.
CTX	An electronic funds transfer format compatible with X12 which carries information about a payment as well as transferring value. Also refers to Corporate Trade Exchange.

Glossary

Data Interchange Standards Association, Inc. (DISA)	DISA, the secretariat of the ASC X12 Committee, provides non-profit administrative services to the committee, communicates with ANSI and the public on behalf of the committee, manages the standards database, and plans and manages ASC X12 meetings and the annual EDI conference. DISA also services as the secretariat of the Pan American EDIFACT board.
Data Mapping	The relationship between the user's data and the X12 message syntax.
Delete	An AT&T Mail service command used to remove a message.
Delivery Options	Delivery options define the features which apply to message delivery. Options include features such as receipt and urgent delivery and can be specified for a specific message or for all messages.
Directory	An AT&T Mail service command that is used to search for registered users of the service.
EDIFACT	The EDI document standard being developed by the United Nations to be the global EDI standard and primarily used in Europe. EDIFACT stands for EDI for Administration, Commerce, and Transport.
Edit	An AT&T Mail service command used to change, add, or delete the message content.
Electronic Commerce	Electronic commerce is the process of doing business electronically, using a variety of technologies. EDI, electronic mail, computer-based fax services, and databases are a few of the technologies or tools used in a company's EC strategy. Companies that adopt an electronic commerce strategy focus on managing changes to organizational structures, selecting tools and applications that match their business objectives.

Glossary

Electronic Mailbox A mailbox is the AT&T EasyLink Services network repository of information belonging to a single user. The mailbox makes it unnecessary for the user to provide dedicated hardware for the purpose of awaiting incoming calls.

Encryption The encoding and scrambling of data. Data are encrypted at the sending end and decrypted on the receiving end through use of a predetermined algorithm and unique key. Encryption is done for reasons of privacy and security.

Fax A process where both graphics and text documents are scanned, transmitted (via telephone lines), and reconstructed by a receiver.

Folder Logical storage unit which can reside on either the AT&T EasyLink Services network or local storage. All users have In and Out folders on the network. Enhanced AT&T Mail account subscribers may create folders on the network for specific message storage purposes; users of Access PLUS may create message folders as desired on their local computer.

Format The arrangement of message information into a specified order.

Gateway Software or system that connects two otherwise incompatible networks; between VANs, allows customers to communicate with trading partners who are on other networks.

Header Area The Transaction Set Header Area contains preliminary information that pertains to the entire document, such as the date, company name, address, purchase order number, and terms.

Help Folder An AT&T Mail shared folder that contains on-line "help" information about AT&T Mail commands and operations.

Glossary

Hub	A large company, very active in EDI, that strongly encourages its paper-based business partners to begin using EDI. Also called a "sponsor."
In Folder	An AT&T Mail folder that stores received messages.
Interactive EDI	Two applications exchanging EDI directly within a preprogrammed context.
ISO (International Standards Organization)	Organization responsible for development of international data communications standards.
ITU	The International Telecommunications Union; its purpose is to encourage international cooperation and development of radio, telegraph, cable, telephone, and television communications. It is a successor to the former CCITT and sets messaging interchange standards, among others.
Log Off	The process of ending a work session and terminating connection to the AT&T Mail service.
Log On	The process of connecting to the AT&T Mail service and beginning a work session.
Message-Enabled Applications	A message-enabled application is one in which sending capabilities are built into the application. Examples include EDI, order entry using a hand-held device over wireless communications, and a spreadsheet application. A message-enabled application allows a manager, after preparing the spreadsheet data, to send the spreadsheet directly to another manager's application without having to exit the spreadsheet or go into an electronic mail application and attach the spreadsheet to an electronic mail message before sending.
Originator/ Recipient Attributes	Attributes used to address mail to X.400 systems. They consist of: Country Code, Administrative Management Domain Name, Private

	Management Domain, Personal Name, Organization Name, Organizational Unit Name, and Domain Defined Attribute.
OSI (Open Systems Interconnect)	Structure based on a seven-layer model developed by the International Standards Organization (ISO) which will allow different computer manufacturers' machines to communicate with one another.
Password	A string of characters (usually up to eight) entered during the login process that permits access to the AT&T Mail service.
Private Network	A network belonging to a private organization or corporation and used solely by its internal employees.
Prompt	A message displayed by AT&T Mail requesting instructions from a user at a terminal.
Proprietary Standards	An industry/company-specific data format developed for transmission of data to and from trading partners. Proprietary formats do not comply with the ASC X12 series of standards.
Protocols	A set of rules for the format and control of information exchanged between two communications devices.
Quick Response (QR)	The process similar to just-in-time manufacturing which is found in the retail industry; it depends on EDI. The process allows retailers to respond quickly to customer orders.
Quit	An AT&T Mail command that is used to exit the AT&T Mail service.
Read	An AT&T Mail command that displays the content of a message.
RJE	Remote Job Entry. A protocol, for IBM-compatible systems, used to transfer files between computer systems.

Glossary

Send	An AT&T Mail command that is used to send the messages to their specified addresses.
Sent Folder	An AT&T Mail folder that stores messages that the subscriber has sent. Also known as an Out folder.
Service Grade Options	Options that allow users to specify whether a message is sent by standard electronic, priority, urgent, or nonurgent delivery.
Session	The connection of a data terminal or personal computer to the AT&T Mail service.
Shared Folder	A file that other users (subscribers to that particular shared folder) can have access to.
Show	An AT&T Mail command that displays information about messages.
Spoke	A trading partner of a hub (a large company very active in EDI) that will implement EDI as a consequence of the hub's desire to trade electronically.
Subscriber	A registered AT&T Mail service user.
TDCC/EDIA (Transportation Data Coordinating Committee/Electronic Data Interchange Association)	TDCC/EDIA is now under the ASC X12 umbrella for standards maintenance. This United States non-profit organization was the facilitator of standards efforts for a message standard and a communications structure based on EDI transaction sets.
Teletypewriter	A generic term meaning a teleprinter terminal.
Telex	Teleprinter exchange, the transmission of information via teletypewriters connected through automatic exchanges. This communications service is a predecessor to electronic mail and is still used extensively in some areas of the world.

Trading Partner	A company active in EDI viewed from the perspective of the company that does EDI with it.
Transaction Set	A complete business document such as an invoice, a purchase order, or a remittance advice.
Translation Software	Software which converts a data file that is in a proprietary or Internal corporate document format to the EDI standard format.
Uniform Communication Standard	The Uniform Communication Standard (UCS) defines both a message format standard for EDI and a telecommunication standard for EDI.
UN/TDI (United Nations/Trade Data Interchange)	A cross-industry EDI standard predominantly used in the United Kingdom and Western Europe.
User Group	A collection of AT&T Mail subscribers specifically placed into a closed group on the service for administrative and billing purposes. Usually, all the users are from one company or association and need to limit communications between themselves and other service users. A "super group" is a collection of several user groups.
VAN (Value-Added Network)	Vendors of value-added networks typically provide customers with network services and additional services such as customer support, standards expertise, training, and implementation support. An EDI VAN typically provides electronic mailbox capability, audit, control, and security procedures. Gateways on a VAN allow communication between trading partners with different EDI VANs.
View	AT&T Mail service command that displays all message envelope lines as well as the content.
Wastebasket Folder	An AT&T Mail folder that stores messages deleted during the current session.

Glossary

X12	The United States standard developed by the American National Standards Institute which defines the format of EDI documents.
X12 Mailbag	X12 Mailbag facilitates interconnections between VANs and mailbag-registered users. AT&T EasyLink Services supports this standard as an interim solution until the industry as a whole has reached a state of X.400 readiness.
X.25	An ITU-T international standard protocol for inter-network packet switching. The standard defines the interface between data terminal equipment and data communications equipment for terminals operating in the packet mode on public data networks.
X.400	The international standard for store-and-forward messaging. The purpose of X.400 is to provide a standard way of connecting different messaging systems, allowing users on different systems to exchange messages. X.400 is primarily used for interpersonal messaging (electronic mail). However, this standard was designed for all electronic messaging in general. Benefits include reliability, end-to-end message tracking, fast, event-driven transfers, integration of email and EDI, highly secure, global, and open standard, and standardized services such as grades of service, deferred delivery, etc.
X.435	A recent addition to X.400 that provides EDI-specific services such as EDI notification and advanced security.

Bibliography

1. AT&T Archives. 1992. *Events in Telecommunications History.* Warren, N.J.: AT&T Archives.

2. Fagin, M.D., Ed. 1975. *A History of Engineering and Science in the Bell System.* pp. 684, 686. Warren, N.J.: Bell Telephone Laboratories.

3. Pool, Ithiel de Sola. 1983. *Forecasting the Telephone: A Retrospective Technology Assessment.* Norwood, N.J.: ABLEX Publishing.

4. Pool, Ithiel de Sola, Ed. 1977. *The Social Impact of the Telephone.* Cambridge, Mass.: MIT Press.

5. Smith, George David. 1985. *The Anatomy of a Business Strategy.* pp. 35–36, 76–80. Baltimore, Md.: The Johns Hopkins Press.

Index

A

A-GATE, 231 - 233
ABA/net, 11 - 12, 41 - 45
    colleague directory, 42
    communications software, 44
    FAXsolutions, 44
    information services, 44
    legal conferencing, 43
    legal research , 43
    LEXIS/NEXIS, 43
    Master Calendar, 42
    WESTLAW, 44
Access
    options, 96
    worldwide, 17
Accountability, 17
    VAN and Internet, 68
ACCUNET Packet Service, 248
ADMD, 248
Advantage
    competitive, 67
Advantages
    business , 17
Agreement, telephone patent, 3
Air express companies, 23
Application
    integration, 226
Applications, 11 - 45, 101 - 105
Architecture
    access control, 127 - 128
    ACCUNET Packet Service, 132
    ADMD, 132, 134
    AT&T EasyLink Services, 107
    AT&T Electronic Data Interchange, 121
    AT&T FAXsolutions, 120
    AT&T Global Messaging Services, 118
    AT&T Information Services, 121
    AT&T Mail, 120
    AT&T Mail 400 Service, 132
    AT&T Network Notes, 117
    availability, 125
    backup, 127
    barrier removal, 117

Architecture, *continued*
    business messaging, 109
    client/server, 111 - 117
    content description, 119
    contingency plans, 125
    cooperative processing, 111
    devices, 110
    enterprise integration, 107
    frame relay, 143
    GOSIP, 138
    groupware, 115
    heterogeneity, 111
    human interface, consistent, 111
    infrastructure, 108
    integration, 107
    interconnectability, 111
    Internet, 141, 144
    interoperability, 111, 133
    InterSpan, 143
    LAN integration, 107, 117
    Lotus Notes, 115 - 117
    MailTALK, 130
    message protection, 128
    message transfer, 119
    messaging functions, 138
    mission statement, 115
    multimedia, 107
    multiple-platform, 116
    network access, 122 - 123, 126
    network design, 122
    network operations, 122
    Network Program Members, 146
    objectives, 110
    Organization Name , 133
    Organizational Unit, 133
    OSI reference model, 131
    patent, 118
    platform, 118
    Private Management Domains, 132
    private X.400 connectivity, 134
    public network, 116

Architecture, *continued*
    sales and support, 146 - 147
    Sales Program, 146
    scalability, 111
    self-administration, 128
    SMTP, 142
    software, 130
    software-defined network, 140
    standards support, 131
    strategy, 108
    unified mailbox, 107
    Unified Messaging Architecture,
        107 - 108, 110, 114, 117, 131
    user validation, 126
    Value-Added Reseller, 146
    WAN integration, 107
    Windows '95, 116
    Windows NT, 116
    workgroup integration, 107, 116
    X.25, 132
    X.400, 116, 118, 130 - 131
ASC X12, 251
AT&T
    current operations, 4
    firsts, 5
    internal messaging, 5
    mission statement, 5
    structure, 6
AT&T Business Multimedia Services,
    91 - 92, 94 - 105
AT&T EasyLink Services
    AT&T Business Multimedia Services, 6
AT&T EasyLink Services Enterprise
    Network Management, 70, 73, 75
AT&T EasyLink Services SNADS, 246
AT&T EasyLink Services Sync FEPS,
    244
AT&T EDI, 251 - 283
AT&T Enhanced FAX, 27 - 30
    see also AT&T FAXsolutions
    benefits , 30

Index

AT&T Enhanced Fax, *continued*
   computer forms, 27
   engineering, 30
   fax mailboxes, 27
   high-volume, 27
   hospitality, 30
   host applications, 27
   insurance, 29
   network-based, 27
   personal computers, 27
   privacy, 27
   sales applications, 29
AT&T FAXsolutions, 285 - 319
AT&T FORMsolutions, 25, 203 - 217
   automation savings, 25
   extended reach, 26
   strategic advantages, 26
AT&T Mail, 149 - 176
   access methods, 155
   Access PLUS, 153
   addressing, 157
   AT&T Enhanced FAX, 150
   AT&T Mail Catalog, 164
   audit trail, 161
   autoanswer, 165
   autoforward, 165
   autoresponse, 166
   basic, 153
   billing, 175
   bills, project coding, 166
   binary file transfer, 151
   broadcast, 151, 163
   capabilities, 150
   closed user groups, 151, 176
   commands, 159
   confirmation options, 172
   courier delivery, 170
   delivery, 159
   delivery notification, 162
   delivery options, 169, 171
   directory services, 156 - 157

AT&T Mail, *continued*
   encryption, 169
   file attachments, 167 - 168
   file transfer, 167
   file transfer, large, 167
   format options, 170
   forms, 165
   forms/files, 153 - 154
   FYIInfo Boards, 164
   gatenames , 167
   Group Partitions, 176
   individual user administration, 160
   legal applications, 43
   logos, 167
   mailbox capabilities, 154
   mailbox, combined, 155
   MailFAX, 169
   MailPRINT, 170
   MailTALK, 152, 155
   menu prompt, 165
   message options, 170
   mobile devices, 170
   online directory, 150
   online help, 150
   online storage, 151
   other networks, 151
   overview, 149
   postal service, 170
   PostScript printing, 152
   Pricing, 175
   protocols, 168
   receipt, 162
   reverse billing, 151
   service and support, 152
   service grade, 172
   service reporting, 161
   shared folders, 163, 173
   shared folders, autodelivery, 164
   Shared Lists, 175
   signatures, 167
   storage, online, 161

AT&T Mail, *continued*
  telex, 169
  user interface, 152
  user-defined administration, 151
AT&T Mail Connectivity, 219 - 249
AT&T Mail Gateway400, 248
AT&T messaging history, 1 - 10
AT&T NetWare Connect, 91 - 99
AT&T Network Notes, 91, 94, 100 - 105
AT&T Organizational Units, 379 - 385
  AT&T's Joint Ventures and Alliances, 381
  Business Units , 379
AT&T PersonaLink Services, 12
AT&T Professional Services, 14
AT&T School of Business, 52
AT&T Synchronous Gateway, 244
Axint Technologies, 212, 215

B

Backbone applications, 13 - 14
Bell Patent Association, 2
Bell, Alexander Graham, 1
  letter, 8
Binary Synchronous Communications, 244
Bridges, native, 222
Broadcast, 16
Bulletin boards, 21
Business Multimedia Services, AT&T
  see AT&T Business Multimedia Services

C

Closed user groups, 41
Collaboration, 102
Collaborative platform, 95
Connections, external, 14
Connectivity, 18

Connectivity, universal, 11
corporate workflow, 219

D

DEC All-in-1, 240
DEC VMS, 240
DEC VMS Mail, 240
Delrina Technology, 210
Distribution, wide, 19
Document Assembler Disassembler, 246

E

EDI
  access, 261
  ACCUNET, 252, 261
  administrative interface, 274
  applications, 31 - 33, 35 - 40
  architecture, 259
  AS/400 Platforms, 271
  ASC X12, 251, 254, 256, 258, 264, 269
  asynchronous support, 261
  AT&T Professional Services, 282
  audit trails, 276
  billing, 279
  billing, hierarchical, 280
  billing, split, 280
  data interchange standards, 251
  definition, 251
  EDIA/TDCC, 269
  EDICT, 254
  EDIFACT, 251, 254, 258 - 259, 269
  enveloping, 264, 266
  enveloping, network, 268
  enveloping, premises, 268
  file transfer, large, 263
  FreeForm conversion, 269
  GTDI, 251, 254
  human-readable, 269
  IBM environment, 269
  INFOTRAC, 261

Index   401

EDI, *continued*
   international, 253
   investment protection, 259
   ISOCOR, 252
   Jensnet, 261
   LAN , 270
   mainframe, 269
   message tracking, 277
   Message transfer agents, 253
   Messages, 253
   network dial-out, 262
   notifications, 277
   Odette, 251
   open mailbox, 262
   PC, 270
   pricing, 278
   purchase orders, 255
   security, 278
   software certification, 265
   software testing, 266
   software, network interface, 265
   standards, 251, 258
   support, 280, 282
   synchronous interconnections, 253
   synchronous support, 262
   System 36/38, 271
   TDCC, 251, 258
   TDI, 254
   Tradacoms, 251
   trading partners, 251
   Transaction Types, 254
   UCS, 251, 258, 269
   UNG/TMI, 258
   Unified Messaging Architecture, 252
   UNIX, 272
   User agents, 253
   VAN connections, 263
   VANs, 258
   X.400, 251 - 252
   X.435, 252
   X12 Mailbag/TA3 Acknowledgment, 278

F

Fame Computer, 213, 215
Faults, network, 72
Fax
   Access PLUS for Window, 318
   AT&T Enhanced FAX, 289
   AT&T FAX Catalog, 307
   see AT&T FAXsolutions
   AT&T MailFAX., 317
   Combined mailbox, 294, 318
   computer-to-fax, 316
   EDI-to-fax , 287
   Fax Mailbox, 289, 298
   Fax Sender, 318
   Fax Services, 316
   Fax Viewer, 318
   FAXAFORM, 317
   features, 299
   FreeForm conversion, 319
   high-volume, 285
   international, 289
   network benefits, 287
   network-based, 285, 290
   North America, 289
   Pacific Rim,, 289
   productivity, 288
   SDN Enhanced FAX, 306 - 307
   terminal-to-fax, 316
   traffic peaks, 286
   Unified Messaging Architecture, 290
Finance operations, 20
Financial management, 20
Financial messaging applications, 24
forms, electronic, 203
   AT&T Mail, 207
   benefits, 204
   cc:Mail, 212
   designer package, 208
   development cycle, 206
   external messaging transport, 207

Index

forms, *continued*
  FormLink, 212
  forms filler, 208 - 209
  intelligence, 203
  Liberty, 210
  mail-enabled forms, 207
  Microsoft Electronic Forms Designer, 216
  Microsoft Mail, 212
  open systems, 209
  overview, 210
  routing-based, 217
  software, 206
  transaction oriented, 212
  Visual Basic, 216
  wide-area networking, 212
forms, paper, 203
  costs, 203
  development cycle, 204
Functions, process-linked, 12

G

Gateways, native, 222
Global Messaging Architecture, 107 - 147
Government OSI Protocol
  see Architecture, GOSIP
Gray, Elisha, 2
groupware, 219

H

Hall, E.J., 4, 6
History, AT&T messaging
  see AT&T messaging, history
Hubbard, Gardiner Greene, 2
Human resources, 21

I

Information distribution, 12
Information exchange, electronic, 102
Information gathering, 12
Information Services, 321 - 365
  abstracts, 341
  Airport monitors, 358
  AT&T FAX Catalog, 327
  AT&T FYI Service, 327, 345 - 348
  AT&T InfoMaster Service, 338 - 339, 341 - 344
  AT&T Mail integration, 323
  contents, table of, 323
  databases, selecting, 342
  directories, 340
  ECLIPSE EXPRESS, 323, 333 - 336
  forms, 350
  frequent flyer, 358
  full-text, 340
  FYI categories, 358 - 365
  FYI InfoBoards, 325, 349 - 350
  FYI NewsAlert, 350 - 352
  FYI NewsLink, 345 - 346, 352, 354 - 355
  FYI use, 351
  gateways, 336, 347
  industry-specific news, 348
  InfoMaster, 327
  information distribution, 324 - 325, 349
  information retrieval, 323
  international data, 348
  Investment ANALY$T, 344 - 345
  keywords, 352 - 353
  LEXIS/NEXIS, 335
  librarian, free reference, 338
  market information, 348
  menu, custom, 337
  network, virtual private, 321
  news, 348
  NEXIS EXPRESS, 323, 327, 331 - 333
  Official Airline Guide, 345, 355 - 358

Index

Information Services, *continued*
  on demand, 322
  online searches, 324, 343
  private, 321
  provider, 321
  PUBCITE, 323, 327 - 330
  public, 321
  Reed-Elsevier, 331
  research on demand, 324
  researchers, professional, 331
  session capture, 323
  shared folders, 326
  subscriptions, 324
  travel, 348
  vendor, 321
  weather, 348
InstantCom//MS for LAN, 238 - 239
Internet, 68
Investment protection, 16, 18, 222

L

LANs, 220 - 221, 240
  off campus connectivity , 224
Leeson Howe Associates, 238
Location independence, 15
Lotus, 91
Lotus Notes, 100
LU6.2, 244

M

Mainframes, 244
Management
  Access and egress, 77
  accounting, 70
  ACCUMASTER Management
    Services., 73
  administration, 70
  alarm correlation, 72
  alarm escalation, 75
  alarm filtering, 74

Management, *continued*
  alarm ownership, 72
  AT&T BaseWorX, 73
  AT&T network, 71
  AT&T OneVision Network
    Management Solutions, 72
  backbone, 76
  central, 68
  configuration, 70, 74, 78
  configuration database, 71
  domains, 70
  dynamic fault, 77
  element systems, 75
  elements, 74
  event thresholding, 74
  expert systems, 79
  fault, 70
  Hewlett-Packard's OpenView, 73 - 74
  hierarchical resolution, 76
  infrastructure, integrated, 80
  integrated network, 70 - 72
  maintenance, 70
  messaging network, 70
  multi-vendor networks, 70
  network architecture, 70
  network, industrial-strength, 69
  open system platform, 75
  operations, 70
  performance, 70, 74, 80 - 81
  physical, 78
  physical network, 70
  proactive, 76
  problem, 70
  reactive, 76
  real-time expert systems, 75, 80
  response, 76
  revenue base, assured, 68
  security, 70
  SNMP, 73
  standards, 83
  trouble ticket, 79

Management, continued
    Unified Network Management
        Architecture, 71, 75
    unified portal, 75
    VAN reliability, 88
    WAN, 76
Marketing, 20
Messaging
    commercial, 68
    formal, 12
    in-house, 13
    informal, 12
    non-commercial, 68
Messaging redefined, 17
Microsoft Exchange, 226
Microsoft Mail for PC Networks,
    225 - 229, 231
Microsoft Mail Remote for Windows, 226
Microsoft-AT&T
    strategic relationship, 225
Midrange systems, 240 - 243
Migration path, 18
Military contributions, 2
Mission-critical, 2, 12 - 14
    applications, 67 - 69
Mission-critical applications, 85
Modification of Final Judgment, 4
Morse, Samuel, 3

N

Networks, linking, 16
Networks, private, 11
Novell, 91

O

Off-campus, 19
OfficeAccess, 240
OfficeAccess for IBM AS/400, 242
ON-Technology Corporation, 231
Outsourcing, 14

P

PC software, 177 - 202
    Access PLUS, 178 - 179
    Access PLUS, Macintosh, 196 - 198
    Access PLUS, MS-DOS, 182 - 188
    Access Plus, Windows, 60, 189 - 195
    agent software, 179
    alliances, 178
    application mapping, 186
    AT&T Mail driver, 200
    AT&T Mail-enabled applications, 180
    Background Mailer, 182
    combined mailbox, 195
    Dynamic Data Exchange, 189
    Fax Sender, 195
    Fax Viewer, 195
    general-purpose, 178
    hybrid design, 179
    Instant Information Inc., 178
    InstantCom, 178
    InstantCom//MS , 178
    Microsoft Mail for PC Networks, 178
    Microsoft Mail Remote for Windows,
        178, 200
    Microsoft/AT&T Mail benefits, 201
    online message preparation, 179
    overview, 177
    PC stand-alone, 178
    preview mail, 62, 189
    problems, 178
    scripts, 179
    selection criteria, 202
    Windows overhead, 179
    wireless support, 189
Petrochemical companies, 22
PRMDs, 248
Productivity, 18
Professional Services, 373 - 378
    consulting, 373
    education, 373

Index

Professional Services, *continued*
   implementation, 376
   implementation support, 373
   installation, 376
   process re-engineering, 374
   program design, 375
   ramping, 377
PROFS/DISOSS, 246
Protocol Format Converter, 246
Public messaging networks, 67 - 89

R

Reach, extended, 11
Remote Job Entry, 244
Risk, 68

S

Sales automation, 21
Sanders, Thomas, 2
Security
   business continuity, 87
   commercial network, 84
   disaster recovery, 87
   encryption, 68
   Internet, 85, 87
   reliability, 84
   tracking and audit, 85
Services, customized, 41
Single source, 18
StarGROUP
   AT&T Mail gateway, 237
   Microsoft Mail gateway, 237
   MS MAIL, 233 - 236
Start-up, immediate, 17
Systems Network Architecture, 244

T

Telegraph monopoly, 3
Telegraphy, 3

Telemarketing, 20
Telephone, 2
Telephone caveat, 2
Telephone patent, 2
Telex, 367 - 371
   access, 368
   accountability, 369
   database access, 370
   delivery options, 370
   funds transfer, 367
   integration, 368
   LANs, 368
   mainframes, 368
   midrange systems, 368
   mission-critical, 369
   Personal computers, 368
   real-time, 370
   store-and-forward, 370
   test-key codes, 367 - 369
   UNIX, 368
   value-added services, 371
Telex applications, 41
   banking, 40
Telextester, 238
Time independence, 15
Time-to-market, 11
Travel information networks, 24

U

UN/TDI, 251
Universal service, 6
UNIX, 247
Use, ease of, 17
User groups
   closed, 11
   open, 11

V

Vail, Theodore N., 4, 6
Versatility, 17

Virtual workplaces, 47 - 65
   1990 Clean Air Act, 49 - 52
   Access PLUS, Windows, 60
   AT&T EasyLink Services, 47, 53
   AT&T Mail, 48, 54
   AT&T Mobile Messaging, 48
   AT&T PersonaLink Services, 64
   benefits, 48
   business strategy, 47
   cellular access, 54
   cellular phone access, 61
   computers, 54
   EMBARC, 58
   Intel Mobidem AT modem, 58
   intelligent agents, 64
   location-independent workers, 48
   MailTALK, 54
   messaging infrastructure, 48
   Microsoft At Work, 63
   Microsoft Mail Remote for Windows, 60
   mobile messaging developments, 63
   Mobile messaging software, 60
   mobile workers, 48
   MOBITEX, 59
   Motorola, 58
   NewsCard, 58
   NewStream, 58
   non-traditional locations, 47
   packet radio, 54, 60
   pagers, 54 - 55
   PDAs, 54, 64
   pen-based devices, 54 - 55
   personal organizers, 54
   portable office, 47
   preview mail, 62
   product integration and support, 48
   productivity, 47
   professional services, 51
   public network services, 48
   radio, 55
   RAM Mobile Data S, 58

Virtual workplaces, *continued*
   remote workers, 48
   RF modems, 56
   satellite transmission, 54
   SkyStream, 58
   SkyTel, 56
   telecommuting, 47 - 49
   wired connectivity, 48, 55
   wireless connectivity, 48, 55

W

WAN applications, 13
WAN,connectivity, 229
Western Union, 3
Western Union EasyLink
   acquisition, 6
Western Union, control of, 4
Wireless, 224
Work process improvements, 22
Workplaces, virtual
   see Virtual Workplaces

X

X.400, 219, 221, 248
XCOM6.2, 244

About the Author

Ira Hertzoff is an author specializing in inter-enterprise internetworking technology and implementation. He founded iLAN, a pioneer LAN integration company, served as CIO of GateKeeper Telecommunications Systems, and has been a columnist for *LAN Technology*. Mr. Hertzoff is also the author of several Datapro and Auerbach research portfolios on UNIX networking, LANs, and telecommunications.

Important Bookbuyer Offer

As an expression of our appreciation, AT&T EasyLink Services is making a special offer to all *AT&T Global Messaging* book owners. You may receive a choice of

1. "Access PLUS for Windows Mini-Pack" (version 2.5), accompanied by a Quick Reference Guide—FREE!

2. "Access PLUS for Windows," which includes the latest software version as well as a complete set of documentation—at a 50% discount.

Additionally, for all NEW subscribers to AT&T Mail, this certificate is worth up to $25 in savings toward one month's usage (email charges only).

To register for AT&T Mail, or for more information about AT&T EasyLink Services and its products and services, please call 1-800-242-6005, Dept. 6860.

(Promotional offers good while supplies last.)